Dancing in Your Head

DANCING IN YOUR HEAD

Jazz, Blues, Rock, and Beyond

Gene Santoro

New York   Oxford

OXFORD UNIVERSITY PRESS

1994

Oxford University Press

Oxford   New York   Toronto
Delhi   Bombay   Calcutta   Madras   Karachi
Kuala Lumpur   Singapore   Hong Kong   Tokyo
Nairobi   Dar es Salaam   Cape Town
Melbourne   Auckland   Madrid

and associated companies in
Berlin   Ibadan

Published by Oxford University Press, Inc.
200 Madison Avenue, New York, New York 10016

Oxford is a registered trademark of Oxford University Press

Library of Congress Cataloging-in-Publication Data
Santoro, Gene.
Dancing in your head : jazz, blues, rock, and beyond / Gene Santoro.
p. cm.   Includes bibliographical references and index.
ISBN 0-19-507887-X
1. Popular music—United States—History and criticism.
2. Jazz—History and criticism.   I. Title.
ML3477.1.S25   1994
781.64'0973—dc20   93-15186

9 8 7 6 5 4 3 2 1

Printed in the United States of America
on acid-free paper

Preface

Putting this compilation of previously published pieces together has been exhilarating and scary. Exhilarating because during my work on it, from assembling the list of potential entries to editing and updating them, some things became clear to me—well, clearer than they had been. I couldn't help noticing, for instance, that I had actually been up to something relatively coherent over the last few years. It was quite a kick to scan the assembled table of contents and find that, despite its originally deadline-driven nature, it was actually held together by some kind—my kind—of historical and critical sense—an overview. The feeling was a bit like being a little kid who recognizes his own reflection in the mirror for the first time.

Like most of the writers I know, I never think anything I'm working on is done. Deadlines are just tools for structuring my time. And again like most of the writers I know, I like to think I've learned more since each and every one of these pieces got untimely ripped from my harddisk drive. But I can now admit that they have a value aside from my own ongoing education in print. Despite obvious gaps, they form a view of music's history and development.

As a kid I'd been exposed within a very short period of time to three major sonic explorers who blew me away: Jimi Hendrix, John Coltrane, and Béla Bartók. I was too young to have much of a technical grasp of what the last two were doing, though I played enough guitar to be able to grasp the basics of Hendrix's revolutionary attack. But I could *hear* what they were doing; I could *feel* the reaction in the pit of my stomach. I could intuit that they had more in common than not. That sense of wonder and discovery is what happens when you've been hit by art's immediate vatic power; it's quite possibly art's most essential cultural by-product. It has never left me, has been touched and renewed by each encounter I've valued. These pieces chronicle some of the results.

In that sense, they represent my coming to intellectual grips with that first brain-addling set of experiences. They don't avoid formal categories and distinctions, though they leaven them with enough anecdotes and asides so that their value is limited, as it's meant to be, to the merely descriptive. So the musical subjects in this book range literally across lines of all kinds, whether geographical or formalist. In and of itself, that's not the point. The point is that music travels along with other forms of commerce and, as it collides with other cultures, changes. So good listeners have to be willing to stretch and bend and learn and be willing to discard, however provisionally, what they think they know in order to be able to understand afresh. In other words, to become a little more like the artists they're listening to.

So my job has, I think, two distinct aspects to it. Sometimes they overlap; sometimes they clash. But in any piece I write there's always play, if not tension, between the roles of critic and advocate. I think that's true of any critic who ever mattered, from Plato to Erich Auerbach and Edmund Wilson to John Berger. For me starting to write about music, two of the most important models were Robert Palmer and Gary Giddins. Both writers seemed learned and broad-minded to me. But what hooked me on what they did time and again was the passion that glowed through their words, their attempts to translate the immediate experience of the music that moved them into prose and thus communicate it to others. Enthusiasm was the key to understanding. If I've ever had a goal for what I do, it's been to emulate that talent. This book is the natural product of that hope.

There are many people who have to be held responsible for my being able to make this book at all. Several years ago, when I was editing books about music, two of my writers who are now my friends, Allan Kozinn and Peter Guralnick, persuaded me that I'd be good at scribbling about the stuff. Kozinn especially counseled me on everything from how to lead the freelance life without starving to where to line up editorial contacts, and often knocked on doors for me. Other established writers, like Palmer and Giddins, encouraged me to believe I really did have a clue about what I was supposed to be doing. And then-*downbeat* editor Art Lange boosted my self-esteem by putting me on that long-lived

Preface

magazine's masthead while helping me take a more conceptual tack toward reviewing.

Elizabeth Pochoda, then the arts editor at *The Nation*, brought me, via Giddins, into that venerable journal as non-classical music columnist. Besides handing me a practically limitless portfolio, she let me discover, via her incisive line-editing and rapier comments, just what I could make that job mean, where it could take my thinking and writing. The column has been my laboratory ever since. Elsa Dixler and Art Winslow, her successors, have been consistently supportive and insightful. Maria Margaronis, whom I met at *The Nation*, and Giddins both opened up spaces for me at the *Voice* that let me stretch in other directions. Marilyn Lipsius, head of RCA's publicity department, suggested to Don Shewey that I'd be perfect for his Arts section in the then-unborn *7 Days*, where he let me run consistently amok over the areas I loved. Again thanks to Lipsius, Cathy Cook let me do likewise in the pages of *Taxi*. Sue Byrom, then the arts editor at the *New York Post*, let Pochoda and Diane Stefani persuade her that I was what that newspaper's music coverage needed. My time there was an education in itself; as—again thanks to Pochoda and Ron Givens—my time at the *New York Daily News* has been. And many others, like Brian Cullman, then at *Spin*, Thom Duffy at *Billboard*, Jim Oestreich at the *New York Times*, Charles McGrath at *The New Yorker*, Chris Smith of *New York*, and Laura Jacobs at *Stagebill* opened their pages to my stuff.

And of course, Sheldon Meyer, my editor at Oxford University Press, not only accepted my proposal for a book but worked up a head of enthusiasm for topics that must have seemed even more foreign to him than Alma-Ata.

To all of you, my deepest thanks.

My friends, musicians and non-, have been amazingly willing to suspend disbelief about what I thought I was doing without letting me get away with too much. The ever irascible Bob Quine taught me more about music history than any professor I ever had. Ornette Coleman, Muhal Richard Abrams, Henry Threadgill, Geri Allen, John Zorn, Marty Ehrlich, Tim Berne, Mark Helias, Mark Dresser, the Neville Brothers, Nile Rodgers, Bernard Edwards, Ronnie Drayton, Melvin Gibbs, and Vernon Reid taught me more about how to think about music and the music industry in larger contexts. Music-industry workers like Lipsius, Karen Goldman, Bob Merlis, Gregg Geller, Howard

Preface

Thompson, Bill Levenson, Jerry Rapaport, Brian Bacchus, Mary-Claude Nouy, Peter Clancy, Yale Evelev, Verna Gillis, Bruce Ricker, Craig Street, Jim Fouratt, Terri Hinte, Andy Caploe, Jonathan Rudnick, Steve Karas, Mary Melia, Fred Kelly, Margot Core, and Wayne Rosso ushered me inside the music-biz maze and helped me believe that what I was doing made a difference. Friends like Kozinn, Guralnick, Geller, Cullman, Oestreich, Billy Bergman, Leslie Berman, Ricky Martinez, Joe Milner, Bar Bizsick, David Dunn, Yvonne Tost Ervin, and Ellen Spross all spent time listening to me whine my way through some tangled idea, and usually managed to translate my bellyaches into a direction via a few well-placed questions.

Then there's my family. My parents didn't live to see this book, but before they died they'd realized that I was getting serious about that childhood dream of becoming a writer, and they'd seen enough of what I'd done in print to know I wasn't bluffing. My wife Tesse and my children, Donna and Linda, have put up with the peripatetic, not to say frantic, life a writer covering the turf that I do leads. They seem to think it was worth it. As one of my cousins put it at a recent family reunion, "You made up your own job, you created something where nothing was before. And you get to have a blast and get paid for it. I think it's great." I have to admit, so do I.

New York City/Shokan   G. S.
June 1993

Contents

Contents

Contents

Dancing in Your Head

Phonograph Blues

When Robert Johnson recorded it, in November of 1936, his "Phonograph Blues" was one of the first blues references to the technology. Recording hadn't yet transformed the blues from a collection of widely variant regional styles, each with its own salient characteristics, into a more homogeneous approach that, by the 1960s, had become virtually generic. For though an essential part of his myth (and life) was rambling, Johnson's own blues reflected not just his actual travels, where he picked up different regional attacks—the minor-key broodings of Skip James, the slashing Texas call-and-response vocals-plus-guitar, the ragtimey Piedmont jaunts, and the hardcore "deep" Delta blues of his Mississippi birthplace. Instead, his blues also pivoted around what he heard on records. And as blues historians like Peter Guralnick and Robert Palmer have pointed out, Johnson's compacted, crafted songs differed from most of his contemporaries' (with rare exceptions like James's or Leroy Carr's) because they were clearly shaped (or could be) for the three-minute recording limit 78s carried.

Bluesmen (and the very few women who played the blues) performed primarily for dancers at juke joints, outdoor parties and picnics, as well as on street corners—wherever an audience with spare change and spare time could gather. Armed with preset verses, like the Homeric bards wandering ancient Hellas, they could plug parts in or yank them out, depending on whether a particular song reached their audience. As a result, many blues lyrics from Johnson's time and before can seem anything from disorganized to borderline incoherent: their plots simply had less to do with their formatting than audience reaction did.

Like Skip James, Johnson apparently pruned his lyrics, honing them to a terrifying edge. Also like James (and unlike most of his contempo-

3

raries, at least from the recorded evidence), he seems to have formatted his musical accompaniments very tightly: alternate takes from his 1936 and 1937 recording sessions display some shifts of detail from one take to the next, but always within a set arrangement. (The one exception is "Come On In My Kitchen," where the alternate take lacks the menacing, hovering atmosphere of the issued take—a clear argument for the taste of Johnson's original producer, Don Law.) Besides offering mesmerizing virtuosity, Johnson's arrangements rotate around individual, distinctive riffs that mutate during the song's course to underline its lyrics. They whipsaw crossbeats back and forth between Johnson's piercing high-pitched singing and his achingly vocalic bottleneck guitar, and in the process foreshadow the latticework of rhythms webbing the postwar electrified urban blues pioneered by the likes of Muddy Waters, Howlin' Wolf, and Johnson's stepson Robert Jr. Lockwood. Eventually, of course, Johnson's feels found their way into the blues' stepchild, rock and roll.

In 1962, when producer Frank Driggs compiled *Robert Johnson King of the Delta Blues Singers* (Columbia) from the masters for the blues legend's 78s, he understood that Johnson's art was highly wrought, even though little was known of the bluesman's life at that time. So Driggs shaped the album to reflect the curve of an imagined performance: kicking off with the haunting supernatural loneliness of "Crossroads Blues," taking listeners through the double entendres of "Terraplane Blues" (Johnson's only regional hit), and building on the bitterly rising ironies of "Last Fair Deal Gone Done," "32-20 Blues," and "Kindhearted Woman Blues." Fittingly, he wrapped up the album's 16 cuts with what may well be two of the most frightening blues of all time, the aching Faust-in-Mississippi "Me and the Devil Blues" and its jagged, twitching companion piece, "Hellhound on My Trail."

A few years later *King of the Delta Blues Singers Vol. II*, which collected 16 additional Johnson tracks, including alternate takes of "Kindhearted Woman Blues," "Rambling on My Mind," and "Preaching Blues," was issued. Other alternate takes surfaced over the years on specialty labels, like "Milkcow Blues" on *Bottleneck Blues* (Yazoo).

In nearly three decades since the first Columbia compilation, Johnson's musical influence changed from being indirect (via his blues disciples) to stunningly direct; rockers from the Rolling Stones and Eric

Clapton on down reinterpreted a lot of his material for young audiences who'd never heard of Johnson, and in the process redirected the genre's sound. Then too, thanks to the untiring detective work of historians like Mack McCormick, who doggedly pursued flimsy decades-old leads to dig up Johnson's relatives and friends, the biographical slate gradually filled in. By the time Guralnick's *Searching for Robert Johnson* (Obelisk/ Dutton) was published last year, it could (with generous acknowledgments to McCormick) present a fairly complete and compelling picture of the seminal blues great's life and times.

So now, to the usual major-label fanfare, comes *Robert Johnson/The Complete Recordings* (Columbia). This two-CD set is just what the title says: for the first time, all 41 takes of Johnson's 29 tunes are collected in one place. But the digitally remastered sound is no better than the earlier Driggs albums'. And the added come-on—the 48-page booklet, which boasts fan's-eye appreciations by Keith Richards and Eric Clapton as well as an essay, lyric transcriptions, and discographical data written and gathered by would-be Johnson biographer (and the reissue's co-producer) Steven C. LaVere—is less than it seems.

I say "would-be" because LaVere's lack of insight is, along with corporate unconsciousness, what keeps this long-awaited compilation (it's been in the works for over 15 years) from being more than just a collection. Certainly his notes don't have me panting for his book on Johnson. The biographical section does present the facts, but it devolves too often into uninspired rehashes (especially of McCormick and Guralnick) alongside colorful but fanciful stretches of the known data. On the other hand, the section called "The Music" is simply appalling. Some samples:

> The dilemma of playing music for the rural mentality, while striving to divorce himself from it, not only served to extend to its furthest reaches the form and capabilities of the country blues, but since a strong element thereof is one of self-destruction, it quite logically and perhaps predictably, destroyed itself—its form and more importantly, its relevancy to its culture—and its practitioner as well, as a direct result.
>
> The obvious strife within a sensitive mind like Johnson's not only was the seat of his self-destruction, but its existence pre-created an urban neurosis.

Regardless of what Johnson was singing about, the reality of his situation can be powerfully felt. Certainly he felt this and knew it, too, but it is obvious from his own words that he didn't understand it.

This unconsciousness or awareness of the subconscious without a thorough understanding of its implications is the most pathetic aspect in all of Johnson's being. It is the underlying element of and key to his romantic appeal, both to women in his own time and to others, years and lifestyles removed.

Johnson shrouded his ignorance while confessing his confusion in four main thematic communities. Those of love, mainly unrequited; traveling, usually fleeing; evil thoughts, especially wrongdoing by himself or a lover; and intent mental activity dominated his work. He acknowledged being out of control with his surroundings, his fate, his destiny and yet he wasn't satisfied to blindly accept that fact, at least not without a good deal of thought.

Certainly LaVere could never be accused of a good deal of thought. Johnson's music is so tough-minded and taut, so rife with rich imagery and rippling with sexual and supernatural energy, so supple with humor and double entendres and so variegated in texture at the same time it repeatedly faces the echoless places within the human psyche, that the only explanation for LaVere's alleged aesthetic characterizations is Romantic racism. What he gives us is Johnson the nach'l nigger, anatomized, as by a lobotomized Northrop Frye, into his ridiculous "four main thematic communities."

Almost as unfortunate are LaVere's lyric transcriptions, which include phonetic inconsistencies supposed to represent some, but not all, of what LaVere calls "Johnson's dialectic pronounciation." Then there are the misrepresentations, errors, and omissions that riddle LaVere's version of Johnson's words and their meaning.

Of what value is an annotator who cites Webster's to explain "crossroads" and "hellhound" and "break down" but neglects to explain any of Johnson's double entendres—like the shrimp in "Dead Shrimp Blues," a term for whore that originated in the 17th century? Who points to "the only instance in Johnson's lyrics where he uses the uncontracted present participle" but underlines several passages of meaningless syllables which, he explains, "are phonetic approximations of what Johnson sings, which, in truth, may be nonsensical"? And as a transcriber—well, let's just say that LaVere drops the last verses of "32-20 Blues."

Phonograph Blues

In some key ways, the flaws of *Robert Johnson/The Complete Recordings* reflect more than LaVere's foolish incompetence. With the triumph of the CD, the record companies—those corporate custodians of our cultural history—have been rushing to unload the vaults they'd so blithely ignored for the last 20 years. Some of the reasons are simple: CDs are more profitable than LPs were; old material can be resold to its audiences with a minimum of effort in time and dollars; thanks to massive advertising, "digital" has become a word that automatically means "better," even though the translation of any single piece of music from analog to digital technologies is a matter of myriad small decisions that each producer and engineer makes differently, thus creating a highly variable meaning for the words "digital transfer"; and so on.

So right now, for the record companies, CD boxed sets—collections of musical careers—are all the rage, and Johnson's boxed set illustrates the strengths, weaknesses, and limitations of the genre. It's obviously important and valuable that the widespread musical treasures of this country's regionally and ethnically diverse populations be treated with deserved respect, not be left to molder away unheard, be made available so people not content to be segmented by radio-prescribed formats can find it between the marketing cracks. But *how* to do that is the question, and an unresolved one.

Only a collector or a critic would want to sit down and listen to two or three takes in a row of the same song, and even a critic would probably tire of the archivist posture pretty quickly. Records, after all, are aesthetic experiences that, like any other, are meant to have a form: artists and their producers make decisions about which takes of songs to release based on their aesthetic assumptions. With the advent of the album, even the order of the tunes became an important art, and not only with such '60s "concept" albums as *Sgt. Pepper*. Musicians and producers strove to create an overall aesthetic impact, a meaningful shape that would make an album more than just a collection of pieces—a portrait in time.

When a historical compilation covers a long career, there's a real argument to be made that chronology can be a useful key to an artist's evolution. Hearing an Eric Clapton grow over a sensitively thought-out selection set like *Crossroads* (Polydor), for instance, can teach initiate and fan alike something about the guitar hero. But it can only do that because of pleasure involved; only the weird eat spinach because it's good for them, and they're the only ones who'll suffer through even an exemplary by-the-numbers chronology just to learn something. If the tracks chosen and the order in which they are presented don't grab their listeners, they won't have any. That's one defining distinction between an album and an archive. To release 10 CDs with all of Bird's Verve recordings (*Bird: The Complete Charlie Parker on Verve*, PolyGram) is an enormously important archival act to be applauded and appreciated and bought by any reasonably serious jazz lover (and library), but it's not a picture of the essence of Bird's art that will reach beyond the already converted. To do that, PolyGram has rightly re-released individual Bird albums.

As far as Robert Johnson's art, the case for presenting his small body of work in purely chronological order is as weak as it can get. (And besides, as a couple of reissue producers pointed out to me, if the matrix numbers for the original masters were out of sequence—a common occurrence—this set's supposedly strict chronological order is fictitious anyway.) Johnson's entire recording career consists of a handful of sessions over an eight-month span. Nothing in the tunes suggests any major or minor shifts in his talent or vision. Of course, he predated the LP and CD, but since his three-minute performances were so highly conceptualized, it's easy to see that Frank Driggs's original LP compilations extended and articulated Johnson's own aesthetic frames. After listening to the Driggs, listening to LaVere's timetable approach is about as meaningful as hearing a sentence after it's been taken apart and restacked in alphabetical order. If you're curious about chronology, you can always check the discographical info that's included.

Fortunately, for the Johnson set, as well as for the countless reissues of individual albums that have alternate takes implanted to break the original conceptual flow, technology, which is part of the problem's source, is also the solution: program the original sequence into your CD player. In Johnson's case, use the order of the two Driggs albums, followed, if you're interested, by the alternate takes. That way, you'll get some sense of why Robert Johnson could inspire literally hosts of musicians like Keith Richards, who's quoted in the booklet as saying, "You know, you think you're getting a handle on playing the blues, and then you hear Robert Johnson—some of the rhythms he's doing and playing and singing at the same time, you think, 'This guy must have three brains!'"

After all, in many ways musicians understand their art best. Eric Clapton has never been accused of being a critical theorist, but for an aesthetic understanding of Robert Johnson's music he's a more useful guide than a dangerous geek like LaVere—who, in addition to his other flaws, had the gall to copyright Johnson's tunes under his own King of Spades Music. (Peter Guralnick was originally scheduled to write the notes for this package, which would have made them intelligent and useful; he set up the interviews with Richards and Clapton, but, thanks to corporate indifference, his Clapton transcription is marred by randomly italicized portions—an unfortunately apt symbol for CBS's approach to this project.) So it's worth pondering when the guitarist says of his idol's music,

> His best songs have never been covered by anyone else, at least not very successfully—because how are you going to do them? In some ways a song like "Hellhound on My Trail" is hardly there, it's almost in the air—what he doesn't say, what he doesn't play, it's so light and menacing at the same time. . . . It would be just great if people could simply appreciate his music for what it is, for its truth and its beauty, without its having to be a scholarly event. [1990]

chapter 2

Hellhound on His Trail

In 1989, it's hard to imagine that anybody who listens half-seriously to American popular music could not know who Robert Johnson was. After all, many of his tunes, like "Love in Vain" and "Stop Breaking Down," "Crossroads Blues" and "Walking Blues," have been repeatedly covered by folks like Muddy Waters, Howlin' Wolf, the Rolling Stones, and Eric Clapton. But long after his shadowy murder—its actual date, place, motives, and methods weren't confirmed until two generations passed—Johnson remained a mythic figure whose legends were unencumbered by historical data and fed only by his music. Intense and sly, supple and omnivorous, Johnson's blues are raunchy, terrifying, sophisticated, and different from nearly every other bluesman's. Like Skip James's, they represent a highly wrought set of conscious aesthetic decisions that, when Columbia gathered together an LP from his late-1930s 78s, justified crowning Johnson "The King of the Delta Blues Singers."

Nearly everyone who's ever played that album remembers the first time he or she heard it, usually with a mind-boggling circumstantial vividness—as if Johnson's raggedly keening voice, astonishingly agile guitar, in-your-face creative abundance, and haunted sense of the supernatural's day-to-day power impresses itself on listeners so deeply that they become poets-by-proxy. Nearly everyone who's ever played that album has wondered what forces drove Johnson, where the inspiration for his towering achievement came from, what made him him—when they weren't wondering about who he was and whether he'd really existed.

Peter Guralnick isn't nearly everyone. A renowned music critic and historian (*Feel like Going Home, Lost Highway, Sweet Soul Music*), Guralnick is dauntingly knowledgeable and an engaging stylist. He seduces you with the flow of a sentence before you realize you've just swallowed a chunk of history or critical analysis. That's because Guralnick combines heart and head; he wears his knowledge with the easy grace born of real love, and since he genuinely wants to share what he knows he writes with an honest, direct emotional attachment. So while he reconstructs the music's genealogy and structural components and larger social pictures as few others could do, he also vividly remembers the first time he heard "The King of the Delta Blues Singers."

Which is how *Searching for Robert Johnson* begins. Guralnick instructively reminds us, who are drowning in the glut of undifferentiated information that now doubles as a kind of censorship in this culture, of the impact "The King of the Delta Blues Singers" had in the info-black-hole of 1961, when he was a blues-loving freshman at Columbia:

> I had perhaps fifty albums of country blues . . . it seemed as if there could scarcely be any more. Names that are as familiar as presidents' today, touchstones for anyone familiar with the roots of contemporary music, were the exclusive province of collectors then. My friends and I studied the little that was available, attempted to piece together virtually indecipherable lyrics, pored over each precious photograph, constructed a world of experience and feeling from elliptical clues.

. . . I don't know if it's possible to recreate this kind of feeling today—not because music of similar excitement doesn't exist, but because the discovery can no longer take place in such a void.

From there, with a thoroughness that belies his book's slender size, Guralnick traces Johnson's lineage in the history of the Delta blues, from Charley Patton through Muddy and Wolf; reconstructs the chronology and paths of his development as a key player whose influence via recordings swept the blues; re-creates the two recording sessions from which the two LPs released in the '60s were compiled; and develops a circumstantially detailed picture of his family, loves, and travels, thanks partly to painstaking research by historian Mack McCormick and partly to extensive interviews with Johnson's disciples/companions Johnny Shines and Robert Jr. Lockwood, whose mother was one of Johnson's regular female stops on his endless road.

Nor is Guralnick content with reconstructed data. He locates Johnson's life in a context that makes it, and the process of building a narrative about it, resonate more meaningfully:

> The thing most commonly misunderstood is just how shadowy was the world in which Robert Johnson was moving about. . . . Communication . . . was almost exclusively oral . . . contacts were almost always tangential; the stories . . . were in a sense as mythopoetic as those of the ancient Greeks. Johnny Shines and Robert Lockwood, playing partners today, met, for example, through Johnson and became friendly years later in Chicago, but though each was well aware of the other, neither shares a single experience or memory of their time with Johnson. In a certain sense, in fact, each is suspicious of the other's memories and of the memories of others, because in their experience *it simply didn't happen that way.* Shines remembers an illiterate Robert Johnson, and Lockwood scoffs at the suggestion, which in turn seems to prompt a shift in Shines's memory.

Sifting and recording such treacherous but illuminating shifts, combining the results with the researches of others and his own acute critical insights, Guralnick has outlined as good an answer as we're likely ever to get to the question of who Robert Johnson was. But as he points out, the real mystery of Robert Johnson demands a never-ending search through its timeless clues, his slashing, ribald, aching blues.   [1989]

chapter 3

Lift Every Voice and Sing

Anybody who's attended urban storefront or rural clapboard churches or tuned in to their Sunday evening radio broadcasts has been hit with a sense of raw power: the stomping feet that shudder the walls, the yearning vocals that swell out of any proportion to the congregation's size, the incantatory preaching with its fervent call-and-response. This is the heartland of African-American gospel, whose intense and highly wrought musical styles have seeded the breeding grounds for leaders from W. E. B. Du Bois to Martin Luther King to Jesse Jackson. Not coincidentally, gospel provided some of the civil-rights and antiwar movement's most stirring anthems.

Black gospel grew out of the mongrelized American spirituals tradition and the Pentecostal revivalism rampant during the early part of this century. It's as peculiarly American a hybrid as its contemporaries and cultural antagonists/partners, blues and jazz, and its secular stepchild by them, rock and roll. As Anthony Heilbut put it in his recently revised *The Gospel Sound* (Harper & Row/Limelight Editions), which is still the best overview of the style, "Its language combined the stately periods of 18th-century prose with the richness of southern country talk and ghetto slang." Back in 1971, Heilbut was also among the first to point out rock's roots in gospel—a notion others, like Peter Guralnick in his *Sweet Soul Music* (Harper & Row/Perennial Library), have since detailed.

Gospel's internal conundrums are twisty and rich. Deprived of their own cultural identities once they were hauled here, black slaves were gifted with massa's religion. White Protestant hymnals served as a foundation for a very different musical approach. The slaves and their descendants felt free to adapt what they were given—at least when massa wasn't looking. (In the early 1800s, slaves held their own "brush arbor" services after the official ones, whence come allegorical "sorrow songs" like "Swing Low, Sweet Chariot.")

In *The Souls of Black Folk* (Bantam), W. E. B. Du Bois explained,

As bard, physician, judge, and priest, within the narrow limits allowed by the slave system, rose the Negro preacher, and under him the first church was not at first by any means Christian nor definitely organized; rather it was an adaptation and mingling of heathen rites among the members of each plantation, and roughly designated Voodooism. Association with the masters, missionary effort and motives of expediency gave these rites an early veneer of Christianity, and after the lapse of many generations the Negro church became Christian.

Given the historical context, maybe it's not surprising that African-American gospel songwriters described biblical figures like Solomon and Jesus as black. In the process, they nourished an Afrocentric tradition that enters our culture's stubbornly recurrent bouts of historical reinterpretation—like those that now have hardcore canonists and politically correct deconstructionists tearing at each other's throats.

Also ironically, gospel's fierce undercurrents of sexuality are enough at times to make you want to tear somebody else's clothes off despite the idiom's apparent prudishness and sanctified lyrics. According to Heilbut and other observers, that's just what happens very frequently indeed when gospelers meet their church groupies. Jubilation is a mighty aphrodisiac. This may seem unsurprising in our post-Jimmy Swaggart era, but its significance in the black gospel scene, as Du Bois and others have pointed out, lies elsewhere. In African cultures, the line between ritual and sexuality—between ritual and life—is usually placed quite differently than it is in Christianity. There rites are an integrated part of the social fabric, mark key passages and turning points in ways that parallel the relationship devout urban-ghetto and poor-rural folk in this country have with their churches.

Like most theologians, gospel adherents divide the world into the saved and the un-, which has yielded odd and ironic but enriching cultural by-products over the last few decades. Take the manifold but always uneasy (and sometimes downright acrimonious) dialogue of the last half-century between African-American gospel music and its popular counterparts, from blues to rock and hiphop. Plato's portrait of the artist as partially sighted, parasitical misleader is no stranger to gospelers. Gospel vocalists take well-justified pride in their jazzy flights of improvisation, but almost always cite their virtuosity's end as transcendent salvation. Art without a theological or philosophical harness is out of control. So churchgoing folk have always despised blues players, for instance, for their refusal to abide by "traditional" values, their racy lyrics, the sexual innuendo of their rhythms, the goings-on where they perform, their references to black magic and other vestigial descendants of African belief systems.

In their turn, the feelings of blues folk toward their religious brethren have run an apparently bewildering gamut. Many blues greats shuttled between the sacred and the profane. Some of them, like Skip James, lapsed into silence for decades because they wouldn't sing "the devil's music" once they returned to the church. If they had, of course, they would have been expelled. That's part of the reason for the venom of the great Son House's "Preachin' Blues." As a boy, House dutifully learned the church ways his father practiced. By his own account (to Sam Charters in *The Blues Makers*) he was sincerely devout. Then he dropped it all to become a bluesman, and wrote the jabbing "Preachin' Blues," whose opening lines are, "I'm gonna get me religion and I'm gonna join the Baptist church / You know I want to be a Baptist preacher so I won't have to work."

Interestingly, there's also a small but dynamic tradition of spiritual blues singers. (Some are collected on *Preachin' the Gospel: Holy Blues*, Columbia/Legacy.) Blind Willie Johnson, a truly scary bottleneck guitarist who was a contemporary of Blind Lemon Jefferson, drew haunting renditions of now-classics like "Dark Was the Night." Charley Patton, the fountainhead of Delta blues, recorded religious as well as secular tunes. For his Library of Congress field recordings, Muddy Waters played spirituals. Adherents like the Reverend Gary Davis backed religious lyrics with ragtime guitar. Sister Rosetta Tharpe, propelled by her guitar and a jazz-band backing, scored gospel's first crossover best-seller with the hard-swinging "Rock Me." And in the Caribbean, where the white hymnals-meets-blues tradition is remarkably like ours, Bahamas guitarist Joseph Spence in his unique way recaps the street-singer tradition that includes Blind Willie Johnson's religious duets with his wife.

This meeting of the sacred and profane has flowed in the other direction as well. The '40s harmonies of groups like the Mills Brothers and the Ink Spots were gospel-derived, and paved the way for the '50s doo-woppers who likewise crossed gospel into pop. Sixties soul music and soul-jazz also grew directly out of gospel, which turns on pyrotechnic vocal exhortations and improvisations. Many r&b performers did like Ray Charles, who appropriated a gospel ditty for his sexy shout,

"I Got a Woman." Singers like B. B. King, Bobby "Blue" Bland, and Dinah Washington all annexed churchy melismas and moans to their secular heartaches. Early soulsters like Solomon Burke, who himself vacillated between church and secular worlds, crossed over preaching-style monologues and call-and-response female backup vocals. Wilson Pickett's gruff confessing came right out of the gospel-quartet tradition he'd been raised in. And Aretha Franklin, whose father C. L. was one of the black church's famed preachers, heard heaven's door slam shut behind her when she testified with a ferocious vengeance in top-40 hit after hit.

Like Aretha, some artists were faced with hard choices because of the gospel world's harsh attitude toward secular backsliders. Sam Cooke started his career singing with the famed gospel quartet the Soul Stirrers, but had to change his name when he secretly cut his first soul singles. Once he decided to go overtly secular, his gospel career was instantly over. (His murder at a motel, complete with sexual scandal, had gospel folk shaking their heads with a grim sense of expectation fulfilled.) Then there's the Reverend Al Green, whose silky Cooke-ish singing has been transformed into a kind of incandescent religious ecstasy—a St. John of the Cross for soul music. A house-rocking preacher with his own con-gregation in Memphis these days, the Reverend has changed almost nothing about his music and lyrics except their putative addressee—which makes him feel (with some justification) still unaccepted by his peers. As you might expect, he also projects a more tolerant attitude toward pop culture than most of his brothers of the cloth.

One of the few links in the tradition who reconciled his secular and sacred sides was Thomas A. Dorsey. Dorsey was, in essence, gospel's godfather. He recharged the sentiments of widely used hymns like Dr. Watts's and Dr. C. A. Tindley's (who at the turn of the century merged black folk material with poor-white evangelism) with bluesy structures, composing thousands of gospel standards that became the movement's bedrock. With singer Sallie Martin, he founded the Gospel Singers Convention, and helped pave "the gospel highway," the touring routes that established the music as the lingua franca of black (and many white) churches throughout the land. (As Heilbut rightly argues, populism coexists with reaction in the evangelical movement: Aimee Semple McPherson's services, for instance, were always integrated, and in 1936 featured Martin.) In his earlier incarnation as bluesman Georgia Tom, he'd accompanied Ma Rainey and Bessie Smith, and as partners with guitarist Tampa Red penned and recorded any number of highly sugges-tive tunes like "It's Tight like That." But 20 years ago, Heilbut reported,

> He is completely secure in his several roles and feels no qualms about his life in show business. He remains a member in good standing of the Chicago Musicians' Union, and his attic studio is filled with pic-tures and records of Georgia Tom. "No, no," his voice cracks calmly, "I'm not ashamed of my blues. It's all the same talent, a beat is a beat whatever it is."

Since ritual is art's earliest source, it's no surprise that gospel music radiates a visceral power that can thrill the most devout atheist. And it continues to evolve a long ways from its bluesy "folk" early days and the barbershop-quartet-based jubilee style of the '30s with its simple piano or guitar backing. In the '60s James Cleveland, gospel's "Crown Prince," pioneered more complex melodies and harmonies, and in the '70s the likes of Andrae Crouch and Edwin Hawkins led choirs that mimicked contemporary pop formulas. Today, younger contenders like Green and Philip Bailey take on hiphop rhythms and synthesizer sonics as well.

Getting a sense of the spread and wealth of gospel music is a bit easier now than it's been for a while, since the new audiences and higher profit margins created by the compact disc have moved record companies to rummage through the vaults for this material as they already have for blues and jazz. So it happens that three fine compilations, each with a particular purview, have hit the marketplace recently. *I Hear Music in the Air* (BMG) offers a solid intro to the early folk-quartet days with the likes of the Rev. J. M. Gates and the Golden Gate Jubilee Quartet. *The Gospel Sound of Spirit Feel* (Spirit Feel)—from Heilbut's own tiny but outstanding label—casts its nets wider. It serves up important contribut-ing artists who include Clara Ward, Mahalia Jackson, and Sister Rosetta Tharpe, as well as seminal sweet-gospel quartets like the Dixie Hum-mingbirds, the Fairfield Four, and the Sensational Nightingales.

The Specialty label was central to gospel in the '50s, as it ironically was to rock and roll. Owner Art Rupe recorded not only the cream of contemporary gospel quartets but emerging gospel-driven rockers like Little Richard and Sam Cooke. *Greatest Gospel Gems* (Specialty) is a sterling selection from the label's mother lode, dazzling gems like Sam

Cooke with the Soul Stirrers, the Travelers, the Silvertones, Alex Bradford, Dorothy Love Coates, Sister Wynona Carr, and Cleveland.

For many observers, gospel's golden age comes with the postwar period, the so-called "sweet gospel era." That's when record companies began capturing the sounds of male quartets like the Soul Stirrers. During this era the quartets grew into quintets and sextets, and moved from the simpler antiphonal and chordal backings of jubilee to close harmonies supporting contrasting dual lead voices (usually a liquid tenor and a gruff light baritone) that trade off and improvise within a denser call-and-response format. Specialty plans to reissue Stirrers' classics with both Cooke and his mentor/model, Rebert Harris, as well as the bristling and intense material by the heart-stopping Dixie Hummingbirds. In the meantime, grab the Swan Silvertones' *My Rock/Love Lifted Me* (Specialty) or the Pilgrim Travelers' *The Best of the Pilgrim Travelers* (Specialty). The Silvertones' tenor Claude Jeter is another whose lilting, fiery flights became a model for soul, and the group's smooth-but-pulsating harmonizing remains a gospel hallmark. The Travelers were massively influenced, as were many, by the Harris-era Soul Stirrers, but that doesn't diminish their yearning musicality.

The next decade saw the triumph of "hard gospel" quartets like the Original Five Blind Boys of Alabama, whose appearance a few years back in the wonderful Greek-tragedy-goes-gospel *Oedipus at Colonnus* stopped the show. Lead vocalist Clarence Fountain is an incandescently ragged stylist who incarnates the physical growling and piercing screams of this period on *Oh Lord—Stand by Me/Marching up to Zion* (Specialty).

Women also rocked out in small groups. *The Best of Dorothy Love Coates and the Original Gospel Harmonettes* (Specialty) is a collection of one of the finest examples. Coates folds race consciousness and poetically charged recastings of received images into her scintillating songs, then fires them via her torn but amazing voice, which dips and whirls and leaps over intervals with throaty abandon. You can hear her echoed in Mavis Staples (whose own background is gospel, with guitarist-father Pops and siblings) and Irma Thomas, the soul queen of New Orleans who still sings in church every Sunday.

The great women soloists, like Sallie Martin, Mahalia Jackson, and Clara Ward, have been tireless and indispensable gospel workers. One of the greatest vocalists in the Bessie Smith tradition is Marion

Williams, whose sturdy, nuanced *Strong Again* (Spirit Feel) finesses older styles. (It boasts a version of Billie Holiday's "God Bless the Child," for instance.) Heilbut has written tellingly, "She defines and reconciles her twin dispositions, for she is both a modest saint . . . and an overwhelming showman. The two impulses . . . aren't always balanced, but when spirit and style converge, the result is unparalleled. . . . If she's saved to the utmost, she's also as worldly as any gospel singer."

That duality is at gospel's heart. In the end, by lifting their voices with the incredible expressivity and dazzling technique that they've developed, gospelers resemble the great medieval cathedral builders. Their labors intend to reflect the glory of God, but they shout as loudly about the glory of humanity, its ability to triumph over its apparent limitations.   [1991]

chapter 4

Doing It to Death

On September 24, 1988, in an office complex he owns in his hometown of Augusta, Georgia, James Brown brandished a shotgun at an insurance seminar. He complained that someone there had used his private bathroom next door. The cops were called, Brown dove into his pickup truck, and they pursued him for 10 miles—with between 10 and 14 vehicles at speeds up to 85 m.p.h. Surrounded during the *French Connection*-style chase in an abandoned lot, Brown slammed his truck into reverse, and the cops shot out his front tires. (Brown, who'd been convicted of assault and battery involving an officer that February, said he'd been stopped for ten minutes before the cops showed up.) Though he had his shotgun with him throughout the incident, the police said he didn't threaten them with it or attempt to use it. Brown's truck had 23 bullet holes in it when he finally ran into a ditch. As he told one interviewer, "I was scared to death." And to another: "They're trying to make you antagonize 'em so they can kill you."

On December 15, 1988, Brown was convicted of failing to stop for police—a felony in South Carolina—and assault of a high and aggravated nature (trying to run down his pursuers). His time: 6 years for the so-called "blue light" offense, and two concurrent 5-year terms for assault that were suspended to 5 years of probation not concurrent with his 6-year sentence—which, for purposes of parole eligibility, was equivalent to an 11-year term. His lawyer, Reginald D. Simmons, said, "It was extremely harsh, not commensurate at all with the crime."

As Dave Marsh points out in a new epilogue to *James Brown* by James Brown with Bruce Tucker (Thunder's Mouth Press), the fine autobiography reissued in 1990, the media weren't much kinder. They certainly weren't addicted to the facts. Marsh cited *Rolling Stone*, which muddled actual charges against Brown with allegations. But *Stone*, as usual, wasn't alone. Tabloids like *New York Newsday* hoisted Brown with the headline "Cell Brother No. 155413." *Time*'s rather sneering piece, entitled "Soul Brother No. 155413," inaccurately suggested that he had long been sliding into musical irrelevance. Nor did the music world Brown has been crucial to for three decades seem interested in sorting things out: there were no organized demonstrations, and only an embarrassing handful of individual protests, on his behalf before his parole. (Marsh duly outlines racist hypocrisy within the music industry—and by implication, the country at large—by contrasting Brown's fate with the treatment given famous white rockers in trouble with the law.) And when he was finally released early this year, *People* ran a mocking piece that focused largely on the 57-year-old's teeth implants, tattooed eyebrows and permanent lower-lid eyeliner, use of Lysol to clean his cell, and work in the prison kitchen.

Despite the jabs and the silence, James Brown was paroled after putting in two years and two months for trying to flee arrest. He'd served 15 months of his sentence at the State Park Correctional Facility near Columbia. Then he was transferred to Aiken, where he worked for the nonprofit Aiken and Barnwell Counties Community Action Commission counseling youth about drug abuse for 11 months. (Although South Carolina police said Brown tested—voluntarily—positive for PCP use when they finally corralled him, although he'd been busted earlier that year for possession of PCP and again on September 25, 1988, for driving under the influence of PCP and pot, he was not convicted on either charge. Jesse Jackson, who visited Brown two months into his term, read a statement by the singer that said he wasn't on drugs and hadn't engaged in any violence toward the cops.)

The Hardest Working Man in Show Business went right back to it. (During his stir time, a constant if ironic refrain in interviews was, "I'm rested, well rested.") On the Potomac Productions has produced and marketed a video documentary called *James Brown: The Man, the Music & the Message* that's been airing via syndication around the country. On June 29, Brown began a summer-long tour. And then there's *James Brown Star Time* (Polydor), a four-CD compilation of digitally remastered seminal cuts from Brown's long and varied career.

Few artists can claim the far-reaching influence on the pop music of the last three decades that Brown can. *Star Time* boasts 71 cuts that illustrate how he managed to go from motherless street urchin, who lived in a shack, scoured through garbage for food, danced for World War II troop trains for pennies, and served an 8- to 16-year term for breaking into four cars at age 16, to The Godfather of Soul, whose international disciples include jazzers, rockers, disco-ites, Afropoppers, reggae-ists, and rappers. (Brown has guessed that about 150 of his tunes have been sampled without royalties by hiphoppers. Estimates of how many hiphop tracks ride JB samples run as high as three thousand.) Sly Stone, George Clinton, the Rolling Stones, the Electric Flag, Chic, Bob Marley, Tower of Power, Talking Heads, Sunny Ade, Fela Kuti, Michael Jackson, Prince, Public Enemy—all bear his mark. Like few other bandleaders—Count Basie, Duke Ellington, Muddy Waters, Miles Davis, Charles Mingus, Ornette Coleman—he has both maintained a core of loyal players and molded changing lineups into his musical image. In the process he's trained some of the era's outstanding musicians while redirecting the evolutionary flow of pop culture worldwide.

For a while along the way, he acquired visibility, wealth and holdings that swelled pride in the black community—his 12-room mansion in St. Albans, his Lear jet, his limos, his string of radio stations. But the corporate institutionalization of pop music and radio, which promoted disco and realigned markets, shriveled much of his music-based empire. In 1971 he moved to Polydor from the small indie King, which theoretically should have sustained, if not extended, his huge multiracial reach. But he claims with at least some accuracy in *James Brown* that Polydor helped derail his hit-making via insensitivity to his live-in-the-studio recording methods and lack of insight into his audiences. (Not surprisingly, *Star Time*'s notes indirectly dispute this.) Then in the mid-1970s one of his managers was convicted of payola to get airplay for the previously invulnerable Godfather's discs. Soon after, his jet was repossessed. He sold off the radio stations one by one. He sunk a million dollars into an abortive TV show. And since 1985, his 62-acre farm outside Augusta has been under lien by the IRS.

The IRS claims Brown owes $9 million in taxes—$4.5 million for 1969 and 1970 alone. On the video he taped with Dick Cavett, Brown asks, "Why do all black people wind up penniless? Why do they come and take tax from me? That case is 25, almost 30 years old, and was never about but $211,000 from the git-go." Whatever the actual numbers, with his IRS overseers Brown joins a long line of successful blacks who've come under harassment, from Joe Louis through Chuck Berry. Still, he thinks of himself as an African-American version of Horatio Alger. He meant it when he told *Time*, "I've been the American Dream."

In many ways, his life reflects in intensified form the contradictions many African Americans feel about this country's promise even when they affirm the myth they're only partially included in. As JB hornman Fred Wesley told Cynthia Rose in the interesting, if sometimes over-reachingly interpretive, *Living in America* (Serpent's Tail), "Contradiction is the very thing which feeds his nerve. . . . He is just as fragile as he is tough." So there are his hardhitting anthems like "Say It Loud (I'm Black and I'm Proud)," his talk about payola as a method of financial redistribution between white station owners and their underpaid black DJs, the street-jive realism of his lyrics. There's his endorsement of Nixon and hobnobbing with Reagan and Bush. There's his ceaseless entrepreneurial drive and patriotic tunes (which caused cries of "Uncle Tom") like "America Is My Home." And there are his longtime friend-ships with the Reverends Jesse Jackson and Al Sharpton.

But mostly, and most importantly, there's his music, which in its insistent individualism arising from a wealth of diverse influences is very much a culmination of at least one aspect of the American Dream. *Star Time* picks from the panorama of Brown's nearly 40-year-long evolution by emphasizing both hits and significant musical turning points—a solid strategy for dealing with his enormous, syncretic, and idiosyncratic output.

In his early days (collected on *The Federal Years, Vols. I and II*, Solid Smoke) JB extended the silken gospel-based cries of Roy Brown with the frenetic jump-blues of Louis Jordan. His ballad stylings—he told me, "I've never really been an r&b singer, I was always a lot more of a ballad singer, and then I started singing more uptempo songs"—owe a lot to his other heroes, Jackie Wilson and Little Willie John. (John's hit "Fever" made more money for Peggy Lee than for him; he died in prison for manslaughter at 30.) Fusing them and models like fellow Georgian Little Richard, Brown fashioned the nonstop stage show that climaxed with "Please Please Please" and half an hour of the famed cape routine he'd adapted from '50s wrestler Gorgeous George. It all culminated in the universally acclaimed 1962 album *Live at the Apollo* (Solid Smoke), which Brown cut despite record-label opposition. The disc topped the pop charts for over a year—a rare feat for an r&b artist.

The New Breed Thing—what became funk—kicked off with 1964's "Out of Sight," and deepened with the landmark "Papa's Got a Brand New Bag." Harmonic movement disappears in favor of vamps and the primacy of polyrhythms. The coiling instrumental lines intersect, pair at different but cyclically repeating points, then expand away from each other until the next touchdown, creating an irresistible chug-a-lug effect. Riffing over, under, around, and through this whole percolating juggernaut is the band's rhythmic key, *that voice:* the battle-scarred grunts and "Good Gods," the torn screams, the jagged phrases, the calls for the bridge that pushed generations of happily frenzied young whites and blacks alike onto the dance floor with hit after hit, like "I Got You (I Feel Good)," "Cold Sweat," and "I Got the Feelin'." The way JB explained it to me, "The horns are really gospel with jazz licks. That's where soul music comes from, y'know. It was totally different from anything else that was out there. I was too far ahead of the people, though. So I recorded 'I Feel Good' twice. I cut it first like jazz, but then I went back and cut it again." (Both tracks are on *Star Time*.) During this period, he literally changed the face of popular music around the world.

By the early 1970s Brown's music had modulated the violently syncopated popcorn rhythms into heavier funk grooves. Tunes like "Funky Drummer"—a favorite of hiphop samplers—and "Brother Rapp" illustrate just how far ahead of his time Brown still was. It's a disparity that's been pointed up over the last decade-plus by the differences between his burning stage shows and his often mediocre recordings. He put it to me this way:

> I would rather record live, because I want to have that live feel in there. If you hear my band, it's so far ahead of what I'm doing on record it's scary, y'know. But they don't ever let me put that on record anymore, and I can understand that, y'know—it's also so people can grasp it a little bit easier. I actually have to go back to more elementary things to put on a record as opposed to the way I do it live, because when we do our hard thing we speak very very fast, y'see. But I think the audience can handle it. I don't think the record companies can. They don't want you to be different, an Einstein in an ABC world.

That problem—the inability of his record companies and even his audiences to keep up with his relentless musical changes—plagued him from the mid-1970s on. After a series of black-power anthems like "Say It Loud (I'm Black and I'm Proud)," "Soul Power," "I Don't Want Nobody to Give Me Nothing," and "Funky President," many whites began to avoid his shows while many blacks began to embrace the pallider disco beats he'd helped spawn. A cadre of his key musicians, like Maceo, mutinied and signed on with George Clinton's Parliament-Funkadelic, that fabulous sci-fi/funk cosmological groove academy. His empire was crumbling, despite solid efforts like the pathetically titled *The Original Disco Man* (Polydor). Stabs at movies—he had cameos in *The Blues Brothers* and *Rocky IV*—didn't really lead anywhere. In 1984 he hooked up with rapper Afrika Bambaataa for *Unity* (Tommy Boy), where phrases from outstanding JB tunes swirl through a rap-meets-funk entreaty for peace and brotherhood and against nuclear holocaust. Material he cut with reggae rhythm masters Sly and Robbie and a gospel album with Sharpton didn't manage to find label homes before his imprisonment.

Four years in the making, *Star Time* traces this remarkable and unsettling achievement with sensitivity and intelligence. Including unedited cuts, for instance, allows us to hear Brown and his crackerjack bands shaping tracks in the studio live as the tape rolls. The digital remixing clarifies individual lines without sterilizing the overall result. The accompanying booklet supplies a good intro to Brown's life and music. The set's only real drawback is its 6- by 12-inch case. This new industry standard, the result of retailer pressure, makes box sets unsuitable for either CD- or LP-sized shelves.

But swell package aside, the ultimate thing about James Brown is the contradiction-healing groove. Densely filigreed, it lifts you with an easy inevitability. It's like a brief return to Paradise. As JB told me in his purring, gospel-preacher singsong,

> Y'know, one thing about music: it's the key to *every*thing, the universal language of man's commitment to be together. Yeah, a baby can *feel* before it can *see*, so the *feeling* is far beyond sight, *sound* is far beyond sight, umm-hmm. So that we ought to have music *every*where: in the churches, in the political meetings, in hospitals, in dentists' offices. 'Cause see what the music is doing? It's so *vast*, or *beyond* our thinking, because it reaches your soul and you can feel before you can see, that it's mind over matter. You say ouch and don't even know where the pain's coming from, but the *feeling* is *real*.

And more than anyone, James Brown's got the feeling.   [1991]

chapter 5

Take It to the River

"I am an artist," says the Reverend Al Green, "and what I do is supposed to be enjoyed as a work of art. If the church world today were more open to that, I think I could cut more songs that would be more art-oriented instead of always religious-religious-religious oriented. But in the church, y'know, we have our way of doing things and we're kinda set in the pattern, so therefore you're kinda in a bind about what you can do a little bit. Except me—I'm the black sheep, liable to do anything. I mean, I still cut songs like 'The Mighty Clouds of Joy' that was done by B. J. Thomas some years ago. It's just art; that's what I think it is, anyway."

Whether as Al Green, the '70s' sensitive soul singer with a sinuous falsetto the rival of Smokey Robinson's, or as the Reverend Al Green, for

the last decade the soul-shaking pastor of Memphis's Full Gospel Tabernacle, a low-slung space-age structure not far from Graceland, he's been
honing that art for twenty years. On secular hits like "Tired of Being
Alone," "Let's Get Married," and "Sha-la-la" or church-oriented outings like *He Is the Light*, Green unleashes a voice supple and sinewy
with the right pauses, curlicues, twists. As he insists, he's just moved his
artistry to the sacred side of the musical aisle.

The split between the sacred and the secular runs through the history
of the blues, rock and roll, and soul music, as well as Green's own
musical career. Born Albert Greene in Forrest City, Arkansas, in 1946,
his home reflected that polarization. "My father played bass in different
r&b groups, but he only played Christian gospel records at home. Eventually he formed a gospel group with me and my brothers called the
Green Brothers. I got bounced out when I was nine for listening to
Jackie Wilson, 'cause at that time it was kinda taboo, y'know."

So by age 16 he'd transferred his guitar playing and singing from the
sacred to the secular realm. "Soon I kinda joined this r&b group, the
Creations, in Grand Rapids after we moved up there." (Green's family
moved from Arkansas when he was 13). In 1967 the group, by then
called the Soul Mates, cut "Back Up Train," which got Green booked at
the Apollo Theater.

The Soul Mates soon fell apart, leaving Green to tour the chitlin'
circuit and get nowhere for the next year or so. Then he walked into a
Hollywood-style scenario for being discovered. A 1968 night found him
in a Midland, Texas, club opening for trumpeter Willie Mitchell, then
riding a crest of instrumental hits like "Soul Serenade." Mitchell doubled as chief producer and a&r man for the small but important Memphis Hi label.

Watching the young man loosen up, Mitchell heard in his softer-
voiced but passionate soul a sound he'd been searching for. "I wanted
somebody who could sing pleasant enough to appeal to black and white
audiences with the same record, not like some of the rougher-voiced
singers," he says. So he called Hi's owner Joe Cuoghi to tell him he was
bringing Green back to Memphis. After a lot of coaxing, Green bounced
along on the hump of Mitchell's band van for the several-hundred-mile
ride. Time and conversation—and the fact that Mitchell loaned him
$1500 to pay off Grand Rapids bills—convinced him this was the right
road.

A few weeks later they were in the studio cutting cover tunes like "I Want to Hold Your Hand" and their first hit, a Southern-style funkified version of the Temptations' "Can't Get Next to You." But Green had been writing songs, and obsessing on one in particular, for years. "After we had cut almost the whole first album I said, 'Well, I have a song.' So everybody says, 'Yeah, right, right (laughs). Maybe we could cut . . . Let me see. . . .' I said, 'But you haven't heard my song.' So finally I got a chance to play it on guitar, and it turned out to be our first million-seller."

"Tired of Being Alone" outlined the soul-man turf Al Green would claim as his distinctive own. Until he'd met Mitchell, Green's vocalizing was, in his own words, "more in the harder vein. I'd been listening to Otis Redding, James Brown, Wilson Pickett, B. J. Thomas—all the stars who were singing with a certain, you know, strength. That was the thing at the time. But Willie wanted me to just relax and not sing so hard, just to find Al Green. So there I was, trying to create myself as well in the middle of all this recording. Apparently I stumbled across it (laughs)." Apparently he did: "Tired" hit number 11 on the *Billboard* charts, the first of Green's nine million-sellers.

The string of hits and big-venue tours ran pretty much unbroken until 1976, punctuated by a searing experience at Disneyland in 1973. "We'd played with Smokey Robinson in San Francisco, then got a private jet to take us down to Anaheim for this special midnight show," is the way Green tells it. "I went to bed collapsed and exhausted, and woke up in the middle of the night praising God. It was amazing; I'd never experienced anything like that before. I ran into the bathroom and tried to keep it from coming out, stuffed a towel in my mouth, but that's impossible to do—even if you have a towel."

His co-workers weren't exactly thrilled to learn of his conversion. "When I was telling Willie and the others about it, at first they found it difficult to believe. Oh, man, there's a great current pulling back and forth in there within the (music) industry, between secular rhythm & blues/pop and Christian gospel. It's tremendous to try to change from one place to the other. You have to be mentally strong to do that. There was so much stress and strain from everyone in the industry: the managers, the promoters, the booking agents, the club owners."

In fact, Green himself spent over three years seesawing back and forth across that line. "I spent a lot of that time doing songs where the lyrics were deliberately ambiguous about what their object was, whether I was singing to a woman or someone else," he grins. His life reflected that ambiguity. He'd become involved with a woman who, unknown to him, was married with three children. It was a recipe for the disaster that struck in 1974. "I was in my apartment in a separate part of the house. She had just proposed to me, and I'd said I didn't know whether I wanted to marry her, what I wanted to do." Her reaction was to take a pot of boiling grits, bring it to Green's quarters, and toss it all over his back, scalding him severely. She then went downstairs and shot herself.

The sensational case recalled how Sam Cooke, one of Green's biggest vocal influences and himself a singer who crossed from gospel to r&b, was killed in a cloud of sexual innuendo. It pushed Green into painful skin grafts and convalescent seclusion for almost eight months. Coupled with his Anaheim conversion, the trauma led Green to recross to the sacred, so he bought the somewhat dilapidated Full Gospel Tabernacle and began preaching there in the mid-1970s. He continued to record and perform what sounded like soul music with increasingly ambiguous lyrics. "I did an album called *The Belle Album* where that's kinda evident. There's one song that goes, 'It's you that I want, but it's Him that I need'; that's the epitome of the pyramid, the tip of the iceberg, if you will. That's where I began to say it out loud."

It was also the first time he'd produced himself, since longtime producer Mitchell bowed out. *The Belle Album* sold well, but it marked the last of Green's soul music. By 1979, after nearly being badly hurt by a fall from a concert stage, he dedicated himself solely to gospel. With that, his audience too began to shift. "That was inevitable. But it's like anything else: if you go for the flashy, high-roller-type life you get the flashy, high-roller-type people. You know, if you live more down-to-earth, you draw that kind of a crowd. So when you change like that people are gonna disagree about whether it's a good thing or a bad thing." As they continue to do to this day about the Reverend Al Green, with his Grammy and his gold records and his 1982 stint with Patti LaBelle in Broadway's gospel smash *Your Arms Too Short to Box with God* and his performance of sections from Duke Ellington's *Sacred Concerts* and his Sunday midday preaching into a sweat—from both sides of the aisle.

I Get Joy (A&M) is likely to stir everybody up a bit more—especially when they catch the video for the single, "As Long as We're Together."

According to Green, "Our concept is about love, and I suppose if I could save a soul from hatred I'd be saving a soul from death." Still, the gyrating dancers aren't exactly holy rollers. Two years in the making, built with overdubs from Green's basic guitar-plus-vocals tracks, rounded off with churchy lyrics over backings from jubilee shouts to dance-floor beats, *I Get Joy* is shot through with jubilant vocals.

And for his supporting tours he's been reincorporating secular hits like "Let's Stay Together" into the light- and smoke-filled show. For the message the Reverend Al Green serves up at the Tabernacle and New Orleans Jazz & Heritage Festival and the Beacon Theater stays constant:

> Love is universal, and love is meant to be broader than just a little narrow box. If I'm to love my neighbor as myself, I don't know who my neighbor may be; I ought to check and find out. The commandment is simply love each other as we love ourselves. And since that's the case, it's true no matter who our neighbor is. One may want to listen to Duke Ellington, one may want to listen to Count Basie, one may want to listen to Mozart, one might want to listen to Bruce Springsteen. You see what I'm saying? But the commandment is what it is. So therefore, should I take your music from you? Should you take my music from me? Not so, I don't think.   [1989]

chapter 6

Born on the Bayou

Outside New Orleans, between Baton Rouge and the Louisiana-Texas border, stretches the swampy, waterway-laced countryside familiar from films like *The Big Easy*. It's called the bayou, and from the mid-1700s on it became a refuge for the French-speaking inhabitants of the Canadian province Acadia. The British government began uprooting them after the French loss of Canada; though the Crown tried to resettle them elsewhere, many successfully fled to New France, where they re-established their communities and culture and became known as Cajuns.

Their cultural baggage included the informal back-porch sounds of scraping fiddles and percussive guitars, wheezy squeezeboxes and scratched rubboards; high nasal vocals arched over modified waltzes and simple but driving two-step dance rhythms. The mix thrived in the bayou, where it began to rub against some of its neighbors and exchange characteristics.

The other large group of bayou settlers were French-speaking blacks, the Creoles. Though descended from runaway slaves and freedmen, the Creoles shared more than a fractured *patois* with the white community. Creole and Cajun culture developed along similar lines in many areas, like cuisine; in music, they crossfertilized to the point that their sounds were frequently interchangeable stylistically, with instrumentation, rhythms, and mournful vocals in idiosyncratic French staying fairly constant across the color bar.

At least until the '20s and '30s, when other influences on the music's development entered the bayou via records and later radio. For Cajuns, the key new entrant was country music—the early raw hillbilly kind derived from the Anglo-Celtic folk traditions of jigs and reels and ballads, not Nashville's corporate product. For Creoles it was blues, which thrived along the Mississippi River in bustling ports and on backwoods plantations alike. Not surprisingly, these musical strains continued to crosstalk, with Creoles picking up on country stylings and Cajuns adapting blues elements.

The single most important name in zydeco, as the Creole gumbo of black, French, and country traditions is known, is still Clifton Chenier. Accordionist/vocalist Chenier, who died in 1988, earned his title King of Zydeco by fashioning a unique rollicking hybrid from his early recordings in the '50s on. Especially as captured on essential albums like *Clifton Chenier Live* (Arhoolie), he transformed a more laid-back rural music into an electrified rhythmic dynamo. Singing now in French, now in English, over the insistent rasp of his brother's metal rubboard and the powerhouse backing of a band boasting ripsnorting sax, B. B. King-ish guitar, and unstoppable rhythm section, Chenier cut such blues-drenched masterpieces as *Boogalusa Boogie* (Arhoolie). His stamp continues to define latter-day practitioners like his son C. J., Buckwheat Zydeco, Boozoo Chavis, and Rockin' Dopsie.

Zydeco, like its Cajun cousin, is the music of a community; unlike the commercially produced musical formats we're used to hearing on the radio, it reflects a particular way of life and values. To get a better sense of what those are, grab documentary filmmaker Les Blank's *Red Beans and Rice*, which captures Chenier and his music on their home turf.

Despite Louisiana's horribly depressed economy in the wake of the oil bubble's bursting, Cajun musical life on the bayou has, like its zydeco cousin, been enjoying a revival of its own. That's thanks in part to fiddler/vocalist Michael Doucet and Beausoleil, his band named after the leader of the 1755 Acadian uprising against the British. Playing in a duo with accordionist Zachary Richard, Doucet became inspired to dig into his culture's musical roots, which, like many local traditions in this country, was being steamrollered out of memory by the media onslaught of the commercial mainstream. So he studied with old Cajun masters like Dennis McGee and the Balfa Brothers as well as Creole fiddle great Canray Fontenot, then formed the nucleus of Beausoleil in the mid-1970s.

Though the band got attention in folkie circles early on, their regular appearances on Garrison Keillor's *A Prairie Home Companion* in 1984 were what broke them to a wider audience. Meanwhile, Doucet has loosened up from his early stiff preservationist correctness with mix-'em-up albums like *Hot Chili Mama* (Arhoolie), *Bayou Boogie* and *Bayou Cadillac* (both Rounder). And if Beausoleil's soundtrack for *Belizaire the Cajun* displayed their continuing concern with their history, their culture-crossing song for *The Big Easy*, "Zydeco Gris-Gris," demonstrated their entwined black and white roots, versatility, and potential pop-audience reach via those foot-stomping beats.

Laissez les bons temps roule!   [1989]

chapter 7

New Orleans's Hidden Treasures

Everybody knows that jazz was born in New Orleans. But the range of music born there before and since is more diverse than you'd think from just stopping in at Preservation Hall or wandering along Bourbon Street, and it's thriving in the otherwise economically depressed Cresent City.

The conceit that New Orleans is really a Caribbean city helps explain its musical diversity. The percolating rhythms of military marching bands mingled from colonial days with the African-derived polyrhythms and call-and-response forms of slaves (who were brought from Africa) and free blacks (who migrated from Caribbean islands) eventually to yield early jazz. That mix was replicated differently in the Europeans' Caribbean colonies, but it set up a continuing exchange: Jamaicans tune in New Orleans radio stations and New Orleans musicians pick up early on Caribbean developments like soca and reggae.

So New Orleans is a kind of paradox: a near-foreign city where music is a more natural part of the cultural fabric than in any other U.S. place, it's produced quintessential American sounds. Take its famed Mardi Gras Indians, who've combined African roots with a commemoration of an Indian-aided slave revolt to create elaborate pageantry and a loose-limbed, exuberant parade music for the family- and neighborhood-oriented tribal organizations. Driven by fierce percussion and call-and-response vocals, their ornate costumes and street celebrations have to be witnessed to be truly appreciated, but recordings like the Golden Eagles' *Lightning and Thunder* (Rounder) can give you a taste. And for the VCR-lover there's *Always for Pleasure*, the fine documentary by Les Blank that captures the omnipresent music and unbusinesslike attitudes toward life and time that define New Orleans.

For a long time the brass-band tradition thrived in the Crescent City, but even there it began to peter out along with cultural holdovers like funeral processions, which were among the bands' work staples. (The catchphrase "second-line" used to describe New Orleans's parade-based rhythms comes from processions: the band, or first line, would lead the strutting dancers, or second line.) Then a few years ago the Dirty Dozen Brass Band bent the moribund format's perceived limitations. Playing traditional marches back-to-back with bebop or Rolling Stones tunes, the DDBB lace it all with a good-time rhythmic feel that makes not moving impossible. Check out *My Feet Can't Fail Me Now* (Concord Jazz) or *Voodoo* (Columbia). Other participants in the current revival are compiled on *Down Yonder* (Rounder).

The piano has been basic to New Orleans since the days of barrelhouse "professors" and houses of ill repute, and two of the best pianists of recent days are having posthumous revivals. Henry Roeland "Professor Longhair" Byrd and James Booker III were musically omnivorous, dextrous, and rhythmic with a catchy complexity that can baffle even drummers. Not surprisingly, they reached legendary status among locals—the famed club Tipitina's was named after a yelping party-down mambo by Longhair. Standout recordings include Longhair's *New Orleans Piano* (Atlantic) and *James Booker Volume One* (JSP).

Which brings us to one band that embodies New Orleans's cultural diversity and spirit. The Neville Brothers, after years of working separately in different lineups (like the amazing Meters, the Big Easy's funky answer to Booker T and the MGs, who opened a Rolling Stones tour) and scoring some hits, united in 1975 to play with their uncle George "Jolly" Landry, a chief of a Mardi Gras Indian tribe. The resulting classic, *The Wild Tchoupitoulas* (Island), crossed parade tunes with rock and roll—like Mardi Gras on the dance floor.

The history of the Neville Brothers encapsulates the problems facing New Orleans musicians. Off N.Y.'s and L.A.'s beaten corporate paths, operating with a casual, tribally based trust that has repeatedly left them open to rip-offs, a racially mixed group who attract racially mixed audiences, the Nevilles have until recently seemed trapped by commercial pressures and pigeonholes, though their infectious funk and astonishing voices have repeatedly crowned them champs of the New Orleans Jazz and Heritage Festival.

Yellow Moon (A&M) mixed Bob Dylan covers and horn work from the Dirty Dozen Brass Band with the Jamaican rapping called toasting, party-down funk with spacey textures and bluntly political lyrics dealing in racism and war and imperialism. Subsequent albums like *Brother's Keeper* (A&M) extend the mix. As their always amazing concerts show, the Nevilles can wreak their special magic on anything from Ellington to Mardi Gras standards, from raunchy rockers to delicate soul ballads. And as they stir up traditions from far and wide, they, like their home-town, make an unmatched musical gumbo that has to be tasted to be believed.   [1989]

chapter 8

Soul Queen of New Orleans

Now in her early fifties, she's beautiful and sassy and the mother of four, and she wields her rich, throaty voice with the nuanced command born of long experience. New Orleans's very own Queen of Soul, Irma Thomas, has been winning back the national spotlight her musicianship and spinetingling vocals deserve.

Born in Pontchatoula, Louisiana ("The Strawberry Capital of the world," she laughs), and raised in the Crescent City, Thomas has been immersed in music from her earliest days. During the week she was glued to the radio listening to hits by r&b greats like Percy Mayfield, and on Sundays she sang, as she does to this day, in church, where she, like so many other soul singers, draws out her gospel-derived vocal swoops and swerves, from the aching catch in the throat to the flat-out belting scream.

Her break into show biz came in 1958, while she was waitressing at the Pimlico Club. "Tommy Ridgley and his band were playing there, and I asked myself up onstage to sing a tune with them," she says, grinning at the memory. Ridgley, a key musical figure in the Big Easy, liked what he heard; and so when Thomas was fired ("The people in the club didn't mind me getting up on stage, but the man who was paying me to be a waitress did"), he set up an audition for her with the local label Ron Records. "He took me to the audition on Monday, I recorded on Wednesday, and I had a record out the following week," she recalls.

33

"That's how it happened in those days." The tune, "Don't Mess with My Man," had a refrain that ran, "You can have my husband, but please don't mess with my man," and put her lusty contralto squarely on the musical map.

It also launched her on the checkered, label-hopping career typical of New Orleans artists, partly because of that scene's neglect by major U.S. record companies. So Thomas worked for a succession of labels over the next 15 years, cutting big regional and r&b hits like "Time Is on My Side" but making it onto *Billboard*'s national top-40 pop charts only once, in 1964, with a primo tear-jerker called "Wish Someone Would Care."

In the course of moving around, she got to work with most of the region's acknowledged masters, like pianist/songwriter Allen Toussaint. Toussaint was one of the driving forces behind the legendary Minit Records, and at various points nearly all the great New Orleans artists passed through Minit's studios. Among them was Thomas, who remembers the association with the same easygoing but blunt candor that characterizes her generally. "I didn't have any choice about what I sang," is how she puts it.

> He'd write a song and say, This is for you, and I'd do it, just like everybody did in those days. See, at that time I was 19 years old; what did I know about choices, anyway? I'd only been in the business for a few years, I was still very naive, and all I was doing was just trying to hang in there. Besides, if there's some degree of success, you have to respect the people you're working with; and he obviously hadn't done me any great injustice with the material, so why not go along?

Which is what she did until Minit, like Ron before it, collapsed financially, leaving her contract to be picked up by Imperial, where she cut "Wish Someone Would Care." When Imperial folded not much later, Thomas found herself scuffling from one project to the next. By 1970, in fact, she'd left New Orleans and music for L.A. and a day job clerking in a Montgomery Ward, singing only sometimes on weekends. "Opened for James Brown on a tour, and cut 'It's Man's Woman's World' (a female-ized version of Brown's early hit "It's a Man's Man's Man's World") for one of his labels. Even went back and recut some of my old hits for different labels. Did a disco thing for RCS in '79 that was just a little too late for the disco craze; so even though it was a good record, and we made a video that ran on HBO, it was down the tubes again."

In 1984, Thomas began her association with the Boston-based indie label Rounder, hoping that the combination of their track record at selling her kind of music and the resurgence of interest in '60s-style soul could coalesce into something better. *The New Rules* brought her honey-smooth voice to lesser-known soul classics like "I Needed Somebody" and "The Love of My Man," as well as pumping new tunes full of the good-timey soul grooves and silken vocals she and her band specialize in. *The Way I Feel* found Thomas's stunning renditions of "Dancing in the Street," which roasts that soul chestnut in her sexy heat, and "Baby I Love You," where her darker-voiced, focused, torchy intensity couples with the spare, almost reggae-like instrumental backing to create a very different feel from Aretha Franklin's slower-paced, gospel-driven, pyrotechnic original.

Part of the albums' sheer punch derives from the way Thomas and her band work; for them, there is little distinction between how they perform live and how they record. Where many artists in this age of the 48-track studio assemble a tune fragment by fragment, one instrument on tape at a time, Thomas takes her chances by cutting the entire band and her vocals as if they were on stage. Aside from occasional punch-ins to fix a bum note here or there, those performances find their way to vinyl undoctored, and so can hit home with the stunning impact Thomas unleashes in a club.

When she graciously drives me back to my New Orleans hotel after our interview, we get to talking about kids, and she offers to pick up a present for mine—a T-shirt sporting an embroidered crawfish with tiny removable sunglasses. She drops it off the next afternoon—to the astonished, worshipful reactions of doorman and concierge alike, who ask incredulously, "Do you *know* Irma?" Well enough to know that the Soul Queen of New Orleans is one of the great overlooked singers of our time, that she's finally coming into her own again. When I come back to New Orleans Jazz and Heritage Festival, she's always one of the biggest reasons.   [1988]

chapter 9

Uptown

The Birthplace of Jazz and the Blues. The Paris of America. The Crescent City. Mardi Gras, Bourbon Street, gumbos and jambalayas and pralines, riverboats and levees and Cajun queens and wrought-iron railings. New Orleans is more than just a city, it's a mythology, a cultural stew, an intersection where different ways of life meet and merge and shape new forms.

And has been from its beginnings, this home of Louis Armstrong and Jelly Roll Morton, washed with the tides of Delta blues and warmed by the same humid sky that kisses other Caribbean ports. No accident, then, that the Big Easy was the place in the late 19th century where Latin beats unleashed a firestorm of syncopation within the marching bands so popular here, as in the rest of the U.S. Nor was it an accident that ragtime and Delta blues, flowing downriver with the Mississippi, collided here with those tangy beats—dubbed by Jelly Roll "the Spanish tinge"—to create a hybrid called jazz. Nor is it surprising to learn that Caribbean islanders in the '50s began listening to the powerful signal from New Orleans radio stations like WINX, picking up on the early r&b sounds of pioneers like Fats Domino, which they then reworked into rock-steady, ska, and reggae. So with roots reaching to such diverse musical styles, it seems inevitable that this town should produce a musical institution as flexible, subtle, and propulsive as the Neville Brothers. The musical mix that scrambles over their second-line syncopations marks them instantly as a New Orleans band, a part of the relentless hybridization process that produced first jazz, then rock and roll. But the voices hold the key to their identity. If the Everly Brothers sing like the tailored halves of a single voice, then the Neville Brothers meld a single voice from four seamless doo-wop parts.

Still, despite their unparalleled abilities, until lately they'd garnered little exposure and less financial reward. Critics have raved over their previous LPs, putting *Neville-ization* on every Ten Best of 1984 list from

Rolling Stone to *Time*. Musicians like Keith Richards, Ron Wood, Ronnie Lane, Jimmy Buffett, Rod Stewart, and Patti LaBelle have praised them to all comers. They've opened tours for the Stones and Huey Lewis, among others. So if you've never had the chance to hear them, maybe the problem lies with the record companies and radio programming directors, who can't seem to find easy marketing slots for the band's earthy, good-time groove, its blend of r&b, funk, gospel, jazz, Afro-Cuban, blues, and soul music.

The tangle of roots that thread through their music has been sketched by an excellent two-disk compilation called *Treacherous*. Starting with Art Neville's first 1955 hit, the Hawketts' "Mardi Gras Mambo," *Treacherous* boasts selections from virtually every phase of the Nevilles' careers, both as solo artists and together. Not that they are relics from the reissue bin: their fifth LP as a group, *Uptown*, is full of chugging beats and soaring harmonies. It rates high on what Art, at 49 the eldest of the four Neville brothers and their spokesman/patriarch, calls "the chill-bump factor."

As Art tells it, there is no mystery to the band's cult status:

> The record companies didn't know how to sell Neville-ism. The stuff we did for them was so raw, I figure at some point on our career we *will* be able to do some stuff like that and get away with it—I mean *really* get away with it, where people *want* to buy it. Then it won't be one of those deals with the marketing shit, where the guy don't know how to sell it 'cause it don't have no label on it. Well, everybody was afraid to touch us because they got all round holes and we're a square peg. We're just as hip as all those round holes, but there just ain't no place to put us. So there's the problem. You got a predominantly black band, and they figure right away, Black means r&b. And when *I* hear r&b, r&b means *real* black to me. But here you got a band that's got a 95% white following all over the world. This totally baffles the record companies, to the point where they would just say, These cats can't make it, we don't want to touch 'em, we can't change 'em. That's when they go and send producers in on you. They may send a producer that really loves the band, and he'll let you do a lot of the stuff that you want to do; but then when you finish, the company can't sell it. They're used to selling grapes and bananas and here you done give 'em a hip watermelon [laughs]. So they don't know what to do. I mean, when they go to talking 'bout r&b, we couldn't compete with the groups that are doing r&b out there right now, if they would try to

call our stuff r&b. That's going backwards for us, saying crossover, you
got to go to the black stations first and then cross over from there.
That's bullshit, when you got a 95% white audience: somebody out
there just don't know how to do their job in a situation like that, man.
That's the bottom line.

With *Uptown*, the bottom line may meet the Nevilles' second line
for the first time. The Nevilles have, with this LP, ventured into the
mainstream realms of synthesizer-driven pop. The very notion may
horrify their longtime fans, even before they've heard the disk itself. But
remember, after all, that Fats Domino, Louis Armstrong, Jelly Roll
Morton, and other Crescent City innovators—including the Neville
Brothers—never intended their music to be a fossilized art form.

For the Nevilles' story is the tale of a way of life and of the city in
which that lifestyle flourishes, a New Orleans which tourists catch a
glimpse of once a year at Mardi Gras, far from the riverboats and
picturesque French quarter and the Superdome. For this story, we've
got to go Uptown, as the locals call it, to the 13th Ward.

St. Charles Avenue uncoils south out of downtown New Orleans
through a brief bit of East Village-type scenery: purple teased hair, torn
punkers' clothes, splashes of neon, eyes heavily ringed with mascara.
Then suddenly it opens out to become a broad, tree-lined boulevard
whose old and often large houses face each other with a settled quiet
across the oldest American streetcar line in continous operation. But
when Mardi Gras comes, St. Charles explodes into a riot of colors and
smells and sounds. Here the Wild Tchoupitoulas Indians—one of many
black "tribes" that painstakingly create elaborate Indian-inspired costumes for the pre-Lenten celebrations—make their annual parade along
the avenue to the ageless marching tunes handed down from generation
to generation. Traceable to the slave rebellions of the early 1800s, which
were apparently fomented by free blacks from Santo Domingo and
possibly Haiti, the tribes continue rituals which memorialize how the
neighboring Indian nations hid escaping slaves from their owners' vengeance.

Where Valence crosses St. Charles marks the heart of the Nevilles'
home turf; a left turn and a few blocks, and we pull up to a small one-
story frame house whose wooden shingles are peeling from lack of new
paint. In the driveway sit two late-model American-made cars; their
dashboards and rear decks groan with stereo equipment. The kitchen

door swings open, and Art Neville rubs his sleep-rimmed eyes and suggests we meet him at the other side of the house, which is where the band rehearses and records demos. The others will drift in as they can: they worked late last night, they're leaving for the road day after tomorrow. We walk back around the front of the house and pull open the front door.

The room isn't that big to begin with—maybe 12 feet by 12 feet—and in an odd way it looks even smaller now that all the equipment is gone. Somewhere between here and L.A. the rig rumbles over superhighways with its load, rushing to Burbank to answer the last-minute summons that calls the Neville Brothers to *The Tonight Show*. "Our hair done turned gray together, but brother, but we still here, man, we made it," grins Art as he imagines the conversation he and America's longest-running talk-show host will have. The last few weeks have been a blur of rehearsal for the Nevilles' two-week minitour of the Pacific Northwest, then it's back to New Orleans in time for Mardi Gras, and then off to Europe for a two-month swing. Art settles into a battered leather chair in the second practice room, where the Teac open-reel four-track and the Tascam four-track cassette studio sit amid the welter of Tandy electronics and stereo gear. Cartons holding electronics gear—wires, jacks—huddle at the floor's edges, while in one corner a lone keyboard rack stands, left behind from the rig. Covering the walls are bits of memorabilia plucked from a career that stretches back 32 years. There's a poster announcing that the Funky Meters will play at Tipitina's for a week in 1969, a poster from the Police's first U.S. tour, a small fading photo of Art at around seven on the back of a pony, a sepia-toned photo in an oval frame which depicts Art as a Chicago-style mobster complete with tommy gun, the cut-out front panel of the *Neville-ization* LP. . . .

Now Aaron drifts in from down the block, huge-shouldered and tattooed ("They say I couldn't go on *The Dick Clark Show* because of the tattoo on my face, but that's not true," he says at one point in his soft-spoken but no-nonesense way), and hunkers down onto the hastily refolded chairbed that tech-wiz Eric Kolb ("Mr. Spock running the show here," grins Art) had flopped on until we arrived to roust him. Soon Cyril shows from across the street, lean and sharp and topped with a Rasta's knitted cap; he drops onto the long-legged stool that squats beneath one of the elaborate speaker setups with outboard tweeters.

Wiry Charles fingers his Fu Manchu moustache as he considers answers, and three-year-old Ian, Art's son, scampers around clutching drumsticks and occasionally working at his drums in a room farther back.

You Can't Stop Running Water: 1954–61

The second line has always taken precedence over the bottom line for the Neville Brothers. Music has filled their homes, no matter where or how poor they were—a genetic link for this family-centered group that pulses with the blood in their veins. "Our uncle George Landry and our mother, who was his older sister, were a dance team, run it down to us that they were the best dancers in New Orleans—even had an offer to go on the road with Louis Prima," Aaron begins with obvious pride, adding with a laugh, "Good thing my grandmother wouldn't let them do it, or there'd've been no Neville Brothers." Art continues, "They put on shows around town. My mother and father listened to the same music: Charles Brown, Nat King Cole, Wynonie Harris, Louis Jordan, Louis Armstrong. It all influences what we're doing today."

It was natural for the next generation of Nevilles to absorb as much as they could—though not always by orthodox means. "I learned to play piano by playing other people's," Art laughs. "Any chance I got to play around this neighborhood I did." For the others, musical training consisted of messing around at home and in the neighborhood, and various school band programs.

By age 16, Charles, a year younger than Art, had already taken his sax on the road, while the oldest Neville slid into a group of fellow high schoolers called the Hawketts. "By that time," he recalls, "we'd moved from the 13th Ward into the Calliope project, and I started doing these little talent shows at NORD, the New Orleans Recreation Department. So these guys the Hawketts had a singer/piano player named Mac Mollette that had a bigger gig: he went out with Fats Domino—that's a long time ago (laughs). There were seven pieces: two trumpets, trombone, tenor, alto, guitar, bass, and drums." Which cut the now classic "Mardi Gras Mambo" at the studio of local radio station WWEZ; reissued every year at Mardi Gras time, it's sold over a million copies from which Art says he's never received a penny. It was the first link in a chain of alleged financial deceptions and legal sleights-of-hand that has grown to bind the Nevilles until today. They claim to have reaped little financial reward from their music, asserting that until their recent success with *Yellow Moon, Brother's Keeper,* and *Family Groove* (all on A&M) their earnings have gone to a succession of colleagues, managers, and the like employing shrewd or shoddy business practices. If such allegations are all too common in the record industry, the sad fact is that they are all too often true.

However, while many first-generation rockers got ripped off, few have had the musical and spiritual staying power that has enabled the Nevilles to face trial after trial. "I see a lot of guys are bitter," says Art, "saying, Man, I didn't get no money, I'm mad with everybody. But man, if we're sounding so good today, and we're all together, and we're getting ready to unleash some stuff that's *cold-blooded,* so then all those people who saw fit to take and take and didn't put nothin' back in didn't stop us. We must have something that's real genuine, that's real meaningful, else we wouldn't still be here." Aaron prompts him: "It's like running water, mon." Art nods, smiles, and explains, "Had a friend from Trinidad used to tell me all the time, You can't stop running water. So hey, here we are—we must be like running water. Now it's beginning to be *cool* running, man (laughs)."

After "Mardi Gras Mambo," Art's next shot at recording came via famed Crescent City reedman and arranger Harold Battiste, who inked him to Specialty Records in 1956. "He was one of the top-line musicians here," is how Art tells it, "and so he got a job with Specialty. That's when we did 'Cha Dooky-Doo,' 'Zing Zing,' 'Oooh-Whee Baby,' all that stuff like that." All of it classic New Orleans rock and roll of the '50s, brandishing push-pull rhythms and Art's warm, smooth vocals.

Among the other local legends that Art and Aaron worked with during this period was pianist/vocalist Larry Williams, whose two 1957 singles, "Short Fat Fanny" and "Bony Moronie," cracked *Billboard*'s top-15 pop charts. "I hooked up with Larry first," Art explains.

> Larry knew the whole family from right out here, with the '54 Ford station wagon with the Hawketts painted on the side of it. So he asked us, You cats wanna go on the road? We didn't know nothin' 'bout no road—Baton Rouge was the road far as I was concerned (laughs). So we went out with Larry, which was real real real good experience.

Played behind people like the Spaniels, Screamin' Jay Hawkins, who's one of my favorites, on package tours. We played the Howard Theater, the Regal Theater, Chicago. Used to play the Brooklyn Paramount all the time before they messed Alan Freed around with that race music and devil music stuff. Rock and roll won't last ten minutes—that's what they said then (laughs). I was 18, just about to turn 19, and things was looking pretty good.

Until Uncle Sam came looking for him in 1958: his touring had made him miss the Naval Reserve meetings he'd signed up for in high school in order to avoid the draft. Since the Hawketts clearly needed a stand-in for Art while he served out his two-year stint, his father, who was now managing the band, plugged brother Aaron, three years younger than Art, into the slot. "Singing doo-wop in the high school bathroom's where I got my education," Aaron laughs. "Doo-wop was the beginning of *all* of this stuff, we all had it," Art chimes in. Aaron continues, "But my singing heroes, besides people like Nat King Cole and Sam Cooke, were Roy Rogers and Gene Autry. When I was little I wanted to be a cowboy, and I used to go to the movies all the time to see shoot-'em-ups; whoever was the main character, that's who I was when I came out (laughs). So I used to do the yodeling like they did, like Gene Autry and Hank Williams." And so Aaron took over his brother's band. "I was the front man, singing 'Cha Dooky-Doo,'" grins Aaron. "I didn't even hear it on the radio until I was in the Navy, and didn't get the chance to sing it till I was out," Art grins back.

Once Art came back from the service in 1960, Aaron started his own solo career, scoring a hit ("Over You") that featured his effortless crooning and the yodeling technique he'd refined into a soulful version of Sam Cooke's lilt. All this over a classic New Orleans bump-grind beat, rolling piano, and a bleary, good-natured horn section. "I wrote the other side of that, called 'Every Day,' when I was in jail for auto theft," he says softly. The A side was penned by another local legend named Allen Toussaint. A mainstay of the New Orleans session scene as a pianist/arranger/composer/producer, Toussaint often credited his songs to Naomi Neville, apparently his mother's maiden name. And as house writer/arranger/producer at Minit Records until it was absorbed by L.A.'s Imperial Records in 1963, Toussaint crafted tunes for Aaron that would maximize the effect of his eerie voice and hybrid yodel.

Tell It Like It Is: 1961–68

Joe Banashak, who owned a number of small New Orleans labels like Instant and Minit, had been impressed by Art and Aaron as individual artists. And so, when Specialty Records, where they were first signed, moved to L.A. in 1960 he bought their contracts and set them to work cutting records for him.

"That was through Larry Williams too," explains Aaron. "I had went on the road with him, and he turned me on to Minit Records, him and this disk jockey named Larry McKinley. Worked every day, split sessions between me and the Del Royals—I'd do two songs, they'd do two songs." Unfortunately, according to the Nevilles Banashak rarely paid them—or any of the other musicians—anything like a regular wage. "He was a trip," says Aaron with a mixture of irony and disgust. "Get a hundred dollars from him, you done good. Then after he give you the hundred dollars he see one of the other fellows coming and looking, say, Don't tell Ernie K-Doe or anybody that you got no money from me (laughs)."

Just about two years after he'd bought their contracts from Specialty, Banashak had to fold Minit and its affiliated labels; and so Art and Aaron found themselves no richer, a little better known, and without contracts. "I started doing odd jobs, driving a truck, working on the riverfront, whatever, taking care of family, y'know," says one of the most unique vioces ever to waft over the air waves. "Every once in a while they'd put together a show with me and Ernie K-Doe and Benny Spellman and Irma Thomas, things like that. And all in between them times I was leaving town, going to California with Cyril—we left with five dollars and a bag of chicken (laughs), going to this place and that to seek my fortune (laughs). I had a few little episodes, y'know."

Four years later, in 1967, the lightning finally struck when Aaron hit number one on *Billboard*'s national pop charts with "Tell It Like It Is," a silky-smooth skein of entreating vocals. "I went for about a year on that," says Aaron, "making all kind of gigs. Had a tour with Otis Redding, then the Apollo Theater. That was like a dream, the Apollo, I'd heard so much about it: stayed there for two weeks, they kept us over for an extra week, myself and Billy Stewart and a bunch of others. Then we went up through Canada, even got to the Virgin Islands." He adds, characteristically, "I never even got no gold record; the record company got the gold record." Given their intense family loyalty, it's no surprise to learn that Art accompanied him on the road, backing him on keyboards.

By the time Aaron got back home in 1967, he and two of his brothers—Art and Cyril, at 36 the youngest—banded together in a seven-piece group called the Neville Sound. "It was me and Art and Cyril and Gary Brown and the Meters," says Aaron. That lineup worked for over a year around the Crescent City. "Then," continues Aaron, "the deal came up with Art and them going to this other club, 'cause the gig just called for four pieces."

Second Line Strut: 1968–75

If that gig meant the end of that first Nevilles-dominated lineup, it also marked the start of one of the funkiest four-piece rhythm sections outside Memphis, where Booker T and the MGs and the FAME/Muscle Shoals crews backed virtually every soul singer in the '60s at some point. The Neville Sound rhythm section—at first called the Funky Meters, then the Meters—became *the* leading proponents of New Orleans-style funk. The popcorn feel propelling the hits of James Brown blended with Sly Stone's more psychedelicized excursions and Stax-Volt soul, all leavened by the Crescent City's characteristic good humor. The lean syncopations and spare arrangements that resulted marked a dramatic shift in style from the work of earlier New Orleans artists like Battiste and Dave Bartholomew, whose charts wove thick saxophone textures everywhere.

And when the Meters hooked up with Sansu Enterprises partners Marshall Sehorn and Allen Toussaint, they burned a lot of wax that more than holds up, backing vocalists like Sansu artist Lee Dorsey as well as out-of-town stars like Robert Palmer, Patti LaBelle, and Paul McCartney. In addition, three LPs of their own were cut on Sehorn's Josie/Jubilee Records; their first release, a single called "Sophisticated Cissy," jumped almost immediately into the top 20.

Art left, then returned to the Meters in the mid-'70s, when Cyril and Aaron went back to doing the Soul Machine, the other half of Neville Sound. That group played around New Orleans for nearly seven years; then, as Cyril says, "Everybody started going to Nashville, so we moved the Soul Machine up there." Meanwhile Aaron had been cutting records for Sansu, covers of soul hits and original material like "Hercules," which boasts wah-wah guitar and falsetto vocals in the Curtis Mayfield mode.

By the early '70s Warner's Reprise arm began leasing the Meters' recorded output from Sansu. In the process, as still often happens when major labels face sounds that don't fit their marketing-determined categories, Reprise bent the Meters' slinkiness to fit something called the mainstream. Even the band's recording methods were forced to change. "That was all head charts," says Art of the earlier material—meaning that the Meters, like most soul house bands, invented arrangements on the spot, working around the vocalist's idiosyncracies and the demands of the song to produce something that would use both to the maximum effect. "After the fight, we'd play some serious music," is Art's line, which cracks the room up.

The Soul Machine, too, had hit some brick walls, which led to a decision. "Cyril and myself left Nashville and went to New York, where Charley was," says Aaron.

Fiyo on the Bayou: 1975–82

In New York they hit the streets with the same intense determination that they'd hit stages all over. "By then I'd been on tour with all kinds of people, like B. B. King, Bobby 'Blue' Bland, Wilber Ware, George Coleman, lots of folks," observes Charles, while Aaron notes: "We just called ourselves the Wild Tchoupitoulas. I was playing piano, Charles was on horn and washboard, and Cyril was on congas." "We did a little of this, a little of that; played places like 'Catch a Rising Star,'" interjects Cyril. And Aaron declares, "Got a chance to talk to people, some saying, Hey, man, I'd like to record you but I can't 'cause you're under contract to Sehorn and Toussaint."

But in 1975 came the event that pulled the four brothers back together and gave them a chance to pool their interlocking talents. "That thing with Jolly's what did it," declares Aaron, and everybody nods agreement. He's referring to the uncle who nearly toured with Louis Prima, who'd encouraged and helped train his nephews in the ways of music and the Indian ways, George Landry, Big Chief Jolly of the Wild Tchoupitoulas tribe. Art was already in New Orleans, working with the Meters; he'd called Cyril back after four months in the Apple so he could put vocals and percussion on the last Meters LP. So when Charles and Aaron returned, the foursome began using their roots in the black Indian cultural traditions not only to reinvigorate their music but also to honor the older generation.

Hence *The Wild Tchoupitoulas*. Charles recalls the making of it this way: "It was the first time we'd done anything together in I don't know how many years. It turned out so magical, with all the tunes and words my uncle had written based on the traditional Indian chants. There were no real arrangements until we got into the studio, where it all just *happened*. That record had so much magic in it, it was obvious we should all get together." Magic indeed. With the Meters—on what would be one of their last recorded collaborations—pumping out the stuttering syncopations that dared all hearers to keep their seats, the four Nevilles wrapped their rich harmonies around Jolly's gruff growl to create a spellbinding rendition of Mardi Gras Indians' music.

"He was more than just Uncle to me," declares Cyril of Landry.

He was Big Chief Jolly: I had followed him in the street, you know, to the Indian practices. He taught me this whole thing, the Indian culture, an altogether different culture than I thought we were. I found out we had a lot more going for us than I had been taught previously. Putting one of them Indian costumes together is *serious*, it's one of the highest forms of primitive art. Then there were all the other rituals that went on at the Indian practices; they go all the way back to the times when the Indians and the Africans had to get together to—well, we all know why they had to get together [laughs]. It taught me all about myself and how unique we as a people are. Not just anybody could be no Indian, and certainly not just anybody couldn't be no big chief. These are all working-class people, but they find the time and the money to make these costumes. So to be able to go in the studio and document this culture—that's what it all meant to me. Even though I didn't get no money for it, it's something I can pass down to my children and my grandchildren.

While this record did little for the Nevilles financially—they claim they were told it sold only a ridiculously small quantity—it put major labels on the alert about them, which led to their signing with Capitol and cutting *The Neville Brothers*. Their next project, three years later, was *Fiyo on the Bayou*, and if they didn't exactly get rich off that one either, at least it captured what they do better than anybody else.

But with no promotion or airplay ("The producer and management cats spent much more bread than they were supposed to," says Charles, "but the company thought *we* got it, so some of the money that should've gone for promotion went to them"), the Nevilles hung in something like major-label limbo. Three years passed before they released anything new. And when they *did* roll the tapes in 1982, it was live at the club named after one of Professor Longhair's most famous tunes, Tipitina's.

Whatever It Takes: 1982–87

As a result, *Neville-ization* (which wasn't released until 1984 due to legal hassles) marks the only time the rhythmic crossfire and incredible vocals that are this band's onstage trademark have made it to wax undoctored. "All the record company people had seen us," says Charles. "What we kept hearing was, Yeah, the albums were really good but they didn't capture the thing that happens on stage. Tipitina's was the most magic place to play, it was the first gig in New Orleans the Neville Brothers ever did. The atmosphere was highly electric, highly charged with fans ready to get down, and the music has always been at its peak there." Indeed, the disc is a succession of peaks. And followed by the gradual breakthrough to mainstream America of *Uptown*, *Yellow Moon*, *Brother's Keeper*, and *Family Groove*, it's meant the Nevilles are, for the first time, riding the airwaves and making hard cash. Few bands have worked harder to get there, or deserve it more.   [1987/1992]

chapter 10

Country Comforts

More than any other American musical form, maybe more than any American genre but its cousin the movie Western, country music is based around commercially generated nostalgia. The Grand Ole Opry, the industry's ideological centerpiece, has traded in its retrospective image's value from its 1925 beginnings on Nashville's WSM. As Opry founder George Hay wrote of his audience, "They were hungry for the rhythm of the soil and the heart songs, plus the rural flavor and humor which spiced it." So while the salesmen for the National Life and Accident Insurance Company, WSM's owner, used free tickets to see the Opry as icebreakers for their pitches, Hay exerted strict control over every aspect of his performers' presentation, from how they dressed and talked down to their biographies and politics and instrumentation. The solemn Old Judge, as Hay was known, thus set the pattern Nashville's country-music establishment follows to this day.

Although the past country music evokes (almost invariably at the present's expense) is, like the movie cowboy, a largely idealized fabrication, it's also a mirror that reflects American history as it refracts the present through its guilty dream. Think, for example, of how this nation's deep-seated anti-urban prejudices are outlined so clearly in country music. For every song about a soothing pastoral landscape, where even the hardest times can produce a transcendental moment (via religion, family, or true love), there's another about adulterous honkytonkers adrift on a post-industrial sea of pain.

One aspect of that city-as-sinkhole-of-iniquity stance stems directly from the population displacements brought by the Great Depression and the postwar economic shifts. But another is as American as cherry pie and brokers a complex interaction of nativist myths. That second strand stretches from Thoreau and the Jefferson/Jackson mandate for a nation of sturdy white British yeoman farmers. It meanders through the Progressives' fear of European-immigrant hordes, who were mostly penned into large urban centers once they got here. It underlies the creation of our system of now-endangered national parks, conceived by the likes of John Muir and Theodore Roosevelt as outlets where urbanites beleaguered by the alien onslaught could retire to revitalize via the healing forces of Nature. And it finds its present outlooks in everything from jingoistic patriotism and kneejerk political reaction to the attitude of many Americans, which seems to mix a sense of divinely ordained retribution and glee, toward the decay of our once great cities.

Of course, a hundred years and more ago, back before country music was manufactured in L.A. (not coincidentally the World's Movie Capital) and Nashville, there were the hymns and ballads and schottishes and fiddle tunes and so on that the early WASP colonists brought with them, which became the roots of so much American popular music. Today, preservationist folkies—a too often self-righteous and over-solemn lot who nevertheless perform an invaluable service—tend those roots. For what until the postwar era was disparaged as hillbilly music is as much a recent set of hybrids as any of its cousins, from the blues and jazz to rock and rap. Like them, too, country music is an umbrella term sheltering a broad set of styles.

Country's historical interactions with other genres have been considerable, and the results diverse. More often than not, they've also been in defiance—at least initially—of the Nashville music establishment unless they've served an obvious commercial purpose. (As far as chronicling the nervous insularity and negative attitude toward cultural/social innovation that marks the Athens of the South, Robert Altman's blistering epic *Nashville* is right on the money.) In the 1930s, for instance, Nashville pushed the tie-in with ersatz movie historicism that spawned the singing cowboy; the marriage was an obvious way to broaden its audiences. So too with the soft-focus Nashville Sound of the mid-1950s on: by glopping strings and chorales onto Tin Pan Alley lyrics, it responded to rock's commercial success, which knocked postwar crooners off the airwaves, and thus opened a space where country could recoup its own sagging sales.

But most other upstart styles have generally been either ignored or marginalized by the country-music powers-that-be until they could follow the dollar signs. Take a few examples. A lot of the "old-time" music first recorded in the 1920s grew up side-by-side with the blues, which was being recorded at the same time; each showed the other's influence.

Western swing grew out of big-band dance music and the popularity of the Hawaiian guitar. Honky-tonk, based largely in Texas and then Bakersfield, was country's postwar analog for the hardening beats and dislocated cries of electric urban blues. Rockabilly welded urban blues with the bluegrass revivalism that reacted against Nashville's poppier bent. In the '60s, groups like Buffalo Springfield and the Byrds spearheaded a remating of rock and honky-tonk that led to still widely prevalent country-rock. And the Austin-centered outlaw movement of the mid-1970s—actually a group of relocated, dissatisfied Nashville singer-songwriters—infused country with r&b, rock, and Tex-Mex angles.

In time, Nashville (and its L.A. partners) accepted and capitalized on all of these movements. That's when the myth-making machine has always kicked in. Suddenly outcasts become retrospective heroes; insiders are transformed into retrospective rebels. Approaches that were condemned by their contemporaries as heretical become orthodox. The process can be almost as fascinating as watching Reagan and his Nauts laying claim to the mantles of Lincoln and FDR. A rash of reissues has made it possible once again to look at the process while listening to some of country music's rich historical reservoir of material.

Almost at the beginning of what would become country music looms the Singing Brakeman, Jimmie Rodgers. *The Early Years, 1928–1929* and *First Sessions, 1928–1929* (Rounder) are the first two installments of what will be an eight-CD set compiled by Richard Weize, who's worked on some of the staggering multi-CD compilations put out by Germany's Bear Family label. Rodgers dealt in a variant of what Ralph Peer, the legendary Victor talent scout who first recorded him, called "nigger blues." Though you could see him that way as a kind of '20s Elvis, Rodgers wasn't unusual. White and black string bands of the time played overlapping repertories, for instance, and blues greats like B. B. King have cited Rodgers's recordings as influential. While Rodgers's rhythms are usually less complex than most used by his blues contemporaries, his yodeling bent and fluttered notes in astonishing ways that presaged both singing cowboys like Gene Autry and r&b greats like Aaron Neville. The exemplary recording quality and notes of this set make it a fine introduction to country's roots.

While it also does some of that, the five-CD *Columbia Country Classics* (Columbia) sits at the other end of the compilation spectrum. It's basically a solid, if obviously chosen, greatest-hits sampler that spans eras and styles, from old-timey to the current New Traditionalism. The good sound and in-depth notes by Rich Kienzle make each volume worth having for devotees, but to my admittedly prejudiced ears the music is far more uneven. The first two volumes, *The Golden Age* and *Honky Tonk Heroes*, span from the Carter Family and Roy Acuff to Lefty Frizzell and Roy Price—by far the more interesting stuff, if only because it's less processed-sounding than what's to come. Volume 3, *Americana*, gathers novelty tunes like Fess Parker's "Ballad of Davy Crockett" alongside classics like Frizzell's "Long Black Veil" and swill like Charlie Daniels's "The Devil Went Down to Georgia." The last two CDs, *The Nashville Sound* and *A New Tradition*, demonstrate all too clearly the music's mainstream decline into formulas.

The Country Music Foundation is Nashville's academic arm. It publishes learned monographs in the *Journal of Country Music*, for instance, and does serious historical research as well as filling a convenient PR function. In that way, it recapitulates some of the Music City's larger schizophrenia. So it's no surprise to find that its first five ventures into major-label partnership—the *Country Music Hall of Fame* series, kicking off with *Ernest Tubb, Red Foley, Bill Monroe, Kitty Wells*, and *Loretta Lynn* (MCA)—are meticulously annotated and well engineered. In this series, each CD is built around a well-conceived greatest-hits approach to an individual artist.

Tubb was Jimmie Rodgers's most fervent disciple, and Rodgers's widow Carrie helped him promote himself as the Blue Yodeler's successor. But he didn't hit until "Walking the Floor over You," a genial if soft-edged proto-honky-tonker that landed him some roles in Hollywood. Most of his tunes are standard-issue country weepers, but a few of the more interesting stick closer to the blues he learned from Rodgers and elsewhere. And "Two Glasses, Joe" is a good example of the early honky-tonk surrounding Hank Williams.

Foley was one of the reasons country-music recording finally shifted from Chicago and New York studios to hometown Nashville after World War II. During the process, he shaped the mold in which the Nashville Sound then congealed country's regional roots: he established, for instance, a set group of session players who did "head" (unwritten) arrangements of tunes for everybody who recorded in the studio. Though these were accomplished players, a certain sameness settled—perhaps inevitably—over their work as they ground from session to session. This album, aside from its treacly sentiments, demonstrates that easygoing boredom.

Mandolin virtuoso Bill Monroe reached back to string band days to invent bluegrass, a kind of bluesier version of old-timey music. (Like Rodgers, Monroe learned to play in part from black musicians.) Pitting fiddle breakdowns against guitar, banjo, bass, and his own vigorous picking, Monroe created a rhythmic filigree—not something any form of country is noted for—that he laced with his high lonesome vocals in a kind of neo-Appalachian blues, complete with Rodgers-ish yodeling for punctuation. Nice as these selections are, however, none is drawn from what aficionados regard as the quintessential Blue Grass Boys—the 1945–58 group featuring banjo genius Earl Scruggs, guitarist Lester Flatt, and fiddler Chubby Wise.

Wells embodies an older country-music female template—the stay-at-home woman who's gentle and understanding and righteous and tough and true and plaintive and passive and usually, though not always, hangs by her man through whatever comes down. In other words, a familiar part: morality's underpowered arbiter. Newer country women like Loretta Lynn are allowed anger and divorces and even, lately, affairs of their own, although for Lynn's generation the role of moral guardian remained intact. Lynn, as the "Coal Miner's Daughter," personifies one of country's favorite fantasies, where sturdy families overcome grinding poverty through strength of spirit. Her tunes also depict her spending a lot of time sparring with other women about just who's gonna get the man in the middle. If the dull-witted morality plays aren't enough to make you skip these, imagine Wells's nasal dentist's-drill of a voice and Lynn's patented syrupy twang gracing the insipid, repetitive arrangements from *The Nashville Sound Handbook*, pages 54–62.

One of the most mythologized figures in country music is Hank Williams. Depending on the perspective of the storyteller, he was either Mr. Inside or Mr. Outside with the Nashville establishment and music critics—one of his least scrutinized accomplishments. I guess his composing talent, performing style, burn-it-at-both ends lifestyle, and resulting early death are flexible enough to be rhetorically useful to different camps.

Williams probably came closest to the cry of the blues than any country star since the Blue Yodeler himself. A friend of mine once described them without irony as slit-your-wrists music. But in fact,

Williams's highly self-conscious craft spanned a host of styles, from Tin Pan Alley to rawly gut-churning. So it was fascinating when, a couple of years back, Polydor's archivists issued an exhaustive 8-volume, 16-record set of his complete recorded output. Unfortunately, as satisfying as it was for critics and fanatics to listen to Williams's skills grow and develop incrementally, for less dedicated or crazed types it was just exhausting and expensive. So now there's *The Original Singles Collection . . . Plus* (PolyGram), which, as three CDs, is more compact and cheaper but still cuts a pretty revealing cross-section.

The power of Williams's tunes comes from their apparently unadorned directness. Like all the best country tunes, they tell simple stories. No deep ironist, Williams churned out plenty of emotional mush in the country-weeper vein. But the jagged-edged aches that make you want to open your own veins—"So Lonesome I Could Cry," for instance—turn around spare metaphors that pack a pain as seemingly artless as the torn yodels racking his voice on "Lovesick Blues" or "Long Gone Lonesome Blues."

Of course, like the best tunes of Jimmie Rodgers, like the blues of Rodgers's contemporary Robert Johnson or Williams's contemporary (and Johnson's musical offspring) Muddy Waters, Williams's songs are highly crafted and self-conscious. But like Rodgers's and unlike Johnson's or Muddy's, they often betray the stiff sense of rhythm that underpins nearly all country music, even the stuff you're supposed to dance to. Commentators have often claimed honky-tonk is the white man's blues, but if I'm right in saying that country music is a guilty dream of America, that comparison misses a point. Country's mythology masks its fears and its real past, while the blues stands up and looks it square in the face. Maybe that's one reason the blues and its descendants can dance more freely: unlike their masters' music, they're not dragging the luggage of nostalgia.   [1991]

Androgyne with a Lariat

She sports a modified ducktail haircut and a startlingly direct candor. Deliberately makeup-less, she's as likely to wear a man's Nudie suit as a cowgirl's fringed dress onstage, where she'll erupt into a slam-dance-gone-hoedown. She's copped the prestigious Canadian Juno award and been nominated for three Grammies, appeared with the likes of Bruce Springsteen and Elvis Costello on Roy Orbison's Cinemax special, become a *Tonight Show* regular and done the *Pee Wee Herman Christmas Special*.

She's k. d. lang, and she raises some serious questions as she moves her big, supple alto voice from country weepers like Patsy Cline's "Three Cigarettes in an Ashtray" to her own offbeat "Watch Your Step Polka" (picture newlyweds swirling through a cow-pie-littered gym).

"Country music is this *huge* thing," says lang, who lowercases her name in homage to e. e. cummings.

> There's more country radio stations than any other kind in North America. It doesn't reflect in sales, because those audiences don't buy records, but they listen to the lyrics. And the subject matter is mostly *so* myopic, *so* sexist and stupid.
> I don't mean to sound like I'm above it, but I just saw so much room to talk about things that need to be talked about. That's one of the things that has drawn me to country music: the potential to work a different sort of thinking and consciousness into it.

lang's sort of thinking, manifest in her androgynous look, her some-times loopy and satiric humor, and the topics of her songs, violates Nashville's usual norms. According to those rules, men, women, and children have well-defined roles; Christianity and political conservatism combine to create a passive acceptance of authority; and songs and arrangements—and the images of the artists performing them—take well-worn, predictable forms.

"What you see on t.v. / all them sparkles / it ain't me," drawls lang in pointed parody of just that mindset during a typical verse of "It's Me," a tune from *Absolute Torch and Twang* (Warner Bros.). After 1988's *Shadowland* (Warner Bros.), a nostalgic outing with Nashville vet Owen Bradley (who produced lang's idol Patsy Cline nearly 30 years ago), *Absolute Torch and Twang* marks a return for lang.

Once again doing her own material with her own band, the reclines (named in honor of Cline), she extends the highly charged, category-bending contemporary style she outlined with her 1984 indie-label release *A Truly Western Experience* (Bumstead) and her critically acclaimed 1987 major-label debut, *Angel with a Lariat* (Warner Bros.).

Like other younger musicians—Jason and the Scorchers, Lyle Lovett, Dwight Yoakam, Lucinda Williams, Nanci Griffith—lang wants to release the populist power of country music from the string-infested, self-serving clichés of the Nashville Sound. So *Absolute Torch and Twang* draws from all over the musical map. Says lang, "My music is a hybrid of a lot of things, but really the biggest influences on it are jazz ballad singing—torch music—and hillbilly twang, with some sort of polite balance between the two of them."

Raised in a house filled with classical music and Broadway show tunes in the 650-person town of Consort, Alberta, Kathy Dawn Lang began writing songs and performing as a kid; later she listened to model popsters like Janis Joplin, Joni Mitchell, and the Carpenters. After studying painting in college and working as a performance artist, in 1982 she landed the role of country-vocal great Patsy Cline in a play. It turned her on to country music, which she'd grown up disliking in its saccharine Tammy Wynette/Kenny Rogers form.

Soon lang had shaved her head and donned outrageous parodies of Nashville stage-style country—sawed off-cowboy boots, a wedding gown to accept her 1985 Juno award for Most Promising Female Vocalist—and was penning tunes no Nashville producer would touch, like "Watch Your Step Polka."

But though she started her country shtick as a performance artist, lang's goal went beyond snotty parody. "First of all, the thing that pulled me into this was the love of the music. My first reaction to it was more on the rebellious performance-art side. Then the more I performed it and wrote it and sang it and listened to it, the more real it became. So it just became easier for me to be completely honest."

Which is why she wins over audiences wherever she tours. As she puts it, "I think it's just a matter of people seeing me. It's hard to capture the wind on a piece of wax." [1989]

chapter 12

Even Cowgirls Get the Blues

Around its edges, country music is sprouting fascinating hybrids. Younger musicians like Dwight Yoakam, Steve Earle, and Lyle Lovett consider country music their natural heritage, but they're also fed up with Nashville's syrupy sound and greeting-card sentiments. So they and others like them are seizing that heritage and remaking it.

Among the others are two young women whose songwriting chops are matched by their interpretive skills. In many ways, Nanci Griffith and Lucinda Williams are polar opposites, but they share the country music tradition that encompasses tough-minded females from Maybelle Carter to Loretta Lynn.

Griffith first. Born in Austin, Texas, a center for outlaw-style country, she began picking guitar at age six to imitate some of her dad's favorites: Woody Guthrie, Hank Williams, and Buddy Holly. A few years later she was gigging steadily at local dives, and slowly, by word of mouth, developed a devoted cult.

It's not hard to hear what drew them. After four albums on independent labels and another two on MCA, Griffith has honed her music to an understated edge—the unexpected fist in the velvet glove. She may look like a little girl, she may be soft-spoken and friendly, she may sing in a quavery twang that recalls Emmylou Harris, and she may write and cover songs that seem folky-gentle (she calls her music folkabilly), but Nanci Griffith has some razor-sharp twists to her.

One Fair Summer Evening (MCA), recorded live in the Houston club where Griffith used to go as a teenager to hear older Texas songwriters, illustrates how. Take the wry heartbreaker called "Looking for

56

the Time (Workin' Girl)." Through a series of deft, novelistic images—her favorite authors are Larry McMurtry and Carson McCullers—Griffith paints a scene of hard-bitten regret: a street prostitute has to turn away someone she's clearly attracted to for, er, business reasons. This minor tragedy of love-for-money pivots on its ironic shrug of a chorus: "If you ain't got money / Take it down the avenue / 'Cause I ain't got the time for you / 'Til daylight."

One Fair Summer Evening offers a potpourri of voices and moods. Alongside slices of life from America's Midwestern past, when shy folks met and fell in love in what city slickers think of as unlikely places, is an eloquent plea for this country's credit-drained farmers. This disc is more than a fine collection of songs—it evokes an entire way of life.

That's exactly what *Lucinda Williams* (Rough Trade) does, in its own way. Like Griffith, Williams somehow projects vulnerability and strength simultaneously. In large part that's because she too has paid her club-circuit, small-label dues while she's pursued her craft and nurtured a following.

Born in Louisiana, home to some of the U.S.'s most vibrant sounds, Williams started on music early; not surprisingly, country blues came naturally to her. She tried her luck on the club scene in New York about a decade ago; she cut two previous albums for the Folkways label, one a collection of blues covers and the other original tunes in a country-blues style. When personal problems broke up a potential major-label deal, she picked up the pieces to head west. For a while she lived in Houston and Austin, prime incubators for the new wave of country-rockers; there she met and competed for attention with folks like Lovett and Griffith, but eventually settled in L.A. Wherever she landed clubgoers discovered her and drew record execs in their wake, but for years labels would get excited by her earthy music and then back away because they didn't think they could package her. Until last year, when Williams finally landed a deal with a major U.K.-based indie.

Lucinda Williams illustrates her broad musical background and tough heartache perfectly, over a deliberately ragged, roadhouse-style mix of country touches, Cajun reels, gutbucket blues, and rock beats. Her songs are barstool tales shot through with pathos and humor and resignation and grit; she scrawls their contours with a voice whose aching pathos, smoky burrs, and threatened loss of control recall late Billie Holiday.

Like Griffith, Williams unfolds her stories from unusual perspectives. But the capper is "Changed the Locks," a hilariously paranoid catalog that acerbically sums up the peculiarly depressed/exhilarated/frantic state of mind that hits right after a relationship has ended, that fragile time when even your ex-lover's shadow still wields immense power: "I changed the lock on my front door / I changed the number on my phone / I changed the kind of car I drive / I changed the kind of clothes I wear / I changed the tracks underneath the train / I changed the name of this town." That oughta do it. [1989]

chapter **13**

Austin's Eraserhead

Pencil-thin, nattily dressed, smiling through a rough-hewn face that looks like the product of a stone ax, crowned with extremely tall curly hair that recalls *Eraserhead*, Lyle Lovett doesn't much resemble country music's Hollywood-handsome new traditionalists, like Randy Travis. He doesn't take himself as seriously either. Without cutting off its country roots, Lovett's music is broader, more self-conscious, more offbeat, and just plain funny.

Take his breakthrough second album, *Pontiac* (MCA). The surrealistic "If I Had a Boat," pictures a seagoing cowboy on horseback. "L.A. County" describes how a jilted lover, "with my old friend at my side," pursues his ex and her new boyfriend crosscountry to the altar; the old friend turns out to be a .45, and when he gets to the wedding he blows them away.

Lyle Lovett and His Large Band (MCA) extends his musical boundaries. Kicking off with Clifford Brown's hard-bop instrumental "Blues Walk," the album hits its oblique stride with "Here I Am," which alternates apparently simple-hearted pleas and a monologue punctuated with hammy pauses out of Jack Benny: "Hello / I'm the guy who sits next to you / And reads the paper over your shoulder /

Wait / Don't turn the page / I'm not finished / Life is so uncertain."

If the ironically mixed feelings behind the satire are familiar enough to New York straphangers, they've also landed the 31-year-old, Texas-born-and-bred Lovett in the midst of some misunderstandings.

"I realize that with some of my stuff, you can't listen with half an ear," he explains. "If you do, it'd be really easy to misunderstand some obvious things. For example, 'The Wedding Song' off the first album (*Lyle Lovett*, MCA). There have been places that I've played where people take it *exactly* the wrong way. It's like, 'Yeah, right on, white is the color of the big boss man.' That's a very scary thing, but that's the kind of stuff that happens. Irony is like that."

Not that it stops Lovett: despite charges of misogyny (which he denies) he persists in writing tunes with titles like "I Married Her Just Because She Looks like You" and lines like "She's no lady, she's my wife." But at the same time, he can pen touching portraits and frame complex emotions.

Lovett's ability to switch deftly from satire to straightforward emotion owes a lot to the models he absorbed in Texas clubs and from records friends turned him on to rather than to country-radio staples. "I feel I was influenced more by people that I used to actually go and see, guys like Michael Murphey," he says. "The stuff that I would find out about and get really interested in, like John Prine or Bonnie Raitt or Ry Cooder or Little Feat, Randy Newman or Jesse Winchester or Tom Waits, was stuff you didn't hear on the radio.

"The idea of a big-time commercial success didn't enter into the songwriting," he continues. "I think that makes for a different kind of song. It's an attitude that was influenced by the late '60s, when Guy Clark and Townes Van Zandt—who are songwriters' songwriters—lived and played in Houston."

Born in the small Houston exurb of Klein, founded by and named after his great-great-grandfather, Lovett graduated Texas A&M with a degree in journalism—which accounts for the slice-of-life feel to many of his lyrics. Doing cover versions of his idols' tunes, he worked the restaurant-coffeehouse circuit in the '70s. "I remember one night, I was doing a set and all of a sudden I heard this *thwack*. I figured I'd busted a string. I looked down at my guitar and saw a tomato stain—somebody'd thrown a pizza crust at me."

Persistence built him enough of a following to put him on a six-week tour circuit. In 1983, a lucky accident threw him together for a month with a band called the Rogues at a big Luxembourg fair. "They'd listened to my songs and liked them, and they felt sorry for me because things weren't going real well with the audience for me," he grins.

The temporary alliance was cemented into a long-term relationship when Lovett & Co. began recording tunes that would eventually find their way onto his three albums. In 1984, though, cutting them was just a way to get a record out, to try to grab Nashville's notice for a deal. So for a year Lovett bounced between Country Music's Capital and Phoenix, where he and the Rogues, who still form the nucleus of his recording and touring band, would hit the studio.

The result was a contract with MCA and his 1985 debut, which yielded four hit singles. After the last year of racking up appearances on TV shows like *Night Music* and *David Letterman* as well as knocking live audiences out with his barbed asides, Lyle Lovett has clearly arrived.   [1989]

chapter 14

The Layla Sessions

Twenty years after its release, some of what makes *Layla and Other Assorted Love Songs* a pivotal album in rock history is clear.

There's the crackling energy—the key ingredient in the best rock and roll. Derek and the Dominos ripple and burn with a high-voltage passion that infuses the entire album, gives it that unifying feel that makes even the order of the tunes seem inevitable, predetermined somehow. They were a *band*, not a made-in-the-studio confection, a garage band writ large.

The quintet's personal chemistry was crucial. It pushed Eric Clapton and Duane Allman to strafe each other in mock battle to the edge of their considerable limits and beyond, especially on songs like "Key to the Highway" and "Nobody Knows You When You're Down and Out" and Clapton idol Freddie King's anguished tune about fooling with your best friend's wife, "Have You Ever Loved a Woman." It pushed Bobby Whitlock to keep pumping vocals that drove Clapton's, to keep swirling keyboards to get a foothold amid the bristling guitar army, to keep scribbling lyrics that transformed jams into songs. It pushed Carl Radle and Jim Gordon to come up with offbeat material from their own backgrounds and invent startling, shifting rhythmic patterns that force your feet to move by sounding deceptively simple. Take "Bell Bottom Blues," where Gordon virtually turns the beat around for the whole song and drops deep-toned tablas into the chorus to stunning effect.

Their interaction joined with the quality of their material to unleash their imaginations and impose structure at the same time. So they remade Big Bill Broonzy's "Key to the Highway," a gently insistent on-the-road-again boogie, into a slash-and-burn eighteen-wheeler rumbling directly at your brain; Clapton, for effect, deliberately garbled lyrics that were perfectly intelligible when Broonzy sang them. More ambitious formats like "Nobody Knows You" (where Allman wails on bottleneck through one of Whitlock's Leslie cabinets) and Jimi Hendrix's "Little Wing" set high standards for their own material: the tunes Whitlock co-wrote with Clapton, for instance, reflect the Memphis native's sure grasp of soul-music song forms.

The edge-city finesse with which Derek and the Dominoes hot-wired their staggering assortment of influences and ideas has made *Layla and Other Assorted Love Songs* into a kind of inadvertent monument. An era was ending, and *Layla* was one place where it found both its final voice and one of its finest summations. Beginning with the English Invasion of 1964, the period marked the revitalizing of American rock and roll, mostly by forcing it back to its roots—the blues and r&b and country—for inspiration. (Remember whose tunes the Beatles and Stones and Yardbirds and Animals were all scrambling to cover.) The jams-away excesses of the psychedelic summers that followed came out of the roadhouse, where bands played for hours while folks partied and danced. It was only toward the period's close that audiences collapsed back into their seats to watch the performers put on a show.

But while the emerging forms of proto-metal and jazz-rock fusion shed their danceability in favor of long solos, soul music percolated with can't-sit-down beats and taut song structures that foregrounded ensemble work instead of solo flash. On *Layla*, Derek and the Dominos combined the two. As Clapton explained to Robert Palmer in a 1985 *Rolling Stone* interview, "We didn't really have a *band* with Cream. We rarely played as an ensemble; we were three virtuosos, all of us soloing at the same time."

So Derek and the Dominos embodied many of the era's possibilities, played them, brought them to a kind of fullness and fruition, and then, in the best Romantic manner, blew apart. But their legacy lives in *The Historic Layla Sessions*. Digitally remixed, remastered, and issued for the twentieth anniversary of *Layla and Other Assorted Love Songs*, this set includes never-before-heard jams and alternate takes that, besides being good music, offer fascinating peeks into the process of creation.

From late August through early September 1970, then again for a couple of days at the beginning of October, Clapton, Whitlock, Radle, Gordon, and Allman were ensconced at Miami's Criteria Studios. By now, the circumstances behind the blues-and-soul-driven rage of *Layla* are well known enough to need only a quick recap.

Cream had finally blown apart in 1968. Despite enormous hype, Blind Faith never realized its potential during eleven months of life. So Eric Clapton, weary of the frontman's role, joined Blind Faith's opening act, Delaney and Bonnie Bramlett and Friends, as a semi-anonymous guitarist; Delaney taught him to sing with gutsy fervor. Then *Eric Clapton*, his eagerly awaited debut as a leader (which included future Dominos), put Clapton's take on J. J. Cale's "After Midnight" on the airwaves.

The guitarist's personal life was, if anything, more turbulent than his professional life. His blues had been made flesh: he'd fallen madly, despairingly in love with the wife of one of his best friends, ex-Beatle George Harrison. Pattie Boyd Harrison would eventually leave her then husband and marry Clapton, but in the period before the *Layla* sessions she'd basically just flirted with him at parties. At the same time, he started to read *The Story of Layla and Majnun*, by the Persian poet Nizami. So inconsolable that even his deepening involvement with heroin couldn't dull his ache, Clapton was speared to the core by Nizami's obscurely metaphoric, romantic tale of an apparent madman who falls hopelessly in love with a moon-princess whose father marries her off to someone else. It inspired him to fashion one of rock and roll's greatest albums from his pain. (The gently yearning "I Am Yours" sets some of Nizami's words to music.)

The Dominos came together out of a combination of chance and previous contacts. All of them had been members of the Delaney and Bonnie troupe of Friends—including Duane Allman, who'd preceded Clapton in the group. As Bobby Whitlock tells it, "Delaney was a little James Brownish—real hard to work with, him and Bonnie fighting all the time and carrying on. Everyone got disenchanted with the situation." So when Leon Russell passed the word that he was recruiting for the Mad Dogs and Englishman tour behind Joe Cocker, most of the Friends jumped ship. Only Whitlock stayed—and even he split after a while.

He called Clapton from L.A., and the guitarist told him to come on over to England. For the next several months, Whitlock lived at Clapton's house while he and the guitarist hung out and jammed and wrote the tunes that would become the core of *Layla and Other Assorted Love Songs*. When the Cocker tour wound down, they called their Delaney and Bonnie buddies Dave Mason and Carl Radle, who brought Gordon along. (That bumped Jim Keltner, who'd been slotted for the drum chair. "Of course, Keltner wasn't real pleased," drawls Whitlock.) That quintet became the house band for George Harrison's *All Things Must Pass*. Says Whitlock, "That album is essentially Derek and the Dominos with sundry guest artists. We were jamming all the time—that's where 'Apple Jam' on that album comes from." And so passed another few months.

Meantime, Whitlock and Clapton were tightening up as a songwriting team. Whitlock recalls,

"Any Day" we just sat down and wrote. "Why Does Love Got To Be So Sad"—same thing. We started doing that intro on the bottom end of the guitar neck, then Eric whipped up to the top end and it started sounding right. Songs just evolved, like they did with Issac Hayes and David Porter. We weren't writing to have great songs; we wrote just to have something to play.

"Tell the Truth" I wrote one night after we'd been up for days on one of our marathons: we used to just play and play and play. We would play literally for three days without stopping. Anyway, I was up by myself sitting in Eric's living room when this thing just hit me. I wasn't reflecting on Otis's "Tell the Truth" [the '50s r&b smash by Lowman Pauling's Five Royales that Redding and James Brown both covered], even though that's my roots. I was thinking about "The whole world's shaking, can't you feel it?" I was a young man, gaining experience and getting older; that's what I was thinking about. I wrote the whole thing that night except for the last verse. I made up the chords on an open tuning Duane had showed me. Then I went into Eric the next day, and he thought it was great, so we sat down and wrote the last verse together.

The initial version of "Tell the Truth" made its short-lived debut as a single, backed with "Roll It Over," which added Harrison to the band. (Both cuts are included on *Crossroads*, the four-CD anthology from Clapton's 25-year career issued two years ago.) Produced by Phil Spector, it was drastically different from the attack the group put together a couple of months later, and was quickly recalled because, Whitlock says, "We didn't think it was a good representation of the band, and we wanted something that was more like what we were sounding like."

What they were sounding like was a mix of grungy, overdriven guitars and soul-style material and vocals. Says Whitlock,

> The basic concept of Derek and the Dominos—and this was from when Dave Mason was in the group, at the beginning—was that we didn't want any horns, we didn't want no chicks, we wanted a rock and roll band. But my vocal concept was that we approached singing like Sam and Dave did: he sings a line, I sing a line, we sing together.

After a brief tour around small clubs in England, the Dominos wound up at Miami's Criteria Studios, the domain of Tom Dowd, longtime staff engineer/producer at Atlantic records who'd helped pioneer eight-track recording and stereo. Dowd had worked on everything from Bobby Darin's "Mack the Knife" and John Coltrane's *Giant Steps* to Aretha Franklin's "Respect" and Cream's *Disraeli Gears, Wheels of Fire,* and *Live Cream;* Clapton, who has called Dowd "the ideal recording man," asked him on board as the Dominos' executive producer. (The group itself is credited with arranging and producing.)

Criteria was where much of the late-1960s soul material for Atlantic was cut, and Dowd had moved down there from New York to handle the flow. (The stream of material out of Criteria was so large that Atlantic installed a mixing room in Dowd's house so he could work whenever he wanted.) In many ways, the world of pop music was smaller then; career tracks overlapped more frequently. So it was with the Dominos: Dowd had used a Clapton fan named Duane Allman on some Aretha Franklin and Wilson Pickett sessions.

It's a nice historical irony that Dowd got a call from Clapton's organization while he was producing the Allman Brothers Band's *Idlewild South*. (He'd later produce their breakthrough album, *Live at the Fillmore East*.) "We never did an entire album at a sitting," he smiles.

> We'd do three or four songs, break off, and they'd go back out on the road, rehearse, and then we'd record some more. We were in the middle of that process when [Clapton's then-manager Robert] Stigwood's office called me from England and said Eric would like to record with me in Florida. Now, when the call came I was in the studio with Duane. I said, "Hey, that's a hot one, kid; that was Eric Clapton's management talking about him coming here to record." Duane looks at me and says, "You mean the guy from Cream? Do you think he'd mind if I just came by to watch?" I told him no problem.

When Clapton turned up, Dowd was floored by his equipment. "When I had done the Cream sessions," he explains,

> I'd had to protect Ginger (Baker) from the electrified instruments, because Jack (Bruce) and Eric were using double stacks of Marshalls. So my problem was recording the drums; no matter where I put a microphone I had enough of the guitars. So for these sessions Eric walked in with a (small Fender) Champ and a (tiny battery-powered) Pignose. He was getting more intimate with his technique, and he'd gone back the other way, in terms of equipment. So we set it up with camp chairs holding up amps. If you walked into the room and sneezed, you made more noise than they were making.

The magic of the studio: it's hard to believe when you're hit with *Layla*'s whipping gusts of sound.

Whitlock adds,

> It was just getting the quality of the sound—that's what was important. The piano had this big boatlike thing on top of it for a cover, the Leslie was in the sound room, Jim Gordon was in a carousel. It was isolated but open; the amps were in the room, so we got a little of that bleed.

Which let them jam to create and get into material.

For despite the band's months of work, their first sessions were tentative. Dowd remembers,

> Whitlock had two or three songs, Eric had one or two blues he wanted to do, and we were looking for old records so we could be authentic about this or that lick. Carl Radle was into Chuck Willis, for instance, and so we dug out a bunch of Chuck Willis records—which is how "It's Too Late" made it onto *Layla*.

Originally a supplicant's doo-wop-style ballad, it was transformed by the Dominos during their jams into a grittier *cri de coeur*.

The arrival of Duane Allman helped catalyze the Dominos into that kind of exploration. The way Dowd tells it,

> We fumbled along for a couple of days like that while we were getting sounds and breaking ice. Then the phone rings one afternoon and it's Duane. He says, "Hey, the band's doing a benefit concert at the Civic Center down there on Saturday, can I come by?" No problem. So I put the phone down I told Eric who it was. He says, "You mean that guy who plays on the back of (Wilson Pickett's) 'Hey Jude'? You know him?" I tell him he's doing the concert, so he says, "We have to go."
>
> So that Saturday we went into the studio about two or three in the afternoon, fumbled along till about six or seven, and called down to get in. They snuck us in. They had a barricade between where the public was and the riser for the band, sandbags and gobos up there to keep the people back. They got us in by the side of the stage and we crawled in on our hands and knees so we wouldn't obscure the stage and propped ourselves against these sandbags, sitting on our butts looking up with our hands holding our knees together.
>
> Duane was in the middle of a solo; he opens his eyes and looks down, does a dead stare, and stops playing. Dickey (Betts) is chugging along, sees Duane's stopped playing, and figures he'd better cover, that Duane must've broken a string or something. Then Dickey looks down, sees Eric, and turns his back. That was how they first saw each other.
>
> So we piled into cars and Winnebagos and whatever the hell and went up to the studio at about three o'clock the next afternoon with nobody having gone to bed. They were trading licks, they were swapping guitars, they were talking shop and information and having a ball—no holds barred, just admiration for each other's technique and facility. We got back, turned the tapes on, and they went on for fif-

teen, eighteen hours like that. I went through two or three sets of engineers.

It didn't take much to insinuate Allman musically into the Dominos. Jam V, which features what became the Dominos' final lineup, is nuanced with sudden dynamic turns, throttled into high gear by Duane's daredevil bottleneck as it skids up the fretboard until it digs in somewhere over the pickups—dog-whistle territory. It's a snapshot of what's to come. Then, lifted from the random bits and pieces of those jams that pepper the multitracks, is the most complete picture of what the post-concert day was like: Jam IV, which basically takes off from Howlin' Wolf's "Killing Floor," features the Allman Brothers Band, Clapton, and Whitlock. (The piano at the very end is Gregg Allman, who apparently arrived just in time.)

As Dowd remembers it, the Allmans had a couple more shows they had to do, but Duane promised to come back as soon as they were done. "That," he says, "was when the band got serious about what they were doing. All of a sudden the catalyst was there; it was just a matter of putting things into shape." Whitlock agrees,

> He brought the best out of us, even with the songwriting, 'cause the songwriting came out of the jamming. Like "Any Day": Eric and I had already written it, but then Duane came up with that slide part. He said, "Hey, check this out; let's make it like a Roman chariot race." He was doing that kind of stuff all the time. You can tell, listening to all the jams you've got now, that the whole album just evolved. We were just getting ideas, shaping them afterwards.

Like on the two "Tell the Truth" jams included here: the testing of different speeds, the boxiness of running the riff on the beat, all illuminate the small creative decisions the musicians made along the way as they searched for what they wanted to hear.

The sessions' rock-and-roll spontaneity is encapsulated in the story of how "Key to the Highway" made it onto *Layla*. As Dowd recalls,

> Sam the Sham (Samudio) was in the studio, and the chaps heard him doing a number in the adjacent room. They thought it was a great tune. Eric or Duane picked up on it, Radle jumped in, Whitlock, who knew all those tunes, jumped on it, and before you knew it everybody was trailing along and I turned around and yelled, "Hit the goddamn machine!"

It was one of the few times Dowd was caught off guard: on the original multitrack tapes, the tune opens mid-solo, which is why it fades in on the album.

The loose atmosphere was famously thick with drugs and booze. Says Whitlock,

> We didn't have little bits of anything. There were no grams around—let's put it like that. Tom couldn't believe it, the way we had these big bags laying out everywhere. I'm almost ashamed to tell it, but it's the truth. It was scary, what we were doing, but we were just young and dumb and didn't know. Cocaine and heroin, that's all—and Johnny Walker.

The sessions finally burned to their end on the title track and the all-acoustic "Thorn Tree," which was recorded live, with the band sitting in a circle around a stereo microphone. Then they took off on tour while Dowd listened to what they'd left in the can. The way he tells it,

> I sat down and did a rough mix, and lived with it for a couple of days. Then I got serious and remixed the whole thing myself, and sent copies to Eric. Then the Dominos were doing a concert in Miami and came by to listen to the whole thing. They decided they wanted to re-mix three or four of the songs, change a part here and there. Thank God we had good notation by the staff so we could get back to where we were. You've got to remember, everything was done much quicker in those days—which is ironic, because there wasn't any automated or computerized equipment. But I dare say, my initial mix probably took a day or a day and a half. Then for the final mix I took maybe three or four days, with another two days with them when they came back in.

One measure of how things have changed in the art of rock and roll and its attendant technologies: engineer Steve Rinkoff and producer Bill Levenson spent 16 days digitally remixing this boxed set.

One track that got touched up when the Dominos pulled back into Miami was "Layla" itself. Dowd says,

> "Layla" stood up until the back end, when they wanted to add on the finale. So we had to go back and get as close as we could to the original mix up to the point they liked, then figure out how to cut in this other part. I think we wired two or three tapes together to get the transition the way it was supposed to go, then readjust the front end to fit

the back end—there were weeks between the way it was originally recorded and the time we put the back end on.

The Dominos continued on their drug-powered tour (minus Duane Allman, who'd returned to his own band after the sessions), and cut their live double album. Clapton told Palmer,

> By the end of the tour, the band was getting very, very loaded, doing way too much. Then we went back to England, tried to make a second album, and it broke down halfway through because of the paranoia and the tension. And the band just . . . dissolved. I remember to this day being in my house, feeling totally lost and hearing Bobby Whitlock pull up in the driveway outside and *scream* for me to come out. He sat in his car outside all day, and I hid.

(In fact, the band recorded at London's Olympic Studios in May 1971 and, before its drug-induced dissolution, cut some tunes, five of which were included in the *Crossroads* anthology released by PolyGram.)

At this point in time, of course, *Layla* is an etched-in-stone classic, but when it came out twenty years ago it didn't make much noise over the airwaves or on the charts. Dowd sighs when he recalls what went down:

> When we finished it and were mastering it, I felt it was the best goddamn album I'd been involved with since *The Genius of Ray Charles*. And (Atlantic Records heads) Nesuhi and Ahmet Ertegun and Jerry Wexler were absolutely enamored of the album, but they couldn't get the goddamn thing on the air, they couldn't get a single out of it. Nothing. I kept walking around talking to myself for a year. Then suddenly it was the national anthem.

For all the reasons discussed at the beginning of this essay—and more—*Layla*, along with other masterpieces like John Coltrane's *Impressions*, Ornette Coleman's *Free Jazz*, and Jimi Hendrix's *Electric Ladyland*, remains a brilliant monument to its time. But like them, it's no nostalgia piece. Like the moon-princess receding from her madman lover's embrace, *Layla* is always dancing at the edge of its creators' reach, stretching their resources and stamina, demanding more than they think they can put out and yet somehow manage, time after time, to come up with. It's an album musicians and people who can't carry a tune play over and over and over again with equal awe. Which is, after all, the democratic knockout packed by the art form we call rock and roll: one hit to the body and another hit to the soul. *Layla* hits you on every level. That's why, twenty years after it was made, we're still listening to and celebrating it.   [1990]

chapter 15

Beckology

The guitar may slash and burn or sigh an aching melody, blaze a fusillade or arc a lyrical air—but from the touch, the phrasing, you know it's him. He's idolized by several generations of guitarists because along the way he's helped invent psychedelia and heavy metal and change the shape of jazz-rock fusion.

Since 1963, when he first put it down on tape, there's been no doubt about it: Jeff Beck has a *sound*, a unique and characteristic way with the guitar that's instantly recognizable yet constantly evolving. His strong vibrato, his fierce attack and fat tone, his acute microtonal sense of pitch when he bends or slides into a note, his sophisticated sense of rhythmic and melodic phrasing, his ability to wring painfully true notes from up by the guitar's pickups, his continuing use of the electric guitar to generate textures as well as notes—add them up, add the spontaneous magic of inspiration, and you've got a sense of why a Jeff Beck guitar solo sounds like no one else's.

Like most of the Brit rockers of his generation—the Stones and Beatles, Eric Clapton and Jimmy Page—Jeff Beck (born in Surrey, England, on June 24, 1944) backed into the then-fledgling sounds of rock. At eight, he was made to practice piano for two hours daily until, as he recalls, "I ripped one of the black keys off. My mother got the idea than that I wasn't too keen on it." Abortive violin and cello lessons with an uncle followed, leaving as their residue a love of legato melody.

By the mid-1950s, rock and roll was beginning to filter into the U.K., then dominated by trad-jazz and skiffle. But information about its components was scarce. A poster for *The Girl Can't Help It* outside his local movie house inspired the 13-year-old Beck to build his own electric guitar and plug it into the back of a radio. At 15, he joined a local band, the Del-Tones. "We played a lot of Shadows—Hank Marvin," he recalls. "It was easy stuff that any band with the slightest bit of proficiency on their instruments could learn in a day, like 'Apache.' Cliff Gallup is one of my heroes; the stuff he did with Gene Vincent sends me up the wall every time I hear it. The things James Burton did with Ricky Nelson are still incredible." Then a year or so later came soul music: "Once people started getting into Booker T and the MGs, I never wanted to go back to copying Gene Vincent." And in 1962, the craze that swept a generation of British rockers, the blues: "There were the same people that Eric (Clapton) got inspired by, Otis Rush and people that just took your face off, Buddy Guy and Chicago blues. I didn't get off on the bottleneck-scratching kind of stuff—I didn't have any ear for Jimmy Reed, because it wasn't really *useful* enough. I prefer the wildness of Buddy Guy."

By 1963, when he'd joined the Tridents, Beck started scrambling those basic guitar premises with the sonic approach of his idol Les Paul, whose gizmos, from soundshaping boxes to overdubbing, pioneered modern technology. On his '50s recordings with then wife Mary Ford, Paul mustered multiple guitars via overdubs and speed shifts, transforming them into a sweeping impressionistic backdrop that presaged guitarists like Beck, Jimi Hendrix, Adrian Belew, Bill Frisell, and Robert Quine.

Says Beck,

> Les was at his peak during an era of great melody, all those lovely chords, so he had a whole ocean of stuff to put his expertise onto. Mary Ford sang great old standards, then he'd go bananas with all his effects, showers of notes and what not. We were anchored by one chord and a big beat; it was a whole different thing. But I still wanted to get those atmospherics. I was just as unrestricted, in a way, as Les because our music was a wide open sea of emptiness where I could do what I wanted.

The Tridents sides—demos cut to help land better club gigs—show how early and intensely Beck got into painting with sound. On "Nursery

Rhyme," Beck's guitar howls with snarling abandon. Nothing else out there, not even Link Wray's "Rumble," sounded quite like it. "I had a German echo unit, a Klempt Echolette, I messed around with," he explains. "It had alternate delays. I knew how to hot-rod the sounds without actually touching a soldering iron to it. It was an advanced little box for the time, but it broke down a lot at gigs. There'd be a temperature change, and the tape would snap halfway through the first number and all my tricks would be gone."

Playing at Eel Pie Island, a Richmond club in the middle of the Thames that was a center of the British blues revival, the Tridents peaked for several weeks in late 1964, when they packed in 1000 rabid fans. Says Beck, "It was an elite club; people wanted you to imitate their idols. That's when I started to kick some butt. I remember detuning the low E and A strings and just whining the hell out of 'em, making ridiculous noises, and everyone went berserk. There wasn't an ounce of musical sense to it, but they loved it because it was different."

The young iconoclast shared his sonic interests with another fledgling guitarist named Jimmy Page, who had gone to art school with his sister. Their first meeting ("He played us a Buddy Holly song while his mum made us cups of tea," Beck grins) began a long relationship that proved to be Beck's entree into a raunchy, blues-based rave-up outfit called the Yardbirds.

With Clapton on guitar, the Yardbirds were, despite no hit records, becoming well known in the burgeoning circles of the '60s U.K. blues revival that also sired the Rolling Stones and the Animals. But in late 1964 they decided (with producer/manager Giorgio Gomelsky) to mount an attack on the pop charts via a harpsichord-flavored tune called "For Your Love." So they brought keyboardist Brian Auger into the studio and relegated Clapton the blues purist to boogie runs in the bridge. He decided to call it quits; he wanted his music, he said, to be taken more seriously. He went on to join the seminal edition of John Mayall's Bluesbreakers that led to the formation of Cream.

Meanwhile the Yardbirds approached Page, who was then doing constant session-guitar work for everyone from the Kinks and Stones to Donovan and Jackie DeShannon, about replacing Clapton. Page's high-dollar demands and reluctance to leave the security of the studio led him to suggest Beck. Beck remembers the results:

One night, when I was playing with the Tridents at the 100 Club, Giorgio and his sidekick Hamish Grimes, the artist who did all the Yardbirds' logos and worked in the office, came down and dragged me off after the set. I was all sweaty, had hair down to my ankles. They said, "You're coming with us." I said, "Can I swear?" He said, "You're gonna be in a top fucking band. Be at this address tomorrow." It was the Marquee Club. When I turned up there was a Yardbirds van outside. "Let's go," I thought. There were other guys auditioning, but I think they knew I was gonna be the one.

He sure was. Although rock iconography stresses the Yardbirds' mighty triumvirate—Clapton, Beck, and Page—Beck's 20-month stint marked the group's apex; his guitar was the raw octane fuelling the band. As former Yardbirds drummer Jim McCarty sees it,

> The great thing about Jeff was, because we leaned on him so much— we relied on him to fill up the sound—he developed a lot of his futuristic ideas, things that people called gimmicks at the time. We'd been used to playing with Clapton, who was playing much straighter r&b solos, and then Jeff was something much wider. He was interested in people like Les Paul, and all these footpedals and fuzztones and feedback, something we hadn't had before that was very exciting and always unpredictable.

Former Yardbirds rhythm guitarist/bassist Chris Dreja agrees, and adds, "We all feel, I think, that the period Jeff spent with the band was the most creative. His scope of inventiveness was probably the widest of the three guitarists we played with—and none of them were exactly slouches."

Which is why so much of *Beckology*'s first CD is devoted to that period. Beck burst out of the frame immediately. As he recalls,

> The very first track I cut with them was "Steeled Blues." We cut the B side first to warm up and get the balance. Two takes, boom, that was it. For "Heart Full of Soul" they had a sitar player. They'd liked the way that Brian Auger worked, putting an unusual instrument on their sound, and they wanted to do it again. But I was thinking, "I've just joined, and already they're getting these other guys." The band was saying, "Don't worry Jeff, you'll blend in with these guys." And I said, "Well, are they coming on the road with us, then, 'cause there's not much point otherwise." The sitar player couldn't get the 4/4 time sig-

nature right; it was a hopeless wasting of time. So I said, "Look, is this the figure?" I had the fuzz machine, a Toneblender, going. We did one take, it sounded outrageous. So they kept the tabla player, who could just about make it work. They rushed that out, and the rest was a rollercoaster ride.

The rollercoaster started off slowly, however. According to Beck,

The tours were four or five weeks of England, just up and down, up and down. (Singer) Keith Relf's father would drive us in his builder's van; there were sand and bricks all round underneath the bench seats in the back. When the band took off it meant that there were less bags of cement in the back. The less cement, the more successful we were. It was a clear equation. Then Hamish sign-painted the front of the van, The Yardbirds, and we knew we'd gotten somewhere, 'cause we had a painted van. The first time we were on *Top of the Pops*, it was still quite clean, when we parked it outside the BBC studio in Manchester. When we came out it was smothered in lipstick—the windows, the windshield, everything plastered with girls' names and phone numbers. I thought, "This is great! Not only am I enjoying the shit out of what I'm doing, but I get fame as well." So we did one TV show, and I raced home to tell my mum, and the people next door cutting their hedges said, "Saw you on the telly, very good." They were the same people who, up to this point, were yelling for me to turn it down all the time. All of a sudden, I was somebody. It was a mindblowing experience.

It got even more mind-blowing when the Yardbirds hit the States. The way Beck remembers it,

We were halfway across America when we did "Shapes of Things." We were at Chess Records, the home of our heroes—we were thrilled to bits to be there. We didn't have any songs written; we just did it. Like "I'm a Man": we heard the playback and just went berserk. The bass drum was shaking the foundations of the building. We weren't playing that loud, but the engineer did Muddy Waters and Chuck Berry stuff, so he knew how to get that. We'd jam, Keith'd rush off and write some lyrics in the toilet—it was exactly like that. Somebody'd say, "Let's do something modern and exciting; we know we can get a good blues sound, so let's spread out a little bit." It was all spur-of-the-moment, man: "I know: after four verses, let's go into this raga thing." I kept changing guitar sounds all the way through. So we did two or three takes of my guitars and blended them all together. But the solo on 'Shapes of Things' was pretty honest up until that feedback note that comes in over it.

With classic intuitive insight, Beck made a virtuoso's virtue of his equipment's limits, learning to play the sounds other players at the time avoided. He continues,

I started fooling with feedback because we began playing larger gigs where we couldn't be heard. The equipment we had was woefully inadequate, and we all had beer running down into the amp imputs anyway. Those AC-30s would still work, but they really weren't up to the size of the places. In the end I just got berserk and turned it flat-out. I thought, "Wow, that whistle's controllable; it's coming from the string." So I'd just bend the note around the feedback. The more I got into it, the more I found I could control it. I started finding the reso-nant points on the neck where it came in best. I loved it because it was a most peculiar sound that contrasted wildly with a plucked string, this round trombone-like noise coming from nowhere.

Though he erupted into U2-style scratch-picking and near-feedback on the studio "I'm a Man," Beck had forgotten nothing about the blues; even a quick listen to the Buddy Guy-meets-Elmore James solos on "The Sun Is Shining," a James tune, makes that plain. Nor had he abandoned Les Paul, as "Jeff's Boogie" demonstrates. But he was spin-ning off into increasingly outrageous experiments, since the Yardbirds kept opening the spaces for and reacting to his sonic inventions. Thus they pointed the way into the then uncharted realms of what would be called psychedelia.

By the time they recorded the landmark *Yardbirds*—the first album they recorded as an album, which they did in a week—they'd forged a new musical synthesis of Eastern sounds, jazz, blues, rock, and noise. "Happenings Ten Years Time Ago" kicks things off with Beck at his most impressively manic: sirens whirl, chords rumble and explode, hot rods raunch and rheum. The rave-up section of "Lost Woman" rides out on a recurring feedback-and-whistle cloud of powerchords; the first section of "The Nazz Are Blue" solo closes out with a single sustained note spiraling into feedback—and this in 1965, a full two years before Jimi Hendrix's revolutionary *Are You Experienced?* All told, *Yardbirds* is a primer of the Jeff Beck Sound, and was studied as closely as any primer by both the guitarists of San Francisco's Summer of Love bands and the embryonic heavy metallists of the late '60s.

Dancing in Your Head

For a brief while in 1966—long enough to film their bit in the movie *Blow Up* and start a U.S. tour—Page and Beck shared guitar duties in the Yardbirds. "I remember Phoenix," says Beck,

> where we were playing in this unbelievable place, packed solid, with the ceiling onstage just above our heads. And the air-conditioning had gone. So I had one of my tantrums. I pushed this amp speaker out the window, but it hung on by a cannon socket, swinging about an inch over people's heads. It was a Dick Clark tour: 600-mile-a-day jaunts in the bus with Gary Lewis and the Playboys and Bobby Hebb. I suppose it was mix-and-match, but it was dreadful: there was no camaraderie. I stayed about two weeks. Then right in the middle of Kansas I felt like I'd die if I stayed another day. I broke down in the bedroom and told Jimmy (Page) I was out of there. It was awful, because I had to shove all the duties onto him the same bloody night.

Right before Beck split the Yardbirds in 1966, he recorded with Page, John Paul Jones, and the Who's Keith Moon, who was thinking about exiting Townshend's group. One track was called "Beck's Bolero," a kind of shriekback tip of the hat to Ravel shot through with insane guitar slashings and billowing feedback. Beck explains, "We did 'Bolero' and a couple of other outrageous things in one day. Halfway through 'Bolero' you can hear Moonie screaming. He hit the mike and smashed it off, so all you can hear from then on is cymbals." When the foursome's plans to form a band stalled on contractual hassles, "Beck's Bolero" became the B side to Beck's first solo single "Hi Ho Silver Lining." One of Beck's few ventures as a vocalist, it's a cut he's had a 20-odd-year love/hate relationship with.

"Silver Lining" was the opening salvo of Beck's brief career as a singer-guitarist. After leaving the Yardbirds, he returned to England and signed a contract, all too typical of the time, with Mickie Most. "It was a fabulous contract that guaranteed that I wouldn't get anything no matter what," he laughs ruefully. But he felt he had no choice, if he was to keep his career going:

> So I did what he said. I didn't like the song—it was ghastly, stupid. But it's still a mega-success all around England: they play it at the end of discos now, turn it off halfway through and everyone sings along. That double-tracked guitar solo, where everything is slightly off, sounds like two guys playing? I was actually trying to get it right but couldn't, because I had all these little inflections in the first take

that I couldn't copy. "That'll do," Mickie said. He was one of those guys who always said that: "Next. We've got Suzie Quatro coming in."

The way the first Jeff Beck Group came together and survived is characteristic of the late '60s. At the time, the world of rock was in transition. From models like the do-it-yourself British blues revival and American folk renaissance, underground scenes began to spring up. They were more spontaneous and less dependent on hits than the record industry. With them came clubs and radio stations that hosted non-top-40 material and print outlets that covered alternative sounds and lifestyles. So even without a tune on the charts, a group with a following could support itself by performing. Some, like the Grateful Dead and Jefferson Airplane, surfaced to land major-label contracts. Because audiences were open-minded, many rock bands experimented with a fluidity and freedom of expression more typical of jazz. The Dead and the Velvet Underground, for instance, cited influences like Ornette Coleman and John Coltrane for their noise-driven jams.

If the world of rock was in transition, it was also much smaller than it is today. The way Beck tells it,

> One very slack night at a club, there was one guy there plowing into some food and getting drunk on his own: Rod Stewart. He didn't even look at me, so I went over to see what was happening. He was really drunk. So I asked him whether he was still playing with Steampacket; I'd seen him with them, and he was outrageous. He said, "No, I'm not gonna stay with them." So I said, "If you ever want to put a band together . . ." He said, "You're joking." I said, "No." He said, "You ring me tomorrow, I'll leave Steampacket." So I rang him and that was it.

As Ron Wood remembers it,

> I knew Jeff from meeting him at various clubs, so I rang him when he left the Yardbirds. A lot of people don't know that when I first joined I played guitar along with Jeff, and we had Dave Ambrose, who used to play with Brian Auger, on bass. Jeff couldn't take him, though, so he asked me, "Would you mind switching to bass?" I'd seen the Yardbirds a lot at the Crawdaddy in Richmond, so I picked up a lot about bass from watching Paul Samwell-Smith. But I also learned from sticking with Jeff's licks.

Substituting Mick Waller for Aynsley Dunbar ("Mickey didn't have the drive Aynsley did, but he was funkier, more Tamla-Motown, and could still play blues," Beck observes) rounded out the final lineup.

Though Led Zeppelin's debut album is usually cited as the opening blast of heavy metal, *Truth*, along with some of Beck's Yardbirds sides, is clearly where Page copped his ideas about how to thicken and mutilate sound. That first Beck Group made some of the music molten, barbed, downright *funny* noises of all time—and helped spawn Page's paler-sounding, more studio-bound group in the process.

A feedback-riddled reworking of the Yardbirds' "Shapes of Things" kicked *Truth* off. Says Beck,

> We had a great sound, but nobody'd written anything. Rod wrote folk songs then, which wouldn't really have worked out for us. So he suggested "Shapes." I said, "Let's slow it down and make it dirty and evil." I got a Sho-Bud steel guitar and messed around with it. We were always messing around with other instruments to see how they'd work. "Superstitious" was an early wah-wah novelty. I like the Crybaby pedal because it was bloody irritating after a while. Clapton and Hendrix were using it differently; I wanted it more like a warclub, so I found the holes for it. I put slap echo on it to accentuate the edge in it.

Even their management wasn't quite sure what with this beyond-the-edge lineup. Beck explains,

> We were literally down on our last crumb. We had nothing left. But Peter Grant, who'd been over to America with the New Vaudeville Band, was smart enough to see there was an underground scene happening, where bands were making it without being seen on the surface—newspapers, records, none of that. So he said, "I'm gonna put you out there." It was a last-ditch thing, to keep the band going. So we rehearsed. But we had just one set of good clothes that had to last us the whole tour.

Rolling the dice, they landed at that alternative-music Mecca, the Fillmore East. Grins Beck, "We played two numbers in a segue to open. Finished with a big RRRARRHHHH. Rod came out from behind the amps—he sang from offstage—in a mackintosh and a hat, ready to go off home. I said, "I think you can take 'em off; they liked it.'" The next day's rave review in the *New York Times* was headlined, "Beck Upstages Grateful Dead." Recalls Beck, "It said, 'Beck and Stewart were playing like two angels with a Pinter script.' Wow! I'll never forget that magic night in New York, the warmth that came from the audience."

But after a year audiences wanted more material, not just ever wilder variations on what they'd already heard. According to Beck,

> We cut the tour short, went back home and straight to the studio. We did *Beck-Ola* in about two weeks: four days for the tracks, a week for the overdubs and mixing. That whole album was pretty much dreamt up on the spot. I didn't know what I was gonna do in the morning at breakfast. That's one of the things that's lost these days: spontaneity.

Two chunks of Presley gold, "All Shook Up" and "Jailhouse Rock," get rudely blasted into new shapes as Beck's multitracked guitars screech and wail over Wood's galloping bass to hedge Stewart's sandpaper vocals.

It was too good to last. Ironically, the high-tension egos that fired the high-wire musical acrobatics were the very ingredient that blew the band apart—on the eve of the mammoth Woodstock Festival, where the group was scheduled to appear. Says Beck,

> I deliberately broke the group up before Woodstock. I didn't want it to be preserved. Even though we were playing really well, the vibes in the band were totally shredded. So I figured, "It's only one gig." Of course, it *was* the biggest gig ever. But I couldn't face it. I didn't have any control over the P.A., anything. I couldn't have stood the failure.

So it was back to England and a new idea: combining Stewart's vocals with the dense, slamming bottom of ex-Vanilla Fudgers Tim Bogert on bass and Carmine Appice on drums. Stewart opted out; he was headed on the singer-songwriter course that threaded early '70s pop. Then, in November 1969, Beck's car hobby took a wicked turn. When a tire blew out on his '23 Model T Ford, he careened into a small Morris. The Morris's driver sustained a broken knee, but the guitarist was thrown onto the road; he broke his nose and opened the back of his head. Lucky to be alive, he was sidelined for six months, and suffered recurrent headaches for a long time thereafter.

In mid-1970, looking to get back into it and hooked on the Motown Sound, Beck took drummer Cozy Powell with him to Detroit, where they recorded eight vocal-less tracks, including "(I Know) I'm Losing You," released here for the first time. Beck shakes his head:

Talk about going a long way to get something! Let me put it this way: we went to Motown to get the Motown sound. The first thing Cozy does is remove the Motown drum kit and put his own in. (Bassist James) Jamerson said, "You want the Motown sound? You've just taken it out."

Still, the session led Beck to form the second Jeff Beck Group. After producing *Rough and Ready* himself, Beck decided he wanted to combine Motown with the Stax sound, so he asked MGs guitarist Steve Cropper to produce the follow-up. "Steve tried to explain to Cozy that you play soft, and it comes out loud," he says.

Steve was used to playing with Al Jackson, who was so understated. See, I wanted to play like Booker T and the MGs, but we had the totally wrong impression of their music because it was always played loud. They recorded it soft. I mean, look what happened to "Going Down" when we did it. We took that song and turned it inside out. But honestly I didn't know what I was doing; I was walking around with headaches all the time.

In late 1972 Beck finally hooked up with Bogert and Appice, a lineup that can still make him wince:

It was miraculous 100-mph boogie stuff—when it worked. But they overplayed everything. And I heard only a fraction of it, with the monitors the way they were then. But we flattened Japan: they loved it. Smoke pouring out of Carmine's drums, enveloping the drum riser, and he'd filter in a tape recording of a drum solo, so that when the smoke cleared the drums were still playing. It was impressive at the time. It was like in *Spinal Tap*, "Spontaneous Combustion"; I think that's where Rob Reiner got some ideas.

Although BBA was guilty of excess, it offered Beck the room to move sonically: he introduced The Bag. "It was a horn driver encased in one of those Mexican drinking-bottle bags," he explains.

Instead of having the horn deliver the sound, it was unscrewed, and we put a piece of plastic piping in the little round threaded hole where the horn used to go. The whole thing was encased in rubber to keep the sound in and drive it up the tube. So the extension leading from the amp used this as an amplifier. You put the tube in your mouth, and form a voice box where you mold the sound by the shape of your oral cavity. You don't sing at all. Then it comes over a mic to be re-amplified. People were quite amazed.

You can hear why on "Black Cat Moan" and "Blues DeLuxe/BBA Boogie."

BBA's patented showstopper came from yet another soul-music source: Stevie Wonder. The multi-instrumentalist had hunkered down in Electric Lady Studios soon after Jimi Hendrix's death; his contract with Motown was running out, and he wanted to renegotiate for more money and artistic control while he stockpiled the sounds that later surfaced on albums like *Talking Book*. Among the contributors to that breakthrough disc was Beck.

"Somebody at Epic told Stevie that I love the shit out of him, and asked him if he could maybe write a song for me," remembers Beck.

> Forget it—I was 20 feet tall at that. So I did a couple of tracks on *Talking Book*, which went down very well; he liked what I did. Then it was his job to write us a song. One day I was sitting at the drum kit, which I love to play when nobody's around, doing this beat. Stevie came kinda boogying into the studio: "Don't stop." "Ah, c'mon, Stevie, I can't play the drums." Then the lick came out: "Superstition." That was my song, in return for *Talking Book*. I thought, "He's given me the riff of the century." We played a version that he quickly put down. Stevie is a businessman; he said, "Hold the session, I'm paying for it from right now." He went out and jotted it down; he knew he'd hit gold. So he took our quickie demo to Motown and got his contract. My band had a great stage number with it, but we didn't get the hit.

Two years later, after passing on an invitation to join the Rolling Stones, who needed to replace Mick Taylor, Beck ripped out *Blow by Blow*, where his spectacular overdubs, newly expanded chordal vocabulary, and razor-sharp technique built rich textures from modal and fusiony material as well as two more Stevie Wonder tunes. Powered by FM radio, it shot to the top of the album charts, a rare feat for an all-instrumental disc. One Wonder cut, "Cause We Ended as Lovers," is dedicated to the late Roy Buchanan—with good reason, since Beck duplicates Roy's partial-harmonic picking and severe note-stretching.

Partially thanks to producer George Martin, *Blow by Blow* brought out Beck's ballad side—a consistent thread in his playing from singles like "Love Is Blue" and album cuts like "Greensleeves" on *Truth*. According to Beck,

"'Cause We've Ended as Lovers" is one of the most beautiful tunes I've ever played. I first saw Roy Buchanan in Boston in the early '70s; I was locked up in a hotel room with two guards because there was a threat on my life. So I was checking the TV out. I didn't have the sound up, but there was this guy playing a Telecaster on a rock program. Amazing sound: it was Roy. He gave me another supercharge up the bum, you know: you *can* get away with playing like this, people want it, they love it.

I went from heavy riff tunes to things that were a bit more classy. I guess I have this natural understanding of where chords are going, and what they enable me to do. Max (Middleton) was always hitting me with nice chords. I'd have to be like a twerp for about two hours while I fumbled around with them. That's what I've always done, though: just opened myself up and said, "I can't play guitar, but I'll have a go at this." And being totally honest and open and willing to start from square one works better than to try to force something that you already know over something new.

A year later, *Wired*, with its haunting rendition of Charles Mingus's "Goodbye Pork Pie Hat," marked the beginning of Beck's fruitful if conflict-laden collaboration with keyboardist Jan Hammer. Says Beck,

George Martin was a gentleman in every sense of the word. And he was a middleman to stop the musicians from wrangling. It worked really well on *Blow by Blow*. But by *Wired* I'd gotten the power bug back again. I wanted more vicious power, but with more concise playing— the way Jan plays, that spitfire thing, a million notes but concise. I wanted to take a chance with Mahavishnu-type blasts. I just lost George with that. "I don't know where the hell you're going," he'd say. But we toured with McLaughlin and went down really well.

Actually, I first heard "Goodbye Pork Pie Hat" when John (McLaughlin) played it on acoustic. One day I was fooling around with it and Max said, "I know that song." He played some of the beginning chords, but he didn't really know the rest, so he came out with his own version. The Mingus chords are unbelievable. With the voicings Jan used, I used to think I was playing the wrong notes: every night onstage I would have to watch my hands.

Jan loved to take my guitar licks and feed them back to me; it was like musical turbocharging, total self-propulsion. We were having our own party onstage. That's what I sensed: it was too self-centered for people to handle, which is why I backed off. The size of gigs we were playing, we couldn't get away with that stuff; it was for clubs, really, where you can sit and enjoy every note. But in a huge arena with 86,000 people nobody was really hearing it. It must've sounded like a jet engine.

Two years after touring Japan in 1978 with Stanley Clarke, Tony Hymas, and Simon Phillips, Beck recorded *There and Back*. Using Hymas, Phillips (one of his favorite drummers), and some bass lines by Jan Hammer and others by Mo Foster, Beck recapitulated the chameleonic styles of his long career. That lineup toured extensively. Then five years later, *Flash* tried to harness his lunacy to a techno feel with little success; that shouldn't have been surprising, since, as Beck puts it, "I always need a strong drummer to play off, to get me going. Someone like Simon is just the ticket." Of course, *Flash* did reunite Beck with Rod Stewart for "People Get Ready." A short-lived tour, instigated by Stewart, foundered. The way Beck tells it,

He wasn't forthcoming with any ideas which involved me, and I was slotted to about fifteen minutes. I just couldn't see the sense of touring the U.S. in that context. When my fans turned up, they'd be thinking I'd gone mad . . . or moody.

For all his virtues as a sonic explorer, Beck is no overall conceptualizer—which is why, like Roy Buchanan, he's sometimes seemed like a guitar genius in search of a context. As the man himself admits ruefully,

I'm no good as a bandleader. Years and years of lack of responsibility and application to the job, I guess. I always think some magic's gonna happen and someone else is gonna do it. Then I realize that it's me who's meant to be organizing it. When I really gave it authority, it bloody well worked. As soon as I went iffy and namby-pamby, it was the too many cooks thing. It's probably a hangover from the Yardbirds days. I don't want to have anything premeditated, or else I'm not able to do what I do, which is come out of the woods with all the guns blazing. I just like to hear the thread of an idea, and I'll beat down the door—you don't have to open it and usher me in.

Beck's car-building fanaticism nearly cost him his thumb in 1987:

I was in my garage working on the hot rods. I have a deep six-foot pit, an inspection pit; I don't have a cover for it other than these oak planks, which are really heavy. I picked up one of them and pulled it, and the other end went about four feet down into the pit and kicked and pinched my finger up against the chassis. It was just squashed, broke. I had two bottles of whiskey to kill the pain and went to the hospital. I practiced with the remaining fingers for six months, and started using the thumb even though it was bound up—I'd get sticky plaster all over the strings. Then the feeling didn't come back to the tip for about a year.

Two years later, the ironically named *Guitar Shop* used Beck's scattered sensibility as a structural tool, surrounding his alternating rage and lyricism, tempered by his inevitable wit, with varied styles. As he sees it,

It's got some very basic early-Beck-style elements, like from *Beck-Ola*, in it, which help people recognize my playing straightaway. But I added new elements, like electronic keyboards.
    Recording it was incredible. When I saw Terry's drums go up I got the old heartbeat going. I suggested he get into some wild jungle grooves, because I couldn't handle going to thousands of nightclubs and seeing people trying to get into a non-happening groove. You know what I'm saying? That mechanical nonsense. People have never danced to that in thousands of years, and all of a sudden everybody's dancing to a fake, perfectly spaced mechanical beat. I can't believe that's what music's about. All the great records from the '50s that I love were recorded in real time: you pushed the button and that was it. You got the electricity when you performed, and it was captured. That's what we wanted to do. And before we knew it we were going from cassette to two-track to twenty-four track—we had the twenty-four track rolling in half an hour! I was trying to capture that *now* thing.

Beck's recent work has also featured him in more congenial settings. Of the U.K. single "Wild Thing," for instance, he remarks, "It explodes, right? Totally solid overload. I wanted to bust back out, Hendrix-style, to establish that I was still kicking after *Flash*."

Looking back over a career that's lasted more than a quarter-century isn't easy for Beck. He's an incessant risk-taker who prizes in-the-moment spontaneity above all else. "I don't think about the past at all, really," he shrugs.

Yesterday is gone. I do flip back in my mind to what's worth keeping sometimes. I mean, I've skated through this business without any hit records. I've never wanted to be flavor of the month. In fact, I get frightened by the things that I know people like, 'cause then that sets the standard for what they expect of me. So you've gotta quickly rub it out: "Try this instead." That's the attitude I keep a strict hold on. I want what I do to be fresh; whether it's in the right direction or not, time will tell. But there's gotta be that stab. That's the way I play. The only thing I carry is the memory of what people have said to me, genuine appreciation, not bullshit. That's enough for me.

For the rest of us, there are the blazing, heartfelt, indescribably outrageous sounds of his guitar.   [1991]

chapter 16

Rockin' in the Free World

Neil Young has always been one of the scariest rockers around. It's not just his screechingly inventive torture of the electric guitar. It's not just the seized-up quaver of his thin nasal voice as it wobbles precariously around notes. It's not just his willingness to shift (with wildly uneven results) from grungy rocker to delicate folkie to technohead. It's the truly frightening intensity those qualities grow out of. Even at his worst—which he often is—Young is always emotionally naked, and he doesn't care who's looking. He's rock's shaman, a holy fool.

Ragged Glory (Reprise), which reunites him with the late '60s garage-band trio Crazy Horse, characteristically tackles head-on two central problems '60s rockers and the fans who grew up with them have been facing: aging and history. It's not just coincidental that rock's last few years have been marked by the deepening grip of nostalgia. The cycles of repetition draw closer and closer together as sanitarily repackaged decades come on and off the market as "memories"; the pace is so hectic that soon we may be officially nostalgic for the '90s.

Right now, though, the '60s are back, for the second or third time in recent memory, in every manifestation from clothes to graphics to vocabulary to drugs of choice. And so reformed bands and ghost bands from the period have been reprising hits and near-hits, sounds and attitudes and gestures for the graying folks who were kids then and their kids.

It can be an enjoyable and fascinating and even comforting phenomenon to watch the two- and three-generational crowds at, say, Grateful Dead or Eric Clapton concerts. (In fact, those two '60s icons have genuinely pursued their music, even if the results have been mixed.) And unpretentious reunion concerts can be the easygoing fun they're supposed to be, despite the abusive rage many critics have been heaping on them. But the overall thrust of this '60s redux, whether from older players, like The Who and The Band, or younger recyclers, like the English wave of neo-psychedelic groups being highly touted throughout the industry right now, is eerily disembodied by nostalgia. It recalls Reaganism's repeated gestures at a fictitious '50s. But where the connection between Reaganism and the '50s was ideological, the only real cultural link between now and the '60s is commercial. (This round of revivalism was solidly in place long before Operation Desert Storm gave commentators the mistaken opportunity to compare the Middle East to Vietnam.)

So even if rock's current obsession with the '60s seems to be analogous to the Reagan-era retreat of young jazzers into pre-existing languages like bop and hard bop after the creative ferment of the '60s and '70s, it's not. Of course, culture goes through cycles of exploration and retrenchment, and so what's happened recently within the two genres looks superficially alike. But rock isn't jazz. There's no obvious place in rock for an elder statesman like a Duke Ellington. Outside of garage bands doing cover versions, there's no standard repertory, and only a limited sense that songs can—or might, or should—be detached from their original performances. From that perspective, part of the struggle within this wave of nostalgia is a renewed attempt to find out whether it's possible to develop a sense of history within the music itself that goes beyond simple imitation, pastiche, and genealogies of influence.

In a curious way, because it was marketed from its beginning as "youth culture," rock is powered by a relentless pseudo-romanticism that doesn't allow it to acknowledge its own lengthening history and the age that implies. Live fast, die young is still the template, and it's a major semiconscious source of critical rage at the so-called dinosaur bands that have been touring around with more frequency and more fanfare since Woodstock's 20th anniversary two years ago.

Whatever you might think about the too-often cynical motives driving these revisitations, it's still true that the best (and the far-less-than-best) of this usually disposable music can and does find lasting meaning in people's lives. If it didn't, we'd need a radically new definition of culture. But that points to a central conundrum rooted in rock's romanticized contradictions: the commercial cult of the perpetually new can't face its past organically, doesn't allow for either continuity or growth—two of culture's primary functions—outside narrow genealogical limits. In response, some critics have elevated disposability itself into an aesthetic, consciously or unconsciously buying into a kind of corporately administered planned obsolescence for pop culture. That seems like a dead end, a blinkered and contradictory stance, unless you're willing to concede that pop music is a totally manufactured commodity foisted on an unsuspecting gullible audience—which I'm not.

On the other hand, it's also true that once most rockers are divorced from their historical moment, they become purely commercial propositions, not engines for development. If Neil Young is one of the rare exceptions, it's because he understands the passage of time and its inevitable distancing, acknowledges the distance but refuses to lapse into its nostalgia, remains determined to be as naked now in his forties as he was as a teenager in the seminal Buffalo Springfield. To a large extent, in fact, that's exactly what *Ragged Glory* is about. In "Over and Over," for instance, while Crazy Horse snorts barely controlled explosions and his guitar snarls, Young sings, "Remember the nights of love and that moment on the beach / That wasn't really too long ago / But we paid the price of time and now it's out of reach / And so the broken circle goes / Over and over again."

Most of the rest of *Ragged Glory*, as nasty and brutish and exuberant and creative a garage-band guitar bash as rock has ever had, is just as to-the-point. Take "Mansion on the Hill," which appears to be an unapologetic evocation of flower-power days. The first verse runs,

> Well I saw an old man walking in my place / When he looked at me, it could've been my face / His words were kind but his eyes were wild / He said, I got a load to lug but I want one more try / There's a mansion on the hill / Psychedelic music fills the air / Peace and love live there still / In the mansion on the hill.

That's a characteristic Youngian (pun intended) metaphorical land-scape. In "Love To Burn," for example, he sings about "walking through the Valley of Hearts"; there he finds the desolate couples who perpetually argue because they've lost themselves by refusing to spend their ability to love on each other, and tells of his own Orphic encounter with a spirit who advises him "you better let your guard down / you better take a chance on love."

Young has always projected his emotions as a world, however para-doxical or inexplicable—which is why at times he can be utterly awful, and why at times he can write such powerful and terrifying songs. He refuses to protect himself with pat judgments and revisionism. He nei-ther ignores the past nor irradiates it with a nostalgic haze. As in "Man-sion on the Hill," he stares into his aging face, acknowledges its history, seizes the multiple ghostly images that trail from its present, and then melts his selves down in the fury of the immediate creative moment.

Young's insights into the interactions of time and pop culture could—should—offer a model for rock that's as far from the bored stage antics of founders like Chuck Berry and Bo Diddley as you can get. It's equally far from the extravagant onslaughts, however successful, of bands like the Rolling Stones and The Who, who are effectively trapped by their own images and aesthetic within a perpetual time warp. As Keith Richards said to me before the last Stones tour, "We've got to find a way to make rock and roll grow up." Ironically, the Stones haven't. The Steel Wheels road show boasted terrific performances, but the Stones haven't generated memorable new material, a new sound, a new direction, for over a decade. That's at least partly because they can't face growing up in their music; they can only doctor their romanticized images. Neil Young, who's a true romantic, isn't afraid of or trapped by time in that way.   [1991]

chapter 17

Still Alive: The Grateful Dead

In this Woodstock 20th-anniversary year of 1989, the Grateful Dead have logged a quarter of a century in a peculiar countercultural nether-world where they thrive long after their contemporaries have either bailed out, gone stale, or started churning out corporate ads. The Dead's sheer longevity—they're releasing a solid new album, aptly titled *Built to Last* (Arista), on Halloween—is ironic for several reasons. A typical Grateful Dead concert—like those in mid-October at New Jersey's Meadowlands Arena, part of a national tour running through De-cember—defies the apparently ironclad rules of arena performing: no massive light show, no choreographed band steps, no constant patter, no fixed set list. Then there's the Dead's legendary willingness to break open any song for extended jamming—a strategy that takes uncontem-porary chances even as it bucks the current sound-byte mentality.

That's partly due to when and where they come from. Their original nucleus—bluegrass banjo/guitar picker Jerry Garcia, folk/jazz guitarist Bob Weir, and blues-drenched organist/harpist Rod "Pigpen" Mc-Kernan—hooked up in 1964 to play Bay Area coffeehouses as Mother McCree's Uptown Jug Champions, then soon added r&b drummer Bill Kreutzmann and jazz trumpeter/electronic composer-turned-bassist Phil Lesh. The off-kilter sounds that came spilling out of this odd mélange tossed musical ingredients in ways that transcended Summer of Love sloganeering.

The Dead paralleled 1960s jazzers in their desire to explore and appropriate Caribbean, African, Middle Eastern, and Far Eastern sounds; they also picked up on the "free" ideas of Ornette Coleman and John Coltrane as well as the modal approach of pre-fusion Miles Davis. So their acid jams began to deepen in texture, to become more than guitar solos stretched over a three-chord rock backing repeated ad infin-itum. Spearheaded by Garcia's spidery, Django Reinhardt-inspired off-beat triplets and spiraling arpeggios, the Dead remade their rock lineup into something more flexible: Lesh's loping, octave-jumping bass would bounce in loose counterpoint or doubling of Garcia, Weir's increasingly sophisticated chordal and rhythmic variations would cluster around the dual drummers' polyrhythms, and the tune at hand would gradually mutate into free-form space. That approach eventually inspired bands from the Allman Brothers to Television.

Especially since the punk outbreak of the mid-1970s, with its much-needed attack on the arena-inspired, corporate-rock flatulence of bands like Yes and Journey, the Dead have often been criticized for their meandering jams and hippie ways. And in fact, they've had bleak patches of pointless four-hour-long concerts topped with fingernails-down-the-blackboard vocals. The last couple of years, though, have brought renewed vigor to their shows and their first-ever hit single, "Touch of Grey"—a statistic they can add to being the first band to record on 16-track equipment, to invite fans to private-tape their free radio broadcasts, to create the forerunner of the modern arena P.A. system, to play at the Sphinx, and to stay consistently popular without radio hits among several generations of rockers.

For the Grateful Dead's audience reaches across generations with fanaticism. Tie-dyed fans who weren't even born by the time the Dead got to Woodstock as well as those who were follow them literally around the globe from show to show, like Pirandellian characters out of a period movie. Part of what draws them is the dialogic sense of community that, during the Dead's late-1960s heyday, found voice in the counterculture. The band still infuses that spirit into its extended-family attitudes toward its followers (e.g., by funding hotlines and magazines to disseminate info) and its longstanding political affiliations (especially with environmental groups like Greenpeace).

As it updates the Dead's core sound with appropriate synth washes, *Built to Last* touches on timely concerns like drug addiction and the earth's rape as well as sometimes fuzzily expressed ones like love and hope—which, after all, were always the message sent by the Dead's engaging way of being. It's not a great album, but it'll do. For when they're playing as well as they're playing now, their balletic, democratic communication validates the old slogan: there is nothing like a Grateful Dead concert. That may explain why they, unlike most of their contemporaries, have avoided the irrelevance of nostalgia.   [1989]

chapter 18

New York Lou

The Velvet Underground has had an amazing posthumous career for the last twenty years. History, if you like, caught up with them about a decade ago, when the punkers and incipient New Wave rediscovered the virtues of sonic assault and coupled nerve-shredding decibels with hyper-alienated lyrics. So it is that Sonic Youth and Husker Du, Jesus and Mary Chain and the Smiths, and countless others can claim the Velvets for ancestors.

Taken up by Andy Warhol soon after their formation in 1965—he put them on the road, produced their first album, and furnished the artwork that makes its "banana" cover a MOMA exhibit and collectible today—the Velvet Underground became notoriously chic in some New York circles. That enthusiasm didn't exactly mushroom: their shows, especially outside New York, were sparsely attended, and their albums sold in microscopic figures.

And no wonder. While the counterculture was painting itself day-glo and ingesting consciousness-expanding substances, organizing its politics and becoming a kind of cartoon guerrilla army that parodied the Asian military buildup, Lou Reed, at the V.U.'s creative core, was penning lyrics about heroin and homosexuality, sado-masochism and street violence. The music was shot through with grungy feedback, spewed nightmare screeches from Reed's howling-at-the-abyss, brutal guitar and Cale's sawed-to-the-bone electrified viola and droning keyboards; underneath rumbled the pummeling of Maureen Tucker's drums and Sterling Morrison's guitar and bass. It was a deadly and riveting mix, heightened on their first album, *The Velvet Underground & Nico* (Verve), by icy Dietrich-pretender Nico's vocals. Between that and *White Light/White Heat* (Verve), the V.U. brought the Marquis de Sade's jaundiced ironies into the 20th century.

Or at least, that describes the Velvets of classic tracks like "Heroin,"

"Waiting for My Man," "White Light/White Heat," "I Heard Her Call My Name," and "Sister Ray." But they had their other sides too: the odd folkiness of "I'll Be Your Mirror," the inflated psychedelia of "All Tomorrow's Parties," the jejune schmaltz of "Sunday Morning."

The V.U. staggered along for two years after Cale left in 1968, but the dialectic of astringency and excess that powered them had fractured. By the time Reed went solo in 1970–71, he was on his way to parodying what would make him a cult hero years later. He spent a lot of the '70s recycling or unearthing songs he'd written during the Velvets period; he seemed to be wandering through identities, trying them on, discarding them without even a shrug—as if irony alone would save his muse. He attacked the first wave of his disciples, glam-rocker proto-punks like the New York Dolls, but reconfigured himself to emulate glam-rocker supreme David Bowie on *Transformer* (RCA). He stopped playing the guitar on and offstage, and left his live music to uneven bands. He got bloated from booze and drugs, sped and vitamined himself down to Dickensian thinness (the Bowie Look), cut his hair, dyed his hair, and cut some utterly spectacular tunes (the hilarious space-shot sendup "Satellite of Love," the grimly funny jive of "Sally Can't Dance") along with lots of crap. The Street Poet of New York, as he was billed, rode a creative rollercoaster to nowhere in particular, but his credentials appeared on his album sleeves via titles like *Growing Up in Public* (RCA).

The punk/New Wave revolt penetrated Reed's solipsistic universe. On the one hand, the bands spearheading the move, like Television and their offshoot Richard Hell and the Voidoids, drew plentiful creative ideas from Reed's V.U. material; on the other, they simply disregarded most of what he'd done since. Faced with a new musical vanguard, Reed's reaction was again to co-opt, but this time he got lucky: when Hell's Voidoids ground to a halt, he picked up guitarist Robert Quine (and later drummer Fred Maher), added bassist Fernando Saunders and drummer Doane Perry, and thus assembled the band that would push him back up to the front ranks of rock and roll.

Their only album, *The Blue Mask* (RCA; o.p.) pits pastoral breathers against Reed's genuinely harrowing descent into the hells of sex-and-drug-driven terror, rage, and violence—a place that nobody else can plumb with his scarred power. Even the apparently gentle songs bite. Saunders's growling, octave-jumping lines and Perry's vicious rhythms kick the rockers into bloodcurdling shape while the dual guitars chime and slash.

Quine, a hardcore Reed fan since the '60s and a seminal guitarist on the post-punk scene, pivoted his idol's direction. He not only convinced Reed to play guitar again, but deliberately recreated the Velvets' grinding, droning chordal textures and riddling solos. The band helped refurbish Reed's mordant ironies, which run on disjunctions—between words and music, between socially accepted values and id-like horrors, between apparent meanings and actual events.

"The Gun," a Peckinpah-like nightmare of robbery and rape, packs a wallop because of the arranged control, the tension between the icily restrained music and the lurid lyrics; "The Blue Mask" is a litany of self-hating incantations, roars, and rages; "Underneath the Bottle," an alcoholic's rationalizations, gets an almost jaunty setting with melodic country trills. But the killer is "Waves of Fear," a DT anxiety nightmare that rides out on Quine's mewling, puking guitar solo, deliberately raw and formless as a baby whirling in a blender.

That was 1981; a year later came Reed's new mainstream look and sound. He peeled off his band, mixed Quine's wrenching guitar to near-inaudibility on *Legendary Hearts* (RCA). By 1984's *New Sensations* (RCA) he'd become a self-parodic name-dropper.

Then came January of 1989, when Reed and Cale reunited in a Brooklyn church to preview their fourteen "Songs for 'Drella." These will form the backbone of a music theatre piece (to be premiered this winter at the Brooklyn Academy of Music's Next Wave 1989 Festival) about Andy Warhol and the scenes that swirled around him. Even in this embryonic stage the music came across as powerful and promising and unpretentious. I was so relieved and fired-up I went home and plowed through my old Velvets' records, my favorite '70s cuts, *Rock N Roll Animal* (RCA), *The Blue Mask*, and even the videotaped *A Night with Lou Reed* (RCA/Columbia Pictures Home Video).

The very next day brought *New York* (Sire) to my door, along with the predictable chorus of critical raves greeting its release. Lou. The Street Poet of New York. The Archetypal Punk. The Legend in His Own Time. But this is The New Improved Legend. (Maybe record companies are on to something when they call their output "product.") After touring for Amnesty International and appearing on the anti-apartheid

Sun City album, Reed has apparently undergone a political consciousness-raising. Living in exurban New Jersey, he's become an environmentalist; married and settled, he's apologetic about sexism, vehement about anti-Semitism, and virtuously down on crack.

Unfortunately, the product at hand displays just how unsubtle and fuzzy the New Lou Reed's new social awareness is. There's the muddled anti-anti-Semite attack on Kurt Waldheim, the pope, and Jesse Jackson called "Common Ground," the empty rhetoric of "There Is No Time," the implicit sterilize-'em solution of "Endless Cycle," the warmed-over Springsteen Viet-vet homilies of "Xmas in February," and the downright jejune pseudo-myth called "Last Great American Whale."

To be fair, all Lou Reed albums have moments nobody needs, which on a good or great Lou Reed album are overcompensated for by extraordinary peaks not found anywhere else. And *New York* does have good tunes that showcase Reed's masterfully savage ironies at work: "Halloween Parade," set over a bouncy little riff, looks at AIDS and the ghosts conjured up for him by that annual Village street blowout; "Dirty Blvd." slices a patented Reed view of the drug-and-whore netherworld; "Beginning of a Great Adventure," a wry and relentless look at the always tangled motives behind having kids, offers classic Reed lines like, "It might be fun to have a kid that I could kick around create in my own image like a god I'd raise my own pallbearers to carry me to my grave and keep me company when I'm a wizened toothless clod."

But even the best songs here are hobbled by a kind of musical aphasia. There's no tension, ironic or otherwise, between Reed's monotone vocals and the insipid arrangements punctuated by barely competent Keith Richards-type licks. *New York* sounds like a collection of demos with the redeeming vitality somehow drained out.   [1989]

chapter 19

On the Border

The cover for his latest album, his seventh in nine years, is startling. A hulking skull, leering toothily from beneath a Mexican cowboy hat, sprouts from a clothed skeletal body which straddles a horse rivaling Quixote's Rocinante for malnutrition; the right arm brandishes a reverse-field Jolly Roger. Its fierce mouth open, eyes literally blazing, the steed clatters across clusters of worn skulls and pieces of bone against a dour, dark sky. It is a graphic reproduction of an engraving of Emiliano Zapata, possibly by the Master of the Wormeaten Skull; and it serves notice that Joe King Carrasco's *Bandido Rock* has some things to say about how the U.S. conducts its business south of the border. He's come through New York a few times this summer to perform it live for the folks who've been following him and his music while, in the rock and roll tradition, he follows the road.

Not of Latino descent himself, Carrasco (né Teutsch) has drunk in the south Texas musical traditions that find a polka beat firing through so many border sounds. Because of the heavy concentration of German immigrants in both Texas and Mexico, some say partly because of the Emperor Maximilian's abortive reign, the polka was imported from its central European spawning grounds and transplanted to the region, where it melded with Spanish traditions to produce the two-step. The style infiltrated swing music via the territory bands of the region, resounded in the Western swing bands of folks like Bob Wills, then resurfaced in the budding pop idioms of Ritchie Valens and his pal Buddy Holly. During the '60s, Texas-based rockers like ? and the Mysterians and Doug Sahm and California types like Cannibal and the Headhunters and Sam the Sham kept the flame, and, more recently, bands like Los Lobos and the Cruzados have picked up the torch. This long-running current in pop's wide river has, thanks to the massive success of *La Bamba*, suddenly been rendered visible beyond cult borders again.

And so, I hope, will Carrasco. Like the currents in a river, his mongrelized music has flowed in a general direction: from the friendly party-animal brawls of his early days to the still-good-humored, if by turns fierce and ironic, political commitment of his recent efforts. Unlike Los Lobos, who paint devastating portraits of the underclass but look to a kind of spiritual resolution for the dilemmas of economic and cultural imperialism, Carrasco gets ever grittier in search of an earthly revolution. With his last two albums, he seems to have found one, in Nicaragua. In a way, he's become like an updated Woody Guthrie, peeling off song after song that takes a flinty-eyed look at official pieties.

But Carrasco isn't a moldy folky classicist: his medium is the raunchiest of bar-based rock and roll, the slop-it-up, stomp-it-out, tear-this-roadhouse-down variety. You can think about the lyrics, all right, and you'd probably better, but you're gonna have to do it while the urgent beat, the snarling guitars, and the wheezy organ and accordion blast you and your Dos Equis into Partyland. Like all the best descendants of the Stones' "Street Fighting Man," Carrasco's political rock swaggers with compelling dance-floor rhythms that are far from cerebral to put the message across. Take *Bandido Rock* as an example. Picking up the overt political direction he began with *Bordertown*, the LP bristles with self-explanatory titles like the churning, darkly minor-key "Hey Gringo 'No Pasaran'" and the closing track, "Fuera Yanqui," as well as the ironic singsong called "Banana."

Still, it's got live that you really want Carrasco: the clubs strung out along the road are really more his natural home than vinyl, which can only suggest the sweaty, smoke-filled celebrations that follow him wherever he plays. It's often been said that rock and roll is basically a community rite, not an act of solitude; even a narcissist like Billy Idol wants to dance with himself in front of a crowd. Carrasco doesn't have money or fame, doesn't play arenas, and tramps around the country with only a road map and a beat-up van instead of an entourage. But when he and the band pull into town you're guaranteed 100 percent from the heart of rock and roll.   [1987]

chapter 20

Payola Guys

Hit Men by Frederic Dannen (Times Books/Random House) looks at the development and consolidation of the recording industry over the last twenty-plus years. As late as the 1960s, it was still a ragtag collection of hundreds of vari-sized companies that could compete on different but roughly equivalent levels. A tiny label could produce a major national hit partly because everyone shared the same fragmented regional distribution systems, partly because radio was looser and more open, via payola and the independent tastes of individual disk jockeys, to smaller companies' efforts. Now the industry has evolved into a bare handful of major labels that control 96 percent of the U.S. retail market and boast the only national distribution pipelines around—which means their products are the only ones guaranteed an automatic presence in stores, especially chains, across the country.

While it touches on this, Dannen's book focuses on another part of the market-control mechanism at play in the record industry: the industrialized institutionalization of payola. According to Dannen (who's based much of his research on previous reporting), the payola scandal of the '50s that broke the likes of Alan Freed inadvertently led to this situation. First, responsibility for choosing what would go on the air was taken from the DJs and centralized in station program directors; the theory was that that would minimize abuse. What it did instead, as Dannen sees it, was create an opportunity for the major labels and organized-crime affiliates. Dannen's sources estimate that in the 1980s CBS—which, he says, helped formulate the system and used it most heavily—spent $10 million annually to hire independent promoters, who in return supposedly generated widespread airplay for the records they were paid to rep. By upping the ante for the promoters' services beyond the smaller labels' reach, the majors could effectively dominate radio, and thus guarantee themselves a hammerlock on chart-toppers and an ever increasing market share.

The ironic twist came when the promoters began to hold the industry hostage for those vast amounts—and more. Their power, as Dannen notes, derived not from their ability to make hits; contrary to paranoid myth, nobody's ever really figured out quite how to do that. But the promoters could guarantee that if they didn't get their cut for a record, it wouldn't make the airwaves, and thus the charts—the negative power of the gatekeeper. Since radio has progressively stratified stylistically into narrowband formats dictated by PDs and programming consultants over the last two decades, and since experimental, pioneering, and even just-left-of-center sounds have disappeared from the medium that broke rock and roll when it was just a fledgling regional style, it looks like the strategy worked.

Dannen leaves his plot cliff-hanging: some of its major characters are awaiting trials whose outcomes will presumably determine the industry's (and the government's) next steps. The ending doesn't significantly affect *Hit Men*'s value, since its prime virtue is that it collects this story in one place; most of the puzzle's pieces have been exposed before. (Dannen meticulously cites sources in back-of-the-book notes.)

Possibly because of what he sees as the personality-driven nature of the record biz, and possibly because the best-selling books about business are usually driven by insider gossip, Dannen combines solid research and reporting with what seems meant to be an intimate behind-the-scenes flavor. There's amateur psychologizing about label heads' backgrounds and motives and insecurities, for instance, and annoying and unprofessional stylistic tics, like referring to protagonists by their first names. There's a somewhat unsettling tendency to reduce corporate struggles to personality conflicts. Then too, Dannen doesn't always get his factual details right, which isn't reassuring: he woefully underestimates the number of annual releases, for example. But despite its faults, *Hit Men* is a useful and provocative and highly readable perspective on an industry that still likes to pretend it's not.   [1990]

chapter 21

Turn On Your Love Light

Following the resurgence of apparent social commitment in pop music since the punk explosion of the late '70s, *When the Music's Over: The Story of Political Pop* by Robin Denselow (Faber & Faber) or something like it was probably inevitable. Not only because the subject is begging to be covered, but because the entertainment conglomerates that dispense information to us all tend to milk any trend or money-maker that comes up in every format available. And as Tracy Chapman and Bob Geldof and countless others have shown, good politics can translate into good numbers—and good numbers are the only ideology the accountants care about.

You won't come away with that sense from *When the Music's Over*, however. For Robin Denselow—a British journalist who, according to the dust-jacket blurb, "specializes in both pop and politics"—the world of political pop is a relatively simple if rambunctious place that consists largely of good guys (the politically committed) and misguided guys (the politically confused or uncommitted) and bad guys (politicians, corporate executives, and the like). Sometimes the good guys and the bad guys go eyeball-to-eyeball; more often various varieties of good guys engage in the kinds of intramural power/ideological struggles/backbiting the left is so adept at.

Within this reductive frame, Denselow charts a history of political pop that is largely a fair and interesting re-telling. Beginning with folkies like the Weavers in the '50s, he walks us through the '60s civil-rights/antiwar era in the U.S., U.K., Brazil, and Greece (that last more off-the-usually-beaten-path than his other material), the '70s and '80s in the Caribbean and Africa, the '80s in Ireland, and the recent mega-media campaigns against nuclear power, apartheid, Thatcher, and so on.

Most of this comes out about right in Denselow's hands, although he spends a disproportionate amount of his attention on developments in the U.K. and his editor Pete Townshend and Townshend's extremely unpolitical band, The Who. And he gets myriad details wrong—calling Pete Seeger Peter, Keith Richards Richard, Charles Mingus's "Fables of Faubus" *Fables of Forbus*, and so on. Still, he does cover events over a wide geographical and cultural range, focusing primarily on charismatic figures like Ewan MacColl and Bob Marley and Billy Bragg, as well as outlining a generally solid, workmanlike picture of music's interaction with political movements and ideals over the last 40 years.

The terms around which his book revolves, however, are never resolved, or even raised significantly—which both limits and frees him. Since he effectively never defines what he means by the "political pop" of his book's subtitle, he seems unshackled by dogma and able to roam—which he does, literally around the world and across generic lines with what might seem like commendable impunity if it didn't seem more like naivete.

What exactly do Pete Seeger and Elvis Presley and Harry Belafonte and Bob Marley, Miriam Makeba and Harry Chapin and the Sex Pistols and Tracy Chapman, Ewan MacColl and The Who and Bob Geldof and Sweet Honey in the Rock, Stevie Wonder and Bob Dylan and Thomas Mapfumo and Jello Biafra and U2 have in common? Denselow never explicitly says; he just assumes a kind of time line of continuity—the retrospective reasoning of naive history—between old folkies like Seeger and MacColl and rock and rollers around the globe, whether political activists or simply rebels by cultural definition. But where folkies like Seeger and many Third World rockers hearken back to an ageless worldwide tradition of the news-bearing troubador—a tradition Denselow rightly notes—First World rockers (and, as they enter First World-run pipelines into the international marketplace, musicians of every stripe) have another, completely different heritage and milieu to deal with as well.

For while rock was born as a folk music, its surging popularity quickly made it a commercial property whose stock kept fluctuating—and whose managers kept manipulating it to their own ends as best they could. By the early '60s, for instance, the rockabilly rebels of the '50s were dead or in the army, Chuck Berry was in prison, and oodles of Dick Clark-sponsored voiceless wonders were crooning "rock" songs that Bing Crosby could have felt comfortable with.

Unfortunately, the closest Denselow comes to articulating anything about rock as commercial music is in passages like this: "Rock'n'roll was under attack from the start, but this exuberant new style, unsure of its power or even whether it would last, merely tugged a forelock politely at the establishment. [Bill] Haley tried reason, Elvis joined the army, and none of the first generation rockers rocked the political boat."

The civil-rights/antiwar movement of the '60s changed that, of course, with its explicit, folkie-derived recognition that music, as part of culture, can help create a community and articulate shared ideals, values, goals. Bernice Johnson Reagon, longtime activist and leader of the women's harmony group Sweet Honey in the Rock, puts it succinctly: "The singing was used to create the climate, to get people ready to address the issues. So any statement from lawyers, any testimony from someone who'd been arrested, was presented on a bed of song. And the song-leaders were absolutely essential. . . . A job had to be done by the singing, and it wasn't done by someone singing a solo."

But just as Woodstock has now, in the post-Reagan years, become what *Adweek* in late May called "sanitized as both a memory and a marketing tool" so that that Festival's logo can appear on 20th-anniversary ashtrays and barrettes and T-shirts, so too with rock's political edge in the '80s. The key change over the last 20 years has been the sheer growth and consolidation of the entertainment industry.

Rock is now a mega-business—if you don't believe me, just ask Sony-CBS or Time Warner—that grosses some $7 billion annually in the U.S. alone. The bits and pieces of the modern delivery system that began to emerge in the '30s—radio, for instance, which made Woody Guthrie and Benny Goodman folk heroes—have, over the last decade and more, been assembled into a more homogenized and controlled mass-marketing organ. Among its components: playlist-radio and MTV (which functions as the linchpin between Madison Avenue and rock, drawing directors and casts back and forth across the nonexistent line between music videos, which are of course ads themselves, and commercials), corporate underwriting and sponsorships of tours and major events, record companies (owned by larger conglomerates with far-flung interests), retailers (more and more, mega-chains), and, of course, the press.

While this doesn't translate into a cabal of evil geniuses who are able to predict what will go to number one on the charts, it does mean enormous amounts of pressure can be exerted in a casual way to keep other smaller players (in the form of indie record labels or breaking bands, for instance) off the field. If you can manage to find out where the field is: as nearly anyone who's ever worked in a record store can explain, the *Billboard* charts that serve as the industry's sales bible are steadily if quietly manipulated by enticements of various kinds from record companies to the underpaid retailers who report sales figures to that trade magazine.

This massive, sloppy pipeline also intrudes inevitable distortions on virtually any overt political act and/or message sent through it by a musician, however well intentioned. When Amnesty International runs tours sponsored by Reebok, with the TV and radio coverage saturated with ads boasting endorsements of motorcycles and soda pop by the people coming on and off the stage, you have to stop and wonder just what the messages getting to the audience are, even though AI's membership rolls and general-public awareness level obviously get a deserved and needed boost. The same issues can—and unfortunately, must—be raised for Live Aid, Farm Aid, and every mega-event mounted by contemporary mega-conglomerates.

The implications roll on from there. Just one example: What does the outpouring of environmental concern on the part of musicians mean in the context of an industry so dependent on petrochemicals? (Once you've noticed that, it does seem odd and perhaps revealing that so much concern is lavished by U.S. and U.K. rockers on Japanese fishing practices and Brazilian logging.)

Underlying questions remain. Does anyone—can anyone—in a culture as commercially fractured and driven as ours actually respond in a lasting, meaningful way to messages about revolution, racism, poverty, sexual freedom, child abuse, and teenage pregnancy that are sandwiched between the same old 30-second spots about acne medicine and chewing gum? Whether in the form of mega-events or a tune played on commercial radio, 1980s political pop is not, after all, some direct modern analog to the wandering singer setting up in the town square—as much as we all pretend at times that it is, if only because the contradictions are too thick and daunting to deal with.

I don't have any answers to these questions, but I wish Robin Denselow had at least raised the issues. Then we might actually be able to begin talking about what political pop is. In the meantime, at least he's taken a fact-oriented first step on the long road ahead. [1989]

chapter 22

Rock Vaudeville

They scamper onstage, just the two of them and their prerecorded backing tracks and a weird assortment of instruments that includes electric guitar, accordion, baritone sax, and stick—as in limb of a tree. They don't wear Spandex or black leather or funny suits with water-squirting flowers in their lapels or big floppy shoes on their—well, wherever they'd put them. But they do sometimes don gigantic puppet heads and hands and ridiculous wicker hats that look like something the tomb-builders for Ramses II discarded. They twitch and pogo during their tunes in a schizoid frenzy that suggests they're recent escapees from an electro-shock clinic. They are They Might Be Giants, whose whimsical irony and sharp-witted parodies have cut them a path to the high-school and college audience that listens to the Smiths and Sonic Youth and U2 and Run-DMC and has, it seems, begun to perceive the web of social pathology linking their individual angsts.

Whimsy and irony aren't words you find nestling comfortably alongside rock and roll in too many places even though they have a role that goes back to the music's very beginnings. As Robert Christgau has suggested, those qualities explain how a lot of Chuck Berry tunes— "Memphis," "Sweet Little Sixteen," "No Particular Place To Go"— gently overcame the distances separating this black adult (thirty years old and already a prison vet when he penned hit after hit) from white teenage America. Duck-walking across the stage, slinging his guitar over his back and between his legs as he played, Berry is a Founding Father not only of rock and roll, but of rock vaudeville.

Berry and other key performers of that first generation—Elvis Presley, Jerry Lee Lewis, Little Richard—were the main vehicles by which the minstrel show and vaudeville came into rock and roll. Twist Berry's good-natured view of adolescence into the surly, know-it-all smugness brandished by many teenagers and you get the Mothers of Invention. The Mothers' early social critiques were soon squandered on two mutually exclusive (though neurotically connected) directions: increasingly feeble "satire" (largely limited to sneering at safe targets like suburban America's hypocrisy) and inflated musical pretensions (leader Frank Zappa's constant citations of Edgard Varese as his model—the need to justify by appeal to European classicism that infects the American body cultural).

While the Mothers were squatting in the Village in the late '60s, at the theater upstairs from the Cafe Au Go Go, the Fugs were down the block in the basement of the Cafe Wha?, hurling Beat-style lyrics and deliberately disjointed rockabilly- and country-flavored tunes at the tiny audience in a kind of anarcho-hippie cabaret. No small historical irony that this club was where a then unknown guitarist named Jimi Hendrix (calling himself Jimmy James, and his band the Blue Flames), first played on his own. Hendrix, of course, reclaimed and expanded the wilder staging aspects of rock vaudeville, which had been left largely dormant (except for the likes of James Brown and the Velvet Underground) outside the black music ghetto known since vaudeville's heyday as the "chitlin' circuit." Hendrix had played that circuit, and developed his onstage mania, behind stars like Little Richard and the Isley Brothers.

There were other vaudevillians at work in different directions. Beginning with a free-form radio show allowable in the late '60s (and *verboten* ever since on commercial radio), Firesign Theater molded old detective novels, B movies from the '30s, TV channel-jumping, social and political radicalism, and rock and roll into a thoughtful and hilarious Joycean pastiche that became at once an acute social critique and a lot of recycled fun. Monty Python, their British TV counterparts, often worked with Neil Innes, co-conspirator in the collection of zany Brits known as the Bonzo Dog Doo-Dah Band. Less overtly political and more self-consciously arty than some of their contemporaries, the Bonzos shared with their fellow vaudevillians the genre's defining traits: a highly developed sense of parody, a broad knowledge of musical formats, a love of wordplay, a keen feel for the ridiculous.

Which brings us to They Might Be Giants. The Giants have indeed been laughing hard all the way from the now defunct East Village performance club called 8 B.C. (a bomb-crater of a basement where I first saw them years ago) to the Ritz (one of N.Y.'s top-line venues) and MTV. One of the best things about their drawing closer to the bank is that there's no single cause behind it, no simple way to explain how their quirky parodic anthems, their knotted and witty takes on adolescent viewpoints, have reached out to the numbers they obviously have. The Giants have no major-label contract, and so there's no machine grinding out PR releases by the truckload, spitting out pieces of vinyl by the truckload to radio stations and print media, rounding up rock critics by the truckload, hauling in truckloads of TV promo spots on *The Tonight Show* and all. Instead what you have here, as with hiphop, is a phenomenon that is both at the roots of rock and roll and periodically almost forgotten—word-of-mouth, spontaneous appeal through shared values and the call to rebellion. It's no accident that some Giants' tunes have titles like "Kiss Me, Son of God" and "Alienation's for the Rich."

Nor is it a coincidence that the Giants have translated their developed sense of how skewed the world is not only into biting songs but into a mushrooming popularity stoked by their simple, useful, and brilliant insight into how the skewed music biz functions. Since doors did not exactly fling themselves open at the Giants' approach, they devised Dial-a-Song. Pick up the phone, punch in 1-718-387-6962, and you get that day's Giant-penned looney tune (there are over 300 to choose from). To understand how subversive this tack is, especially in light of its success, you have to understand a few things about the U.S. music industry.

It's no news to anyone that over the last 15 years the handful of major labels have come to dominate the release of "product," as they call the items they make from pop music. (Previously they'd limited themselves more to raiding whatever "fad" established an audience for itself, as when RCA bought Elvis's contract after his initial hits on the minuscule Sun label.) This effort to regularize the market, to make a more predictable commodity out of recordings and more predictable and massed consumers out of a jumpy patchwork of audiences, was just another instance of the way top-heavy corporations grew via mergers and mutual monopoly agreements in almost all other areas of the U.S. economy during this period. There's no need to invoke a conspiracy theory of history to understand how this narrowing of possibilities for both musician and audience is enforced: it's in the same depersonalized mode that characterizes the interlocking and self-regulating control apparatus we call industrial bureaucracy everywhere. That way, options are rendered unavailable (I use the passive voice deliberately).

That apparatus, as it currently exists within the recording industry, is built from three main parts. First are the large labels—WEA (Warner-Elektra-Atlantic), CBS, RCA, Capitol-EMI, PolyGram, and MCA, all of which shelter clusters of smaller lines beneath their expansive corporate umbrellas. Their sheer distribution muscle—they own the only truly national pipelines to service retailers—both determines what they release (sales are intended to average six-digits' worth of "product" to break even) and casts them as Charles Atlas to everyone else's 97-pound weakling. Then there are the large commercial radio stations, whose reach over the airwaves via their high-wattage signals and metropolitan locations is all the more damaging given their neurotically focused and formatted playlists. Those commandments take what "product" makes it through the pipelines and break it down even further according to the "demographics" (read racist, economic, and cultural imperatives) the labels and stations share as ways to categorize sound, and decree which are playable on what particular station. (A healthy cadre of "programming consultants" has grown up over the last decade to service just this neurosis; they do the breakdowns, make the playlists, and take the station's responsibility to the audience whose airwaves it rides into their own well-manicured hands.)

Finally (though the bloom has worn off this particular rose in the industry to a certain extent because of its volatile audience figures) there is MTV. Initially owned in large part by Warner Communications, WEA's corporate parent, MTV has since been bought by Viacom, a subsidiary of National Amusements that deals extensively in music videotapes. Whatever its ownership, MTV has in effect appropriated the narrowcast formats that have effectively throttled creativity on commercial radio.

They Might Be Giants neatly sidestepped (and quite possibly undercut) the whole thicket with Dial-a-Song. And when you think about it, what else could they have done, short of accepting their own oblivion as inevitable and just? Outside of college radio, that beleaguered and wildly uneven haven for the idiosyncratic, what programmer would have knowingly (never mind willingly) aired songs like "Youth Culture Killed My Dog," a tragic tale of a puppy whose mind was blown by hiphop and white funk when all he really loved were Bachrach-David tunes; or "She's an Angel," a literalization of that cliché which observes of the winged folk, "When they sing you can't hear, there's no air"; or "Everything Right Is Wrong Again," which traces "the line dividing laugh and scream" (one of the Giants' favorite live ploys is to ask their audience between songs to "scream like you're in hell")?

Surely one reason the Giants have succeeded in circumventing the industrial apparatus between them and their potential audience is that they give that audience credit for brains—something few major-label or commercial-radio execs can be accused of. Not only are their lyrics consistently well worked and able to turn on thought-provoking paradoxes or allusive situations, but their music grips and shakes those lyrics with the tenacity of a grinning pit bull. Thus their brilliantly executed parodies: of Elvis Costello's paranoid Hitchcockian visions ("(She Was a) Hotel Detective"); of The Who's '60s-youth-culture banalities ("Hope That I Get Old Before I Die"); of the pseudo-Rimbaudian babble that Bob Dylan and his ilk all too often palm off as poetry ("Absolutely Bill's Mood"); of that tired country and rock staple, the road song ("Toddler Hiway"); and on and on.

The social implications undergirding their mordant satires and their self-marketing campaign become clear on a number like "Put Your Hand Inside the Puppet Head": "Ads up in the subway are the work of someone / Trying to please their boss / And though the guy's just a pig we all know what he wants / Is just to please somebody else / If the puppet head were only busted in / It would be a better thing for everyone involved / And we wouldn't have to cry / Put your hand inside the puppet head." Whether the puppet head is MCA's, IBM's, or Reagan's, the advice couldn't be better. So put your hand inside the puppet head and pull out their LP (*They Might Be Giants*, Bar/None Records) and their 12-inch single ("Don't Let's Start," b/w three tracks not on the LP, Bar/None Records); they'll give you as much laughter as you can take and you'll help them edge closer to the bank. That's what I call a fair exchange.   [1988]

chapter 23

Good Day at Black Rock

Via the mongrelized sounds of rock and roll, some of the key questions Living Colour pose on their debut album, *Vivid* (Epic), deal with the divisive nature and state of racism in this country. Take the pointed, frantic, punk bash "Which Way to America?," which describes the chasm still cutting between the two Americas a generation after the assassination of Martin Luther King. "I look at the TV / Your America's doing well / I look out the window / My America's catching hell / I just want to know, which way do I go / To get to your America?" Then, over a stomping drums-only backdrop: "Where's my picket fence, my tall cool glass of lemonade? / Where's my VCR, my stereo, my TV shows?" It's an indictment that, flying on rock-and-roll wings, may well reach more ears than the Kerner Commission Report.

In fact, *Vivid* poses two levels of questions, one simply by its existence. That's because Living Colour is led by guitarist/chief songwriter Vernon Reid, who's also co-founder of the Black Rock Coalition. The BRC began in 1985 as a cooperative organization for black musicians dedicated to breaking the color-bar stereotypes and marketing categories slammed across music by the recording industry. In effect, certain areas, like rootsy rock and roll and heavy metal and other college-radio-oriented sounds, are simply designated off-limits to blacks.

Fundamental to how this industry-wide segregation works is a way of organizing and describing sound not stylistically but racially, as if that division were self-evident. Every major record company has a separate a&r department, marketing department, and publicity department to handle r&b (read black) artists. Radio stations, especially in lucrative urban markets, are categorized by the putative color of their audiences, and the music they play is programmed by their consultants accordingly. Retail outlets organize their bins and departments to follow suit. Publications that survive largely on industry support, from fanzines to trades, follow that racist lead religiously; even jazz magazines, covering a field clearly dominated by black players, tilt heavily toward covering whites, especially in big features. So the lock-up is pretty complete.

From the industry's standpoint, this kind of segregation has the obvious advantage of neatening the crazy quilt of sounds it sells. Black musicians are expected to follow one of three or four permissible prototypes for the music they're told "their" audience wants to hear. But however obvious the advantages of this policy may be to a large, established, and ever-more-consolidated industry seeking to control its output and regularize its markets by increasing compartmentalization, the equally obvious problem is that music, like any art form, is messy, and spills over even such apparently airtight borders as race.

Given the relative weakness of the musicians in this marketing game, it's no surprise that the struggle is usually resolved in the circular form of self-fulfilling prophecy. If blacks are "supposed" to play a certain constellation of styles for their pre-assigned black audiences, and if to get a hearing for their music they have to make it fit the pre-existing slots, most times they will.

Nor should it come as a surprise to learn that these racially segregated arrangements aren't reciprocal. White musicians can appropriate "black" styles like funk with the same ease that in the '50s found cardigan-wearing Pat Boone covering the hermaphroditic, gospel-derived raunch of Little Richard for white America's eyes and ears. Since black audiences constantly learn about official white culture while whites have to delve to get into black culture, one ironic result is that black musicians can more easily reappropriate "white" sounds for their own ends—like when Run-DMC incorporated heavy metal into rap.

As Jesse Jackson has done in the presidential forum, the BRC has tried to reformulate the debate about these topics by insistently pointing to the racism and economic inequalities that structure it and seeking ways to escape its contradictions. It uses two basic approaches. One is a regular program of meetings that gather musicians, writers, anyone interested in music to address the free-floating agenda of racism in the industry and how to combat it. Topics can range from how and whether to set up an alternative method of recording and promoting black musicians not playing within their accepted formats to how to combat the dominance of high-priced, high-powered synthesizer technology by whites—who, just by possessing it, automatically gain access to gigs more lucrative and high-profile than blacks can without it.

Dancing in Your Head

The other prong of the BRC's attack has aimed at infiltrating the clubs, the incubators, after all, of music, audiences, and opinions alike. In a kind of floating guerrilla road show, they've staged performances at a variety of venues all over New York: artsy sites like the Kitchen, punk havens like CBGB's, Third World centers like SOB's, downtown hip-rock pockets like Siberia, where their last show was a fund-raiser for Jesse Jackson. The purposes have been several: to raise money, to re-evaluate accepted myths about black and white roles in U.S. pop music history in public, to introduce different member bands/players doing their different musics to different audiences, and—driving all the others—to educate audiences about the racism and politics underlying the musical categories they are forced to hear every day. Reid, for instance, dubs the AOR radio format—the initials stand for Album-Oriented Rock, which translates as '60s-dominated sounds from records by white musicians—Apartheid-Oriented Radio.

The blazing jewel of the BRC is Reid's Living Colour. When he started the first version of the group, Reid was known primarily as one of the younger jazz-based players coming up on the downtown N.Y. scene; he'd played with the swaggering Decoding Society of Ornette Coleman's ex-drummer Ronald Shannon Jackson for years. But he had grown up listening to all kinds of rock-based sounds, like almost all musicians his age, and he also played them. He became determined to find a way to mold them all into a musical shape he could call his own.

This kickass quartet successfully realizes that concept in its astonishing range and surefooted commitment to explore cross-cultural sounds regardless of color, origin, or destination. Like rappers mixing all kinds of records on their turntables, Living Colour thrives on its phenomenal breadth of musical influences. The ingredients they blend so skillfully are—in contradistinction to the industry's unwritten codes—attuned to roots-digging college-radio types and buppies, ghetto posses as well as alienated suburban metalheads: hardcore metal raveups slam into bluesy ballads and psychedelicized pop, lilting Caribbean inflections collide with hiphop scrambles of prerecorded material and touches of funk. One of Vivid's killer tracks is a drastically rearranged version of the Talking Heads' classic "Memories Can't Wait," which sharpens its edge on a long rideout of overdubbed guitars that wheeze and groan like a Cajun band on acid. There's no small irony in covering a cut by a white group that first broke into the mainstream by covering Al Green's "Take Me to the River."

This talent for coming up with the unexpected shapes everything the foursome does. Opening in hiphop fashion with a snippet from the last speech by Malcolm X before his death and closing with "Ask not what your country can do for you" from Kennedy's inaugural and FDR's famous "The only thing we have to fear is fear itself" platitude, "Cult of Personality" thunders its coiled riffs as Cory Glover pumps his big, supple voice along a list of warnings: "I'm the smiling face on your TV / . . . I exploit you, still you love me / I tell you one and one makes three / I'm the Cult of Personality." Reid's guitar solo blisters and screams its anger in response, while bassist Muzz Skillings and drummer Will Calhoun pummel the rhythms into outrage.

If it's obvious from those lyrics that Living Colour isn't shy about its commitment to combining music with social commentary, a quick runthrough of some song titles confirms it: "Cult of Personality," "Desperate People," "Middle Man," "Which Way to America?," "Open Letter to a Landlord." But the beauty of how they sculpt their attack comes not just from what they say but from the way they shuffle up sounds to match words. It's a tack as contemporary as the 48-track studio.

Look at how "Open Letter to a Landlord" is built. It kicks off with a sweet-chording, attackless guitar that floats rubato in mournful anticipation behind the chorus: "Now you can tear a building down / But you can't erase a memory / These houses may look all rundown / But they have a value you can't see." Suddenly the song snaps into a hard strut driven by Skillings's stuttering bass and Reid's crunchy, swerving chords and snarling fills, as Glover wails:

This is my neighborhood . . . I call this place my home / You call this place a slum / You want to run the people out / This is what you're all about / . . . Last month there was a fire / I saw several children die / You sent flowers to the families / But your sympathy's a lie / 'Cause every building that you burn / Is more blood money that you earn / We are forced to relocate / From the pain that you create.

It closes with the rattle of an elevated train. What's created is more than a descriptive song, however evocative: it's a physical, three-dimensional sonic portrait that puts you into the rhythms, the stances, the scene.

Living Colour does that just as deftly for more personal themes as well. The satiric "Glamor Boys" bounces along its nonstop buoyant Afro-Caribbean dance groove as it cuts the superficial party lovers who spend their lives chasing the right club and the right clothes—on debilitating credit, of course. The pseudo-bottleneck swells weeping through "Broken Hearts" match its lyrics' age-old laments with the sound of the blues, '60s style: if it recalls the Stones of *Beggars Banquet* vintage, that's partly because Mick Jagger plays harp on it.

The sheer mastery they deploy to put over their messages is a major reason Living Colour has attracted and held a growing multiracial audience during the long search for a record deal. Another has been their fierce but user-friendly stage show. In fact, the buzz about them going around New York was what lured Mick Jagger and Jeff Beck down to CBGBs one night over a year ago to see them. Blown out by their set, Jagger—whose Stones started life as a cover band doing "black" music—offered to produce a demo they could shop around for a deal. Eventually, they wound up at Epic. To its credit, that arm of Columbia seems genuinely interested in promoting what they've signed.   [1988]

chapter 24

The Godfathers of Rap

As rappers and hiphoppers have become more and more mainstream, most have shed, retargeted, or blunted the edge of rage and truth-telling that drove the wordplay of '70s pioneers like Afrika Bambaataa and Grandmaster Flash. It's the American Way: the closer you get to the center (of politics, the market, whatever), the less likely it is you're gonna say anything that significantly offends your audiences/buyers. Could M. C. Hammer or Vanilla Ice make anyone angry except via their own lack of talent? Do the widely heralded gangster-rappers proliferating up and down the West Coast really serve up anything but swagger and audio versions of bad B movies and Saturday morning cartoons?

The Last Poets don't like the direction a lot of rap has been going in, so six years after their last album they've made a counterproposal with the pointed and musically diverse *Freedom Express* (Celluloid). "We produced this ourselves from scratch," says Sulieman El-Hadi, one-half of the Poets. "We recorded it at the Brent Black Music Co-op in England; they gave us the studio at a good rate because we do a lot of things for them." Shopping around for a distribution deal was no snap, but the disc wound up with their previous label, Celluloid, in the U.S., while in England they hooked up with Acid Jazz, which puts out many of the jazz-rappers currently surfacing.

The Poets have been pushing the envelope—and making it possible for rap to surface—for nearly a quarter-century now. So Sulieman's view of the current rap scene is telling:

> The medium that we deal with is the truth. And so consequently, our stuff is serious. So some of the people we deal with in the media and people that are in the recording business are afraid to deal with us, because of the political content of our work. But they're not only blocking our stuff, they're actively ripping us off.
>
> I've been really hoping to do some things with the young brothers, but we seem to keep missing each other. Some of them are good manifestations of the seeds we planted. I feel like all the young brothers are talented, but the content of what they're saying isn't always positive; in fact, a lot of it is foolishness. The sex stuff, the gangster stuff— I think they should cease and desist from that stuff right there. The blow should be how to uplift the youth and themselves. And they should research their material so they can address more serious themes. That would be much more beneficial, since they have such an influence on their listeners.

Not surprisingly, Sulieman numbers Public Enemy, KRS-One, Doug E. Fresh, Queen Latifah, and the Jungle Brothers among his favorite contemporary rappers.

Coming from the Last Poets, that's no idle evaluation. After all, since they started out in the late '60s by extending the connections between poets reciting and music that go back to the dawn of time and up through Langston Hughes and the coffeehouse-jazz declamations of the Beats, the Last Poets hammered out one of rap's early templates on a series of albums—*The Last Poets* and *This Is Madness*—that became impossible-to-find underground classics. (These two once-again-hard-to-find discs were reissued by Celluloid in 1985. At that time Celluloid also reissued *Doriella Du Fontaine*, the Poets' fiery collaboration with Jimi Hendrix that foreshadowed the rap-meets-metal crossover of later artists like Run-DMC.) "We're just the speakers, the amplifiers for the people," asserts Jalaluddin Mansur Nuriddin, a.k.a. Alafia Pudim, a.k.a. Lightnin' Rod, the other Poet. "What we do comes directly out of reality. There are poems, like people, lined up around the block for us."

The line goes back to Harlem in 1967, the era of black power and Vietnam. There, a group of writers shared a loft called East Wind, where they would gather on Friday nights to read and perform their work for the people of the neighborhood, accompanied only by house percussionist Nilaga. They learned to use their voices like the frontline horns of a jazz combo: one voice would solo with the lead while the others would combine in a kind of riff-like refrain running behind it. Gradually they built a word-of-mouth following because they tackled some major problems that bugged their fellow ghetto dwellers head-on, things like racism and poverty and the struggle to survive.

They were nameless until, with the kind of historical irony that's usually reserved for bad novels, South African poet Willie Kgostile showed up to read his work. The way Jalal recalls it, "He wrote that this would be the last generation of poets before the generation of the revolution, and so that's why we called ourselves the Last Poets."

Their social-activist vision was fired by their Muslim beliefs—a common crosspollination during the late '60s that's recurred in the Afrocentricity of many contemporary hiphoppers. These themes came into play while the Poets explored the technique they'd developed for presenting their work. Dubbed "spoagraphics" or spoken pictures, their declamatory narratives were partially written and partially improvised. Based in part on the long-enduring African-American dialogic format called the dozens, spoagraphics armed the Poets with a verbally dextrous attack for their political outrage. Their following grew, and word about them began to leak out of Harlem.

Soon they found themselves on a PBS show, where they caught the eye of producer Alan Douglas. At the time, Douglas's other ventures included working with the likes of Lenny Bruce, Miles Davis, and Jimi Hendrix—which is how the Poets hooked up with the guitar hero. In the fall of 1969, Douglas was producing a Hendrix recording session with drummer Buddy Miles, and then-Lightnin' Rod was in the control room. Hendrix was late, so Douglas suggested that Rod rap. When Hendrix showed up in mid-improvisation, he was fascinated, so he and Miles stirred up some heavy funk-rock grooves with jazzy inflections while Rod took flight on "Doriella Du Fontaine." It was one of the ways Hendrix, who at that point felt cut off from black audiences because of his management's marketing strategies and black radio's refusal to play his music, tried to reconnect.

Douglas already knew what Rod could do before he asked him to take the mike at Hendrix's session. He'd recorded the Poets that June, but hadn't done anything with the tapes. According to Jalal, "He came up to our loft and listened to us, and said he wanted to record us. We recorded *The Last Poets* in June of 1969, but he didn't put it out. We kept at him, saying either put it out or give it back to us. So he finally released it in 1970."

The Last Poets got virtually no airplay, but still managed to sell hundreds of thousands of copies—some estimates run as high as 800,000. In the process, it helped foment a musical revolution, thanks to what Jalal characterizes as "largely word-of-mouth sales. It was the grassroots people that bought our records, because the record companies found out at the beginning that the Last Poets couldn't be bought or compromised. We wouldn't turn into plastic just to sell records." And so, despite the larger-than-cult success of *The Last Poets* and *This Is Madness*, despite the group's indie release of three more albums over the next six years, they disappeared.

It was an oblivion that they insist, with some justification and some hyperbole, was prepared for them by the corporate record powers-that-be. Says Jalal, "We were in industry-imposed exile because we were too real, too honest. We wouldn't be *stars*, because we wouldn't lose touch with the earth, the people." Denied access to the media, the Poets took their messages back to the places they'd sprung from: the streets, the prisons, the people. The way Jalal puts it, "Media comes from the Greek meaning in the middle, but the way they do it is more like this. (Stands up, gets between two people, turns to one.) Yo' mama. (Turns to the other.) Yo' mama. (Steps out from in between.) Now you dudes are ready to fight each other—and you don't even know why."

Uncovering why is at the heart of what the Last Poets do. "We do research in libraries, where they bury the lies, to get at the truth," puns Jalal in a weirdly Sun Ra-ish fashion. Sulieman explains,

> We keep each other in check, balance each other off, looking to find the light. You find stories in the papers, like how one in every 250 Americans can expect to be murdered this year, but for black males it's one out of every 23. Or companies that make birth-control products that kill the women who use them. Or AIDS, or defense contractors. *That's* reality. *That's* where it jumps off.

In 1985, the Poets got another chance to jump off with *Oh My People*. Produced by Bill Laswell, it sported his patented production techniques that combined hiphop-style drum machines and African talking drums. With that, the Poets moved into the '80s with a vengeance. They sure didn't lose their edge. Take the haunting "What Will You Do," which recites the threats and promises of a Muslim Last Judgment over almost percussive background vocals and Aiyb Deng's polyrhythmic talking drums, congas, chatan, and cowbell. "Let your voice be heard / Train yourself to speak the righteous word," they chant.

Freedom Express continues their pursuit of righteousness. "Un-holy Alliance," for instance, puts an indictment of the European conquest and ruling of Africa over an engagingly floating highlife beat from West Africa. "We used that rhythm because of the subject matter," says Sulieman. "It's the highlife blues dealing with a highlife situation. We always try to fit the music to the thematic sense of the poem. That's why no two of our songs are the same." And it's why the Last Poets' broad-stroked portraits of some of our time's ongoing and basic social conflicts are still a useful and informative corrective to much of our official culture.   [1986/1991]

chapter 25

Don't Believe the Hype

If you strut into a party brandishing an Uzi, even a plastic toy replica, you're gonna get noticed. The image encapsulates the approach, triumph, predicament, limitations, delight, and calculation of Public Enemy. They've provoked commentators who normally don't waste ink on popular phenomena as well as culture pundits. The results: a tidal wave of pronouncements about an attitude, a snatch of lyrics, a handful of interview quotes, and a truckload of hype.

By now, Public Enemy has in many ways become more mirror than entity. The group's attackers and defenders alike often bypass the music for rhetorical flourishes, fanzine gush, and vague sociological analyses scooped from their own preconceptions and fears and hopes. Rarely do you find a simple statement like this: their second album, *It Takes a Nation of Millions To Hold Us Back* (Def Jam/Columbia), released last year, was an inventive, astonishingly varied and textured collection of musical challenges that greatly expanded on the promise of their debut, *Yo! Bum Rush the Show* (Def Jam); its recent follow-up, *Fear of a Black Planet* (Def Jam/Columbia), stands above most competition but doesn't live up to P.E.'s full promise.

The music and its quality should not be irrelevant to the debate raging around Public Enemy. Hiphop, born in the black ghettos of Brooklyn and the Bronx from the dub toasting and sound systems of Jamaican immigrants, is that startling thing, a new way to imagine sound. Looping, defacing, and recontextualizing isolated snippets ("samples") from old records—a bass line's rumble, a horn section's punctuation, a guitar's shrieking wail—DJs who work turntables replace bands as sound sources. Left out of the high-priced music wars by their lack of access to state-of-the-art equipment, the early 1970s black street music artists, concurrent with the rise of graffiti artists, surfaced. They redefined an entire wing of rock and roll by grabbing what was cheap and available: a couple of turntables, old records, manual dexterity, and a new concept jostling shredded musical history into new shapes within a single new tune behind the singsong, usually macho-deep-voiced street-style poetry that descends from the dozens.

In the hands of early rappers like Grandmaster Flash and the Furious Five, that concept had social and political teeth: their 1982 hit "The Message" was a searing indictment of the economic and social decay accelerated by Reagan-era programs. But raps of the lighter sort—variants of the usual teen-tune stuff about sex and posing—were generally what penetrated the commercial mainstream. After a decade as the African-American equivalent of garage bands, after serving as the soundtrack of the streets and illegal clubs, hiphop hit the big time and the big labels with tunes like Run-DMC's "Walk This Way," which reworked the old Aerosmith proto-metal smash.

Turbulent density has been Public Enemy's main sonic contribution to hiphop. Three-dimensional sounds, raw and cooked, crosscut with the zigzagging speed of a dial twirling on a cosmic TV during P.E. tunes like "Bring the Noise," where leader and chief rapper Chuck D., with typically pungent self-awareness, underlines hiphop's pivotal role in recent music history despite the prejudices it's encountered:

> Beat is the father of your rock'n'roll / Music for whatcha, for whichin', you call a band, man / Makin' a music, abuse it, but you can't do it, ya know / You call 'em demos, but we ride limos, too / Whatcha gonna do? Rap is not afraid of you / Beat is for Sonny Bono, beat is for Yoko Ono.

As even that brief sample shows, P.E.'s lyrics turn on a reprise of '60s black power and Afrocentrism; they speak of a repressed American culture for and to a generation of increasingly disenfranchised young black males. Yet, despite the street poses essential to hiphoppers, the most successful, including Run-DMC and Carlton Ridenhour (Chuck D.'s real name) come from suburban middle-class backgrounds filled with most of the same perks, car-cruising, TV and movie images and pop music as their white counterparts. In fact, according to Chuck D., Public Enemy's early audiences were largely white—undoubtedly at least partly as a result of that cross-cultural assimilation and understanding.

While P.E.'s first album was sonically adventurous, Chuck D.'s lyrics opened up on the second, which brought more complex and ambitious political statements into play—and thus manifested some of the other contradictions facing not only Public Enemy but American pop culture. Their first record sold over a quarter of a million copies with little promotion, but their next album hit the million mark, and CBS, their distributor, backed the group's PR reps with cash as they began pouring on the promo hype, exploiting the group's black-nationalist politics to sell product by, for example, organizing extensive media coverage of P.E.'s 1989 "solidarity" appearance at New York's Riker's Island prison.

Then the group's Minister of Information, Professor Griff, parroted a Louis Farrakhan line of anti-Semitism during a May 22, 1989, interview with the Moonie-owned, right-wing *Washington Times*. "Jews are wicked . . . [and responsible for] the majority of wickedness that goes on across the globe." He continued to say that Jews had financed the slave trade, that they are "responsible for what's happening in South Africa," and wondered about whether it's "a coincidence that the Jews run the jewelry business and it's named jewelry." He also noted that he admired Idi Amin, Muammar Khadaffy, and Ayotollah Khomeini.

All hell—if hell is where pundits are properly stored—broke loose in the media. The shadowy Jewish Defense Organization, which claims 3000 members, announced a boycott of P.E., and sent a group armed with baseball bats and chains to P.E.'s management offices. (Fortunately, if comically, they had the wrong address.) The JDO also peppered record company execs and retailers with flyers reprinting Griff's incendiary remarks. In retaliation, Chuck D. announced that the group was disbanding, that it was not disbanding and was preparing its third album but would boycott the record industry (how was unclear), and that Griff was dismissed. For a month, his position on all three points seemed to change with each bulletin.

Griff was P.E.'s in-house ideologue and media brain. A U.S. Army vet and martial-arts freak, he also trained and led the Security Force of the First World (S1W) that brandishes plastic Uzi's onstage at P.E. shows while doing martial-arts steps that look like doo-wop moves—a weird parody of Malcolm X's Fruit of Islam elite that metaphorically draws a line between entertainment and politics. An adherent of Farrakhan's Black Muslim beliefs, as is Chuck D., Griff is the kind of two-dimensional Malcolm X white liberals and conservatives need: he is what they tried to paint Malcolm as. Hence the jubilant outcry, from the *Village Voice* to *Rolling Stone*, from the *New York Times* to *People*.

But P.E.'s connection with Malcolm is vital and revealing, even though any comparison is enormously to Griff's—and P.E.'s—disadvantage. A vocal segment of young African Americans, which P.E. has helped nurture, has become increasingly Afrocentric, in cultural terms. In that sense, they're among Malcolm's heirs; they self-consciously voice his contention that black Americans must elevate their own values, must build their own economic bases, must understand that worldwide political and social movements against power structures are inextricably linked via Eurocentric racism opposing them. The Black Muslims, including Malcolm, identified with the Arabs of the Mideast, an anti-Zionist alignment that fed into an already existing resentment in certain segments of African-American communities like Harlem toward the Jewish retailers, real-estate owners, and bankers who were a visible face of white oppression.

That's part of the historical context for the inflammatory remarks that got Griff kicked out of Public Enemy, after the JDO threats of boycott, enormous media noise, and vacillations by Chuck D. about whether or not he'd fired Griff—which naturally added fuel to the media fire. A month after Griff's interview was published, Chuck D. held a press conference and announced Griff's formal dismissal:

> The black community is in crisis. Our mission as musicians is to ad-dress these problems. Offensive remarks by Professor Griff are not in line with Public Enemy's program. We are not anti-Jewish. We are pro-black, pro-black-culture, and pro-human-race. Griff was to trans-mit these values. He sabotaged this. We are not here to make enemies but to say that the system is the enemy. To use the mechanism that you're fighting against definitely is wrong.

Then came an astutely self-imposed silence, during which "Fight the Power," P.E.'s anthem for Spike Lee's highly charged film *Do the Right Thing*, climbed the charts. (Chuck says now that the reason for his silence was to take the heat off the movie and Lee.) It was followed by "Welcome to the Terrordome" (Def Jam/Columbia), their latest single. The following lines were read as a metaphorical defense of the now departed Griff and the group and a reiterated anti-Semitism:

> Crucifixion ain't no fiction / So-called chosen frozen / Apology made
> to whoever pleases / Still they got me like Jesus / I rather sing, bring,
> think, reminisce / 'Bout a brother when I'm in sync / Every brother
> ain't a brother cause a color / Just as well could be undercover / Back-
> stabbed, grabbed a flag / From the back of the lab / Told a Rab get off
> the rag / Sad to say I got sold down the river.

Not surprisingly, its release stirred the embers of racial controversy back
into blazing life.

So—is Public Enemy anti-Semitic? It's hard to imagine a lyricist as
smart as Chuck D. being unaware that those words reek with age-old
attacks on Jews. Is Griff? Definitely, and anti-white to boot—as is his
replacement Harry Allen, self-described Hip-Hop Assassin and Media
Activist who's been circulating a half-assed recycling of Elijah Mu-
hammed's "scientific theory" that all races derive from the black race by
evil experimental grafting. According to Washington psychiatrist
Frances Cress Weising (whom Chuck D. has endorsed), whites' lack of
pigmentation marks them as genetically and psychologically inferior,
which they make up for by oppressing blacks. (Malcolm X rejected
idiocies like these long before his assassination while retaining his belief
in black nationalism, and split from the Black Muslims to form his own
group while reaching tentatively for broader interracial support—all of
which led to speculation that Elijah's Muslims had killed him.)

Maybe even more to the point, Chuck D.'s justifications for Griff and
his lyrics are the kind no African American would be likely to accept
from a non-black person trying to explain remarks that seem self-
evidently anti-black. But as Malcolm himself saw, that's a problem with
certain aspects of black-nationalist ideology: while American anti-black
racism is uniquely institutionalized, in the hands of rhetoricians like
Public Enemy it can justify black manipulation of racial guilt and slurs.
Conceptually as well as in reality, black racism holds no higher moral
ground than any other, and is a dangerously double-edged sword: witness the flare-ups in Flatbush between Caribbean immigrants and Ko-
rean grocers, the beneath-notice-by-leftists slurs about Guidovilles in
the wake of Yusuf Hawkins's murder, the flattened stereotypes shaping
Spike Lee's *Do the Right Thing*, the claims by some black musicians that
jazz and rock and roll are all-black legacies, which ignore their indelibly
mulatto nature.

Institutionalized racism against blacks in America has deep and un-
arguable historic roots, of course, and there's no denying that blacks,
especially young black males, are stuck at the bottom of the socio-
economic shitstream. That, rather than how the American system deliberately pits groups low on the pyramid against one another, remains
Public Enemy's main point. However reductive, it's been validated over
recent months by scorching articles and TV shows, replete with barely
submerged anti-black racism, about hiphop in the wake of the P.E.
controversy.

In one of the most outrageous manifestations, *Newsweek* ran a bilious
diatribe called "The Rap Attitude" that ranted against hiphop, overtly
because of its sexism, racism, and disrespect. Since heavy metal, mentioned only in passing, covers precisely the same ground—which is, in
fact, one reason rappers have used metalloid backing and samples for
nearly a decade—you don't have to be African American to wonder
about the unstated biases of the article's writer.

"Having an attitude," huffs writer Jerry Adler, "means it's always
someone else's fault: cops who disrespect (or 'dis') you when you walk
through a housing project with a gold chain that could lock up a motor-
cycle. . . . The viler the message, the more fervent the assertion of
honesty that underlies it."

Besides racism, the biased attitude here is generational: hiphop, like
heavy metal, has less depth and resonance than, say, the Rolling Stones
because it's not the creation of the postwar generation that sees itself, in
retrospect, as a repository of history and taste—as if rock and roll wasn't
always about sex and provocation and adolescent attitudes. Check out
any video of swivel-hipped Elvis with his bedroom sneer, pouty Mick
Jagger peacocking across the stage in imitation of James Brown, las-
civious Jimi Hendrix dropping to his haunches, flicking his tongue, and
flailing his guitar-phallus.

But according to Adler's intro,

OK, here it is: the first important cultural development in America in
25 years that the baby-boom generation didn't pioneer: The Culture of
Attitude. It is heard in the thundering cacophony of heavy metal and
the thumping, clattering, scratching assault of rap—music so postin-
dustrial it's mostly not even *played*, but pieced together out of prerecorded sound bits. It is the culture of American adolescent males
frozen in various stages of adolescence: their streetwise music, their

ugly macho boasting and joking about anyone who hangs out on a different block—cops, other races, women and homosexuals. Its most visible contribution has been the disinterment of the word nigger, a generation after a national effort to banish it and its ugly connotations from the American language. Now it is back, employed with savage irony by black rappers, and dumb literal hostility by their white heavy-metal counterparts. *Nigger! Faggot!* What ever happened to the idea that rock and roll would make us free?

In fact, the decade of the '60s was a time of similar contradictions: the racial and economic segregation that marked movements and audiences as earlier, broader political and cultural coalitions gave way to multiple divergent agendas, including black nationalism; the Beatles and Stones, among countless others, getting their starts in the highly commercial project called rock and roll by covering black sounds for a white audience; the Youngbloods' "Get Together" and Sly and the Family Stone's "Stand!" and James Brown's "Say It Loud—I'm Black and I'm Proud" sharing the airwaves with S/Sgt. Barry Sadler's "The Ballad of the Green Berets," the Guess Who's "American Woman," and Merle Haggard's "Okie from Muskogee." Despite the love-and-peace image of Woodstock, the '60s were driven by polarization, and the music, then as now, reflected that.

In the years since, the polarizations have been exacerbated by governmental policies. Is it surprising that the generations that have come up under that ever expanding institutionalized racism, sexism, and violence reflect it? How can they be held responsible for it, when it's what they've been taught? Is it their fault that their schools are less funded, that their textbooks are dullingly simplified, that they've inherited a culture increasingly commercialized and regimented by a handful of international conglomerates that, for instance, make and sell over 96 percent of the recordings available in the U.S.?

Public Enemy recognizes and, to its credit, tries to educate about some of these problems. Take "Burn Hollywood Burn," which attacks racial stereotyping in the media. But the same tune embodies P.E.'s own internal contradictions: the mid-section by guest rapper Ice Cube transforms its pungency to rank sexual boasting. That's all too typical of the slack lyrics on *Fear of a Black Planet*. But dwarfing Chuck D.'s poetic failures this time out is the larger, continuing problem P.E. has created: their salient positions—the need to empower African Americans, to rewrite standard histories to accommodate non-Northern European achievements, to undo cultural stereotypes—are inevitably undercut when they themselves perpetuate anti-white mythologies and stereotypes about Jews and women and gays. Take "Meet the G That Kills Me," which deals with AIDS by saying "Man to man / I don't know if they can / From what I know / The parts don't fit / (Ahh shit)."

It's our loss that P.E.'s points are getting lost in the noise instead of raising real debate, but in the end it's only rock and roll, and it's all good for business. From CBS's perspective, carrying a plastic Uzi into a party gets you those looks, and those looks sell product. With provocation as their entree, Public Enemy has touched a responsive chord in literally millions of consumers. So now political provocation has become a potent marketing tool.

Witness this recent CBS publicity release:

> Music is about change, revolution, forward progress. . . . With the release, in 1987, of their first album, "Yo, Bum Rush the Show," Public Enemy became, instantly, the most important Black spokespeople in America. Their emphasis on Black knowledge and awareness, rather than the wearing of gold "ropes" and buying a "Benz," has become the standard by which rap music is measured in the 1990s. . . . *FEAR OF A BLACK PLANET* is the most eagerly-awaited album in rap— and music—history. . . . The main theme of *FEAR OF A BLACK PLANET* is confrontation, a theme echoed in many a sociological study about what the 1990s held for the races as a whole. There is widespread acknowledgement that society is reaching a boiling point, what with crumbling governmental systems, homelessness, drugs, gangs, the decentralization of Black life and culture. In sixty minutes of *FEAR OF A BLACK PLANET*, Public Enemy supplies uncanny insight and, who knows, possible solutions.

Who knows, indeed: as a friend suggested when I showed this to him, the most obvious "possible solution" is to buy the album. It would be the final sad irony in Public Enemy's convoluted odyssey if their activist rhetoric becomes just another sales pitch.   [1990]

chapter 26

Mr. Ambience

On the 19th floor of New York's Vista Hotel, overlooking the shimmering Hudson on an autumn afternoon, composer/producer Brian Eno sits strumming his new acoustic guitar with the rapturous singlemindedness of a lover. Nothing so odd about that, right? Except that if there's one style of music Eno is *not* identified with, either in his time with Roxy Music or his ambient pioneering or his work with others like David Bowie, Talking Heads, and U2, it's acoustic music.

But then again, if there's one thing Eno isn't, it's predictable. Not only in his own musical career (who, for instance, could've foreseen his investigations of African music after Roxy Music's art-school ironies?) but in his opinions. His take on the New Age phenomenon—which may surprise New Agers who see his ambient music as a forebear—is just one case in point:

> What happened with New Age is that it unfortunately became Music-Minus-Something. What it has generally left out is what I think makes us all dislike it: [composer] Harold Budd said it best when he said, "What I hate about it is that there's no evil in it." It doesn't have to be a clenched-fist kind of evil, but you really have to sense that there's some complexity to the emotion, and that complexity means that there has to be some darkness as well as all this lovely misty light. It doesn't hold your interest otherwise, it doesn't seem like anything *real*.

For Eno wants no part of the psychobabble shrouding New Age; his preoccupations are more material:

> When you make a piece of music, one way of looking at it is that you create a place. That is more than simply metaphorical. By the time I was making records like *Discreet Music* (Antilles) there had been a lot of technical advances in terms of reverberation, echo, digital delay, harmonization, chorus, flanging, phasing—in every studio there were tons of all this stuff that is telling you, the listener, about a place,

about space. Reverb is a description of space; synthetic reverb is a description of a place that doesn't exist. So that means when you are a composer and very actively working with these things, you're building spaces, not just melodies and rhythms.

And in fact *Music for Airports* and *On Land* (both Editions EG) capture that physicality in the often ominous electronic spaces they seduce you into inhabiting. Unlike the unyielding repetitions of New Age music, what Eno calls ambient music refracts worlds through different dimensions; even changing the volume or the level of your attention alters your relationship with the music, uncovers startling aspects that wouldn't otherwise become manifest.

Eno's background makes him unusually suited for thinking about music in these terms. Trained, like many British rockers, in art school, Eno also studied with John Cage disciples like composers Gavin Bryars and Cornelius Cardew. Hooking up with Bryan Ferry, he provided the offbeat electronic flourishes that made early Roxy Music stand out, like the whirring synthesizer line careening through "Editions of You" (on *For Your Pleasure . . .* , Warner Bros.).

After Eno left the band in 1973, he gradually expanded his role as electronics wizard into that of producer for a series of pivotal artists. His credits are staggering: David Bowie's tortured peaks on *Low, Heroes*, and *Lodger* (all RCA); Devo's hilariously crucial *Q: Are We Not Men? A: We Are Devo!* (Warner Bros.); Talking Heads' head-turning classics like *More Songs About Buildings and Food, Fear of Music*, and *Remain in Light* (all Sire/Warner Bros.); his own remarkable pre-*Graceland* exploration and synthesis of African musics with David Byrne on *My Life in the Bush of Ghosts* (Sire/Warner Bros.); U2's chiming attack expanded into an arena-rock colossus on *The Unforgettable Fire* and *The Joshua Tree* (both Island). Big names aside, however, the innovative sonics and mixes on all these discs demonstrated the practical results of Eno's apparently abstract preoccupations with space-creating textures—and in the process helped rearrange the shape of recent pop.

Not content just to shape other people's sounds, Eno continued his own composing, moving past the arty pop of his early '70s efforts like *Here Come the Warm Jets* and *Taking Tiger Mountain (By Strategy)* (both Island). A 1975 sickbed experience had unexpectedly redirected his curiosity about soundscapes and electronics. When a friend brought him a record of harp music, he dragged himself to the stereo to put it on; once he laid back down, he realized only one channel was playing at an extremely low volume, but he couldn't get up to fix it. Ironically, listening that way focused his ideas, and helped lead to the creation of what he calls ambient music:

Fifteen years ago, there was an old-fashioned idea that when you bought a record, you rushed home, ripped off the wrap, and sat there like this (stares fixedly ahead) in front of your stereo—the classical image of how you listen to a record. Well, we all know that that doesn't happen very much any more. People put the record on, they go on doing what they're doing, and they sometimes sit and listen to it; but because of records, music has become a different thing. It's not the special and sacred event it used to be, it's part of the background of one's life a lot of the time. And not only the background; it comes out of that background and into the foreground as well. So that was what I thought about ambient music: it wasn't Music-Minus-Something, but an acknowledgement of another way of using music. It was really a way people *were* using it, but now saying, I'm a composer, and in the knowledge that this musical niche exists I'm gonna work for it.

I would try to imagine what a piano would sound like under the sea, for instance, where the density of the water is constantly changing. What is it like to imagine we are listening in oil or in very thin air? I started to find that what you were evoking could tell you things about climate: you *can* hear the difference between somewhere snow has fallen and somewhere it hasn't. Those are things we're evolutionarily equipped to distinguish, just like my finger knows the distinction between smooth and rough. So with these records I'm very consciously saying I want to capitalize on this body of psycho-acoustic intuition we all have and which composers haven't been able to work with before, except in very limited ways.   [1989]

chapter 27

Them Ol' Bahamas Blues

Underpinning an entire school of folk and rock guitar is the idiosyncratic work of Bahamanian guitar great Joseph Spence. Acclaimed as a mentor by such astute pickers as Ry Cooder, Taj Mahal, and David Lindley, his tunes popularized by '60s trendsetters like the Grateful Dead and the Incredible String Band, Spence first garnered some attention in this country during the early heyday of the folk revival spearheaded in the Boston/Cambridge region. In those days of the late '50s and early '60s, musicians and fans alike went on a search for musical roots with a determined intensity that parallelled the enthusiasm of dedicated Depression-era folklorists like John and Alan Lomax. Taj and Cooder and Lindley, Clarence White (guitarist with the Gram Parsons-era Byrds), Alan Wilson (later singer-songwriter with Canned Heat), John Fahey, Dave Van Ronk, Stefan Grossman, Sam Charters (who recorded for Vanguard and wrote the seminal *The Bluesmen*), Frank Driggs (who assembled the Robert Johnson compilations), Nick Perls (who founded Yazoo Records), historian Stephen Calt, Chris Strachwitz (of Arhoolie Records and Down Home Music fame), filmmaker Les Blank, and countless others embarked on voyages into little towns and villages all across America looking for the survivors of the '30s, or into record stores and peoples' attics looking for worn old 78s, which were then transcribed and later dubbed and reissued on LPs. In the process they turned up such pivotal figures as Lightnin' Hopkins, Son House, Skip James, Mance Lipscomb, Sam Chatman, Rev. Gary Davis, Snooks Eaglin, Clifton Chenier, and Flaco Jimenez, to name just a few, and introduced them to a whole new generation via folk festivals and small clubs.

Thus it happened in 1958 that Sam Charters found himself on the Bahamanian island of Andros to record local musical traditions, and heard about local legend Joseph Spence. His curiosity aroused, he sought out the then 48-year-old picker and, enthralled by his unique sounds, recorded him as he did other indigenous musicians. And so

Music from the Bahamas, vol. 1 (Folkways), brought Spence's unique music—a heady, raggedly syncopated mixture of hymns and sea chanties, Tin Pan Alley and traditional calypso—to a much broader audience than he'd ever dreamed existed.

That music was fully formed by the time Charters captured it on tape. Spence's characteristic attack on his single-pickup hollowbody guitar is based largely around a number of stable components: his dropped-D tuning (not exactly Western-style well tempered but capable of producing resonant microtones); medium-gauge bronze strings and a heavy steel thumbpick (which produce what Ry Cooder likens to "organ tones"); a highly syncopated counterpoint between his thumb on bass and his index on treble, which often skitters and tosses the melody back and forth across the registers with playful abandon; and a broken polyrhythmic accompaniment that, as it sketches the parts for a complete calypso band, clusters around that croaking voice, itself leaping in and out of the melody like a frog in a pond—he may never enunciate a full set of lyrics, but his vocals function as a perfect portable horn section. Add in a fondness for triplets in turnarounds and connecting phrases, as well as a penchant for times other than 4/4, and you've got some idea of what made Spence's music so captivating in its idiosyncracies.

And captivated is exactly what many guitarists were when they caught wind of that first Folkways release, which was soon followed by *Music of the Bahamas,* vol. 4 (Folkways). Taken together these depicted Spence as he assayed both sacred and secular material, backing up other vocalists as well as himself with his typically sweet-and-sour phrases and lurching sense of rhythm. Soon he'd become something of a cult hero, and so it's not surprising to learn that folkie Fritz Richmond (a member of the seminal Kweskin Jug Band that also numbers among its alumni Geoff and Maria Muldaur) took off for the Bahamas in early 1964, determined to find Spence so that Paul Rothschild (who later produced such bands as the Paul Butterfield Blues Band and The Doors) could get more of him down on tape. Success came when ragtime picker Blind Blake, who happened to be in the Bahamas at the time, introduced Richmond (as he would Cooder and Taj) to Spence, who was now living on the island of Nassau. "Bring 12 sets of medium bronze strings and tape recorder," read the cable Richmond sent to Rothschild. He did, and thus was made the delicious *Happy All the Time* (originally Elektra, now reissued on Carthage).

This LP captures Spence on his own (with only his wife Louise supplementing his ferocious vocals) and in his prime. Take "Out on the Rollin' Sea," where his guitar churns up frothy fills while he grumbles his way through parts of verses; "Bimini Gal," which offers a frenzied guitar part meant to approximate the steel drums of a calypso band; the flowing filigrees of "We Shall Be Happy"; the ragtimey intro and overall feel that marks "The Crow"; the punchy slurs that punctuate "Diamond on Earth"; the rollicking "Uncle Lou/No Lazy Man," dedicated to the flute-playing relative who taught Spence music basics. Then there's the waltz-time "How I Love Jesus"; the punning "Conch Ain't Got No Bone," riding on its edgy guitar calypso that ends by dismantling the tune's time and harmonic structure; and the nearly 14-minute tour-de-force called "I Am Living on the Hallelujah Side," where Spence uncorks a fierce and stomping barrage of blistering guitar work to his own guttural vocal accompaniment.

It was probably inevitable, then, that when 21-year-old Peter K. Siegel and 19-year-old Jody Steicher arrived in the Bahamas in 1965 to record spirituals for Nonesuch, they spent their first day in Nassau kicking off their search for Joseph Spence. "We asked everyone," they wrote later, "and the response was uniform and predictable: 'Sure mon, I know Spence'—until we arrived in his own neighborhood. Nobody knew of Spence, and a young woman standing in the doorway of a cottage asked us sternly why we were looking for him. When we said that we wanted to record Spence's music she brightened and offered to take us to his house; gathering several small children from behind her long skirt, she escorted us next door. In the corner was a black guitar and a small amplifier bearing a sign: 'Joseph Spence—the Voice from Heaven.'" When the guitar master himself arrived home, he took the duo on a tour of his banana trees and then recorded roughly half the tracks (alone and accompanying others) that appear on *The Real Bahamas*, vols. 1 and 2 (Nonesuch).

Six years later, Spence made a trip to the home of the folkies, performing in Boston to a delighted cadre of devotees. There he acquired a Martin D-18, and thus equipped recorded *Good Morning Mr. Walker* (Arhoolie). While it reprises a couple of the tunes available on LPs already mentioned, Spence's fertile inventiveness keeps those reprises from being mere repetitions; and this disc offers more than enough in the way of new riches to warrant snapping it up. "Coming in on a Wing and a Prayer," for example, showcases to excellent effect the axman's uncanny ability to unravel the fabric of any tune and reweave it into a denser structure, while his version of "The Glory of Love" has to rank among the great, if skewed, adaptations of all time. Of course, there are also tunes like "Sloop John B" and "Mary Ann," which present Spence performing familiar Caribbean material and working his strange and intricate spells on it with equal and startling fluency.

So there you have it. Joseph Spence's recorded legacy may not rival Les Paul's in size, but for intensity of feeling and depth of technique it's on a par with those left by the great blues masters. And as with most of them, his influence was disseminated more widely than his name. [1986]

chapter 28

Dancing in Your Head

Folks who write about jazz have certain conceits they're fond of. One is the homology between the way a musician talks or acts offstage and the way he plays. Often enough it works. But in the case of Ornette Coleman, the brilliant pioneer who's sketched the main lines of jazz exploration over the last 30-plus years, it breaks down. Yes, he often speaks in gnomic utterances worthy of the Delphic oracle, and he relentlessly circles his ideas concentrically instead of plotting a linear tack—modes of discourse that parallel his prismatic music. But next to his plaintively feverish cries on alto, his distinctively oddball blatts on trumpet, and his fingernails-down-the-blackboard attack on the violin, his Donald Duck-ish voice is jarring. And alongside the fierce density of his music, which even in its balladic forms shoots off sparks of intensity, his genial personality is a shock. You expect him to breathe fire, but he wants you to enjoy yourself. Just don't mess with his music.

His music, of course, still sets the mainstream on edge, even after his decades on the scene. His sheer endurance; his high profile thanks to influential critics like Martin Williams, Gunther Schuller, and Nat Hentoff, who embraced his revolutionary forays early on; and his consequent ability to attract both enlightened record company execs like Atlantic's Nesuhi Ertegun and patrons here and in Europe have made him impossible to ignore, even for people who wish he'd never materialized. So it happens that every few years he lands a slot in the conservative JVC Jazz Festival in New York, as he did in 1991.

Part of the reason Coleman's ongoing revolution makes people uncomfortable is precisely because it's ongoing. At age 61, he remains remarkably unwilling to sit where he, or anyone else, has sat before. Instead, he's been in almost constant motion since the early 1950s, when his quartet—trumpeter Don Cherry, bassist Charlie Haden, and drummer Billy Higgins (later Ed Blackwell)—broke out of what had become jazz's prisonhouse of language: the recurrent cycle of chords, basic to the 32-bar song form, that it acquired by using Tin Pan Alley material as the launchpads for its flights of improvisation. Coleman, a kind of left-wing Charlie Parker disciple, insisted on the primacy of melodic freedom. His tunes, which then as now tend to turn on bluesy boppish figures or near–nursery rhymes, were designed to be open, so that the musicians could modulate—from key to key, chord to chord, rhythm to rhythm—when the need struck them. As Gary Giddins has observed, he also blurred the background/foreground distinction of post-Louis Armstrong jazz, which pits the soloist against the rest of the band. In a sort of mutant Dixieland revival, he's freed everybody to blow.

That notion was put even more severely to the test in the early 1970s, when Ornette went electric and incorporated funk, African, and Eastern ideas into his music on classic albums like *Dancing in Your Head* (A&M). Prime Time, as he's called his shifting lineups since, alienated many of his early supporters. They understood Ornette's intelligible if idiosyncratic language as spoken in a modified jazz format, but, to their ears, it got inaudible and hostile once the volume got turned up and the dialects within multiplied. Harmolodics is what Ornette calls his kaleidoscopically hybridized idiom: the collapse of harmony, melody, and time in a kind of post-Einsteinian universe. No element is dominant; each is developed by the individual voices within the band. This democratic model dares musical anarchy as it flirts with dangerous and expansive energies.

Coleman himself explains it this way: "Bebop deals with only one solo at a time. Even Dixieland, although it's similar to harmolodics, still deals with one solo at a time, because it's using the same device [the chord sequence] to play the way they're playing. Whereas in harmo-lodics someone might be playing minor, someone else augmented, someone else major—all at the same time. It's closer to folk music and church music, where anybody can make a contribution to the emo-tional part of it. Technically, it means transforming the four basics of music—harmony, melody, rhythm, and unison—into your own voice. In addition, it means that you can transpose any chord or melody or change and still maintain the original [compositional] design by mod-ulating to any sound that you hear from that design."

Ornette's refusal to let himself, his bands, or his audiences lapse into stasis is illustrated by a characteristic irony of his last appearance at the JVC Festival in 1987, at Town Hall. He had just released an astonish-ing double album, *Ornette Coleman in All Languages* (Caravan of Dreams). One disc featured the 1950s acoustic quartet, the other his then current edition of Prime Time. It was a neat joke, and a typical comment on hierarchy and linearity, when he opened with Prime Time, forcing antis to sit through (or walk out of) the slashing electric set before getting to what they'd come to see.

From that vantage point, contrasting Coleman with Miles Davis is revealing. In terms of his influence on the vanguards of the last thirty years, Miles is one of Ornette's few peers. At times they've worked similar lines: 20-odd years ago, for example, both moved into exploring electronics and rock, funk, and African beats.

But though he's made jagged leaps into the new since, Miles has seemed to pull back from the brink, the logical if outré extension of where his ideas were taking him, once he upset nearly everyone with *On the Corner* (Columbia). That percussion-foregrounded firestorm, mixed like a hard-rock record, still registers as a key influence for many of the vanguardists on the so-called downtown New York scene. (Both Miles and Ornette, along with John Coltrane, have also had an enormous impact on seminal rockers like the Yardbirds, the Byrds, the Grateful Dead, the Velvet Underground, and Television.)

But Miles didn't follow it out. The boiling jazz-rock fusion he'd pushed into on *Bitches Brew* (Columbia) and subsequent albums was, thanks to its popularity among rock-raised listeners, transformed into a commercial seedbed. Out of it came the repetitive reams of radio-ready but musically pointless noodling that dominate the industry sales charts and clog the airwaves. More disappointingly, Miles's own takes on his music have also become largely codified. His disheartening appearance at this year's JVC found him coasting through Cyndi Lauper's "Time After Time" and Michael Jackson's "Human Nature," which have been the unrearranged, crowd-pleasing staples of his sets since the 1985 album *You're Under Arrest* (Columbia).

Ornette's set at Carnegie Hall eight nights later demonstrated the distance in that respect between the two giants. Fronting an energetic septet that included self-taught Indian percussion master Badal Roy, a former Miles sideman, and keyboardist Dave Bryant—his first keyboard player since Paul Bley—he and his cohorts shook up even the older tunes they played. "Bourgeois Boogie," from his most recent album, *Virgin Beauty* (Epic), which had surprised most listeners with its relatively airy gentleness, grew more raucous. Then there was the way he had Chris Rosenberg pick up a nylon-string guitar and play what sounded like an adaptation of a Villa-Lobos piece (there were no program notes). After a couple of rounds, Prime Time piled in and blew it apart via simultaneous lines of improvisation.

That explosion demonstrates Coleman's incisive understanding of jazz's peculiarly American dialectics—something he's underscored before with drastic reformulations like "The Fifth of Beethoven" on *The Art of the Improvisers* (Atlantic). First is the relation between the role of composition and the role of improvisation—the tension that's jazz's heartbeat. Second, like every important figure in the music from Jelly Roll Morton on, Coleman has sought his own way to reconcile the corollary pull between the individual, whose need to shape a unique voice out of the past's shards is a key jazz axiom, and the group, whose ability and need to interact in close spontaneity and support for the individual is obviously necessary if the music is going to make internal sense.

These tensions draw fine lines jazzers have had to learn to walk. In the European classical tradition, for instance, what had been an improviser's art in the days of Bach and Mozart and even, more rarely, as late as Chopin, shriveled into modes of interpretation, as the professional musician, the written score, and that post-Beethoven invention, the conductor, asserted increasing, then near total, authority over music-making. Along with the disappearance of the amateur musician and the appearance of the phonograph, those made music a passive activity for its audience. Even Wynton Marsalis—normally viewed as the champion of importing so-called classical norms into jazz—balks at duplicating in jazz the pattern that has helped enervate much American classical music and locked its producers into writing largely for each other and grants proposals. As he told me, "The purely intellectual approach, which was designed for the aristocracy in European music, has helped to destroy the classical-music audience. The thing about jazz that really sets it apart from other art forms is that you have that type of intellectualism combined with the communal type of feeling that African music has."

The collection of musical idioms we label jazz has only one thing in common—improvisation. So jazz can only go the purely interpretive route if it's willing to die. Instead, it's sought to reconcile its apparently contradictory pulls—composition and improvisation, the individual and the group, the past and the present. In the process, it's proliferated a vast number of dialects. That breadth helps mark jazzers as avatars of a quintessential American figure, the self-inventor.

That's not the same as saying that jazz musicians are untrained—something Ornette, for instance, has been accused of for decades. But it does mean their relationship to the cultural past hasn't been circumscribed by hierarchical values. (Duke Ellington's famous line, "There are only two types of music—good and bad," underscores that.) Recently, however, many observers, like the neobop revivalists being touted in the mainstream press, have called for more "classical" training for jazzers. Now, jazz musicians have been training themselves since the music's beginnings, by studying their predecessors and each other. It's how they create themselves. It's how they've pushed the musical envelope—of instrumental technique and sonic properties, for instance—far beyond anything imagined or allowed in the European classical world. And on a technical level, there's no difference, say, in harmonic theory from one type of music to the next—the notes stay the same. So the call for standards is misleading and not a little condescending.

What I mean by self-inventor derives from this country's history and mythology: it's the place people come to wipe the slate clean and start afresh. Its cultural development, sometimes to its detriment, sometimes to its advantage, has followed those same lines. After an inevitable period of European imitaters, Charles Ives and James Reese Europe forged idioms derived from American materials and folkways. But their brand of classical music was ironically derailed by the prewar influx of European refugees. As composer/conductor Maurice Peress has pointed out, the émigrés took over the cultural establishment here and turned it back to Europe-gazing. That twist has left arts combines like Lincoln Center with unresolved conundrums about their relationship to the culture around them—conundrums that show in the programming.

But while imported cultural commissars like Theodor Adorno were abhorring what they found here, what you could call the left wing of American classical music went underground and reinvented itself. Hence the barbaric yawps of joyful noisemakers like Harry Partch. Partch, a typical American eccentric, decided that post-Bach European scales were inadequate for his conceptions, and so he simply discarded them in favor of a 43-note system of just intonation he based on ancient Greek and medieval theorists. Naturally, he also had to invent instruments to play the music, and a notation system so musicians could duplicate performances. So he did. The sometimes eerie, often hilarious, always infectious results were beautifully realized during the June 1991 Bang on a Can Festival in New York, where Partch's "The Wayfarer" was performed. Eliding "high" and "low" culture, Partch took Depression-era hobos as his heroes, and their scrambling lot as his plot. The staging at the Circle in the Square rightly bypassed the proscenium-arch division between audience and stage. All told, the production showed why Partch became a major influence on other composers and, via disciples like John Cage, on the broad conceptual frames of American art.

While classical music is usually thought of—wrongly—as a monolithic European import, movies, like jazz, are often cited as a classic American art form. After all, D. W. Griffith, Charlie Chaplin, and Buster Keaton idiosyncratically mapped out the medium's methods of communicating while the Marx Brothers, for instance, were hard at play subverting structure itself. But Hollywood in the 1930s, like "high" culture centers, fell prey to what you could call recolonization: European directors and actors flocked to Tinseltown for political freedom, safety, bigger bucks. Still, a writer-director like Preston Sturges ironically turned an imported giant like Ernst Lubitsch on his head by injecting unarguably American setpieces like the Ale and Quail Club into a Lubitsch homage like *The Palm Beach Story*. And then there's Orson Welles, who got hooked on celluloid by accident, ransacked an ad hoc grammar assembled for him by an RKO editor, then upended everything from cinematography to *mise-en-scène* with his first completed effort, *Citizen Kane*. (He had been planning to film Joseph Conrad's *Heart of Darkness*, something disciple Francis Ford Coppola attempted three decades later.)

So maybe it's not surprising if American self-inventors like Partch and Welles share key techniques (like the lapping voices that fragment narrative structures out of the guise of omniscience, the aggressive emphasis on disjunction that allows the audience—indeed, forces it—to participate in the activity of the artist) with Ornette Coleman, who taught himself composition and theory while working as a house boy and elevator operator. There's a strong Romantic or idealist strain common to revolutionary American autodidacts. Partch, for example, emphasized music's physicality, with its natural roots and role in human life—attributes he considered lost. His homemade instruments were attempts to retrieve that immediacy. Likewise Welles complained to biographer Barbara Leaming, "You have to hate the camera and regard it as a detestable machine because it should be doing better than what it can do. I have this terrible sense that a film is *dead*—that it's a piece of film in a machine that will be run off and shown to people." According to Coleman, "I was so in tune to music that I picked up my first saxophone as soon as I assembled it and played the same as I'm playing today—only I didn't *know* music, I was just *hearing* music. Which made me believe that every human being has some of that quality to do just that. There's a natural instinct that tells people how to do things even before they learn the skills of how to apply them." Which is exactly the premise garage bands and punk rockers act on.

Seen in this context, the emphasis of today's young hard-bop revivalists on standards, both in their selection of tunes and formats and in their insistence on a timeless hierarchy of values, simply underlines their Reagan-era conservatism. Not that there's anything inherently wrong with playing bebop: it's one of jazz's many available dialects, and its going from the fringes to the mainstream hasn't invalidated its beauties. But the emphasis on pedigree—certain figures "in the tradition" are canonized as sources of all that's good—is unsettling and self-destructive. No less sacrosanct a figure than Louis Armstrong, after all, famously dismissed bop as "Chinese music," and the Dixieland revival-ists who counterattacked bop's exploratory ways used arguments that recur when Wynton Marsalis wannabes put down music "outside the tradition"—as if jazz, that continuing accretion of languages, had a neat, univocal history.

That attitude is actually a reach for moral authority. It recalls how critics like Yvor Winters and F. R. Leavis codified literary tradition along narrow and intolerantly proscriptive lines. Ironically, such ideo-logical baggage weighs on its carriers, pushes them to replicate the past's voices rather than use them to discover their own. Ironic too is the fact that none of their heroes, from Satchmo to Duke to Bird, would have understood such a nostalgic stance. They wanted to make their own music to speak to their own times and beyond.

Which brings us back to Ornette Coleman:

> I think music should have meaning for people first of all, and secondly it should have a quality of *you* that people can appreciate. The natu-ralness of music, of sounds, is basic to human expression. When I was young, I didn't understand that music came in sets of categories—music for babies, music for teenagers, music for old people, music for black people, music for white people. I thought it was all just music. We in the Western world suffer from too many categories and classes; we've forgotten that we all still have diapers on. We've separated music from life. [1991]

chapter **29**

The Blackwell Project

Born in New Orleans on October 10, 1929, drummer Ed Blackwell spans an astonishing number of musical worlds. Partly that's because the Crescent City, the U.S.'s Caribbean crossroads, tends to develop multi-faceted musicians: so many traditions collide and entwine there and there's so little work that players are forced to learn versatility.

The Blackwell Project

Blackwell is best known for his long association with Ornette Coleman, which started in 1951 when he moved to Los Angeles, broke off in the mid-1950s when he went back home, and continued from 1960 until Ornette put together Prime Time, his mid-1970s punk-funk outfit. The drummer's greatest achievement, in this context and elsewhere, was how he harnessed the infectious parade rhythms that kick so joyously in his hometown to free jazz. Like Max Roach and Paul Motian, Blackwell reached back to Baby Dodds for his own starting point: the dancing lyricism, the melodic attack, that made Dodds the font of jazz drumming from his stints with Fate Marable and King Oliver, Jelly Roll Morton and Louis Armstrong.

So Blackwell's groundbreaking work with Ornette, Don Cherry, Eric Dolphy, Anthony Braxton, Dewey Redman, David Murray, and others involved redesigning jazz's pulse. Cherry puts it this way: "He started out tapdancing in the streets, played with r&b bands and Mardi Gras parades and funeral marches, and travelled through Africa with [pianist] Randy Weston, where he learned lots of different tribal rhythms. He put it all together as independent beats he played simultaneously." Or, as trumpeter Herb Robertson sees it, "He took jazz's swing and put that New Orleans groove to it, straightened it up just enough so that younger players like me, who were basically coming out of rock and roll, could find ways into contemporary jazz, so that it wouldn't feel foreign to us."

Cutting across generational and stylistic lines, dozens of musicians repaid the debt via the Blackwell Project, a benefit for the drummer that ran on January 7, 1990, at the Knitting Factory and January 14 at Riverside Church. Blackwell has had kidney problems requiring home dialysis since 1973; growing acute, his condition forced him back onto hospital dialysis and, complicated by pneumonia and a hernia, left him unable to work. Thus these two eight-hour-plus cavalcades.

Even Congress and Corporate America finally seem ready to admit that the health-care delivery system in this country is a disgusting shambles that systematically deprives the sick. Most musicians—most U.S. artists—are among the most deprived populations. Workers without "regular" jobs rarely have "regular" insurance coverage; without insurance comes the right to languish in an underfunded and understaffed public hospital (if you're lucky) or to die. Then there's the additional problem of paying the rent: sickness is, after all, one of the main reasons homeless people wind up that way.

With an outstanding contributor mired in that bog, the Blackwell Project revived the jazz world's sense of community. In the process, it showcased the exploratory vitality of the many different stylistic strands that we tie together as jazz, and applauded Ed Blackwell for being central to them.

The first Sunday at the Knitting Factory boasted sets by mostly younger players and (usually) working groups. Kicking things off was a powerhouse trio: flutist James Newton, bassist Anthony Cox (one of the Project's organizers), and drummer Andrew Cyrille. They leapt outside in a constantly unfolding free improvisation so breathtakingly nuanced and controlled that it sounded composed—which it was, on the spot. Newton is, quite simply, *the* jazz flutist of our time. Taking his cue from Eric Dolphy, he's massively reimagined the instrument: he coaxes and yanks tones that range from gentle recorder to near–tenor sax with admixtures of shawms and bagpipes, as he splits tones, hurls multiphonics, bends actual chords. Cox and Cyrille, both prodigiously supple, dug into rhythms from funk to straightahead to African. Mesmerizing isn't a word I use often, but this performance was, for over an hour.

Next up, with Cox still on bass, was a contingent of M-BASErs, that jazz-funk amalgam coming out of Brooklyn: Greg Osby on alto, Gary Thomas on tenor, Graham Haynes on trumpet, Teri Lyne Carrington on drums. What happened during their set reflected the case of many M-BASE players—early promise with little recent development. Osby, for example, has a cutting tone and a lot of chops, especially as a balladeer, but more and more his solos wind up sounding like a bird careening around a cage, looking unsuccessfully for a way out. His compositions are even more imprisoned by his stylistic limits, as the meandering one-chord funky vamp the group closed with showed. Thomas, normally a dynamically barrel-chested soloist, kept getting hemmed in by echoing outbursts from Carrington, who sounded like she misunderstood the relation between, say, Blackwell and Ornette or Elvin Jones and Trane. Haynes alone played near his potential, sharply wrenching dynamics and grooves to his liking, but even he only sustained his ideas over a couple of solos.

Veteran bassist Dave Holland's trio includes M-BASErs Steve Coleman on alto and Marvin "Smitty" Smith on drums; the group often sounds bigger than it is. Smith is an at-the-ready drummer full of odd-meter, African-derived attacks and sonic touches, and he locked up with

Holland's amazing speed, technical control, and sheer zest to create telepathic grooves. Unfortunately Coleman's adept solos were overlong and strangely emotionless, as if he, like his friend Osby, is stuck in what he already knows. That was underlined by the contrast with Holland's solos, which were at once so sure-footed and daring that they almost made Coleman's seem plodding. Still, their set was shot through with epiphanic moments.

Trombonist Ray Anderson led guitarist Allan Jaffe, bassist Mark Dresser, and drummer Pheeroan AkLaff through gutbucket funk that rode either sprung rhythms or second-line struts. Plagued by technical difficulties, their set couldn't really build, but Dresser overcame a broken string to play a dazzling solo punctuated with two-handed taps and slides, and AkLaff filled the time it took for him to change strings with a remarkable, slow-burning excursion that used deftly buzzing cymbals as a foundation drone while expanding in explosiveness.

Bassist Mark Helias is a growing composer whose mosaic-like structures juxtapose feels, themes, grooves. His quintet boasts crackerjack soloists: pianist Anthony Davis, altoist Tim Berne, trumpeter Herb Robertson, drummer Tom Rainey. The combination created an unbroken incandescence. Berne's jagged romps, fierce with boppish angles and blues cries, balanced Davis's more cerebral classicisms to open a space for Robertson's daredevil trumpet, which updates and extends Cootie Williams's vocabulary of growls and snorts into a stuttering, speechlike arc.

Multireed wielder Marty Ehrlich finished with the indefatigable Cox and drummer Bobby Previte, and the trio ended the first night of the Blackwell Project on the high plane that began it. Ehrlich has mastered so many instruments, played in so many groups with so many greats, that it's about time he got more recognition; he's a consistently probing inventor. An iconoclastic composer, Previte drums with conceptual shape and bristling energy. And Cox reiterated that he can fit in with, push, and prod virtually anybody and anything. Not surprisingly, sparks flew and ignited their long, roiling improvisations.

The following Sunday found the Blackwell Project uptown at Columbia University's Riverside Church, where mostly older players, many of them the drummer's cohorts, took the stage. First up was Tailgater's Tales, led by trombonist Craig Harris and featuring clarinetist Don Byron, guitarist Brandon Ross, bassist Kenny Davis, drummer

Ralph Peterson, and special guest multi-instrumentalist Henry Thread-gill. As a composer Harris interweaves sharply contrasting themes and sections, usually with a startling and challenging freshness—a carnival feel is chased by a funky street beat, say. As a bandleader he's attracted top-notch sidemen: Byron pushes his ax far beyond Buddy De Franco via mellifluous, rangy leaps, Ross is successfully plotting his way past Bill Frisell, and Peterson and Davis manhandled the changing grooves with easy precision. Harris himself growls and laughs and smears as he gracefully darts around the pulse, and Threadgill—well, Threadgill is a genius as an instrumentalist, arranger, or composer; he's inherited the mantle from Ellington and Mingus, and his playing with Harris resounded with the canny humor, arching lyricism, and aching, edgy blues that mark his horn.

Where Tailgater's Tales were pretty tightly plotted, Structure IV—vibist Karl Berger, pianist Geri Allen, bassist Anthony Cox, altoist Carlos Ward, tenorist Dewey Redman, and drummer Lewis Nash—was a blowing session that unfortunately went slack. Redman, for instance, started "Take the 'A' Train" with fluidly enjambed lines that gradually lost their bite. There were excellent moments, though. Cox and Nash sharpened incisive grooves, whether behind Ward's spiraling Trane-isms or Berger's flat-footedness. And Allen, an ex-M-BASEr, continues to grow: juggling pulses that she then zigzagged across, rolling barrel-house chords that thickened and mutated into minor-mode smears à la Cecil Taylor, clustering Monk-isms, Oriental motifs, and boppish cascades with stunning confidence, she told gripping stories that stole the set.

Pianist Don Pullen's solo spot showcased his rubber-wrist, scrub-brush-across-the-keyboard attack that creates an eerily imploding feel, almost as if the piano is folding in on itself like a Mobius strip. Individual notes sink into whimpering, startled by sudden left-hand thumps in an almost ragtimey/stride vein as imagined by Henry Cowell. Long overlooked, Pullen is idiosyncratic but captivating and technically breathtaking.

The World Saxophone Quartet—tenorman David Murray, baritonist Hamlet Bluiett, altoists Oliver Lake and Arthur Blythe—followed. With the departure of founding member Julius Hemphill, the WSQ seems to have settled into a rather bland combination of relentless riff tunes and solos-plus-section-drones. It may be that's the dead-end waiting for such a lineup, though Hemphill, probably the group's most inventive arranger, found ways around it. It may be that their growing popularity dictates easy-to-grasp hooks that can launch their spectacular solos: Murray can still astonish with his hurtling runs from low-end blatts to r&b squalls to dog-whistle squeals, and nobody touches Bluiett for reimagining the baritone and extending its range. But the undeniable virtuosity sounded like flash without more variety in their material.

Branford Marsalis led the ever present Cox—who was stage-managing when he wasn't onstage himself—and drummer Jeff "Tain" Watts through an exuberant set that worked through the young tenor's heavy debt to Sonny Rollins. Marsalis has adopted the jagged phrasing and oddly floating spaces Rollins adapted from Monk, among others, and prodded by his energetic rhythm section, he stretched rhythms and reached for fetching substitutions: he's becoming a better narrator by miming a master, though he hasn't yet found his own voice.

But the high point of the benefits came with their close: the reunion of Cherry, Redman, and bassist Charlie Haden, all of whom, with Blackwell, had played with Ornette and then later formed Old and New Dreams. Appropriately holding down Blackwell's chair was Paul Motian.

As a sizable chunk of Blackwell's musical legacy, Ornette's tunes, from "Blues Connotation" to "Happy House" to "Lonely Woman," had threaded both benefit dates and were often stunningly played, but the rich history wrapping these stellar musicians transported them. Cherry's puckered whimpers and angular dartings, Redman's now-burly, now-whinnying tenor, Haden's deep-toned lyricism, Motian's elastically melodic drumming, Brazilian percussionist Nana Vasconcelos's tasteful embroidering, set up a charged sonic force field that warped tempos and lines, suspended pulses and detonated expectations in a truly magical way. Joined for a final jam by Ornette's drummer-son Denardo, Pullen, and Marsalis, the lineup became a living embodiment of Blackwell's wide-ranging musical contribution.

At the show's end an enfeebled Blackwell, clearly moved, said simply, "I must be loved." With reason: he's a cornerstone of postwar jazz, and in one way or another all the participants at his benefit are his lucky heirs. So are his listeners. [1990]

chapter 30

E.S.P.

By September 1964, 38-year-old Miles Davis was already widely acknowledged as one of the most audacious and probing and influential musicians in the history of what we call jazz. As he shifted musical gears from bebop to cool to orchestral to modal approaches, he helped spearhead the music's overall development.

Partly, of course, that was due to his own instrumental prowess: his puckered, often muted trumpet punctured the expected solo forms, ignoring staccato fusillades and high-register pyrotechnics for midregister swerves and floating silences. But it was also due in part to his early emergence as a leader—an ability that linked him to the likes of Jelly Roll Morton and Duke Ellington and Charles Mingus. From his early days, Miles demonstrated an uncanny knack for finding the best musicians available and letting them realize the new concepts taking shape in his restless, fertile imagination. For over forty years, the one constant in the fruitful and controversial career of Miles Davis has been the unpredictable changes that have come as he's shifted from band to band.

As a teenager who'd come to the Big Apple from his St. Louis home under the pretext of studying at Juilliard, Miles had made sure he was present at the rapid maturity of bebop, since he'd missed out on its birth; the language's pioneers—Bird, Dizzy, Bud—were his mentors and bandmates. But in hindsight, it's clear he was with them but not of them. His own conception surfaced in his solos, which tended to be less frenetic and more obsessed with spaces than the typical Bird clone's spew of licks. The shaping of a melody and the structure surrounding it, not the bop epigones' one-upmanship running of changes at a breakneck pace, was what snared (and kept) Miles's interest. In that respect, he shared an ironic kinship with his sometime antagonist Thelonious Monk, another mislabeled bebopper.

Then, in 1949–50, Miles began to explore some of his conception's ramifications with *Birth of the Cool*, his first collaboration with Gil Evans. It was also the first evidence of Miles's leadership technique: basically, he gathers players who are sympathetic to the general directions he wants to head in, then gives them their heads to map out the new territory while he threads the results together with his concept and trumpet. So it was with *Birth of the Cool*: the album was actually a group of sessions that grew from exploratory rehearsals of offbeat orchestrations by Evans and John Lewis. Its unusually instrumented nonet featured high-caliber players like Lewis, Gerry Mulligan, Lee Konitz, J. J. Johnson, and Max Roach, all of whom contributed their ideas while, as Mulligan put it, "[Miles] took the initiative and put the theories to work. He called the rehearsals, hired the halls, called the players, and generally cracked the whip."

Released on 78s, collected on LP only in 1957, *Birth of the Cool* became, along with combos like Lewis's Modern Jazz Quartet and the Red Norvo Trio, a key influence on what was called (misleadingly) West Coast jazz, whose "cool" practitioners—especially the overpraised Chet Baker—did little but clone and dilute Miles's and Evans's ideas. (The label "West Coast jazz," like so many in the history of the music, was misleading for simple reasons: not only was "cool" a dialect spoken elsewhere, but the California scene at the time was itself rich with other dialects spoken by talents like Mingus, Ornette Coleman, and Eric Dolphy.)

With *Birth of the Cool*, Davis and Evans cemented a legendary partnership and friendship whose musical dialogue continued until Evans's death in 1988. Along the way, they scaled orchestral settings on albums like the 1960s' *Sketches of Spain*. Taking Evans's evocative and moody arrangements of Spanish compositions and folk tunes as their departure points, the tone poems against which Miles darted and curved his vocalic trumpet melded the notion of European concertos (which Duke Ellington had already appropriated into jazz via compositions like "Concerto for Cootie") with Bird's pioneering if not fully realized work against string backdrops. But the results Miles and Gil got on *Sketches* were strikingly integrated and quite suggestive, even if albums like *Porgy and Bess* made the conception uneven overall as a body of work.

Typically enough for the ever restless Miles, at the same time he was pursuing the more orchestral and composed sides of jazz he continued to explore different angles of improvisation, the other pole of the dialectic powering jazz's engine. So 1959 witnessed *Kind of Blue*, which followed up on earlier efforts, like *Milestones*, in attempting to combine modes and open-ended improvisation into a band vehicle. Boasting John Coltrane, Julian "Cannonball" Adderley, Bill Evans, Paul Chambers, and Jimmy Cobb, it was a pivotal effort. Other musicians from George Russell (who was heavily involved in the experimentation and theorizing in Gil Evans's basement apartment that yielded *Birth of the Cool*, and with whom Bill Evans had worked) to Sun Ra (whose John Gilmore deeply influenced Trane) had delved into modes as the basis for a new improvising language that would complement or displace the Tin Pan Alley song structures that generated bebop's thicket of chords. But *Kind of Blue* brought the idea into the mainstream.

Ironically, Miles himself retreated from this improvising revolution. (It wasn't the only time he'd do that: after *On the Corner*, where he foregrounded outrageous explosions of percussion against rock- and funk-derived textures, he lapsed back into the by then more formulaic fusion forged on *Bitches Brew*.) Although following *Kind of Blue* he cut the orchestral albums with Gil Evans, his active bands between 1959 and 1964, which were recorded almost entirely live, were still playing early repertoire like "Walkin'" and "My Funny Valentine," standards with set changes—the very approach that *Kind of Blue* had set aside. But that's the nature of revolutions in music as in life: a breakthrough is usually followed by consolidation, retrenchment, and then, at last, a return to the barricades.

So it's no surprise that by September 1964, Miles had finished assembling another group that would help continue his ongoing musical revolutions. While pundits predicted jazz's death—that same year, the Beatles had led the successful English Invasion that resuscitated rock and roll and pulled most younger fans out of jazz venues and record sections—Miles was bent, as he was so often, on reshaping the music into something vital, not mourning its alleged passing. By the time *E.S.P.* was recorded in early 1965, his ace lineup—Wayne Shorter, Herbie Hancock (credited on the original sleeve as Herb), Ron Carter (credited as Ronald), and Tony Williams—was already churning up sounds that would earn it legendary status.

Shorter was the last element in the band's kinetic chemistry to fall into place. Five years earlier, he'd been recommended to Miles by Coltrane for the tenor slot; Trane wanted to spread his own wings, and

E.S.P

Shorter's adroit mix of influences (Trane's achingly acerbic tone chief among them) coupled with his own coiled sense of time seemed, to the older sax great, to mark Shorter as his natural successor. He was ultimately right, but for that moment Miles persuaded him to stay one more time, and Shorter signed on with Art Blakey's perennial Jazz Messengers instead. Trane, of course, left Miles anyway, and though his slot was filled by high-quality players like George Coleman and Sam Rivers, those bands are generally regarded as interim groups.

That changed when Shorter finally joined Miles's quintet. Between then and the time *E.S.P.* was cut, the band's entire internal texture, its attack and crosstalk, mutated dramatically. As Jack Chambers, author of the acclaimed *Milestones* (Beech Tree Books), noted simply, "Shorter was the catalyst." But in fact, all the band members had the unique ability to, in a sense, lead themselves, which, besides their obvious instrumental and compositional prowess, is what made them prime candidates for a Miles lineup anyway.

For like Duke Ellington, like Charles Mingus, Miles set up a feedback loop between his sidemen, himself, and his musical goals. But with a difference: Duke's loop was closed (as was Mingus's), and thus shaped all the material coursing through it to his image. Even when he appropriated the players' input and custom-wrote parts and solos for them, the results became embedded in the ongoing body of work that was the Duke Ellington Band. By contrast, Miles's feedback loop has always been open. When he's listening to his sidemen, he doesn't have a hidden agenda; he's there to hear what happens and then deduce where it can go. That attitude forces the players to be participants in the democratic model we call a jazz combo even as it helps clarify his next direction in the leader's own perpetually searching mind.

There's an archetypal story told by nearly every musician I've ever talked to who's worked with Miles. Melted down, its various versions run together something like this: "We were sitting in the studio jamming, and the tapes were rolling like they always were," says MilesMan. "Miles was just standing with his back to us, and all of a sudden he spun around and looked right at me and said, '(Fill in the blank with some very specific directive like, "Don't let me hear you playin' none of that bebop shit," or, "Why don't you leave some space in there?").' It was about the only straight direction I ever got from him."

From that perspective, Miles Davis as leader is the epitome of Zen, the blank shrug that answers the clichéd question of which, creatively speaking, came first, the chicken or the egg, the band or the concept. He deliberately places his own creativity on the line, surrenders it to be at the mercy of the band he heads; to a large degree, his course is set by the sounds raging from his personnel. Of course he picks them, but less to align with preconceived notions of where he's headed than because he's reacting to how they might get him to someplace—and this is the key operable word in Miles's vocabulary—"new."

What "new" is or will be, exactly, arises from the friction between Miles's studied technique of avoiding imprisoning his players with too much direction and the band members' evolving sense of community and purpose, their gleaning from his oblique hints what salient points he's hearing about what they're doing. The process completes an ironic circle that Duke's men never had to deal with. In effect, Miles's players are always trying to guess what he's making of their attempts to guess what's on his mind, when in the end what he wants—and when it works, what he gets—is what's on *their* minds: he wants them to plot out their own methods for having the musical conversations we call improvisation. That way, his players do more than infuse themselves into his music. They become the music as much as he does. (Which is one underlying reason that Miles since the '60s has usually refused to play old repertoire with new bands. "How can you play that stuff," he once asked me, "without Bill and Trane and those guys? Why would you?")

His players became the music on *E.S.P.*, creating something new from a meeting of hard bop and modal attacks through both their compositions and their improvisations. Most commentators agree that Williams's shimmering cymbals and odd-meter superimpositions provided the music's distinctive underpinnings and signature. The young (he was nineteen at the time *E.S.P.* was cut) drummer's fractionated pulses thrust his compatriots outward with centripetal force; Carter's deep-toned lines spun out the tightropes that the soloists cavorted on, while Hancock's snaky comping and conspicuous absences warped, and let his compatriots warp, the ever looser harmonic structures. Through it all, of course, Miles's now-singing, now-phlegmatic horn jabbed left hooks and poked into brilliant and unpredictable corners and arced with a ferocious grace. The irresistible combination of ingredients made this

E.S.P

Miles quintet the last of his bands virtually all jazz critics and fans can agree to call great.

You can hear why from *E.S.P.*'s outset. The almost singsong sway of the theme for the Miles-penned title track falls away to Shorter's muscular come-on, which deliberately evokes Trane, then Miles's agile and angular romp, then Hancock's sprightly dashes—all of them goaded by Carter's sprinting bass and Williams's sudden slams and bucking cymbal rides. "Eighty-one" takes a characteristically idiosyncratic turn on the soul-jazz so popular at the time (thanks largely to Miles alumnus Cannonball Adderley), mutating into a growling blues for its B sections. "Little One" opens with lush, post-Impressionist piano chords; soon Miles's bleak trumpet scrawls a theme followed by an anguished solo as the rhythm section kicks into modified waltz-time balladeering; Shorter's sax conveys a kind of sophisticated heartbreak that's no less painful for its world-weariness; Hancock, whose tune this is, paints in spare, somber tones—a Rothko in sound. Rounding out the LP's side one, Carter's piece, "R.J." lights out for hard-bop territory with high-strung bass pumping that suddenly downshifts for the turnarounds.

Sometimes the titles jazzers hang from their tunes seem either mysteriously unconnected or banally direct; but "Agitation," which used to open side two, isn't one of those. The Williams solo that lifts it off is no befuddled or frenzied banging. In fact, it continues the album's introspective mood while, like the tempo changes and stalling pedal tones that punctuate the rest of the tune, clearly suggesting the swirling emotions lurking behind the polished surface. "Iris," penned by Shorter, finds first the melancholy sax, then the voice-of-the-wasteland trumpet framed by Hancock's nimble, leapfrogging comping to a rare extent. Rounding things off is "Mood," another Carter piece; filigreed with breathy, muted trumpet and understated sax in a counterpoint that purposely sidesteps dialog, it lingers in the memory like the fog- and smoke-filled *mise-en-scènes* of the *noir* flicks it could accompany.

After *E.S.P.* came the deluge of remarkable albums featuring this powerhouse quintet: *Miles Smiles, Nefertiti, Sorcerer, Filles de Kilimanjaro,* and so on. And then the quintet finally disintegrated as Miles pressed on into fusion, driven by the iron law of change that has shaped his vast but deliberately discontinuous body of music in the same way it drives life itself. For Miles Davis, motion is life, stasis is death—it's as

simple and basic and relentless as that. So change isn't caprice or whim
for him any more than it was for Darwin. Rather, it's a strategic interplay
of forces—in Miles's case, the literal interplay on stage, and the conceptual interplay between himself and the players he picks for his bands—
that allows the chance of adaptation, and hence survival. By its enduring
beauty, *E.S.P.* demonstrates just how successful Miles Davis's aesthetic
strategy could be.   [1989]

chapter 31

Rolling with the Tape

Trace the story of Miles Davis the recording artist, as opposed to Miles
Davis the stage performer, and it means tracing the birth, growth, and
development of the modern art of recording jazz. That may sound
oversimplified and overdramatic, but it's not.

When Miles started recording in the late '40s, jazz records were more
or less cut the same way they had been since the earliest days of the
Edison cylinder. All the musicians gathered in the studio, ran through
the tunes, got set for the red light to blink on, and then did however
many takes it took to get one that would satisfy the producer and
performers—and it was hoped eventually, the customers in the stores.

Working with producer Teo Macero, his longtime cohort and collab-
orator from the '50s until he left Columbia Records in 1983, Miles
changed all that. Instead of being largely transcriptions of live performances, Miles Davis records from the mid-1960s on began to tackle the
studio in ways paralleling those developed by rock-and-roll explorers of
the period.

To understand how revolutionary this was, you need some technological and historical background. For starting in the mid-1960s, the
recording studio became more than a collection of technology; it became a place where musicians could do more than simply hope to
capture an outstanding live performance. That breakthrough amounted

to a reorganization of thought, and is strikingly similar to the epistemological shift that occurred early in the century after the birth of the movies. Then film directors realized they didn't have to shoot their sequences in real time, but could use editing to create the illusion of continuity by shooting their scenes in the most convenient order regardless of the story line, and then paste them together into a narrative after the fact.

Blame the similarly new sense of the recording studio that took hold in the 1960s on Les Paul. By the early 1950s, guitarist Paul—a classic American dabbler whose inventions included the solid-body electric guitar and countless special effects that presaged the huge racks of equipment and synthesizer banks so common on rock tours today—had pioneered a primitive form of overdubbing using multiple records.

Laying down one guitar part on the first disc, for instance, Paul would then play that disc back and play another guitar part along with it into the microphone. And so on, and so on, until he developed the dense but sweet sound that marked his highly successful career with his then-wife, singer-guitarist Mary Ford. Their string of million-selling hits included "How High the Moon," "By Bye Blues," "The World Is Waiting for the Sunrise," and "Vaya Con Dios."

Obviously Paul's primitive disc-by-disc method of multitracking, as overdubbing would later come to be called, was cumbersome and far from being the kind of technology that was widely, easily applicable. Still, pop singers like Patti Page and Neil Sedaka took full advantage of the technique to overdub their vocals again and again on a single song, creating the impression that they were harmony groups rather than individuals. And Paul himself, years ahead of anyone else, developed the first (if cumbersome) multitracking tape equipment.

With the widespread adoption of tape after World War II, recording got simpler in some ways, more complex in others. For years, tape consoles in studios were more or less easier-to-use versions of the longstanding disc technology. But tape had a basic advantage over discs: you could reuse it again and again just by erasing whatever you'd put on it. A recorded disc, on the other hand, was a one-shot.

With the appearance of commercial stereo recordings in the late 1950s (stereo recording, in a primitive form, had begun in 1919!), that single difference flowered into myriad applications for tape. First two, then as the technology developed multiple mikes were used to capture the sounds generated in the studio and feed them onto two tracks of tape. Those two distinct ribbons of sound were then mixed down—in other words, were sonically balanced against each other electronically to provide a "realistic" stereo image when played back through two speakers.

So even though the sound was being manufactured in a studio via a process that was growing more and more remote from live performing, the concert hall remained the mental touchstone of everyone from producers and engineers to the performers themselves. The idea of stereo was to make recordings seem more "real"—that is, more like a live show.

As the 1960s progressed, the number of tracks available in the studio increased. Let's take the Beatles as an indicator, since they did some of the crucial pioneering in the studio. Their first album was recorded on a two-track machine; by the mid-1960s they were cutting albums like *Rubber Soul* on four-track machines; by 1967 they'd started using a prototypical eight-track studio (made of two four-track machines yoked together) to produce *Sgt. Peppers Lonely Hearts Club Band*. That intricately laced, farsighted album demonstrated a dense recording methodology and almost futuristic sonic imaging that set standards for years—and in fact still sounds unclichéd.

The Beatles had given up the idea that recordings should be made in real time, and also that idea's corollary, that an album should sound like a captured live performance. Along with a host of other rock and rollers—the Rolling Stones, Jimi Hendrix, Pink Floyd, Led Zeppelin— they demonstrated that far from being simply an extension of stage shows, a recording could dare and achieve things no touring unit could effectively duplicate. To put it simply, they raised the use of the recording studio into an art form in its own right.

They also established the recording format that, despite some changes due to technological developments since, has remained the typical pop approach to working in the studio. First come the basic tracks: rhythm section, maybe another instrument or two. Then are overdubbed lead instruments and/or vocals, usually one at a time. The isolation of each stage of the recording process is intended to guarantee the finest signal quality for the final mix-down, when the whole jigsaw puzzle is reassembled into a performance that never actually took place.

Which is why both the classical and jazz communities basically shrugged their shoulders at this imaginative leap. For their different reasons, each of those genres posited the automatic primacy of live performance. In the jazz world, of course, the whole point of what was at once one of the music's greatest achievements and its fundamental language—the language of improvisation—seemed to demand direct transcription to disc. Anything else was deemed inauthentic and even downright fraudulent, because it tampered with the real-time flow of invention and could be used to cover up mistakes and faulty ideas that would have had to stand onstage.

And yet, as brilliant producer Brian Eno—for whom Miles's "He Loves Him Madly," a tribute to Duke Ellington on *Get Up with It*, triggered many of his own sonic insights—put it to me,

> When you make a piece of music on record, one way of looking at it is that you create a place. This is more than simply metaphorical. By the time I was making *On Land* there had been a lot of technological advances in terms of reverberation, echo, digital delay, harmonization, chorus, flanging, phasing—all those kinds of things, which had been quite exotic when I started recording, but now every studio had tons of the stuff.
>
> And what all that stuff is doing to you, the listener, is telling you about a place, about space. Reverb is a description of a space. Synthetic reverb is a description of a space that doesn't exist—which is *very* interesting. So that means if you are a composer, and actively working with those things in the studio, you're building spaces, not just melodies and rhythms.

Miles Davis was one of the first jazzmen to grasp those implications, thanks at least in part to friend and colleague Teo Macero. Macero had played tenor and baritone saxophone with Charles Mingus in the early '50s, and had been one of the cofounders of Mingus's revolutionary Jazz Workshops. Along with friends like Mingus, scholar/composer Gunther Schuller, and Modern Jazz Quartet pianist/composer John Lewis, Macero wrestled with shaping the classical-jazz fusion they called Third Stream. Hired at CBS initially as a music editor, he became a record producer with one of Miles's most important albums, *Kind of Blue*; amid the literally thousands of other recording dates he's worked on since, he produced Miles Davis albums until 1983.

Over those years and in the process of working so often with Miles,

Macero—who estimates with a shrug of the shoulders and a laugh that he must have worked on around 3500 records in his long career—also changed the concept of what producing Miles Davis—and in his wake, many other jazz artists—meant.

Still ruffled because Miles said some derogatory things about him in print a couple of years ago, Macero spoke only grudgingly about his revolutionary work with one of jazz's most revolutionary figures:

> He claims he did it all himself. All those ideas that he had, like taping his live concerts and using them as raw material—where the hell do you think he got those from? Not from his own head, but from my head in the studio, from watching me remixing and cutting the tapes up and all that crap. Even the idea of using electronic instruments— he never did that except for once in 1968. But he never gave me any credit for that or anything else.
>
> It's very strange when you consider that I was only with him for about 27 years, and made almost every record he ever made except the first two, and I worked on the second one, *Porgy and Bess*—I did all the editing for Gil (Evans). But he hasn't talked to me in four years—I can't believe it. So they asked me to be on a PBS television show to talk about him, and I wouldn't do it; and somebody who's writing Miles' biography wanted me to sit down and do interviews, but I'm not really interested—I don't need it.
>
> But at the time we worked together we were really pretty tight—we were like two brothers. I got him through both of his sicknesses; his life was not a pleasant one, and I went through it all with him. Not only in the studio, but personally.

How he did it in the studio was, in part, by adapting rock ideas about recorded media to a jazz sensibility.

> The whole way we made records was much more like rock and roll of the time. In those days, the late '60s and '70s, we used to do things in the editing room that were extremely radical, especially in a jazz context. But if you look back at Miles' career, you'll recall he stopped playing twice. During all those periods when he was not playing, his career went on—thanks to me, working in the studio, with the tapes we'd amassed. Without that, he would've been in the soup.

Macero is referring to periods like the early '60s, when Miles had basically taken himself out of the studio and stayed on the road—partly because he was riding a crest of popularity, partly because his band's personnel turnover was so frequent. CBS, of course, needed product to release to the growing crowds of Miles Davis fans.

It fell to Macero to reconcile the two distinct, and somewhat opposed, priorities. Which he did, ingeniously. Using some of the first sophisticated mobile sound studios, Macero tracked Miles from hall to club, and reshuffled the reams of live tape he collected into albums like *Live at Carnegie Hall 1961* and the two-album *At the Blackhawk*. With that, Macero started serious tape editing.

The insights he gained from that process, the ways it reorganized his own thinking about the studio, tape, and sound, allowed Macero to make the next step. By the time Miles, incapacitated regularly by a host of illnesses from 1975 to 1981, needed albums to release, Macero could concoct outstanding studio recipes like *Water Babies*.

Actually recorded in the late '60s, *Water Babies* wasn't released until 1976. But in the seven or eight years that passed between the time the raw material was taped and the album hit the stores, much changed. In a way that became paradigmatic for nearly all of Miles's albums from the late '60s on, Macero's forceful editing skills were put to the test in patching together performances out of long, often rambling jam sessions.

More and more Miles's studio approach boiled down to something like this: take a group of players into the studio with a few scraps of music and a deliberately vague sense of general direction, turn on the tapes, and go. Via the painstaking process of splicing selected segments together, Macero and Miles created compositions, textures, effects that as often as not hadn't even been imagined by the folks who were playing when the red light was on. It was the beginning of a whole new era for jazz recording, one whose implications have only come clear over the last few years. Concludes Macero,

> We revolutionized the way jazz records were made, though no one gave me any credit—not Miles, not CBS, nobody. In fact, compared to some of the records they're making today, which sound flat and dull, the things we were doing even as early as '59 sound great. I would never have let that shit go by. I used to fight every artist right down the pike. I wanted all the records I produced to be better than what they were.
>
> So we used to have some battles. But the end result was what I was concerned about, not the fighting. When I got into the studio it was

not a personal thing. I went in there with blinders on; if I didn't like the guy, it didn't make any difference. I went in there to make it better than it would be if I just took the times.

Most guys still go in there and just take the times: take one, take two five minutes, and so on. Who needs that shit? I was out there jumping around all the time with all these artists—with Monk, with Brubeck, even with Ellington I used to go out and ended up conducting the band a couple of times. I didn't like what he was doing and told him so, so he gave me the pencil and gave me the paper and said, "Here, you fix it." And I said, "Fine," and went out and did it.

Once the tape left my hands, as the producer I always felt I should go and sit in for the transfer to the final disc, make some changes there too. It's like a final edit, during the master. I used to do that with all my records at CBS—no record was ever put out unless I was sitting there in the mastering room. Or I'd get an acetate the afternoon the mastering was done, and if I didn't like it I'd go right back and work with the guy all day if we had to.

While Miles may not have relished Macero's insistent input, he clearly learned from its prophetic method—and depended on it. But with a change of labels (from CBS to Warner Bros.) Miles also changed recording direction, leaving Macero and live-in-the-studio recording behind in favor of an even more contemporary pop-inspired approach.

Since multitrack recording had grown to offer 24 and more tracks during the '70s, pop musicians (and their producers) had tried to take advantage of the technology to make the instrument sounds sharper and more defined while also providing producer and performer maximum flexibility in the final mix-down (where individual tracks are balanced into the stereo image you get from your album at home). The best way, it seemed, to accomplish both—and get a performance whose quality would be so good the band would then have to learn how to approximate it onstage—would be yet again to change the method of recording itself.

Thus arose the much more expensive and time-consuming method of recording outlined earlier—track by track, with the final assembly of the finished product only at the end of the process. It's the method that still dominates pop—and now, ironically, a lot of jazz as well.

Not so ironically, Miles has depended on one of his former sidemen for production in this new realm. Marcus Miller played bass with some of the outfits Miles put together during his last years at CBS, but he brought to those groups a distinctive sensibility based less on jazz than on the funk he grew up hearing and learning from. Miller honed his skills on the tunes of funky groups like Mandrill, as well as more jazz-inflected funk by players like bassist Larry Graham, whose Graham Central Station attempted to translate the farsighted funk of Sly and the Family Stone (where Graham got his start) into a hybridized context.

Now, Miles is famous for almost-never-give-direct-orders guidance in the studio. As he once explained to me,

> I don't lead musicians, man. They lead me. I listen to them to learn what they can do best. Like Daryl Jones play a bass line, and he forget it. I won't. I'll say, "Daryl, you did this last night, do it again." He'll go, "What?" I'll say, "It's right here on the tape (of the show)." That's what gives playing that feeling, like when you see a pretty woman and say, "Shit, wait a minute." Listening to what they do and feeding it back to them is how any good bandleader should lead his musicians. That's why athletes have coaches, right?

"A recording is only a guide for what you *might* play," he continues, expanding on the key distinction between live and studio work exploited by the Beatles, alluded to by Eno, and seized on by Teo Macero. "In the studio I play an entirely different music like, I don't know, Alban Berg or one of those composers. But outside it's *social* phrases, you know what I mean? In the studio you have control; you can put in and take out whatever you like."

In this larger context, then, Miller brought his funk-derived concept to the jam sessions that went on while the tapes rolled. He'd been doing jingle dates and other sessions, had made something of a name for himself as a session player and had become technically proficient on his bass, but he admits candidly,

> At that time I didn't feel like I had an identity. Miles was the one who made me nail something down as far as a style. See, the music he was playing really didn't have any predetermined base style to it—I had to come up with something, and that forced me to come up with something of my own. The tape would just be rolling all the time. So sometimes what came out wouldn't be so hip, but sometimes it would be *serious.*

When his stint with Miles was over, Miller began writing tunes and producing records for session wizard saxman David Sanborn; Miles heard them, and liked what he heard. So when he moved to his new label after 30 years with CBS, he tapped Miller's multifaceted talents for *Tutu*.

Recalls Miller,

> It started off that I was only going to do two tunes. See, right after Miles signed with Warner Bros. I was talking to (producer) Tommy LiPuma and he said, "Miles wants something different." So he sent me a tape of the George Duke tune ("Backyard Ritual"), and there was a drum machine on it, Synclavier sax, and stuff like that. I thought, Hmmm, I didn't know Miles wanted to go *this* way. So when I sat down to write, I know I didn't have to be limited to anything, that whatever I did Miles would be open to it. I just kept him in mind, which for me means seeing his face; if I went over the melody and I could see him in my mind playing it, see him with the horn up to his mouth, then I knew it was gonna fit him. It sounds corny—but it works.

LiPuma and Miles clearly thought it worked too. They okayed Miller's tunes before they even heard them, and booked studio time in Los Angeles. That was Miller's first shock. When he flew out from New York, he got his second.

"There was no band there," he remembers of his arrival at the studio.

> Tommy says, "I'd like to try this with a drum machine." I was game; I thought it'd be interesting to hear if Miles could make the drum machine swing. So we worked a while on "Tutu," which is the first tune I came up with, programming the sounds to make them feel like they were breathing. Miles was grooving. When he heard "Tutu" he said, "I think you're in a real creative period. I think you should write some more stuff."

Back home in New York, that's just what Miller did. "I saw the album developing as a conversation between Miles and me," explains the multi-instrumentalist, who played nearly all the instruments from synth to sax on the six tracks of *Tutu* he produced. "You know how jazz artists used to do albums with big bands: they'd play the melody, then solo for 16 bars, then play the melody again? That's how I envisioned this record."

Since he was also, in some key senses, trained by Miles, Miller also found himself incorporating conceptual frames borrowed and adapted from earlier Davis collaborators.

> Gil Evans was a big influence; I knew him, and I've really been influenced by him as a person. But I never really checked out *Sketches of Spain* until a couple of years ago.
>
> What I *did* check out, though, was one of my main influences—Herbie Hancock's writing, especially around his *Speak like a Child* period. He was writing really interesting stuff, using chords he didn't even have names for—they just worked. Then one day I pulled out *Speak like a Child* and I read on the back that Herbie during that period was inspired by Gil Evans. [Miller laughs.] So now I understand when people tell me that *Tutu* sounds like *Sketches* for the '80s.

Still, the operative word is '80s—which Miller's production, from *Tutu* to *Siesta* to *Amandla*, is very reflective of. Again using *Tutu* as the example of his studio relationship with Miles, Miller explains,

> I really wanted to use colors, I wanted it to sound different—that's why you hear a lot of *sounds*, all the synths and sampled stuff. That comes from making other records, other kinds of records. You can use sounds to create all kinds of moods, and they're available now, thanks to the technology.
>
> What you don't want is that they become the main element; a lot of bad writing is covered up by great sounds, especially in the music you hear on the radio. But that background gives Miles a different sound. And he reacts off 'em, they really inspired him.
>
> We recorded *Tutu* in an organic way. I'd lay down basic rhythm tracks, then the two of us would play together. I'd go back in and support what was done, then he'd come back in and play again. I mean, he'd walk into the studio when I'd be putting these weird sounds on and put on the headphones and start playing; it was like an orchestra would hit him in the head through the left ear and he'd go "Ernnnh," just fall over to the side and hit a couple of notes. He was having a ball.
>
> I mean, you've got to figure the cat's over 60 years old, he's heard it all, he's played with all the best. So it's an accomplishment to find something that startles him or inspires him. It was a very controlled setting, a very unusual album, and I'm real pleased with it.

He should be, for with *Tutu* Miles Davis got the opportunity not only to continue his pioneering quest for more modern use of the studio but also to update an outstanding piece of his past. *Sketches of Spain*, which started from the carefully wrought Gil Evans score and had taken so many musicians, takes, and tape edits, had been reformulated by a duo surrounded by machines they used to translate ideas into music one track at a time, only assembling the final work at the end of the process. [1989]

chapter 32

The Serpent's Tooth

Miles Davis is one of the few jazzers who could get away with putting just his first name and picture on the front of a book and still sell more than a handful of copies to aficionados. After all, for the 40-plus years of his professional career Miles has repeatedly been standing at or near the center of one musical earthquake after another.

If he came to New York on the pretext of studying at Juilliard, he soon found his real mentors, Bird and Diz and Monk, and so from the ripe old age of 18 he worked with bebop's revolutionaries. By 1949, he'd decided to pursue a new musical direction with arranger Gil Evans and players like John Lewis and Gerry Mulligan; thus was born *The Birth of the Cool* (Capitol), which gave rise to pallid imitations from Chet Baker on down. After kicking his habit in 1953, he gradually pulled together the landmark unit with Trane, Cannonball Adderley, and Bill Evans that worked modally, rather than simply cycling through chord changes as jazz had done since its beginnings. A few years later his crackerjack outfit with Wayne Shorter, Herbie Hancock, Ron Carter, and Tony Williams pushed that notion beyond its limits, and coincidentally launched what became known as fusion. In love with Jimi Hendrix's guitar and Sly and the Family Stone's straight-up funk, Miles went out *On the Corner*, which not only helped change the way jazz was recorded but earned the undying enmity of jazz critics—including Wynton Marsalis, who has loftily passed belittling judgment on all of Miles's work after the '50s while obviously owing Miles an enormous musical debt. And so on.

So it's more than just a little ironic that Miles is also one of the few jazzers to endure literally decades of bad-mouthing from most of the jazz press. Which, not at all surprisingly, is one of the major leitmotifs running through his autobiography. If Miles is famous for anything outside of his music, it's his running putdowns of the white-run jazz industry, from producers to critics, and his street-style mouth—another of the book's major linguistic leitmotifs.

Actually, tiresome as it gets, that's one of the more endearing traits of *Miles: The Autobiography*, since it accurately reflects its subject. The book reads like Miles talked it into a tape machine, except for the set-piece opening chapter, which strives for a hackneyed epiphanic/prophetic moment between a very young Miles and the blue flame of a gas jet. For the rest, Miles talks his way through his life, his music, his grudges, his fistfights, his persecutions, his addictions, his triumphs. That makes *Miles: The Autobiography* by turns fascinating and irritating and controversial and self-contradictory, lyrical and boring and pungent and self-aggrandizing—in other words, a lot like the man himself.

Most people want spicy backstage revelations and settlement of old scores in "star" autobiographies, and here at least Miles doesn't disappoint. Down side first. Apparently the quick-to-anger Miles is as fast with his hands as he is with his mouth, and doesn't much seem to care which person of what gender he hits. Without trying to justify or excuse how disgustingly often he hits the women who pass through his life "upside the head," it's important to note that Miles—who's abused virtually every drug known—became a pimp during his early '50s period of heroin addiction, and a lot of his lingo and habits come from those dark days rather than his relatively sunny, upper-middle-class upbringing in East St. Louis. Then too, he makes it real plain how much he thought of his father, who appears to have supported him emotionally and financially with virtually no strings attached, as well as how little he liked his mother, who first fought with her husband continually, then divorced him. So there's plenty of fodder for would-be psychologists in his repeated antipathy toward a wide range of women, his myriad casual affairs during his marriages, his recurrent fallback on physical brutality when dealing with wives and girlfriends (and, for that matter, band members and friends), and his shrug-of-the-shoulders attitude toward the whole thing.

Other musicians, even Miles's idols, also get brutalized physically and emotionally, or are paid back for old grudges and/or placed in new contexts. For example, Charlie Parker, shown as a brilliant musician and raconteur, is also depicted as a manipulative creep willing to shovel any mountain of shit, shortchange any friend or bandmate, to feed his habits; the famously caustic Miles is remarkably unsentimental about either Bird's genius or his—and bebop's—excesses, both musical and drug-related. Wynton Marsalis, too, gets some well-deserved lumps for his self-serving posturing.

Although the emphasis is definitely on personalities and events, trials and successes, a sense of the dizzyingly varied musical styles Miles pioneered or helped launch over the nearly unparalleled span of his career manages to twinkle through the sensational aspects. That part of the trumpeter's life got less space and depth than I'd expected, mainly anecdotal peeks behind the scenes, some fascinating, others rehashed from what looks like other sources. And when strictly technical points are raised, they're too rarely properly explained.

But that's consistent with how Miles's personality is presented here: largely unreflective, readily cynical, oddly vulnerable and shy, quick to anger and slow to forget. Outside of the bandstand and the recording studio, where he's plumbed the depths of his being to dredge up sounds and ideas that have consistently turned music on its ear, he seems to keep himself deliberately visceral but shallow—as if too much reflection would dull his intuitive edge. Translated into the book, that means, for instance, that his discussions of racism in the music industry often become more rhetorical or egocentric than they had to be, rants rather than indictments. This disappoints because Miles is one of the few jazzers who's made it with a large enough audience to make big bucks; coming in a more informed and organized way, his slashing verbal attacks on racism in the music biz and America could have been deadly enough to extend the legacy of his father, a man active in African-American movements, and teach the rest of us a few things from the inside.

But that's like wishing Miles was Montaigne. The music will mostly have to continue to speak for itself, as it's done so eloquently for so long;

for those more interested in that side of things, there's always Jack Chambers's academically toned but factually solid *Milestones*. The life, at least, is now officially documented. That split, I guess, fuels my own ambivalence: I raced to get the book, raced to read it, and don't expect to pick it up again for quite a while. Your move.   [1989]

chapter 33

Prince of Darkness

Start by thinking of Miles Davis as jazz's Dante, Cervantes, Tolstoy, Whitman, or Joyce. Like each of those epical and epochal figures, his encyclopedic body of work—40-plus years' worth—both sums up what preceded it and recedes into the future like a challenge, a clarion call. Though he began his career playing with beboppers, he was never really one of them. Though he ended playing frequently shapeless funka-thons, when his health and his chops and his too often lackluster 1980s bands rose to the occasion he could still ignite them with a jabbing run from his incandescent horn. Though he vowed time and again never to go back to his past, his final triumph before his death on September 28, 1991, came at the Montreux Jazz Festival, where he played what was, by all accounts, a stunning version of his old collaboration with Gil Evans, *Sketches of Spain*.

So Miles was, like the looming literary figures above, a great conundrum as well. Impatience and restlessness seem to have dominated his psyche. Acute as he was about music, in other ways he was, judging by his autobiography (*Miles*, Simon & Schuster), profoundly unreflective. But however distressing and hurtful, his impatience with the people around him, and his restlessness even within the successive scenes he participated in or led, fed an overwhelming drive that for most of his career steered him toward upsetting the status quo. The ramifications of his many revolutions still haven't been fully worked out.

Unlike writing, where you spend your creativity listening to influential ghosts while staring at your lonely blank page waiting for something to arrive, jazz, like another great popular American form, the movies, is a collaborative art. For all his vaunted viciousness, Miles knew how to draw his cohorts into his ideas, understood how to let them take possession of what he thought he wanted to hear. Like Duke Ellington and Charles Mingus, Miles set up a feedback loop between his sidemen, himself, and his musical goals. The difference was that Duke's and Mingus's loops were closed. Ellington, for instance, would take the flashing scrawl of an inspired lick by a Johnny Hodges or a Tricky Sam Nanton and ramify it into an arrangement; the codified results became embedded in the ongoing body of work that was the Duke Ellington Band.

Miles, by contrast, led by indirection. His feedback loop remained open: he waited to hear what would happen and deduce where it could go. Thus his impatience and restlessness, balanced by his ability to listen, backed by an irascible toughness that ultimately became at least as much mask as accurate projection, helped him become a rare and successful leader. "Don't play none of that bebop shit," or "Lay off your left hand," or "You don't have to plug every hole" were typical remarks he'd make while waiting for his bands to figure out what to make of his sketchy imperatives. For it was his democratic model of leadership—letting his cohorts fill out his skeletal notions, then seizing and synthesizing the results and pointing them toward an overall goal—that spawned one stylistic turn after another of a career that spanned nearly half a century, one of the most astonishing careers for longevity and productivity that jazz has ever seen.

At the center of that career, of course, was Miles's instantly recognizable trumpet: eerily vocalic with its parched, acerbic tone, its elastic sense of space punctuated by note flurries, and its occasional dramatic stab into the high register. The combination, which may have owed more to Bix Beiderbecke than anyone, made him an alchemical balladeer who could transmute Tin Pan Alley tripe like "Bye Bye Blackbird" into burnished gold. It also marked him as one of the first post-Louis Armstrong hornmen to back off from the rush to stratospheric high notes as a sign of virtuosity. Even if that was because, as has been claimed, he simply couldn't make them, he made a virtuoso's virtue of his limitations, and thus redefined the sound of jazz trumpet. In the process, he helped expand the horizons of what we label jazz, that ever growing accretion of stylistic choices. For if Miles was one of jazz's great conundrums, he was also one of its major nexus points.

One of Miles's key talents was his ability to synthesize the salient points of a seemingly unbounded musical space broad enough to include Charlie Parker, Max Roach, Gil Evans, Tadd Dameron, Charles Mingus, Sun Ra, Bill Evans, John Coltrane, Ornette Coleman, James Brown, Jimi Hendrix, Sly Stone, Prince, Ravel, Debussy, Harry Partch, John Cage, Stockhausen, African sources, technology—it was all the same to him. He took what he wanted from wherever he found it. He once told me, for example, that he wanted Herbie Hancock to lay off his left hand during the mid- to late-1960s partly because he'd seen an African concert with an mbira that turned his whole conception of piano around, and later fed into his use of synthesizers. That imaginative talent could be, and could be seen as, opportunistic. But opportunism is one quality all artists share. As Stravinsky put it famously, "Lesser artists borrow; great artists steal."

His restlessness made Miles anathema to many critics and musicians, who deplored his abandonment of bebop and acoustic jazz for the rock-and funk-driven sounds he pursued from the mid-1960s on. On the other hand, it won him an idolatrous audience among the then kids he touched for the first time at venues like the Fillmores. As a result, he eventually became a wealthy man, which inflamed his detractors even more. But though his turn to fusion seemed like a great treason to those who scorned it, it was only one of the series of watersheds he hurdled, which left him as he came to them: driven and divided.

When Miles came to New York in 1945, it was ostensibly to study at Juilliard. That, at least, is how he sold the trip to his father, a prosperous farm-owning dentist in East St. Louis. Instead, he looked for Bird, who roomed with him while he studied bebop firsthand on the bandstands of clubs and at jam sessions. But Miles, who was cheaply dismissive of Parker in his autobiography, never really played bebop, didn't clone Bird or Dizzy Gillespie's lines the way so many did at the time. That independence and contrast probably made it easier for him to land a gig as Bird's sideman of choice.

On *Bird/Savoy Original Master Takes* (Savoy Jazz), which collects early sessions where he played with Parker, Miles is clearly hearing different harmonies stacked in different ways. Like Thelonious Monk, his sometime antagonist, like contemporary American composers, he was interested in silence as a component of sound. Though he became perfectly capable of boppish note flurries—that's especially evident on his series of adrenalin-charged live recordings, even as late as the excellent 1964 *Miles in Berlin* (Columbia)—he more typically chose to halo his spiky lines with silence. So he never got hung up by sheer velocity divorced from soul or ideas to become its own alleged reward— ironically, much as it would, 30 years later, for the fusion epigones following in Miles's wake.

Bebop spoke to the changing realities of postwar life, which was faster-paced and marked by the fact that millions of black Americans had participated in the war effort, gotten real jobs and salaries or been in the armed forces, and weren't about to go quietly back to sharecropping. As music historian Martin Williams once remarked to me, "The first time I, as a white Southerner, saw Bird's combo, what struck me even more than the music was the *attitude* coming off the bandstand—self-confident, aggressive, it was something I'd never seen from black musicians before." This new generation was not given to accepting Jim Crow niceties; Art Blakey and Max Roach have both recounted how they directly confronted segregation in ways that were unthinkable for earlier jazzers. Miles came directly out of that experience, and fought against racism in the record industry as he encountered it. It's no surprise to learn he never really lost his distrust for white people in authority.

Still, he was deemed a potential leader by the white men who ran (and generally still run) the record industry early on; keep in mind that he was recording with Bird at the ripe old age of 19. But he pulled the first of many stylistic surprises when, taken by the ideas of ex-Claude Thornhill arranger Gil Evans, he became a member of an impromptu musical think-tank that gathered in Evans's basement apartment. The 1948–49 nonet that resulted yielded cuts later collected as *Birth of the Cool* (Capitol). *Birth* not only slowed down tempos and featured ensemble passages as much or more than solos, in direct reaction to bebop, but became the seedbed for the West Coast "cool" jazz scene and the long-lived Modern Jazz Quartet, whose John Lewis was himself an arranger and player on the sides. As Miles recalled some of the sources for the concept, "Gil gave me an album by Harry Partch in 1948, where there were drums and keyboards that really sounded like what John Cage was doing. He played Ravel for me too."

In what would become a characteristic zigzag, Miles didn't follow up on those innovations himself. Heroin addiction claimed the young trumpeter until 1954, when he went home to St. Louis to go cold turkey—which he successfully did. The recordings from this period, many of them collected on *Chronicle* (Prestige), find his playing uneven, and his approach moving toward hard bop, that stripped-down take on Bird that Blakey, Roach, and others were also pushing into. As Gary Giddins has noted, it's ironic and revealing that two seemingly antithetical movements of the time, hard bop and cool, stemmed largely from a single source.

The 1955 Newport Jazz Festival marked Miles's return to the front ranks. According to Jack Chambers in his meticulous two-volume biography *Milestones* (Beech Tree Books), "The public image of Miles Davis was refracted, like an object catching the sun in a clouded pool. He was regarded as inconsistent and undependable, but the addiction that had made him that way was now cured. His records showed him struggling technically and playing indifferently, but he had recently recorded music that was both technically proficient and passionately stated. He was considered by even the well-informed fans as a figure from jazz's recent past, but he was actively working at a new aesthetic and surrounding himself with important new sidemen. The gap between public image and reality narrowed almost overnight." His appearance had critics and fans raving. Suddenly Miles could book his band and was approached by Columbia Records—the beginnings of a long-term relationship.

Later that year, Miles began using a little-known saxist from Philadelphia named John Coltrane; their earliest recordings, which tug at bop with a reckless abandon that foretells some of what was to come, are also collected on *Chronicle* (Prestige). Then Miles transferred his recording contract to Columbia, and his band went through a series of personnel changes that eventually resulted in the lineup—Trane, Cannonball Adderley, Bill Evans, Paul Chambers, and Philly Joe Jones—that created the haunting, groundbreaking five-tune album called *Kind of Blue* (Columbia).

It was the period's capstone. Each tune, organized along different modal principles explained briefly in the liner notes by Evans (which mistakenly reverse the descriptions for "Flamenco Sketches" and "All Blues"), is a classic. Working from those approaches, this amazing band broke open jazz's prisonhouse of chord changes. Soloists could determine the shapes of their melodies without having to refer back to the same irritating chordal repetition. Along with the pioneering work at more or less the same time by Sun Ra's Arkestra, Mingus's Jazz Workshop, and Ornette Coleman, *Kind of Blue* was a glimpse into one of jazz's futures.

The trumpeter resumed his collaborations with Gil Evans for *Miles Ahead* (Columbia), a highly eclectic collection of ideas. In some ways, it's more musically successful than its more famed outgrowth, *Sketches of Spain* (Columbia), which has since become a touchstone for attempts to fuse jazz phrasings, harmonies, and tonal qualities with a classical orchestral scope. The pulses and timbres employed throughout reflect Evans's highly unusual approach to big-band arranging: the rhythms, no matter how syncopated, are always understated, while the instrumental voicings, no matter how strangely tilted toward the bottom end and rare combinations, seem muted, pastel, undemanding. It's as if the surface was set out with a deliberately deceptive sheen, a mirrorlike stream in which the narcissistic listener will hear little but which the deeper, attentive diver can penetrate to glean pearls aplenty.

By 1962, Miles felt he had to redirect his music. Hiring a young bassist named Ron Carter, he plugged into a network of younger jazz-men who helped bring it back to the cutting edge. Drummer Tony Williams was only 17, but did for Miles what Elvin Jones did for Trane: take the metrical flexibility the band needed and stretch it even further, relying especially on his cymbal splashes and extraordinarily subtle sub-divisions of the beat. Pianist Herbie Hancock, fresh from recording on Blue Note, brought his gnarled melodic conception to the fray when he signed on in 1963. George Coleman lasted longest of any post-Trane saxist during this period; he'd briefly filled in for Coltrane years before, and had a fat tone that made him a better foil for Miles's breathy, spare trumpet. For a bit over a year, this was the Miles Davis Quintet. The recordings of the period, all live, rely primarily on standards and ballads, Miles's strong points from the mid-1950s, while, characteristically, they virtually ignore his later breakthroughs.

By 1964, Miles finally added the last key element to his next all-star lineup, a young tenorman from Newark. Ironically, Wayne Shorter had been offered the slot by none other than Coltrane four years earlier, when Trane was getting ready to split himself. Shorter was the perfect fit: his tenor could burn with the rough plangency of Trane's while snaking his unpredictable lines through more implied chords than any arranger in his right mind would have written. The band's repertoire immediately reflected the nature of the shift by dropping the standards and ballads the leader had been leaning on for his post-Trane groups. Everybody was writing—odd, angular, rhythmically supple and subtle tunes that were sharp departures from the preceding four years of watertreading, however graceful.

In effect, only now did Miles pick up the musical threads he'd help unloose with *Kind of Blue*. This quintet developed modally based improvisation to near ultimate flexibility. The tonalities of their tunes were either ambiguous or constantly shifting; the rhythmic underpinnings swung furiously around a basic 4/4 pulse but by overlaying or implying all manner of deviations from that beat, thanks to Williams's cymbals and kick drum. Carter's deep-toned lines spun out tightropes for the soloists to cavort on, while Hancock's snaky comping and conspicuous absences warped, and let his compatriots warp, the ever looser structures. This period is where today's hyped crop of young neoboppers draw much of their inspiration. *E.S.P.* (Columbia), *Miles Smiles* (Columbia), and *Nefertiti* (Columbia), with their brilliantly off-center rhythms, coiled ensembles, and spiraling solos, have inspired jazzers as diverse as Wynton Marsalis and Bill Frisell.

When *Miles in the Sky* (Columbia) added George Benson for a tune, it signaled that, once again, the winds of musical change were blowing. They started relatively imperceptibly, on albums like *Filles de Kilimanjaro* (Columbia), where Miles had Hancock play electric piano—which caused major consternation among jazz purists of the time, just as other changes would. *Water Babies* (Columbia), recorded during this period but unissued until Miles's "retirement" in 1976, documents yet another step along his gradual transition to what would be called fusion: one side offers cuts from mid-1967 by the quintet, the other captures some of the earliest sounds—mosaics that fit their pieces together by stretching out over increasing lengths of time—by an expanded lineup with Chick Corea and bassist Dave Holland.

But *In a Silent Way* and *Bitches Brew* (both Columbia) are usually heralded as the birth of fusion—even though it's arguable that earlier rock albums like the Butterfield Blues Band's *East West* (Elektra), Cream's *Wheels of Fire* (Atco), and Jimi Hendrix's *Electric Ladyland* (Reprise) deserve equal credit. Rock-style beats, heavily electronic instrumentation, a loose improvisational attack, and a growing use of studio editing to create jagged soundscapes combined to create a massive young audience as well as a new kind of music. Miles, in fact, had been very taken with Hendrix's expansive psychedelic blues, and had made plans to work with the rock guitar genius that were foiled only by Hendrix's death. In addition, he'd been listening heavily to the deep grooves of James Brown, the acid funk of Sly Stone, the open-ended forms of Ornette Coleman, and the spacy electronic imaginings of Karlheinz Stockhausen.

Collaborating with his longtime producer Teo Macero, Miles knew just what he was doing by moving the percussive and sonic firestorms he'd unleashed into the foreground on the albums beginning with *On the Corner* (Columbia). Mixed like a rock record, it violated jazz sensibilities by once again using heavy editing to elide deliberately distorted textures into a hypnotic whirl. Miles and Macero had started recording the hornman's groups live during the '60s; Macero actually constructed live albums like *Live at Carnegie Hall 1961* (Columbia) from reams of tape. By the time of *Bitches Brew*, Miles's typical studio procedure was to bring musicians in to jam off a basic script of material, and then, with Macero, build finished pieces out of tape, like a movie director. Rock groups—Hendrix and the Beatles in particular—had pioneered the process; to jazzers, raised on the ideal of live improvisation, that approach was a violation of the premise that recordings should simply document the musicians' thought processes in real time.

Nevertheless, Miles and Macero continued pushing their method to its limits for *Get Up With It* (which boasts "He Loved Him Madly," Miles's offbeat elegy/tribute to Duke Ellington) and the brilliantly evocative *Jack Johnson* soundtrack (where Macero honed his editing skills to new heights of aural collage). But as Kevin Whitehead's astute notes point out, by 1975's *Pangaea* Miles's band was able to create the kaleidoscopic sonic collages and dynamics live. That's all the more remarkable when you consider that *Pangaea* is the funkiest, most overtly Hendrixy of these discs—a kind of Hendrix-meets-Trane hybrid, thanks to the presence of guitarists Pete Cosey and Reggie Lucas and saxist Sonny Fortune. Along with the rest of Miles's output from this period, it combined with Ornette's to wield massive influence on the jazz and rock scenes alike.

A wide variety of physical incapacities, including debilitating knee surgery, led Miles to take a long layoff from 1975 to 1981. When he "came back," the fires of exploration seemed quenched. The quality of his music, both live and in studio, tailed off dramatically. Tunes like "Back Seat Betty" (from *The Man With the Horn*, Columbia) are the gold amid the dross. The same intermittency plagues *Aura* and *A-mandla* (both Warner Bros.). And his 1950s fashion-plate image, which had veered into countercultural style with a high-chic flourish during the fusion-and-funk era, exploded into the near self-parody of oversized sequined tops and balloon-seated leather pants that helped breed the neobop revivalists' fierce polemics against him.

What actually underlies that reaction's intensity is the fear of loss of codification, the broadening of possibilities that represent the fruit of Miles's sonic swerves. Ironically, in that sense he was simply doing what all jazz explorers from Armstrong to Ellington to Bird and beyond have always done: reaching for something new that was his own. But because his career endured, because he didn't die young or record only sporadically, and because he generally refused to dwell in whatever he'd previously carved out, his encyclopedic output threatens the stasis any hierarchical aesthetic demands.

Career, however, is a key word that reflects some of the non-aesthetic tensions informing his music's long and twisty history. Miles Davis was that relative rarity, a jazz star with a broad popular following. (Think of how many jazz musicians the average American can recognize by just a first name.) He represented a peculiarly American confluence of celebrity hype and genuine achievement. Like Wynton Marsalis—one of his greatest denigrators and debtors—a decade ago, the very young Miles was groomed to be star material by his record company—the same company (Columbia, now Sony) that records Marsalis.

Not surprisingly, one of Miles's ongoing dilemmas became bridging artistic goals and financial imperatives—both corporate, since CPAs aren't interested in stringing along former hotshots solely on the strength of past glories, and his own, since fame and wealth create their own momentum and needs. The treadmill loomed. By the early '70s, Miles was frantically recording several albums' worth of material a year, and arguing with Columbia, which sat on most of it, about releasing it faster. As Chambers observes wryly, "[His] increased production . . . still did not succeed in balancing Davis's accounts with Columbia, at least during Clive Davis's term of office [as president]. 'At no time did Miles ever fully recoup his advances,' Davis says."

In the end, his music paid the price. During the ten years after his "comeback," when he wasn't in the hospital with one or another rumored illness, he was usually on the road with bands whose members he'd typically hired by someone else's recommendation, churning out versions of crowd-pleasers like his covers of Cyndi Lauper's "Time After Time" or Michael Jackson's "Human Nature." In the studio, he was more passive, as crossover producer-writers like George Duke and Marcus Miller increasingly shaped his radio-ready output.

But none of that should obscure his many and lasting achievements. For most of his career, Miles Davis was an incredible seismograph, a man whose sharp ears registered the sounds of the future as they shuddered faintly on the horizon. Despite his personal vices, like his penchant for beating women, and his inevitable aesthetic missteps—think of *Paradiso*, the ending of *Don Quixote*, Tolstoy's exhortatory pamphlets, Whitman's self-reviews, or *Finnegans Wake*—he's left that horizon much broader and our culture much richer.   [1992]

chapter 34

Notes from Underground

The last few years, a lot of jazz talk has revolved around tradition. It's a word that can confuse as much as clarify. Used in a reductive way, it creates the illusion that jazz—in itself a blanket term that oversimplifies—is the history of well-known key figures who pass a narrowly defined musical torch from one generation to the next, like Herculean Olympic runners.

The truth, like life, is more complex. After nearly a century, the many different musical strands we tie together as jazz have spread, combined, unraveled, and recombined in more ways than can be counted. That's one reason that today you can find releases like Wynton

Marsalis's *Standards Volume 3* (Columbia) and Muhal Richard Abrams's *The Hearinga Suite* (Black Saint) sharing the jazz racks.

Jazz's diversity of sounds is supported by an undergrowth of musicians' musicians who've eluded notice by the public for reasons that don't necessarily have anything to do with aesthetic value. Take John Dennis and King Fleming. You couldn't drop either name to impress the cocktail-party crew, but the two pianists, who spent most of their careers working lounges, heavily influenced Abrams, one of the pivotal musical minds of the last 30 years and co-founder of the seminal Association for the Advancement of Creative Musicians (AACM) in 1965. Via Muhal, their insights filtered into the AACM, and from there to other musicians like the "downtown" scene in New York.

Abrams, who won the prestigious Jazzpar Prize—one of the few "official" recognitions of his enduring vision—sets the context: "I think the nature of so-called jazz is to change, and to reintroduce itself periodically while it's changing. It's uncanny. It'll change, be rejected, turn over and reintroduce itself years later—it keeps turning. The musician sometimes is caught in a bad position in those turns. Some don't make it, and their output, which finally represents them, outlives them. That's the tragic part of this process."

John Dennis fits that bill exactly. Some of his music, virtually unknown even when it was made, will get a shot at a wider audience in resurrected form, since Fantasy is inadvertently reissuing his work as part of a 12-CD boxed set of Charles Mingus recordings. The Philadelphia-based Dennis recorded two albums on Debut, the small independent label Mingus and Max Roach started up in 1951. One, cut in March of 1955, was a sideman gig on *Thad Jones* (Debut) that showcased the then unknown trumpeter with Dennis, Mingus, and Roach.

Thirty-five years is a long time, and Max Roach says,

> There's so little I do remember about John. He was just coming into town; he never did become a permanent resident in New York, to my knowledge. He played solo piano, cocktail gigs: his solo playing was what was impressive about him. He never was in the mainstream of the Philadelphia jazz scene, like Jimmy Heath was. Mingus and I were caught up with him because he was a new face who could handle the instrument so well. He was probably around the same age as we were at the time.

Jimmy Heath recalls,

We used to call him "Fat Genius." I know he went into the ministry for a while. When I had my big band in Philly—which included people like Coltrane and Benny Golson—there were a couple of occasions where my piano player didn't make it, so he sat in. One in particular I remember. We went to a little place outside of Philly called Darby, and when we got to the gig the piano was so flat, it would've caused all the saxophone players to have to pull way out to the end, and they really couldn't play like that. He told us, "Don't worry about tuning up to the piano. I'll just transpose everything." So he played a half-step up, for the whole night. That's why Cal Massey gave him the name "Fat Genius."

On *Thad Jones*, Dennis plays it pretty straight, probably feeling his way in some awe of his company. Muhal agrees with Max: "In the group playing, he's not that impressive. It seems like he was trying to fit in, because his melodic concept was so different. When he played with small groups he had a kind of funky line that he'd play, which would give one the sense that he was limited to a certain type of approach. But then when he'd play the solo," he laughs, "everything would just open up."

Some of Dennis's work on *Thad Jones*, like his fascinating uses of augmented chords, hints at his two-handed, orchestral approach to the piano. That approach put him out of step with the dominant idiom of his day, since it harkened back past the period's Bud Powell clones, with their vestigial left-hand comps and right-hand speed-demon contests, to earlier masters like James P. Johnson, Fats Waller, and Art Tatum. Mingus and Max must have heard the hints, because that July found Dennis back in the studio with them for *New Piano Expressions* (Debut), the pianist's sole shot as a leader.

Muhal puts the album in perspective:

Dennis was coming from that full pianistic approach, which is why I speak of him in the same breath as Hank Jones—who successfully merged a bebop right hand with a stride left hand; Ahmad Jamal; Ellis Larkins; Dwike Mitchell of the Mitchell-Ruff Duo—who's another pianist people should be talking about, that album the duo did of Strayhorn pieces; and King Fleming, of course.

His solo pieces were complete. All the improvisation and the written parts stayed together even rolling round and round through many variations. I haven't heard a pianist that combines what some people might look upon as a cocktail situation with a more artistic jazz situation and a sort of classical situation into one thing. Yet it comes out as a good jazz feel.

And foreshadows the AACM's mix-and-match musical attack.

The Fantasy set offers outstanding examples of Muhal's point: two previously unissued takes of "All the Things You Are" taken at a distinctly Baroque tempo and filigreed with contrapuntal flourishes that would sit easily on a harpsichord. Dennis's relaxed command of that idiom indicates once again that, hype aside, there's nothing new or spectacular about jazz musicians who can play European concert-hall music—they've been around at least since the days of James Reese Europe. Ironically inverting Charlie Parker's appropriations of Impressionist harmonies, Dennis's Baroque adaptation of a bebop standard is a sly homage that gently implies what John Lewis and Steve Reich, among others, have said: that Baroque music, with its heavy reliance on improvisation, was the jazz of its time.

Unfortunately, because the Fantasy reissue focuses on Mingus, the set doesn't include the four solo pieces that are the high points of *New Piano Expressions*. "Odyssey," a disguised blues, is full of unexpected augmented moves as well as angular, bitten-off lines that wrench it beyond the typical. "Chartreuse" is Dennis's most clearly Tatumesque effort, a ballad swept through with the Impressionistic harmonies and glissandos that innumerable cocktail pianists would mimic and debase by rote repetition—and make harder for us to hear, in their wake. Here, as always on his solo spots, Dennis's elastic rhythms expand and contract with a lilting, graceful subtlety.

According to the liner notes, Dennis spun "Variegations" cold, with no run-through. Its compositional/improvisational shape evokes the silent-movie accompaniments that employed the great stride keyboardists like Fats Waller (another of Muhal's heroes) at the organs of '20s film palaces. Listening to it, you'll find yourself starting to project flickering mental images as it shifts moods around its theme, using those emotional changes of tone to build and develop its main motif. Last and far from least is "Someone To Watch Over Me," which surveys increasingly imploding chord substitutions over subtle rhythmic variations as Dennis tosses functions back and forth like an effortless juggler between his right and left hands.

Back in Chicago in the early '50s, Muhal learned a lot from King Fleming's two-handed attack, which pointed him to Tatum and Teddy Wilson. Fleming was leading a big band around town when his arranger, Will Jackson, who'd taught Muhal arranging rudiments, brought the younger pianist down; Fleming hired him as second pianist and arranger. Unlike Dennis, Fleming is alive, and working around suburban Chicago in restaurants and taverns.

That Fleming had a sleeveful of rhythmic invention is clear from his *Stand By* (Argo), where none of the 11 tunes repeats a beat. It was his second album, recorded in Chicago on March 2 and 9, 1962. (His other albums are *The Weary Traveller* and *Misty Night*.) Fleming's trio for the date was bassist Malachi Favors, then a year into his work with Muhal's Experimental Band, the AACM precursor, and drummer Royce Rowan. There's an occasional vibist unidentified in the album credits; according to Fleming, his name was Stephen or Stephanie, which Muhal says means he was probably Charles Stepney, who later wrote and produced a string of hits for Earth, Wind & Fire.

Fleming himself is an expansive talker who, understandably enough, has some trouble remembering details from a session from 28 years ago. He begins,

> I had classical training for six years before going into jazz, from Professor Turner. When I first started playing all I played was classical—"Flight of the Bumblebee," "The Warsaw Concerto," that caliber. Jazz wasn't in it at all. Then I saw Tatum and Teddy Wilson, so I switched over. I had a 17-piece band for several years back in the '50s; I've had small groups since; now I have a trio.
>
> I wrote seven out of the eleven tunes [on *Stand By*], and them and the arrangements are all copyrighted. [As did Dennis's, Fleming's reliance on original material foreshadowed the AACM dictum to avoid standards partly because they're owned by the publishing arms of the major labels, whose royalty fees further cut the musician's already small percentage of the profits from what the industry calls "product."] I try to stay melodic, to be pretty and listenable. I want people to enjoy what I'm doing. Of course, I have to enjoy it, or else I don't think anybody else is going to, but I want you to be able to just listen.

In fact, *Stand By* stands up to most of the piano discs put out in its day. Like Dennis's work, its uneven surface can be deceptive: Fleming is obviously checking out a wide musical vocabulary that he cloaks in lounge-lizard congeniality. "Time Out," his theme song ("I still use it today," he says), is a sneaky shuffle that can lull you if you're not intent; astringent spareness à la Basie crosses with Wilsonesque lyrical arpeggios. He transforms "Green Dolphin Street" into a cha-cha, where his piano twinkles in characteristically understated fashion. His attack, generally light though not always delicate, often couples nuanced shadings of expression with a fondness for the keyboard's upper register.

But Fleming was hardly locked into one idiom. There's Ramsey Lewis-type soul-jazz and thundering Rubensteinian chords in cuts like "Stand By Part 1," a minor-key blues, while "Song of Paradise" coils right around "Yellow Bird." "Then I'll Be Tired of You," a standard associated with Fats Waller, lets Fleming show off stride roots. The breakneck bopper called "Gypsy in My Soul" finds him distinctively cutting the time, racing only in short bursts and jabbing chords, and dropping Paderewski's famed "Minuet in G" into the last few choruses.

But the album's killers are farther out. "Between the Toes" sounds like it stepped out of the Book of Professor Longhair: its rolling barrelhouse rhumbas dovetail with chromatic left-hand slams for a partydown. "That sold pretty good for us in Chicago," notes Fleming proudly. And as for "Stand By Part 2"— well, there just wasn't a whole lot of stuff like it around in 1962. Picking up the minor-key blues of "Part 1," the trio breaks it down completely. The piano drops out to reappear only in fits; voices trade African (possibly via New Orleans Mardi Gras Indians) call-and-response vocals in an unintelligible argot, with one voice taking a griot's role; a firestorm of percussion chatters through it all, a constantly rising and falling wave of propulsion. "It was my drummer's idea," shrugs Fleming when asked about this astonishing piece. "He studied classical music too, I think at the Roy Knapp School. We just expanded on what we were doing in clubs at the time." Along with Dennis's and Fleming's shared willingness to use musical vocabularies wherever they found them, "Stand By Part 2" would feed directly into the AACM's preoccupations with African sounds, percussion, and presentations; Favors, after all, went on to become the Art Ensemble's bassist.

So like *New Piano Expressions*, *Stand By* illustrates how misleading it can be to focus on major trends as explanations for jazz's many evolutionary paths. Bebop may have overwhelmed other postwar languages in New York; cool jazz may have smothered different West Coast dialects. But that doesn't mean other paths weren't taken by players whose time may not have come yet, but whose subterranean influences have already been at work before it does.

Muhal explains why Chicago could breed a King Fleming, when other places with more proscriptive attitudes didn't:

> Look at all the different themes that he used just on *Stand By*. In Chicago, most of the musicians were like that. That's why you could have an AACM and a Sun Ra come out of there. It was an atmosphere where one could pursue his or her own approach to the language of the music. That atmosphere allowed us the liberties that we took. See, there are creative and inventive people all over the world, but whether there's a community for them to grow and thrive in—that's the question. In Chicago there was such a community, and no one dialect that was dominant.
>
> Everything was there. I remember older musicians who'd played with Pops and Jelly Roll and them, a lot of New Orleans guys who were still on the scene when I joined the musicians' union. They had brass bands that'd play in parades and in the parks. That's different from either coast, 'cause a lot of those people just settled in Chicago before they came here or there. It really was a source of nourishment for all kind of approaches. You couldn't get really strange in Chicago. You could get outside, but after a fashion it wasn't strange. We had a tremendous audience. Playing total improvisation for hours, even before the early '60s, we could pack the place.

Resurrecting *New Piano Expressions* and *Stand By*—and albums by Clyde Hart and the Mitchell-Ruff Duo—could also remind us that the broad tangle of jazz traditions should be an energizing force, not a limiting one: its function is not just to conserve the past's breakthroughs and values but to empower the present and future to find their own voices by revising their understanding of what's gone before. The way Muhal specifies it,

> Fleming and Dennis don't play licks; they play ideas. That's that older school again. Those guys weren't interested in a body of licks that were set down by one or two people that they could grab and make cliched connections with. It's a different way to think—trying to tell a story instead of showing off flash. That's one thing that impressed me about them and contributed to my approach.
>
> All these impressions encouraged me to go further into doing things

my own way. At the same time, I'm always trying to maintain the kind of control they have. That's the work in it: shape the story, don't just spit it out. No matter how original the approach is, it's very interesting how your mind can rework certain ideas, certain impressions, to make a situation for you. Yet the essence of the impression is still there.

There never has, and never will be, any best of this or that. What we have is a lot of talented, creative people. That's the challenge of the scene: to be able to function in that atmosphere on your own without thoughts of being the best, just being strong in what you are. There's nothing that can happen now to remove Ornette or Coltrane or Cecil Taylor or the AACM or Charlie Parker from the scene. If people like John Dennis and King Fleming had gotten even the publicity that I've gotten over the years, who knows where they'd be? [1990]

chapter 35

Hidden Histories

Allan Bloom has his analogs all over the cultural landscape, and jazz is no exception. The One Great Tradition theory currently popular in neocon jazz quarters—the Jelly Roll to Louis to Duke to Bird lineage that sounds like a triple-play combo—is its chiseled-in-stone pantheon. And yet it takes nothing away from such indisputable greats to admit that there have been numberless musicians whose names have rarely become known to general audiences, or even to most jazz fans, yet they've exerted a profound influence on the folks they played with as well as on those who've come after them.

Take, for example, the impact on Muhal Richard Abrams, founder of the seminal Chicago-based Association for the Advancement of Creative Musicians, of two historical ciphers, King Fleming and John Dennis. Fleming led a big band in Chicago in the early '50s, and gave the then fledgling pianist Abrams his first arranger's gig. In 1962, Fleming cut *Stand By* (Argo), an extraordinary excursion into rhythmic invention. His recordings never got out of Chicago in any significant way; now in his seventies, he plays lounges in suburban Illinois and the Midwest. In 1955, the Philadelphia-based Dennis made one record as a leader, *New Piano Expressions* (Debut), for the label founded by Charles Mingus and Max Roach, which was also poorly distributed. Nobody's quite sure what happened to him afterwards, except that he's probably dead. But the two-handed approach to the keyboard he and Fleming favored caused Abrams to rethink the post-Bud Powell attack that, with its atrophied left hand and lightning-bolt right, dominated postwar jazz for a couple of generations.

As Abrams—who, along with the AACM, is now based in New York—sees it, "Fleming and Dennis don't play licks; they play ideas. That's the older school, like Fats Waller and Art Tatum, again. Those guys weren't interested in a body of licks that were set down by one or two people that they could grab and make cliched connections with. It's a different way to think—trying to tell a story instead of showing off flash." In line with that way of thinking, over the last 30 years, since his Experimental Band and the founding of the AACM, the incredibly open-eared Abrams has consistently expanded his own vocabulary to include everything from stride to swing to serialism to post-Ornette Coleman, post-Albert Ayler breakthroughs to international musics.

To cite just one example, on his 1991 album, the deftly brilliant *The Hearinga Suite* (Black Saint), he wittily combined gorgeously written ensembles and thick-textured charts à la Duke and Mingus with blithely skipping playground-type tunes à la Ornette for an 18-piece band of first-rate players, including multi-instrumentalist Marty Ehrlich, trumpeters Cecil Bridgewater and Jack Walrath (a Mingus Dynasty veteran), and bassist Fred Hopkins. And in mid-September 1991 at New York's Symphony Space, he led an eight-piece ensemble that included six percussionists through the beautifully articulated jazz-meets-gamelan piece "Percussion 26 (1)"; it projected a vivid three-dimensional sonic image as it moved gracefully from section to section. In some ways, it was the conceptual extension of *On the Corner* (Columbia) Miles Davis never made. And on his 1992 *Blu Blu Blu* (Black Saint), he updates and redefines the gritty electric blues of his Chicago youth: the title cut is dedicated to McKinley Morganfield, a.k.a. Muddy Waters. As Abrams characteristically puts it, "It takes me backwards and forwards."

Subaural pioneers like Fleming and Dennis—and, for that matter, Abrams himself, whose influence on three generations of musicians via the revolutionary AACM is as incalculable as it is largely unknown to the general public—are the knots tying jazz's history together just below the surface. So when you discover one, there's often a sense of déjà vu, because you've heard his stuff before through the scrim of the folks who've picked up on him. But that's counterbalanced by the wonderful zest of strangeness, which reminds you that you've only caught the refraction, not the light source itself.

Horace Tapscott is just another outrageously powerful example of this underground current of history and duality of perception at work. Beginning as a trombonist until he was sidelined by a car crash in the early '60s, Tapscott played in his Los Angeles school band with Eric Dolphy and Don Cherry, and later worked with bandleaders Gerald Wilson and Lionel Hampton. Switching to piano—his mother had trained him—after the accident, he settled back into the Central Avenue scene that had nurtured him. As John Litweiler explains in his definitive *The Freedom Principle: Jazz After 1958* (Da Capo), "Back in 1961, four years before Chicago's AACM, the long-experienced Horace Tapscott founded the Union of God's Musicians and Artists Ascension (UG-MAA) to produce concerts by his Pan Afrikan Peoples Arkestra." Along with the late clarinet great John Carter and cornetist/trumpeter Bobby Bradford, he helped spawn a new generation that includes David Murray and Arthur Blythe of the World Saxophone Quartet; Blythe, in fact, made his recording debut with Tapscott.

All of which makes the incendiary but disciplined sounds of Tapscott's *The Dark Tree* (hat ART) very welcome indeed. Art Lange's detailed, insightful notes point out that the pianist's releases over the last ten years have rarely made it out of L.A. So this stuffed-to-the-soundbytes two-CD set joining Tapscott with Carter, bassist Cecil McBee, and drummer Andrew Cyrille opens into a panoramic view, a retrospective culmination of what we've been missing.

As a composer/arranger, Tapscott can wax complexly lyrical, like on the haunting "A Dress for Renee," where he strides from Impressionism to ragtime in a beautifully dovetailed art-song ballad. Or he can plug into a genially loping blues-with-a-twist like "Bavarian Mist." But on *The Dark Tree* he focuses primarily on driving ostinatos that power the soloists into post-Ornette territory. With the fabulous rhythm section and soloists the album boasts, that's a recipe for a hypnotic force packing the wallop of Hurricane Bob.

Carter, like Bradford, was a boyhood pal of Ornette's and one-fourth of the underrated Clarinet Summit quartet—himself, Murray, New Orleans great Alvin Batiste, and longtime Ellington sideman Jimmy Hamilton. The group released finely wrought albums during the '80s on small labels like India Navigation and Black Saint. Although all four reached beyond Benny Goodman's swing and Buddy DeFranco's bebop, Carter in particular brought the reed instrument out of its then somewhat anachronistic status. His astonishingly vocalic clarinet sometimes recalls Dolphy's as it cries and whinnies, sings and screams with a stunningly rhapsodic abandon.

He was also, of course, a frighteningly ambitious composer in his own right; his five-album series *Roots and Folklore: Episodes in the Development of American Folk Music* (Soul Note and Gramavision) was one of the last decade's outstanding achievements. It traces in musical form the intersection of pre-slavery African civilizations and Western cultures and their ensuing entwined history, without ever lapsing into static allegory. Drawing, for instance, on forms of the various periods it covers, from field hollers to blues and swing, it reinterprets those sounds into contemporary idioms, including noise, dissonance, and chromaticism, in order to create a compelling sonic narrative. Voices, either scatting or singing pointed lyrics, appear periodically. And fierce ostinatos, like Tapscott's, are used to suggest the thrusting drive of postwar life. But while the series made a number of critics' end-of-the-decade ten-best lists, it didn't make much of a dent in a marketplace, and Carter only got to perform sections of it on a couple of rare occasions, like for an underattended performance at the Brooklyn Academy of Music in 1989.

Local scenes, like the '60s L.A. scene that Carter, Bradford, and Tapscott played key roles in, are more often than not underdocumented in recordings, and what records there are are more often than not poorly distributed, since the only true national distribution pipelines in the U.S. are owned and operated by the six major labels. European and small U.S. labels, the typical sources for non-mainstream material, typically either have to rely on a patchwork of regional distributors, who are notoriously unreliable, or else piggyback on a major's network, which leaves their relatively small-selling releases at the mercy of an uninterested sales force. Even the 1991 major-label reissue *West Coast Hot* (Novus), which collects some terrific Flying Dutchman sides from the Ornette-inflected 1969 Carter-Bradford quartet and Tapscott's 1969 quintet, including an earlier version of "The Dark Tree" that features Blythe, was simply dribbled out unheralded.

Worse still, recording for a small label is not necessarily helpful these days when performers are looking for gigs. Promoters and most club owners, like radio program directors, prefer to deal with artists who have big-company "product" in their pockets, if only because of the promotional budgets that then back them. But even if a small- or no-label player lands a live date, it doesn't necessarily follow that it will be covered by the press. The farther away from the media margins you get, the more likely it is that editors want stories tied to current recordings and chart positions. While that's understandable from the standpoint of circulation, it also completes the closing of the vicious circle that ties together recording and distribution control, record company promotion, press coverage and airplay. (To get a hint of how that circle can work, take a look at the enormous orchestrated media play a commercially successful rock band like Guns 'n' Roses can currently command.) So whether you're a jazz or rock musician, if you don't have a big record on a big label, more often than not you won't get noticed except for ever decreasing segments of the music press and the occasional review in a local daily or "alternative" weekly paper. And thus your anonymity, and misleading notions like the One Great Tradition theory, become mutually re-enforcing.

At least some of the many music festivals held around the U.S. every summer try to partially correct that misperception by featuring local artists along with national headliners. The New Orleans Jazz and Heritage Festival, for instance, puts the big touring acts on two big stages, and reserves the many small stages and tents for regional musicians who generally have no record deals and rarely, if ever, get outside the Deep South. There you could have seen saxophonist Edward "Kidd" Jordan, an omnivorous player who's willing and able to share the stage with boppers, lounge lizards, free jazzers, and rappers alike. Later in 1991, you could have caught him at the edges of the Chicago Jazz Festival, where he hooked up with some of Chicago's little-known legends at South End MusicWorks, a small loft-style venue. Along with saxists Fred Anderson and Douglas Ewart, and Art Ensemble bassist Malachi

Favors, and drummer Dushun Mosley, he created a Pharoah Sanders-inspired set full of dynamically shifting overtones so finely calibrated that the room itself felt like it had begun to vibrate along.

Like the New Orleans shindig, the Chicago fest always includes regional acts, like pianist John Young or violinist Johnny Frigo or second-generation AACMer Vandy Harris, who don't get out of the Windy City. And because it's free to the public in lakeside Grant Park, it draws curious crowds who, in the course of any evening's varied program, can get turned on to music they didn't know anything about beforehand. Like any big festival, it also acts as a magnet that energizes more outboard segments of the local scene. Since folks from around the country come to town for it, after-hours jams at small clubs like South End or Joe Segal's Jazz Showcase can introduce the curious to new sounds, like the music of Hal Russell.

Like Tapscott in L.A., multi-instrumentalist Russell is an offbeat local hero in Chicago, an elder statesman who works consistently with younger players, most of whom also double on various instruments. Russell's music, however, stays pretty far from the dark anger that fuels much of Tapscott's. His NRG Ensemble can slide easily from broad vaudevillian humor to outside blowing, sometimes in the space of a few bars. So on *Conserving NRG* (PJP), the quintet swerves from off-the-wall ensembles to pure blasts of angular outside improvisations to wickedly funny jumpcuts and parodies, while *Hal on Earth* (PJP) boasts a hilarious medley-tribute to Fred Astaire, complete with the sound of dancing feet. Finally, in spring 1992, ECM, a decent-sized German label with reasonably credible U.S. distribution, released *The Finnish-Swiss Tour*. A typically probing and wacky combo, it's the first Russell album to make it out of Chicago, except for the copies the man himself sells from the stage at the end of every performance.   [1991]

chapter 36

Gunther Schuller's Memory Palace

Gunther Schuller—musicologist and scholar, musician and critic, tire-less advocate of the offbeat, from the classical-jazz fusion (which he helped pioneer) called Third Stream to Ornette Coleman—is, to put it mildly, a daunting figure. They *loom*, he and the first two parts of his overarching *History of Jazz*. Each volume clocks in at several hundred pages of densely informed (if not always elegant) prose, riddled with numerous (and often lengthy) musical examples and explications, the obviously thick undergrowth of knowledge and listening and, yes, even pure pleasure that he's compacted so richly and suggestively into a sweeping narrative. The footnotes alone bristle with more fascinating background info and critical insight than most entire books of what passes for jazz criticism. Put it all together and you've got the most amazing effort to systematize and sum up the dispersed, underexamined, and undervalued history of what we call jazz that I've ever read. Period.

Not surprisingly, over 20 years stand between the publication of Schuller's first (*Early Jazz: Its Roots and Musical Development*) and second (*The Swing Era: The Development of Jazz, 1933–1945*) volumes. Because of the project's prodigious scope and ambitions, after the sweating messenger arrived with the package from my editor and I sat down and opened it and started to read I felt like I was back in grad school for Comp Lit. First year, actually, and getting overawed by Germanic giants like the Schlegels and Curtius and Auerbach and their encyclopedically knowledgeable tomes, their imperturbable Olympian certainty not only that they knew exactly what they were doing with their innumerable languages and texts and easy cross-cultural familiarity, but *that it really mattered*—enough to devote, in Baconian fashion, a lifetime or several to.

Schuller is a more direct descendant of folks like Curtius and Auerbach than critics like Foucault, Said, or Jameson could or would want to

be. His methodology is downright old-fashioned. His unflagging posi-
tivist's insistence on irreducible (and utterly fascinating) facts like the
historical transmission of musical data (who influenced Coleman
Hawkin's revolutionary approach to soloing, where did the breakaway
from the Fletcher Henderson choir-by-choir system of structuring big-
band charts first come into play, and endlessly so on) will no doubt seem
primitive to devotees of intertextuality's more speculative philosophic
sophistication and more nebulous claims. I guess it is. But in this case it
also delivers—big.

That's fitting, since the subject of this second volume is basically the
big bands. Unravel Scorsese's deft marriage-as-metaphor depictions in
New York New York and you've got one of the plot's hairy strands, the
conflict between the commercial tugs of Tin Pan Alley, managers, and
record labels on the one hand, and jazz on the other: their sudden
heated affair, their temporary and productive détente, their final cata-
clysmic divorce. The big bands, as Schuller sees them, formed the
battleground where American musical tastes and sensibilities were
fought over. If the gladiators (commerce vs. art) at times seem drawn too
patly, think of them (Scorsese did) as escapees from a medieval play,
moralistic "types" rather than "realistic" characters whose aesthetic
function resides precisely in their general applicability, their non-
specificity.

For like all the great cultural critics, Schuller writes from within a
defining set of moral perspectives that he is resolutely unembarrassed by.
He makes a consistent, sweeping indictment of the racism and mindless
commercialism—the modifier is crucial for him—that permeates
American culture and all its artifacts. Along with the growth and development of the musical formats of swing's heyday, those moral bifurca-
tions form his story's spine.

And what a helluva narrative it is, covering those glory days of the
new receding American Century. It begins with a chapter called "The
'King' of Swing," where Schuller debunks some Benny Goodman myths
without fully tearing the mantle off—he simply knows too much not to
be fair. Goodman was a salable white-bread version of the music that
had been sweeping the black ghettos of New York and Chicago and L.A.
as well as countless towns and college campuses throughout the Midwest and Southwest—the Elvis or Sting of his day. But even though he
was crowned by the media for achievements that were not really his—

the charts swinging his band came from the pens of folks like Fletcher Henderson—he could, and did, play real hotshit jazz, Swing Era edition, and cast a huge shadow over other reedmen because of his apparently effortless fluency and usually flawless technique.

Schuller understands the contradictions here only too well, and seizes them to put much of the "King"'s achievement (and the era he's come to symbolize retroactively) into perspective. There were the small groups (and editions of bigger units) that didn't swing as well as their historical rep would lead you to believe, largely due to Gene Krupa's show-offy, old-fashioned drumming. There was Goodman's stubborn resistance to change, his natural reluctance to tamper with a hit-making formula to go in any different musical directions, his somewhat lazy faith in his own technical finesse.

Yet Schuller balances his tale of the ego and the reed with acute observations about the band's invaluable musical legacy. Of the swaggering '40s outfit sparked by the innovative arrangements of Eddie Sauter he writes, "The Goodman orchestra—and Goodman himself—played with a dazzling brilliance that was the envy of all the other bands. The emphasis was not on soloists—as with Basie, for example—but on the orchestra, and on jazz *as* arrangement and composition. The more purely improvised jazz was relegated to the Sextet performances and recordings." He also cites Goodman's own fluid jazz playing, his early and prophetic "crossover" experiments with Béla Bartók's material, and—most important—his creation of "an alliance between national popular taste and a creative music called jazz" as proof of the clarinetist's true accomplishments.

Because truth is what's at stake here. This ain't no postmodernist's party, this ain't no duck-walker's disco, this ain't no market of loose-lipped ideas. The table of contents nearly stands at attention with the names that count, from Duke Ellington and Jimmie Lunceford to Claude Thornhill and Woody Herman, from Coleman Hawkins to Lester Young and Ben Webster, from Fletcher Henderson and Benny Carter to the Casa Loma Orchestra and the Dorsey Brothers and the territory bands. We're talking musical canon formation, but luckily for those of us who give a shit about this stuff, Schuller is no Allan Bloom or E. D. Hirsch. Yeah, his canon is shot through with a lot of names you'd expect to see. But how exactly do you write an Olympian history of Swing Era jazz and *not* focus on Ellington and Goodman and the like?

And if the short answer is, You can't, then how do you avoid focusing on them to the exclusion of the environment that made them what they became, the musical challenges they heard from their (often now unnameable) contemporaries and responded to with their own, the fruitful dialogues that created history and that history has lost?

For Schuller the long answer—and vital corrective—to a rehashed 100-Most-Beautiful-Melodies survey emerges from within the tradition of the anatomy, the ancient methodology that's bequeathed pleasurable texts from Aristotle and Lucretius through Rabelais and Burton to Joyce and Proust, even up to Frye and Pynchon. With ingenious aplomb, Schuller wields his book's sheer bulk as a weapon on behalf of the previously neglected and overlooked. It's as if Bloom tucked into *The Closing of the American Mind* lectures on Hopi mythology or Shangaan folktales. Partly that's the result of Schuller's inalienably liberal-arts liberalism: he genuinely tries to broaden any perspective he can reach because he's committed to the notion that the best students are those who learn to think for themselves. Partly, too, it's due to his resolute unwillingness to endorse received opinions: he's determined to churn up new facts, viewpoints, ideas even where the material seems dessicated and overplowed. And so offbeat names, dates, perspectives flesh out this historical Anatomy of Swing.

For example, while Schuller tells the tales of outstanding bandleaders and soloists, he also generally tries to recast the history of the big bands in terms of composers and arrangers. So instead of wading through endless lists detailing the chart-topping achievements of the Ozzie Nelsons and Guy Lombardos, Schuller opens the hoods of those sleek 12-cylinder big-band machines and explains how they ran, musically speaking, on what the arrangers pumped into their semi-sized fuel tanks. (That's a crucial point being made on the bandstand now by repertory big bands like the American Jazz Orchestra, which is trying to gather a library of the period's arrangements to preserve and play them.)

But if Schuller reinstates the arranger in his rightful place for the period, he doesn't do it in a roseate haze. Here is his characteristically careful distinction between composer and arranger:

> An arranger is not necessarily a composer. He is rarely *creative* in the full sense that fine composers are. Great composers, whether their names are Ellington or Beethoven, develop and expand their musical language, often to the extent that their late works seem barely traceable

to their early ones. With arrangers that kind and degree of creativity is seldom considered desireable. Rather, they are required to be excellent craftsmen, rarely creative *innovators*. (To the extent that one of Goodman's later arrangers, Eddie Sauter, attempted to be innovative and to reach beyond the established Goodman style, his work was largely ignored by the public and, it seems, on occasion by Goodman himself.)

He then goes on to devote much of his long chapter on Goodman to Sauter's groundbreaking accomplishments, their extension of Ellington's rich harmonic and rhythmic languages and their prophetic relation to Gil Evans. It's a pattern he repeats, so that by the book's finish he's uncovered for the general reader a genealogy of the period's major arrangers (as well as a lot of minor ones).

This large-scale redistribution of credit finds its formal mimesis in Schuller's own textual distribution. The footnotes here swell into info-stuffed asides, sometimes even mini-essays, that Schuller uses to limn the sidepaths and back roads off history's main drags. Take as an example his footnote on Ellington vocalist Herb Jeffries:

> One particularly fascinating Jeffries performance is "I Don't Know What Kind of Blues I got," for in it we hear *exactly* the kind of timbre and inflection we know from Billy Eckstine in the mid-forties. I am not certain who was imitating whom, although my hunch is that the younger Eckstine was influenced by the older Jeffries. Coincidentally, both singers sang with the Earl Hines orchestra, Jeffries in the mid-thirties, Eckstine in the early forties. What confuses the picture is that Jeffries generally tended towards a kind of contrived crooning in many of his Ellington recordings, but here "I Don't Know" suddenly came out with a new "voice," whereas Eckstine seems to have been much more consistent and individual over the years with Hines in *his* approach. Perhaps both singers mutually influenced each other at various times. It might also be said that both were not unmindful of Bing Crosby's enormous popularity, even with black audiences—particularly Crosby's success with the ladies for his famous glottal scoops, for which he earned the sobriquet "The Groaner." Both Eckstine and Jeffries worked hard at incorporating this device into their singing styles, although with a black coloration that Crosby did not attain.

Racism and the cultural inferiority complex that haunts America and keeps it from embracing the true achievements of its own artists are sore points for Schuller, as for any thinking American critic. In his remarkable discussion of piano legend Art Tatum, for instance, Schuller argues that Tatum's arrangements of tunes, harmonically far-reaching and overpoweringly influential among jazzers as they were, were largely set-pieces built from European classical techniques the pianist had studied and adapted. Typically, however, he doesn't stop there; he turns the point inside out to make another—in a footnote:

> The long-held myth that Vladimir Horowitz was an ardent admirer of Tatum seems to have no basis in fact. (See the introductory foreword on Tatum to Time-Life's *Giants of Jazz.*) I suspect, moreover, that those classical artists who admired Tatum did so in the generally patronizing way that classical musicians have traditionally viewed black and/or jazz artists, not to mention blind ones. Black musicians have earned renowned white classical musicians' admiration only when they were perceived as emulating classical standards and properties. It is interesting that Tatum's technique was admired by classical musicians in the 1930s and 1940s clearly for its classical leanings and technical perfection, qualities they could relate to. But where were the classical admirers of Thelonious Monk's or Pete Johnson's more "unorthodox" and intrinsically jazz-rooted techniques?

That single footnote blows away many of the ridiculous assumptions undergirding James Lincoln Collier's wretched *Ellington* biography, for instance.

A Rabelaisian catalog of random footnotes turns up a mini-history of the introduction of the electric guitar into jazz by Eddie Durham, Floyd Smith, and Leon McAuliffe; the connections between the diametrically opposed sax sounds of Ben Webster and Lester Young—they played side by side in Young's father's band as kids in Texas and cut their teeth on Frankie Trumbauer's "Singin' the Blues"; a paragraph of (I think misguided) observations about "effeminately voiced crooners" in American pop; a debunking of pioneer arranger Don Redman's status as "the only orchestral innovator in the early days of jazz." One of my favorites—and if that sounds like an odd way to talk about footnotes, all I can say is, Wait 'til you've read 'em—begins "Paul Howard's Quality Serenaders was a now-forgotten nine-piece orchestra that deserves at least a footnote in jazz history." Well, now they've got it.

Of course, in a real sense Schuller's simply skewing the Olympian view slightly to the left. The Hegelian kind of history Schuller has attempted seeks to inscribe its own future corrections within it; it needs to be timelessly true, correct, believed. One of Schuller's most directly apologetic footnotes runs, "It represents a frequent problem for the jazz historian that certain players (and orchestras) who happen not to have recorded prolifically (or at all), or who died prematurely, or who had peripatetic careers not easily traceable through recordings, are difficult to appraise." Uh, yeah, you could say that again several hundred times and still not answer the musical question, How well does the Owl of Minerva fly at dusk wearing mirror shades and smoking dope?

Sure, Schuller's prose and posture is deliberate and measured, at times borderline ponderous, in that academic way, but it's a surface often overcome by its resonating depths of enthusiast's knowledge. Once you start reading you adjust to the notion that *jouissance* in Schuller's terms is the complete transcription of the famed, groundbreaking 64-bar solo that Coleman Hawkins took on "Body and Soul" in 1939. (Gary Giddins tells me Schuller can transcribe music the way lesser mortals write a letter, but from the number and size of the examples in *The Swing Era* that letter-writer would have to be an unreconstructed 18th-century quill-pusher just to qualify for the competition.) Sure, a number of his dominant modes of thought, like the evolutionary models he frequently invokes and the organic metaphors he's so fond of, seem unexamined for the less-than-useful implications, like a faith in teleology and the asssumption of progress, they may harbor (in a way that Foucault et al., for instance, would never allow). But those concepts also stem directly from the Hegelian tradition that informs his work. Much as that tradition's larger and problematic frame sometimes creaks, it gives the book a more meaningful shape than the simpleminded Mount Rushmore model most music critics seem to use to understand the development of the sounds they try to explain.

But maybe what most amazes me about *The Swing Era* is that you don't have to be a musicologist or fanatic to actually sit down and read it—just read it. If you can't follow the many musical transcriptions— and they're not essential since, as Schuller points out, even the best capture only the outlines of the music, not its nuances—you can simply rely on the solid descriptions to get the gist. Just skip the too intensely musicological parts the same way you skim the whale-anatomy sections of *Moby-Dick*. Because like a 19th-century novel, Hegelian history is about a plot, and Schuller's got the makings for a major potboiler: sex and drugs and music and corruption and racism and exploitation and the creation of a musical form that's traveled the world and won honor everywhere but the land of its birth.

Yes, through this music Harlem and equivalent black neighborhoods across the country were overrun with invading whites and left, once the party money ran out, with the legacy of depression and unemployment and numbers and drugs and prostitution and violence and poverty that still defines life for too many of our people. And yes, the vast majority of jazz musicians live(d) and die(d) under those clouds and relentless commercial pressure besides. And yes, yes, yes, despite the very obvious impossibility of it all they somehow forge(d) a new, multifaceted art form that is universal in its appeal, timeless in its reach, awesome in its democratic intensity. Gunther Schuller knows and tells all that; maybe more to the point, he believes in the ultimate triumph the story's self-evident values imply, the victory of art's eternal verities somehow ratified by history. His is a neater, more rounded, more satisfying world than the one I know. That difference is one of the main reasons—aside from everything else he knows that I don't—that he can actually write a history like this one, and I can't even contemplate it. But I'm more than happy and grateful that he's done it; I mean to ransack the hell out of it.   [1989]

chapter 37

Preservation Hall Comes to Carnegie

Don't be deceived because the Preservation Hall Jazz Band appears at Carnegie Hall. Down in New Orleans where they hail from, the loose-limbed music they make, with its crossfire rhythms and its overlapping melodies, is no dusty fossil; it's as natural as red beans and rice and Mardi Gras. You can hear it resounding still when marching bands strut the streets, or in clubs and bars where the musical descendants of the turn-of-the-century cathouse players swing with an easygoing, infectious lilt. And when the PHJB pour their catchy exuberance into every tune from Crescent City standards like "Lil Liza Jane" to Duke Ellington's "Mood Indigo," you'll feel just how alive the music is: it's mighty hard to stay in your seat, however plush.

There is, of course, a historical dimension to what the PHJB does— even to their very existence. Watching the bands (there are several lineups traveling under the name) can be a bit like watching one of the dioramas in the American Museum of Natural History come to life and begin enacting, before your startled eyes, the tumbling flow of a time and place long gone. For as the story goes, it was to New Orleans that the rough-hewn cry of the blues flowed down along the Mississippi; there it mingled in a catchy whirlpool with the snappy march beats of the city's countless brass street bands, so much the rage at the last century's close. Warmed by the kiss of the Caribbean sun and sea, that fertile primeval mix stirred into the first movements of what we now call jazz.

Basically, as it evolved in New Orleans, the music took two forms, both of them, then as now, functional. One style, New Orleans jazz, was for church dances, and emphasized ensemble playing; the other, for jitney dances, sported the hot solos characteristic of Dixieland. Neither style has ever been adequately represented on recordings; like Natural History's dioramas, recordings can only snatch frozen moments from a tumult of development and change.

One of the PHJB's virtues is that, over the course of one of their long, exhilarating shows, they do so much more than that. Playing deftly in both styles, moving seamlessly across the vast catalog of standards in each, they breed contagious enthusiasm because they live and breathe the sounds they play, have learned them from the masters rather than studying them in books. Usually Dixieland bands are hampered by their lack of gut feeling; trying to be historical re-creations, they lack the continuing influence of these sounds that remains so obvious in New Orleans. Minus that context, their music shrivels into superficiality, becomes stylized. Europeanized technique too often overshadows or, worse, replaces, the ragged, stomping vitality, the deliberately altered timbres and skewed intonations at the music's roots: the bleary sweet-and-sour trumpet with its climactic shrieks; the molten clarinet with its New Orleans fingerings and chirpy quality; the boozily grumbling trombone, the brightly splayed piano, the thwacky banjo, the slaphappy bass, the rioting drums. (Contrary to popular misconception, tubas and marching drums were commonly used only in street brass bands, not early jazz ensembles.)

Since they were born at nearly the same time as the century, most members of the PHJB have heard and played these sounds from their earliest days—they don't have to re-create them. All of them have, in the traditional New Orleans fashion, learned their instruments by apprenticing themselves to master musicians and absorbing techniques and tunes by watching their mentors perform and by performing with them; this frees them from nostalgia. Simply put, it makes the difference between joyful volatility and studied stiffness.

The PHJB are anything but stiff, belying their ages. Their utter unpredictability includes refusing to prearrange what numbers they'll perform at a given show; they prefer to trust their own moods and their shrewd sense of the audience's reaction when they call tunes onstage. Given their seemingly limitless repertoire, their endless enthusiasm, and the spontaneous outbursts of snake dancing and clap-and-sing-alongs that seem to burst out wherever they play, it's not very surprising that their shows can often stretch on for two or three hours—or more.

Too bad Carnegie Hall has fixed seats.   [1988]

chapter 38

Nature Boy

His instantly recognizable voice attracts adjectives the way Homeric heroes trail epithets: velvety, silken, intimate. But adjectives can't describe the swinging, ingratiating self-confidence laced with tenderness that colors Nat "King" Cole's singing. His baritone/tenor is so airy and elemental, so palpably physical, it invites you in, then surrounds you glowingly, like the lit cave of a magic mountain emanating song from somewhere deep.

February 15, 1990, marked the 25th anniversary of Cole's death—ironically, given his dense voice, of lung cancer. Folks who discovered Cole through the amiably engulfing sound of hits like "Unforgettable,"

"Mona Lisa," and "Ramblin' Rose" pouring out of radios and jukeboxes may not realize that Cole, a brilliant pop singer, became a feted entertainer because he was also a lot more. In fact, Nat "King" Cole's adventurous musical forays form crucial pivots which helped turn and delineate the directions of pre- and postwar sounds.

It all started in California in September 1937. The year before, pianist Cole, then 19, had joined his bassist brother Eddie, who'd toured Europe with famed bandleader Noble Sissle, to cut his first sides (collected on *From the Very Beginning*, MCA). Soon the Earl Hines-influenced keyboardist had enlarged his band to tour with the 1936 revival of Sissle and Eubie Blake's hit musical *Shuffle Along*. *Shuffle* folded when it hit L.A., and the unknown Cole gigged around solo for a while at bargain-basement prices. Then the owner of the Swanee Inn on La Brea suggested he put together a piano-guitar-bass trio.

Forming a small independent group in the heart of the big-band era was near heresy; forming one with that instrumentation was simply unheard-of. But not long after Cole, electric-guitar pioneer Oscar Moore, and bassist Wesley Prince joined forces as King Cole and His Swingsters, soon renamed the King Cole Trio, they began blazing trails that widened to superhighways once their innumerable followers surged into the openings.

Like the best of the big bands, the trio didn't straddle the often thick dividing line between jazz and pop; they just ignored it. Right from their earliest recording dates for radio-station use only (*Nat King Cole and the King Cole Trio*, Savoy Jazz) they began scrambling an idiosyncratic stylistic mix that included yearning ballads and unison-vocal novelty tunes, bouncy swing syncopations threaded with jump-r&b-ish slurs and rests and thickened proto-bebop chord voicings and lines. Infectious and revolutionary, popular with other musicians and jazz fans, the Cole trio (with bassist Johnny Miller) didn't make a real national splash until 1944, when Capitol Records released "Straighten Up and Fly Right" (on *The Best of the Nat King Cole Trio, Volumes 1 and 2*, Capitol).

Cole's Hines-meets-Teddy Wilson piano, not his voice, defined the trio, but although it defined, it didn't dominate or suffocate. The group's engaging beauty comes from their essentially democratic nature on outstanding tracks like "Sweet Lorraine," "Route 66," "Gee Baby, Ain't I Good to You," "It's Only a Paper Moon," and "Body and Soul." Their telepathic attack finds Moore's astonishingly supple, bluesy lyricism curving and skittering around Cole's gently angular, bop-forecasting chords—and vice versa—to weave a seamless mesh. Percussionless, they insinuate and drive, sway and circle beats with arch displacements only an outstanding drummer could imagine.

Thanks to its riveting if deceptively understated musicality, the King Cole Trio became the model for folks like Art Tatum, Oscar Peterson, Red Norvo, and the Modern Jazz Quartet. Not coincidentally, it also predicted cool jazz a decade before Miles Davis cut *The Birth of the Cool*. And just as Cole's fondness for near–imploding chords, jagged spaces, and lyrical lines points toward Thelonious Monk and Bill Evans, Moore's coiled solos shaping alternate melodies presage Wes Montgomery and Jim Hall. Nor was their influence limited to jazz: via the Louis Jordan combos sparked by novelty tunes, Moore's own late '40s group, the Three Blazers, and no less a fan than Ray Charles, whose early sides are distinctly Cole-derived, the King Cole Trio left its thumbprint on r&b as well.

It may seem incomprehensible now, but until 1946's "The Christmas Song," his first recording with a studio orchestra, Cole's voice basically remained just another instrument in the trio. In the group's early days, Cole was hardly an accomplished vocalist; as Moore explained with delicious historical irony in a 1957 *down beat* interview, "I didn't even think of Nat as a singer." The proof is in the string of female-singer auditions the trio held at its start, not to mention the countless (and revolutionary) unison vocals of their first recordings.

But Cole's warm rasp quickly gained both strength and confidence, as even a casual listen to *The Best of the Nat King Cole Trio* demonstrates. (More dedicated types can hunt up *Any Old Time*, Legend, for 1944–45 radio and V-disc sessions, as well as *The Forgotten Years*, Giants of Jazz, which includes 1945 transcriptions of the trio's appearances on Bing Crosby's *Kraft Music Hall*.) Learning from Billie Holiday (as did his only contemporary male vocal rival, Frank Sinatra), Cole avoided extravagant embellishments, opting instead for a combination of elastic rhythms and flattened melodies that approximate a conversation rather than an aria. Perhaps not surprisingly, his genius found its fullest expression in ballads, which first led him to augment the trio with strings, then go on to record with orchestrations by, among others, the same Nelson Riddle who did so much for Sinatra's flagging fortunes. (These, along with Cole's Capitol trio recordings, have been collected in the mammoth 18-CD set, *The Complete Nat King Cole Trio Capitol Recordings.*)

By 1948's chart-topping "Nature Boy," Cole had dropped the trio and become a pop vocalist. His huge following had grown steadily from his first national hit, "Straighten Up and Fly Right"; combined with his popular appearances and recordings with the 1944–46 Jazz at the Philharmonic tours (with Les Paul on guitar), his broad appeal made him one of the first black jazzmen to have a national radio show in 1948–49. By the 1950s he was internationally known, playing the supper club/concert hall circuit and getting film roles, most notably in 1958's *St. Louis Blues*, where he portrayed W. C. Handy. In 1956–57 he became the only African American with his own weekly TV show, which he left in protest because he couldn't sign up a national sponsor despite good ratings.

This is the period captured on three recently reissued CDs. Recorded in 1956, *After Midnight Sessions* (Capitol) is a good compilation that displays Cole's still-solid piano chops. Misleadingly billed as "Nat 'King' Cole and his trio," it actually features a quartet (with Tatum alumnus guitarist John Collins, bassist Charlie Harris, and drummer Lee Young) augmented by four excellent soloists—altoist Willie Smith, trumpeter Harry "Sweets" Edison, trombonist Juan Tizol, and violinist Stuff Smith.

The other two CDs follow the Cole-with-studio-orchestra pattern that, to these ears at least, cloys around his wonderfully direct voice. *Songs for Two in Love (And More)* (Capitol) is, except for a couple of tunes like "Autumn Leaves," a state-of-the-art recipe for wall-of-dreckystrings blandness; *Just One of Those Things (And More)* (Capitol) at least offers—ironically—some grittier big-band charts. Despite their extended CD times, though, neither boasts the sheer-gold value of an older, more straightforward package like *The Best of Nat King Cole* (Capitol), which includes "Mona Lisa," "Sweet Lorraine," "Too Young," "Route 66," and "Ramblin' Rose"—in other words, the tunes you probably know and want to hear.

Cole's career was shot through with odd turns. But it's a sadder historical irony that his most enduring and influential recordings, *The Best of the Nat King Cole Trio, Volumes 1 and 2* and his Decca material (now owned by MCA, some of which is available on *Trio Days*, Charly), remain out of print in the land of his birth 25 years after his death.   [1990]

chapter 39

The Two Oscars

Pick up a typical jazz history, and thumb to the section on the guitar—if you can find one. You'll find a heavy concentration on two names: Django Reinhardt and Charlie Christian.

There are some perfectly valid reasons for that. The gypsy guitarist certainly transmuted the American jazz he'd taken as his model, especially the collaborations of Italian-American guitarist Eddie Lang (Salvatore Massaro) and his violin-toting Philadelphia sidekick Joe Venuti. Cracking Lang's brief arpeggiated solos open into full lines, Reinhardt overcame the dual problems facing the guitar's entry into jazz soloing: what could it do, and how could it do it.

Since this version of history neatens things into clear-cut stages of development marked by personalities, Christian is inevitably the next up. Emerging at the same time as the electric guitar, he harnessed that technology to a new vision of the instrument, one grounded in scalar rather than arpeggiated runs, that took horn lines as its model.

All this is true—as far as it goes. Problem is, it masks the actual bumping and lurching, the false starts and the roads not taken and doubled back into, that is the sloppy, scrambled, crowded road we all follow through time and space. By singling out towering individuals, this view reduces cultural achievements to a banal triumph of individual wills over (usually threatening) circumstances, like a Punch and Judy version of *Macbeth*. Take Django's burned hands, or Christian's TB and early death, as emblems of how this sort of romanticism reduces history to a series of oppositions between blind adversity and a maimed hero.

While there are, of course, such things as geniuses, they're not isolated. Because of his hookup with Benny Goodman, Christian certainly focused attention on the newfound versatility the electric guitar conferred, and equally certainly bequeathed a vocabulary for it, but he was hardly the lone figure on the scene. Les Paul was inventing the solid-body guitar; Mary Lou Osborne and Eddie Durham and Oscar Moore were among the many dabbling in electronics independent of Christian; Christian himself and T-Bone Walker were influencing each other as they richocheted in and out of territory bands.

This sense of time as motion underlines how history, even at its best, is only a series of Muybridgean photos that try to seize it into stillness. And so it follows that the pictures we take in our never-ending efforts to understand our past gain in intelligence and intelligibility from depth of field and shifts of perspective. Hence this attempt at filling in some background to what Reinhardt and Christian actually achieved so brilliantly. Without it, history lapses into a cartoon.

One place to start filling in the recessions of the real is with Argentinian guitarist Oscar Aleman—not exactly a name that rings through the standard histories. Maybe it should, even though in the U.S. the only available recording of Aleman's fret work is the 16-cut *Swing Guitar Legend* (Rambler). This outstanding compilation starts with the late '30s, when Aleman was based, like Django, in Paris, where he worked from 1931 to 1939 primarily as Josephine Baker's musical director; it spans to the mid-'40s, when he'd returned home to avoid Hitler and World War II. Judiciously slicing selections from that range, it offers some tantalizing glimpses of what Aleman could have offered jazz if he hadn't been so overshadowed by Django in his Paris heyday and then mostly stayed in his off-the-beaten-jazz-track homeland for the last 30-odd years of his life.

Even though some of the tunes feature Aleman in the guitar-violin frontline setting that both Django and he adapted from the Lang-Venuti team, even though they both recorded some of the same standards of the period, like "Sweet Georgia Brown," there's no mistaking Aleman's guitar attack for Django's. What superficial resemblances there are fade quickly under scrutiny. They are no more musical twins than their instruments, differ as surely as Django's Maccaferri ax shares only its rough silhouette with Aleman's National resonator metal-bodied guitar.

Aleman's background—orphaned at ten, he became a young street musician in Brazil by learning to play Afro-Brazilian folk tunes on the *cavaquinho*, a four-stringed ukelele—gave him a fondness for Latinate trilling as punctuation for his solos, a trait the gypsy Django shared. Unlike Django, though, Aleman even on his early discs tended to pepper his runs with accidentals, alter the value of what notes he played against the changes to pursue to the melody he heard in his head. Their very different solos on "Sweet Georgia Brown" or "I Got Rhythm" demonstrate how that works. "Russian Lullaby," recorded in 1939 with another guitarist and bassist, shows spectacularly how Aleman was beginning to search out scalar possibilities, played bob-and-weave with the very arpeggios Django would have used—instead of running through them he swerves around them here, skips over them there with a sly grin.

Then there's the way Aleman incorporates that bedrock element of jazz, the blues, into his Latinate style. Django didn't so much draw on the blues for his solos as replace it with the brooding eastern European modalities so natural to his gypsy melancholy. It was a brilliant manuever, and it opened up new dimensions in both his own playing and the playing of his many followers. Aleman, on the other hand, fused the blues into his Afro-Brazilian background with real understanding. "Doin' the New Lowdown" exemplifies how the blues can inform everything from his note choices to the way he bends.

Aleman's outstanding finger-picking technique—something Django's injured hand didn't allow him to explore—is another surprise. Here too, Aleman seems to have combined approaches that seem inimical, even antithetical. On the tunes he recorded solo, he's clearly drawing from the flamenco- and folk-based styles learned in his youth, but he resolves them into an attack uncannily close to the ragtimey Piedmont feel of bluesmen like Blind Blake and Blind Boy Fuller. "Nobody's Sweetheart," for instance, intricately interweaves the syncopated inner voices of each chord over now-rolling, now-double-thumbed bass lines: it sounds eerily like music that somehow traveled down the Mississippi to the Amazon.

Of the cuts on *Swing Guitar Legend*, it is a solo showcase that is arguably the set's masterpiece. Recorded in Copenhagen in 1938, "Whispering" draws its inspiration from Eddie Lang, who used a similar chordal-plus-arpeggios approach to tunes like "A Little Love, a Little Kiss." Overlaid onto that attack for the rubato opening is a heavy dose of flamenco feathering; when the tempo kicks in, Aleman's ragtimey/bossa finger work shreds the melody and harmony into a thousand subtle subdivisions. Shooting throughout are glissando slides that keen in a way clearly meant to evoke Hawaiian guitar—Aleman, in fact, played Hawaiian guitar with a traveling vaudeville troupe before he went to Europe, and like the old bluesmen (who also tended to use resonator guitars for volume) did all kinds of tricks while he played, like picking the guitar behind his head.

Aleman recorded in Argentina steadily in various formats until the late '50s. He then disbanded his group and dropped out of sight, teaching a few students. In the '70s, the Argentine arm of EMI began reissuing some of his early records, and he began touring and recording again, notably with Jorge Anders's orchestra in a Kansas City swing-type setting. In this country, though, he's known only to a tiny cadre of aficionados. Since he passed up the chance in 1933 to leave Josephine Baker and hit the road with Duke Ellington, who admired him greatly and tried to enlist him in his band, he's remained in jazz oblivion. Despite that, he kept up with the music's development in the U.S. In his later years, whenever he was asked who his favorite guitarists were, he would invariably reply, "Charlie Christian and Oscar Moore."

Even a quick listen to Aleman's work would tell you what attracted him to Moore's. As he told Argentinian critic Tomas Mooney, "Oscar Moore played in my way, though we never met." There's a lot of truth to that, although in some ways the two men couldn't have had careers more different.

Oscar Moore achieved celebrity for almost a decade, while he was playing in the famed Nat King Cole trio, that musical incubator. So much jazz and pop went into the threesome's music and came out the other side transformed that it's impossible not to see them as a major nexus in the music's history: from swing to bop and r&b, their simultaneously laid-back and relentlessly driving sound, their ability to rethink old standards and fondness for novelty numbers made them a major musical influence even as it garnered them enormous popularity. That popularity rubbed off on Moore, who swept the honors in beauty contests like the *down beat* readers' poll and the *Metronome* poll from 1945 to 1948. Besides jazz pickers like Barney Kessel, his most avid fans—who illustrate the influential sweep of his melodic touch—included B. B. King (also a devotee of Django's) and Robert Jr. Lockwood, the revampers of postwar electric blues guitar.

It's not surprising they'd hear the blues weeping in Moore's guitar. Born in 1916 in Austin, Texas, Moore was surrounded by it, like those other seminal players T-Bone Walker and Charlie Christian. But where Walker bailed out of the territory and Western swing styles to burrow deep into his Texas blues roots and electrify them, where Christian assiduously adapted horn lines like Lester Young's to create a swing-to-bop soloist's vocabulary for the newly developed electric instrument, Moore accreted a swirl of ideas from his own past to sculpt a unique attack.

He was, for instance, the first guitarist to develop the modern notion of comping. Earlier axmen had bomped on the beat; Freddie Green, for example, became the rock on which the Basie band built its swagger precisely because of his metronomic intensity. That concept shaped the rhythm attack of all swing band guitarists, and Charlie Christian was no exception.

But in the King Cole trio, the dominant sensibility derived from Cole's pianistic heroes like Earl Hines, Teddy Wilson, and Art Tatum—especially Tatum's Impressionistic chordal voicings, his spinning and hovering rhythms. In the trio's percolating crosstalk, those ideas were parsed into the individual player's rhythmic and melodic attacks which wound like genetic strands, a kind of triple helix around a drummerless core. And so Moore's elastic chordal work formed the perfect complement to Cole's piano. Listen to how the opening chorus on "Too Marvelous for Words" (*Best of the Nat King Cole Trio*, Capitol, o.p.) or his counterpointing chords and fills on "Sweet Lorraine" (*Trio Days*, Affinity) predicts what later players like Joe Pass would perfect. That smoothly jagged approach became the standard once bop shook loose the eight-to-the-bar beat dominating swing.

In the afterglow of Charlie Christian's meteoric impact as a soloist, an entire generation of guitarists from Tiny Grimes to Barney Kessel became "Little Charlies." Possibly because he'd already developed his own voice in some of the very same places Christian had, Moore never aped his more famous contemporary even though their vocabularies inevitably overlapped. Two cuts from *Trio Days* illustrate how. On "Gone With the Draft," Moore's fills snake behind the voice like Prez's behind Billie Holiday's, while his solo spot floats totally un-Christian spaces and intervallic leaps. For the blues "That Ain't Right," he does a kind of aerial act with the typical blues-based riffs of the period, tumbling over the expected phrase, the usual interval, at the last minute; his solo is a marvel of economic precision, its punctuating trills (another trait the two Oscars shared) and melodies spun effortlessly, hung gracefully from the occasional jabbing spike.

Some other stylistic points that would both endear him to Aleman and distinguish him from Christian appear in concentrated form during the instrumental on *Trio Days* called "This Side Up." In call-and-response with Cole's piano, Moore slides chords and slurs glisses for a Hawaiian effect; his solo spots bristle with one of his favorite phrase tags, a fierce double-picking clearly meant to evoke c&w mandolin but kin to the Spanish feathering Aleman often used. Where Christian concentrated on the relationship between scales and chords in a proto-bop manner, Moore was more interested in delving into melodies and refashioning them in his own image—which often happened to foreshadow bop's expanded harmonic sense. A prime example is his solo on "Gee Baby, Ain't I Good to You" (*Best of the Nat King Cole Trio*). Sputtering a mandolin-stinger intro that resolves into a chicken-picked bend a Nashville cat could envy, Moore constructs a sensual, ragged, skittering melody that rivals the original; no scalar run-through, no chordal maze-running, it stretches but never loses touch with the tune's harmonic motion.

Unlike Aleman's, a sizable chunk of Moore's discography with the Trio is findable. Besides the two albums already mentioned, there are *Nat King Cole Trio* (Pathe Marconi/EMI), a reissue of part of the out-of-print Capitol collection; *Intimate* (The Classic Series), a decent-sounding dub of a 1940 New Orleans club date that offers Cole set standards like "Paper Moon" and "Sweet Lorraine"; *From the Very Beginning* (MCA), an electronic-stereo reissue by that corporate giant's U.K. arm of half the Decca material they've left in print in their U.S. catalogue, though that homemade version is difficult to find in stores—the Affinity disc picks up the key titles from it; *Body and Soul* (Topline), an annoyingly recorded L.A. gig from the mid-1940s; *The Forgotten Years* (Giants of Jazz), good-sounding live radio dubs from Bing Crosby's *Kraft Music Hall*, among others; and *Any Old Time* (Giants of Jazz), a novelty-heavy compilation of a 1944 *down beat* radio broadcast and 1945 V-discs.

When Moore left the trio in 1947, he rejoined his guitar-toting brother Johnny's r&b trio the Red Blazers for a while; then he put together his own groups, recording a couple of albums of which only *Oscar Moore* (Tampa) remains available. While it's an uneven effort, when it cooks it burns—as it does on that old chestnut "Brother Can You Spare a Dime," for instance. Here Moore hangs notes at the ends of phrases in an almost cantilevered way, as if daring them to fall off the changes. His heartwrenching bluesy bends avoid easy diatonic resolutions, and he shifts periodically to the broken chordal movements that, wrapped exquisitely around the alternative melody he explores, foreshadow the work of Joe Pass and Jim Hall. It alone is worth the price of the album.

By the time he cut it in the '50s, Moore had already slid into oblivion as far as jazz critics and audiences were concerned. Though in the early part of the decade he'd backed ace r&b vocalists like Charles Brown, Joe Turner, and Ivory Joe Hunter, he never attained the studio prominence of a Mickey Baker. By the time he died in 1981, he'd been inactive for over a decade and virtually forgotten, whited out of the typical textbooks' cartoons because his own weird twists didn't fit their simplified plots. Unfortunately but inevitably, their lack of insight and archaically rigid categories have thus been perpetuated as our lack of knowledge.   [1988]

chapter 40

The Gypsy King

Gypsy guitarist Django Reinhardt offers an early modern (read post-phonograph) example of how pop music travels from its native habitat, is heard through alienated ears, and yields a hybrid no one could have foreseen. Introduced to jazz by an avant-artist pal who played him Louis Armstrong records, entranced by the discs of early jazz guitar-violin duos like Eddie Lang and Joe Venuti, Django and his patrician fiddler/co-conspirator Stephane Grappelli took their models and infused them with a jaunty but fiery feel, a lyrical touch of Old World melancholy and knowingness that was consonant with but distinct from the blues underlying the best of early American jazz. In less impressionistic terms, where Lang had hung his pioneering stabs at guitar solos largely around his chordal work, where fellow trailblazer Lonnie Johnson had leaned on blues-derived pentatonics, Django played with brooding eastern European modalities, broke those chords open into arpeggios and ran them into twisty, spidery figures that belied how three fingers of his left hand had been welded together in a gypsy caravan fire.

The results changed the whole nature of the guitar as an instrument; only Charlie Christian, who a few years later would introduce the electric guitar to jazz and with it, the possibility of the guitarist using long, hornlike, scale-based lines, had a similar impact at the time. To put it even further into context: B. B. King credits Django's records with helping to teach him certain techniques, like tremolo and swooping note bends, that younger rock and blues players have been copping from *him* ever since. Other key Django traits were equally seminal. His manic right-hand slashing at the chords his left hand was sliding around the fretboard and his flight-of-the-bumblebee single-string picking filtered into rock via disciple Les Paul and *his* followers like Jeff Beck and Jerry Garcia. His famed use of octaves in the final chorus of "Sweet Georgia Brown" prefigured Wes Montgomery's and, later, Jimi Hendrix's. And so the spiral continues.

Unlike Charlie Christian, Django lived long enough to record in many different contexts with some startlingly diverse results. From his earliest days as a banjo-picking accompanist to his impromptu recording sessions with Coleman Hawkins and Benny Carter to his matching wits with dual violinists Grappelli and Eddie South on appropriated Bach pieces to his playing classic big-band swing with the Benny Carter Orchestra to his wartime use of Hubert Rostaing's clarinet, *Djangologie/ USA* covers most of the ground. Central, of course, are the priceless Quintet of the Hot Club of France recordings from the '30s, where Django and Grappelli duel and dare each other through early jazz standards like "Limehouse Blues" and "Rose Room" and "Body and Soul" and "Honeysuckle Rose" like a couple of ace fighter pilots strafing in spins and loop-de-loops over their earthbound two-guitars-plus-string-bass rhythm section. There isn't anything else quite like it.

Which is why it's a relief that DRG has taken real care with the sound of this collected set of reissues. The balanced restoration of some previously dimmer top and bottom end lends a nicely consistent sonic sheen throughout. Aficionados—and, for better or worse, how many folks who spring for the money this box costs *won't* be?—will be ecstatic to find the detailed discographical and session info on the cuts included as well as a bonus, a booklet crammed with the minutiae of Django's complete discographical output. My only quibble: the labels on one of my discs were reversed, with side one mismarked as side two.

So let's just put it this way: this collection can usher you into the multihued, panoramic world of Django Reinhardt better than any other single source I know of. Once you're in, of course, it's a whole 'nother story. You'll absolutely *have* to have the two Quintet records (*Django Reinhardt & Stephane Grappelly With the Quintet of the Hot Club of France* and *Parisian Swing*) on GNP Crescendo, since none of their wonderful outrageous tracks is duplicated on this set. Then there's the four-volume Everest set that among other things catches postwar Django trying out electric guitar against Rostaing's clarinet and a regular rhythm section. Then there's . . .   [1988]

chapter 41

The Wizard of Waukesha

Lester Polfus—a.k.a. Les Paul—has a lot to answer for in the history of music. He is one of the prime inventors of the electric guitar: Gibson's Les Paul model, pummeled by the heavier players of rock's spectrum like Cream-era Eric Clapton, Jeff Beck, Jimmy Page, and Duane Allman, has snarled its way through countless tunes. He dreamed up technologies that spawned the racks of modern soundshaping equipment filling recording studios and stages, effects like echo and tape delay and phase shifting. He changed the very way music is recorded: in one of the rooms of his spacious Mahwah, New Jersey, home looms the first eight-track recording machine, each track its own huge (by today's standards) separate tube-filled, VU-metered box. From that came modern overdubbing, the process by which instruments and vocals can each be recorded, erased, and redone individually. Using this process (they called it "The New Sound"), he and his then wife Mary Ford sold over ten million records (a phenomenal figure in those pre-Beatles, pre-Michael Jackson days) by 1952. Their single most famous collaboration, a smoothly upbeat version of "How High the Moon" stuffed with guitars and Mary's multiple vocals, alone moved one and a half million copies. Stacked, the number of records they sold would soar 18 miles high.

An impressive pile of facts, but like most facts they only tell part of the story. What they leave out is Les Paul: the sardonic nonstop talker whose trunkful of memories comes spilling out in answer to a question like the clothes from a ridiculously untidy closet once the door's opened; the unquenchable Tom Edison-style tinkerer who can't resist clambering around the low-slung ceiling at the New York jazz spot called Fat Tuesday's to try to fix the air-conditioning system one hot summer night an hour before his set; the birthday boy who'll show up for his party at Area decked out to hold court over a club full of celeb fans.

Yes, the 76-year-old techno wizard—whose bright, darting eyes, curled-lip grin, gaminish face, and ready, barbed wit belie his age when he takes the stage every Monday night at Fat Tuesday's—has more than made his historical mark. And if he's earned his billing as a "Living Legend" from his guitar playing and showmanship as well as his inventor's prodigality, he's not at all shy about taking full credit. "Robert Moog always says to me, 'Les, if it wasn't for you there wouldn't *be* a synthesizer, because no one else around was doing it,'" he asserts of one of his many techno offspring with his typical combination of ego and blunt candor. Why shouldn't he claim paternity, when his audiences are so frequently sprinkled with stardust? Musicians like Beck and Page, Paul Shaffer and Al DiMeola and Stanley Jordan drop by to pay tribute to and even climb onstage with the man they acknowledge as the Father of It All.

It's a long way from Waukesha, Wisconsin, where he was born in 1916, to the radio, recording, and television success that has made Less Paul a household name, but he started chasing his wide-ranging goals very early on. At the tender age of nine, he was already playing harmonica and building crystal radios; what came over the airwaves first was someone playing guitar, which he—as impulsive then as now—immediately decided to learn. Like most players of that time, his six-string came from Sears, Roebuck, and once he learned a handful of basic chords he added voice and harmonica (jury-rigging a rack from a coat hanger), dubbed himself Rhubarb Red, and began gigging at Lions Clubs, PTA meetings, and the like, playing tunes he picked up from hillbilly discs by the Skillet Lickers and the Gully Jumpers.

Not long after, he found an Eddie Lang 78. "That's what got me interested in jazz," he says. Lang's arpeggiated runs were among the first recorded single-string guitar solos, and influenced key guitarists like Django Reinhardt, another Paul idol. By age 13, he'd built a mini–radio station and a primitive recording machine, and also improvised his first electric guitar. "I ripped the back off my Sears and stuck the pickup on an old phonograph arm through the soundhole, then I turned the record player on so the guitar sound would feed through its little speaker," he explains almost brusquely, as if that bit of technical legerdemain were self-evident to everybody in 1930.

Soon the precocious picker hit the tour circuit with a western band, then formed a successful duo called Sunny Joe and Rhubarb Red, which not only toured the Midwest but played over the radio waves as well. They wound up in Chicago, where, when they broke up in 1933, Paul began a schizophrenic, if successful, career as a DJ and recording artist. Mornings found him on one station as country musician Rhubarb Red, and using that moniker he cut a few hits for Sears and Montgomery Ward. Afternoons he'd become Les Paul and front a jazz combo on another station or accompany "race" artists on recordings.

By 1936 he killed off Rhubarb Red, because he'd started to focus on jamming around Chicago with heavy jazz hitters like pianist Art Tatum and trumpeter Roy Eldridge. A trio he'd formed with Chet Atkins's older half-brother Jim bluffed their way into accompanying Fred Waring and His Pennsylvanians, whose five-days-a-week national broadcast over NBC's radio network ran from 1937 to 1940, and featured Paul on still rare electric guitar. "I used to get more mail than Fred did, and boy, did that make him mad," he grins.

Following a stint as a radio-station musical director and with a touring big band, Paul headed to Los Angeles, where in 1943 he began backing stars like Bing Crosby, Rudy Vallee, the Andrews Sisters, Dinah Shore, and even comedians like Burns and Allen and Jack Benny. Using yet another pseudonym, he also cut an outstanding album called *Jazz at the Philharmonic* (Verve) with a piano player credited as Shorty Nadine—he was actually Nat King Cole.

It was his pal Crosby who urged the ever tinkering Paul to put together the multitrack recording studio he felt he could fashion out of then existing technology. From wax discs and multiple turntables, Paul devised a primitive overdubbing system. After recording on one disc, he'd play it back and record it onto another disc while he added a second guitar line, then repeat the process until he had the dense, one-man-band sound he wanted. With the release of hits like "Lover" and "Brazil" in 1948, the Les Paul sound was unveiled. "It took over 500 wax discs, and an awful lot of time and painstaking—I mean painstaking—care to get the synchronization just right on each of those," he recalls. "If you made even one mistake, it was basically forget the whole thing, and all the way back to disc number one."

The hits launched him into a big-league success that barely missed turning into a major tragedy. In the winter of 1948, Paul was en route from his New Jersey home to a New York gig during a storm when the car he was driving skidded on an icy bridge and plunged 50 feet down into a snowbank. There he lay for eight hours, until help arrived. When he finally got to the hospital, his extensive injuries were cataloged: smashed nose, broken collarbone, six broken ribs, cracked vertebra, pelvis split from back to front, and right elbow joint knocked clean off. In those more primitive days of medical technology, the options about joints in that kind of condition boiled down to amputation. Fortunately for music history, the doctor in the emergency room was a Les Paul fan, and devised a Les Paul-like way around ending Paul's career. He fashioned a metal plate that would hold the guitarist's arm together, but would fix it at nearly a right angle; at least, the pair reasoned, Paul could continue to play. With seven screws holding the plate in place, and a cast that stayed on for one and a half years, the invention worked, though for a long time its beneficiary could use only his thumb to pick while he recorded. In fact, to this day Paul's right arm is welded into a permanent picking position.

By the early 1950s Paul was back in the big time, thanks to the magic of television and his professional and personal partnership with an ex-Gene Autry protégée named Mary Ford (née Colleen Summers). That was partly due to his continuing technological breakthroughs. In addition to pioneering (simultaneously with Leo Fender) the notion of a solid-body electric guitar (as opposed to the basically amplified-acoustic type used by other early electric guitarists like Charlie Christian), he'd transferred his interest in multitrack disc recording to the medium of tape. Working with Ampex, the huge tape and machine manufacturer, Paul designed what would become the standard sound-on-sound feature still found on home tape decks today.

"I just had Ampex drill mounting holes for a fourth head in front of the erase head of a recorder," he says in his matter-of-fact way. "I didn't explain to them why I wanted it." He wanted it to put in a second playback head. "That way," he explains, "things were a lot easier than with the disc-to-disc method. I could record a track, rewind the tape, and play it back so the pickup (second playback) head would read the signal before it passed through the erase head. I'd hear it through headphones and play a second track that would be recorded in synch with it—voila, overdubbing." The frenetically paced classic, "How High the Moon," jammed to near bursting with twining guitars and silky-smooth vocals by Mary, was one of the first products of this technological revolution. By the time the sweetly mournful "Vaya Con Dios" topped the national charts in mid-1953, the couple had arrived as full-fledged stars.

Their marriage and business partnership yielded commercial endorsements, a glut of guest TV shots, and finally their own *Les Paul and Mary Ford at Home* show, which ran seven years. Mary singing at the kitchen sink while Les tinkered and played in his workshop became images (and sounds) impressed on the retinas and subconscious of an entire generation. And of course the hits kept coming through the '50s. But by 1963, the couple had had it, and divorced a year later.

It hit Paul hard, and he put down his guitar for a decade, not even playing at home. In '74 some friends (Chet Atkins among them—their album *Chester and Lester* on RCA is a must-have) prevailed on him to play and record again, which he did for about five years, then quit again. A year later he'd sunk to a physical and mental low, and found himself in the hospital yet again—he'd already had four ear operations because someone accidentally hit him. "It seemed like if I counted up all the years from 1940 to 1980 that I spent in the hospital it would add up to half that time," he says, shaking his head. This time, though, he was facing coronary bypass surgery.

Ironically, his recovery from that drastic 1980 operation combined with the long-term after-effects of his 1948 accident to bring Paul to his now celebrated gig at Fat Tuesday's over nine years ago.

> By 1983 I had thought about playing again, but I had a very serious problem. I have very bad arthritis from that car crash, so it started to really take away my fingers. I didn't mind that so much until I got to thinking about the thing I like to do best, which is play, and that was the one thing that was being taken away. I now have two fingers on my

left hand that are useless, and three fingers on my right. Seeing I was in a mess, the doctor said to me I should exercise and keep what mobility I had left. So I figured the best thing to do would be to play the guitar. It worked. The arthritis got me in here, but what keeps me here is playing for the people. When I see a nice look on someone's face, if I'm making them happy, that means an awful lot more to me than arthritis.

The proof is in the full house at Fat Tuesday's virtually every Monday night since he's started there. In spite of the Hollywood happy-ending quality of his life, Paul is no jazzy Pollyanna: his onstage shtick combines one-liners, occasional stinging put-downs of members of both the audience and his trio in the Don Rickles vein, and a free-floating willingness to stop any song at any time and shift gears into some other tune—his backing band has stay loose and ready, because they can never tell when he might jump from "C Jam Blues" to "How High the Moon." While his disabilities have inevitably taken a toll, his picking still high-steps deftly and even, at times, curlicues his characteristic Django Reinhardt-style phrases to make fun of itself in an impish way. From the looks on the audience's faces, it's clear that after all these years Les Paul still knows how to make them happy.   [1989]

chapter 42

A *Box of Mr. Overdub*

The first time I met now-76-year-old Lester Polfus—a.k.a. Rhubarb Red, a.k.a. Les Paul—was during the summer of 1984. The air-conditioning at Fat Tuesday's, where he'd begun playing Monday nights, was broken, and so this particular legend was crawling around the ductwork an hour before his set—much to the club owner's chagrin—yelling, "Don't call the repairman, I can fix it."

To me, that scene encapsulated Paul: the big but offhand ego, the insatiable curiosity, the indefatigable will. Those qualities help explain why he became the Thomas Edison of the electric guitar, soundshaping gizmos, and modern recording. *Guitar World* readers know he pretty much invented the solid-body guitar. His recordings, whether instrumentals or featuring the vocals of his then wife Mary Ford, created weird and ornery soundscapes stuffed with overdubs. In his agile hands, multiple guitars sped up like Martian mandolins or slowed to a bottom crawl, seesawed and leapfrogged and kicked and twirled in tightly choreographed patterns across trills and arpeggios, and created a sense of textured depth that's often orchestral. Meshing via another of his loopy inventions, multitrack recording, those textures wove a radically new notion of what a pop record could sound like, how it could communicate.

Paul himself, a garrulous man with a biting and sarcastic wit, avoids anything even remotely "highbrow" like the plague. So he wouldn't think of it this way, but he brought into mainstream American pop some of the sonic concepts being explored by contemporary vanguardists like Harry Partch and John Cage. On the other hand, he'd absorbed the easygoing gypsy melancholy and ingratiating, swinging whimsy of his idol Django Reinhardt: the graceful glissandos, the jagged arpeggiated runs, the sudden flashes of musical humor. His hit records, his work on radio and TV, his touring with the likes of Bing Crosby and Nat King Cole all marked him as a key, if somewhat eccentric, player on the field of music history. It's no coincidence that he influenced virtually every important rock guitarist who came in his wake, including Jeff Beck and Jimmy Page (who, when they're in town, usually beat it down to Fat Tuesday's to catch their hero), Jimi Hendrix, Jerry Garcia, Richard Thompson, Billy Zoom, Robert Quine, Adrian Belew, and Bill Frisell. Without Les Paul, the noises that made these guys famous, the expansive sense of soundscape that's basic to their music, wouldn't exist.

Lately there's been an avalanche of boxed sets. The world could easily live without many of them. But *Les Paul: The Legend and the Legacy* (Capitol) makes a valuable contribution to understanding American pop culture since World War II—and is a helluva lot of fun besides. A four-CD set boasting over 100 cuts that have been remixed under the seal of Paul's approval, its first three discs follow the chronology of Paul's career, solo and with Ford. Filling out each disc are segments of his early '50s radio show with Ford, replete with wretchedly funny puns and silly gags. The first has commercials for Robert Hall clothing stores and

Rheingold beer—both defunct. At the time, they must have sounded like they'd been broadcast from a galaxy far, far away. (Fair warning: the ads, shows, and instrumentals like "Goofus," "Brazil," and "Jingle Bells" are among my favorite cuts.) Rarities like his first stereo recordings are sprinkled throughout. The fourth disc, loaded with 34 out-takes and previously unreleased tracks, and the detailed booklet, with in-depth bio and Paul's track-by-track commentary, ices the cake. Since the guitar great's later work for Columbia and RCA pales next to these Capitol sides, this box isn't missing much.

It's a giddy mix. The Wizard of Waukesha's oddball sonic sensibilities altered most tunes he touched, regardless of their quality. His zany antics reached a mass audience—something that would probably be much harder to do now. Of course, he wrapped many of his experiments in novelty appeal and pure schlock. There's sappy schlock like "Vaya Con Dios" and "In the Good Old Summertime." There's flat-footed schlock like "St. Louis Blues" and "Alabamy Bound" and "Send Me Some Money," where Mary Ford's pleasant vocals betray her acute lack of bluesy and rhythmic subtlety. That strategy eventually held Paul captive: listening to these CDs consecutively can make a lot of the ideas seem more formulaic than they were. But then again, most tracks redeem themselves: the original one-man guitar army almost always deploys himself in some bent way no one else could have conceived of. With its authoritative sweep and translucent sound, *Les Paul: The Legend and the Legacy* is a fitting monument to a complex giant of American music.   [1992]

chapter 43

Collier's Ellington Follies

What's strangely off-kilter about James Lincoln Collier's new book, *Duke Ellington*, is that it attempts muckraking without either new information or a fresh critical point of view. The author of a fairly well-received book on Louis Armstrong, Collier has this time out mixed a rather dated and puzzling brew—part formal analysis and part biography, it is structured around a number of fuzzy and outmoded critical concepts. Among them are an oversimplified personality analysis of Ellington and a persistent misreading of what Collier calls "symphonic jazz" as opposed to what he calls "jazz" or "commercial music." Collier objects to symphonic jazz of the Paul Whiteman/Gershwin variety for what he considers its pretentious use of European classical forms. Strangely, he groups Ellington's longer and more ambitious works under that rubric, and then attacks them for not being formally structured along the lines of European models Ellington never used.

On the muckraking front, Collier's claim that Ellington didn't really write many, if any, of the tunes his fame rests on, but instead lifted and adapted themes from his leading soloists, is hardly news. No one who knows anything about the Ellington band is going to be surprised that this or that melody originated on the bandstand or at a jam session or in a recording studio with Johnny Hodges or Cootie Williams or "Tricky Sam" Nanton or Juan Tizol. If Ellington's genius allowed him to recognize the seeds of a good number in a horn line, and then enabled him to polish and set it in one of his dense and inventive arrangements, that just comfirms what has often been said about his music: the orchestra was his instrument, and he played it with an attentive dexterity few others have equaled. But even beyond that, trying to attribute a specific melody line or fragment, in whatever context, seems about as useful as trying to nail Jello to a wall.

Nor is it startling or even useful to explain Duke's borrowings thus:

Ellington carved his creations not so much with raw talent, as did the Armstrongs and Charlie Parkers, but with the chisel of his character. Who Duke Ellington was is critical to the work he produced. If he had been different in this way or that, his work would have been different and might not even have existed.

Can't the same be said of Armstrong and Bird? Were they too "raw" to have characters? Or to reverse the question: What is raw talent, and how can it be spoken of as separate from the individual who possesses it? This dilemma leaves Collier gasping for air at the book's conclusion, when he has to somehow justify the tome's existence by smudging over most of the issues he's raised, like "originality" and "character." But by that time he's into the muck way over his head.

For starters, according to Collier, "character" in Ellington's case was the product of a turn-of-the-century black middle class that shared its values and assumptions with its white counterpart:

> Of particular importance was the presence in this Victorian culture
> of a genteel interest in the arts. The "best" art—the music of the
> "Three B's," the painting of the academic formalists, Greek statuary,
> the plays of Shakespeare, and the novels of Scott—was thought to
> be "uplifting" and to turn the mind to higher things and away from
> depravity and debauchery. Art, and especially good music, had moral
> connotations to the Victorians.

This may well be true; it's certainly clichéd. But, aside from making vague gestures toward the *Zeitgeist* and reciting a short string of family anecdotes drawn from Ellington's autobiography, *Music Is My Mistress*, Collier doesn't really show this worn Victorian ideology at work on the mind of the young man. Since Collier also disparages (rightfully) the truthfulness of that autobiography at other points in his book, his use of it to document his central thesis does seem curiously inconsistent.

Though Collier's sense of character is crude, even lazy, his energy for repetition never seems to flag, no matter how many times he flogs a point. Take as an instance a quote from record producer Irving Townsend, who worked with Ellington during Duke's later years, about *The Queen's Suite*, which Duke composed after being introduced to Queen Elizabeth. In his discussion of the piece, we find a neat microcosmic wrap of what, in Collier's eyes, passes for a critical methodology:

The meeting [between the queen and Ellington] meant a great deal to him. Ellington had always had a weakness for both celebrated people and women, and who could be more celebrated than a queen? He thereupon created this six-part suite. . . . Irving Townsend . . . said, "Ellington went about the composition of 'The Queen's Suite' with greater concentration than he displayed for any other music with which I was associated."

The Townsend quote appears more than once in Collier's book. On its face the remark seems a neutral, or even positive, description of Duke's attitude toward this suite. Not in Collier's eager hands, however. Townsend's passing observation becomes a link in Collier's case against the longer, ambitious works that claimed Ellington's attention later in life, and is moreover evidence of Collier's point that those works owe their existence to the master's being a celeb groupie.

According to Collier, Ellington's crucial character flaw was compounded from his middle-class Victorian snobbishness and his innate laziness, which meant, for instance, that he rarely wrote without a deadline. (Neither do any writers I know.) If Duke's snobbishness led him to what Collier revealingly describes as a "weakness for what he considered 'serious' music," then his lack of formal study and laziness meant that he couldn't organize and structure that art to accord with Collier's quaint formalist canons. As he notes in his dissection of *Reminiscing in Tempo*, one of Ellington's earliest extended pieces:

Ellington, of course, would have said that it did not matter whether the piece fit anybody's definition of jazz, and quite rightly so. But this does force the critic to view it against other than jazz criteria. Jazz pieces are frequently based on quite routine forms: architecture is not an important concern of most jazz musicians. But more formal music is exactly that, and this piece never goes anywhere, but simply meanders hither and thither, almost entirely without direction.

The issues glossed over by that half-paragraph are so numerous: What is jazz, exactly? Why are the "other criteria" available to the listener limited, in Collier's view, to western European classical models? If architecture is not a concern of most jazz musicians, how can they write memorable tunes, build widely emulated arrangements, venture successfully into creating longer forms or even craft improvised solos? In short, the antithesis proposed by Collier, and the one on which his book turns, is the old, discredited one whose culturally and racially imperial-ist rationale takes many forms: high versus low art, trained versus intu-itive artists, and so on. So by those dim lights, if Duke Ellington aban-doned what he did really well, like cobble together unusually voiced three-minute jazzy tunes from other people's input, for things he didn't understand, like large-scale works beyond both his incredibly limited formal training and his slapdash working methods, how could the result be anything but dismal?

The hoary dichotomies and dishonored hierarchies that structure Collier's thinking make his repetitive dismissals of one longer Ellington work after another almost laughable. If they weren't all successful musically—and they weren't, as the majority of critics have long agreed—their failings might be more instructively considered in the context of their persistent influence over other musicians. Ellington's method of crafting parts for individual voices in his band, his juxtaposi-tions of unusual musical ideas and formats, and his constant attempts to extend the ghetto-ized boundaries of the music its creators never named are a major part of his musical legacy, no matter how much Collier may pretend otherwise.

As it is, Collier's pretense of muckraking leads him to twist history, logic, and music way out of shape. Thus, Ellington's putative lack of keyboard skills exemplifies both his laziness and his haphazard approach to his music; his manipulative personality explains how he held together the band he was ripping off; his alleged ignorance of work songs and church hymns as a child is supposed to belie his frequent assertion that he was composing Negro music, not jazz, in his longer works. And so, despite its occasional insights, *Duke Ellington* adds little but distortion to our understanding of one of the 20th century's outstanding composers and his enormously rich and satisfying work. [1987]

chapter 44

Epitaph

Charles Mingus had musical ambitions and abilities as prodigious and far-reaching as his other appetites. An avid student of European composers like Debussy and Bartók, he also saw himself inheriting the mantle of an illustrious lineage that includes Jelly Roll Morton and Duke Ellington.

One central concern for those giants was the relationship between composition and improvisation, the dialectical motor that powers jazz. How to reconcile the more expansive structures made possible by a big band with individual soloing became a subject Mingus investigated as well. His updated vision opened the territory for later investigators like Muhal Richard Abrams, John Carter, Henry Threadgill, David Murray, and Marty Ehrlich.

Epitaph is one of Mingus's major statements on the matter. Hefting a score 500 pages (and 4000 measures) long for a 30-piece orchestra, the ambitious piece was only rediscovered in 1985, by the composer's widow Sue Graham Mingus and musicologist Andrew Homzy. Homzy pasted the yellowing fragments together, in some cases bar number by bar number; then critic-composer-musicologist Gunther Schuller, a long-time friend and professional associate of Mingus's, adapted the results.

So in June 1989, nearly 30 years after it was written and a decade after its composer's death, *Epitaph* debuted to a sold-out Alice Tully Hall. (In November 1962, there was a famous abortive attempt to play and record it at Town Hall, but due to time constraints and poor planning the performance was a fiasco and the United Artists album that resulted was mangled.) Several months later, the two-CD *Epitaph* (Columbia), a recording of the Lincoln Center set, was released, with a 44-page booklet of exhaustively detailed notes by Homzy and Schuller.

Conducted by Schuller, the orchestra boasts all-stars like trumpeters Randy Brecker and Wynton Marsalis, altoists Bobby Watson and John Handy, tenorman George Adams, trombonist Britt Woodman, and pianists Sir Roland Hanna and John Hicks. They tear into the opus's 18 sections with an appropriately fierce vengeance—although had Mingus been at Lincoln Center, in his ever restless way he might well have infuriated the participants (and goosed the proceedings) into an even feistier mode.

The music demands every bit of the players' considerable drive and talent. It's difficult, at times almost inchoate, partly because of *Epitaph*'s sheer magnitude and many shifts. But it's also rewarding: its riotous gargantuan sweep scrambles gutbucket blues and the sanctified church, Morton and Ellington and Monk, Stravinsky and Bartók and Tin Pan Alley.

In classic Mingus fashion, perspectives multiply as styles careen across *Epitaph*'s sprawl. From ominously mournful ballads to grungy uptempo stomps to classically organized set pieces, the orchestra crackles with dense, chameleonic firepower. Sometimes the ensemble work, which is usually taut, hovers with the lush and gradually unfurling harmonies that mark Mingus's introspective side. At other times the band explodes into strutting and swelling, the edge-of-cacophony exuberance that's also quintessential Mingus. Solos, both scored and improvised, sometimes take centerstage and sometimes, in varying numbers, just flicker at the ensemble's edges. Though the work's overarching structure remains hazy, even a casual listener has to be staggered by the music's reach and power. If nothing else, *Epitaph* reaches from beyond the grave to confirm Mingus's power and continue his standard operating procedure—shaking his audiences up. [1991]

bar

Mingus's Sancho Panza

"I topped 'em off last year, but look at the way they're growing back. I'm gonna have to do it again," says Jimmy Knepper. His Staten Island kitchen, like much of the charming little hilltop house he shares with wife Maxine, is under reconstruction. Cabinets sit in the middle of the floor for refinishing. The basement bathroom the Kneppers paid $3000 to have put in isn't done. The path down to the yard needs fixing. The $1500 decorative gates got clamped onto the ground-floor windows after the fourth robbery—the perps got the family silver, the stereo, odds and ends. But in the big yard that slopes dramatically away from the kitchen tower the firs he's talking about. Trimmed, they give Knepper a clear bead from the Washington Bridge almost to the Verrazano. It's breathtaking, and in his understated way he wants it right.

Knepper likes straightforward structure, but he's spent his life within irony. Born in Los Angeles on November 22, 1927, he's marked by his 1957–61 association with Charles Mingus. It wasn't exactly a meeting of the minds. Knepper runs wry variations on phrases like,

> In those days, where could somebody who wanted to play jazz trombone work? The regular bands had trumpet and tenor. To have the opportunity to play jazz, I used to think. "I'm gonna be stuck with this guy for the rest of my life." Even after he's dead I'm stuck with him. The publicity says, "Jimmy Knepper is probably best-known for his work with Charlie Mingus," and it's true. I'm thankful that when I'm eighty years old, if I can still put the horn together, I'll be able to work. It won't be because of my ability; it's because of that recognition factor. And that I owe to Mingus.

Dead on: Knepper made his name with his skin-crawling blues on "Devil Woman," his exuberant lyricism on "The Clown," his pungent call-to-arms on "Haitian Fight Song," his unmistakable voice on a series of albums—*Mingus Ah Um* (Columbia), *Blues & Roots* (Atlantic), and *Oh Yeah* (Atlantic). But the relationship between Knepper, the devout bebopper whom Whitney Balliett has called "the first original trombonist in the modern idiom since J. J. Johnson," and Mingus, the Rabelaisian who swallowed musical viewpoints, feels like the love-hate misprision between Sancho Panza and Don Quixote. To Knepper, Mingus's sprawling legacy is disorganized clutter:

> Mingus's music used to depress me. In fact, it still does. A lot of his tunes I didn't really like; a few I did. A lot of them are illly put together. If Mingus had a snatch of melody and got stuck he'd just put it away. Years later he'd resurrect it, doodle another few bars, and put them together. That's why a lot of his tunes aren't compositionally together.

The instrument that put Knepper's name on the jazz map via Mingus wasn't his choice either. The six-year-old had an alto handed to him at Page Military Academy; he quickly switched to baritone for the marching band. Three years later, his mother decided on trombone: "She wanted something I could play in the marching band and the orchestra." Which the non-Catholic youngster did, through his years in Catholic elementary and high schools. Soon he was playing stock charts with local and touring bands, and joined the union at 15.

He heard swing in theaters and on radio. "But," he says, "I was always kinda disappointed in the trombones. In Basie's band, Lester Young and Harry Edison and Buck Clayton seemed to really dig into the stuff, where—well, it was obvious Dicky Wells could play, but he seemed to treat it like a joke." Knepper hums a mechanical line. "But then Bird came along and turned everybody around." Including a tenor player Knepper met as third trumpeter in the Charlie Cascallas band. His name was Benedetti.

Dean Benedetti taught Knepper standards and how to build alternate chords off piano charts; in 1945, they formed a band with tenor, alto, and trombone. Bird, just out of Camarillo, was at the Hi-De-Ho in 1947 with Howard McGhee, and knocked the duo out even more than his discs. Benedetti, living in Knepper's mother's house, got a disc-cutting machine to capture Bird live—the basis for *The Complete Dean Benedetti Recordings of Charlie Parker* (Mosaic Records). The pair went to the Benedetti family's house outside Reno to transcribe and study Bird's solo flights.

Why Bird?

He was very fluent; it was like he was speaking through his horn. He articulated every note. The saxophone is one of those instruments where you can play a note, then lift your finger, and another note comes out. That's responsible for a lot of saxophonists' technique: they don't articulate hardly at all, just move their fingers like lightning. But brass instruments, especially the trombone, should, in my view, articulate everything. With the trombone, you're playing off a partial harmonic series, so smears are part of the instrument. Knowing that you don't have to articulate everything is a trap trombone players fall into unconsciously.

In early 1948, Knepper and Benedetti, touring with different bands, got stranded in Chicago. There they duped live recordings by other Bird fanatics. Knepper says that's what's behind stories that Benedetti tailed Bird:

Practically everything Ross Russell says about Dean in *Bird Lives!* isn't true. Dean never followed Bird around the country. He never sold any pot. He was a street hustler but not for dope. He'd sell watches that didn't keep time, shavers that didn't shave, stuff like that. The boxes looked great, though. And Russell has Dean as a pimp in New York in 1943–44 when he was in jail, or in Tommy Reynolds's band, or in L.A.

Mingus came into Knepper's life when Benedetti hired him for a San Pedro one-nighter. "All I remember is that he scowled at us all night. Years later, he told me that was the first white band he'd ever played with, and we were all enthused about Charlie Parker. He'd heard of Bird but hadn't paid much attention," says Knepper. Aside from a bop date and an early '50s big-band demo session ("It was Mingus's music, but it was all screwed up"), that was it until 1957.

In late 1956, Knepper moved to New York and joined Claude Thornhill's band, which toured Army and Air Force bases in Europe and North Africa over the holidays. Meanwhile, Willie Dennis called. "He left word he was leaving Mingus's band, and Mingus needed a trombone player," Knepper drawls. "But before I could call him Mingus called me."

Bar by bar, Mingus taught them tunes by playing piano or bass or singing:

I didn't really dig it. It was time-consuming. But Mingus had a prejudice against writing things down, because he'd try to be accurate, and it's almost impossible to read something written down like that with the intended feeling.

Mingus came on like he was as black as the ace of spades, but from what he told me when he was growing up in Watts he didn't fit in at all. Watts was a mixed community, but he wasn't white, he wasn't black, he wasn't Indian, he wasn't Mexican, he wasn't Oriental. He was all by himself. That influenced his perspective on life. Also, it was the Depression when he was a youngster, but his father worked the whole time. Mingus was a rich kid. He always had milk. His family indulged him. He was Charles. I was one of the few people that *liked* him. Dannie Richmond wouldn't even deliver a eulogy for him. To the day he died Mingus gave Dannie a hard time and threatened to fire him. And they worked together for a quarter of a century.

Mingus boiled over at Knepper just before the infamous 1962 Town Hall concert, for which he'd hired Knepper as head copyist a few weeks earlier. (Like most jazzers, Knepper upped his meager income—his 1957 worksheets total some $2000, most of it from Mingus record dates—by doing everything from pit-band work, when he could get it, to playing parades and copying.) "Let me talk about it," Knepper says, "because a lot of the stories aren't true."

Knepper started copying nightly, and soon caught up to Mingus, who'd write a few bars (in concert) just to stay ahead: "It was badly orchestrated. I'd say, 'Mingus, the tenor saxophone cannot play a low G; it's out of his range.' 'Oh, put it up high.' It was surprising: he grew up around horns, yet he couldn't write characteristic parts for them."

As the date closed in, Mingus hired arrangers like Gene Roland:

Mingus gave him a score sheet with a melody line and said, "Expand this into a composition." On *Epitaph*, Mingus gets credit for that piece. He also gets credit for "Moods in Mambo," which had about nine arrangers. I studied that score, and it wasn't Mingus. But for *Epitaph*, all the scores were lumped together and bars numbered as if it was a complete piece. It has more to do with Gunther Schuller than Mingus.

When the last charts arrived at midnight of concert eve, Knepper dropped them at a copying service and figured his job was done. But Mingus called him over the next afternoon:

He said, "I want you to write some background figures for soloists." I said, "Mingus, this is your music. You should write it." At that he said, "You don't want to help me, you white motherfucker, you white faggot," and he hit me. It didn't hurt or bleed or anything. But my front teeth were capped, and he broke off the cap on one. I felt all this gravel in my mouth, so I figured I'd better fall down so he wouldn't try to hit me again. Then I got up and walked off while he cursed at me.

Knepper delivered his copying to the rehearsal, then pressed charges. Mingus was convicted of criminal assault and put on probation; Knepper filed a civil suit that never came to court. Then Mingus apparently tried to set Knepper up by mailing him a few dollars' worth of heroin and tipping the feds the night before it arrived special delivery. He also made threatening calls to Knepper's family.

And the dental fallout?

I lost about an octave, maybe, of range. More importantly, I'd reached a plateau where all I had to do was think of what I wanted to play and it came out. After Town Hall, I had to push everything out. When I play fast, things get kinda garbled. I had to get this special stainless steel apparatus for that one tooth that—hook-hook-hook-hook—needed four teeth to support it. I played like that for years. Now I've had them all pulled, and I've been getting used to my new teeth—for four years.

In 1960, Knepper worked with Gil Evans during a six-week gig at the Village Gate rehearsing what became *Out of the Cool* (Impulse MCA). Here Knepper copied and transposed Evans's sketches. He also inadvertently got the lead for "Where Flamingos Fly," which helped nail his rep. Evans intended it as a Keg Johnson solo, but Johnson didn't deliver so he had Knepper overdub it. Melancholy but spiky, it showcases the smearless legato, the rounded tone, the precise, unpretentious lyricism.

Like most jazz journeymen, Knepper cut a mere handful of his own albums. The tunes are usually standards, either straight or reworked. His 1957 debut as a leader, a four-song EP on Mingus's Debut label, went unreleased (except in Denmark) until the recent *Charles Mingus: The Complete Debut Recordings*. "Cunningbird," which he later re-recorded, boasts a stunning, tautly voiced opening based on Benedetti's intro to "You Go to My Head." "I've changed it considerably," he explains,

to make it more exotic. I put it in 5/4, for instance. The tune came out 9/8, like a blues in waltz time. That's why the little rhythm play—

to set it up. Mingus screwed up that bass part every take we did. And there was nothing hard about it. Finally I gave up, blew my parts, and came in the next day and overdubbed Mingus's part.

None of his discs is revolutionary, but all offer gems. Take the up-tempo title track on *Idol of the Flies* (Bethlehem BCP-6031). After a deftly harmonized, boppish head, Knepper's expansively melodic solo weaves registers with seamless speed. Or the moody ballad "Languid" on *Cunningbird* (SteepleChase SCS-1061), where, damaged mouth and all, he nears his description of Bird's vocalic playing. Or the delightfully limber reading of "My Old Flame" on *Jimmy Knepper in L.A.* (Inner City IC 6047). (All are out-of-print.)

We're discussing Knepper's recordings in his music room. It's dark now, but he doesn't turn on the lights, just keeps talking. Hearing himself on a Tony Scott record taught him how he approaches solos: "I start with some motif, then imitate that motif, then imitate the imitation to lead into something else. That comes from listening to classical composers, where the repeats hold it together." Of producer Ed Michel's line—"Jimmy Knepper never said the same thing the same way twice"—he grins, "It's 'cause I can't remember." That deadpan irony shapes his best playing. So it's no surprise when he says, "I love the trombone because it's a utility instrument that can blend in with anything—including the buzzsaw." [1991]

chapter 46

Rahsaan to the Moon

If Rahsaan Roland Kirk hadn't existed, somebody—maybe Charles Mingus—would've had to invent him. As it is, he invented himself. Not coincidentally, he invented a couple of instruments—the mandello, which he adapted from the B-flat soprano sax, and the stritch, from the E-flat alto; resurrected the Dixieland notion of ensemble improvising; brought circular breathing into jazz; took the vaudeville stunt of playing multiple horns and made it into a musical statement; and ignored labels like Dixieland and bebop and free by playing right across them. A trickster who often cloaked his mind-bending insights within jokes, which brought him some derisory reactions from solemner types, Kirk drew more out of music history—and I don't mean just jazz history— than most other folks hear, let alone use.

The Complete Mercury Recordings of Roland Kirk (Mercury/Poly-gram) is a ten-CD compilation (plus a bonus CD of "A Stritch in Time," recorded live by Kirk's quartet at the 1962 Newport Jazz Festival). It's been lovingly assembled and digitally remastered to a fine clarity by producer Kiyoshi "Boxman" Koyama. (Why is it, several years post-CD, that so much well-thought-out stuff still comes out of Japan and not here? And extra kudos to PolyGram for casing the set once again in a CD-sized box; I'm tired of having to shelve CD compilations in with my LPs.) The set collects the master multi-instrumentalist's sides for Mercury, Limelight, and Smash during the 1961–65 period.

As Dan Morgenstern explains in his excellent notes, this was "Roland in his straight-ahead prime." But in Kirk's case, straight ahead meant a room without walls. His conceptual leaps reach back to Tchaikovsky and Sidney Bechet and Hindemith while zigzagging through the likes of Lester Young, Don Byas, Kurt Weill, Bunny Berigan, Villa Lobos, Charlie Parker, John Lewis, Clifford Brown, John Coltrane, and Barbra Streisand. (The cover of "People" on disc 8 is fascinating and hilarious by turns, finishing up with a characteristically ironic quote from *The Wizard of Oz*'s "If I Only Had a Heart.")

The settings are as varied as the material. Various quartet and combo dates weave in and out of sessions with the Quincy Jones Orchestra; the personnel listing is peppered with names like Art Davis, Hank Jones, Wynton Kelly, Roy Haynes, Tubby Hayes, Walter Bishop, Jr., Louis Hayes, Andrew Hill, Clark Terry, Phil Woods, Jim Hall, Virgil Jones, Richard Davis, James Moody, Harold Mabern, Gary Burton, Major Holley, Benny Golson, Dizzy Gillespie, Jaki Byard, Elvin Jones—you get the idea. If you didn't have a clue about Kirk's deft musical adroitness, just a quick flip through that lineup should tell you.

But broad-ranging as he was in stylistic terms, Rahsaan was no session-sprinting chameleon. Everything he played came out him—odd and gyring turns of phrase, sudden explosions of his one-man horn section, flute-and-vocal conversations, reed squeaks, overblowings, growls and vocal outbursts à la Mingus and horn squalls and all. For to come out "him" meant entertaining as well as provoking. Brilliant and out there as he often was, he wanted to convince his audiences to come along for the ride without compromising either his vision or their need to enjoy what they heard. So cuckoo clocks and windup music boxes—shades of the AACM—made regular cameo appearances on his discs. More often than not, they helped him get to his listeners, then take them somewhere they didn't expect. The serious folks who groused about his alleged buffoonery never got it.

Maybe that was because, no matter how deep his love and knowledge of the past—and he had few rivals in either—he didn't want simply to resuscitate it. No Roland Kirk performance is reducible to a history seminar. In his playing, his compositions, and his arrangements, he bent what he gleaned from it to his time and his needs, updated it, tinkered with it, made it his own while proudly pointing to its genesis. He didn't see history through Reaganesque rose-colored glasses; he heard it, flaws and triumphs alike, through the voracious ears of a musician alive to every possibility he could plug into. *The Complete Mercury Recordings* is an incredible panorama of some ways he did that, and worth its price for that alone, since Kirk remains one of the most undervalued and pivotal figures in a field with more than its fair share of the underappreciated.

Although the terrific Atlantic reissues like *The Inflated Tear* capture Kirk at his conceptual peak, anyone who wants to fill in Kirk's extremely broad musical picture around the edges has plenty of options to consider. Check out *Kirk's Work* (Prestige). Pitting the slippery multi-instrumentalist (often as a one-man horn section) against an organ trio powered by Jack McDuff, this disc isn't the best place to meet Kirk for the first time, but it does offer an unusual perspective on him. Then there's *Rahsaan Roland Kirk & His Vibration Society Paris—1976* (Jeal). This showcases post-paralysis, one-handed Kirk, and it marks his triumph of spirit. Matching wits with Steve Turre and Hilton Ruiz, he plays and sings with such humor and charm on this mostly bop-oriented date that his handicap diminishes. Thirteen months later, he was dead.   [1991]

chapter 47

Space Is the Place

You've never seen a show quite like it, except maybe for the Neville Brothers, Jimi Hendrix, the Grateful Dead, Sunny Ade, James Brown. It's certainly not like any other jazz performance. The musicians snake onto the stage in a long line, stepping in time, chanting a tune like "Space Is the Place" to handheld percussion, wearing spangled headgear and flowing, colorful robes that suggest an extremely foreign origin. Settling in with their instruments, the dozen or more players segue with an easygoing sense from old big-band tunes to ultra-free jazz, sometimes jump-cutting to keep the audience on its toes. A few numbers later, the leader himself ambles out, takes his place behind a bank of acoustic and electronic keyboards, and starts calling tunes from the immense repertory his group has built up during the 30-odd years the core musicians have been working together. Ellington and standards career into spacey blowouts with no beats dropped by onstage or offstage crowds. They know that with Sun Ra, Ruler of the Omniverse and leader of the Omniverse Arkestra, you can only expect the unexpected. Nothing seems alien to him.

And yet, according to him, everything here is alien to him. "I've never been born, I *arrived*," is how he opens the conversation we're having in a two-room suite in Time Square's Edison Hotel. He's sitting on the sofa sporting a straw fedora atop his red hair, a blue chasuble-style robe, and boxer shorts, while we watch the five-minute segment a local news show has pieced together from footage shot the night before at New York's Sweet Basil.

> There are some very powerful forces, an unknown force more powerful than God, Satan, Lucifer, the Devil. It's not written in any books, and it's never been spoken on this planet. That's what's kept me all of these years; I've been knowing ever since I've been a child about these forces. It's the reason I've got a band, 'cause they keep sending me people so I can keep on moving like I've got to. The Creator is using

me, 'cause people are ready for something better. I do what The Creator tells me; I'm not a man—I'm really an angel. I'm not a minister, a preacher, or a politician. There is no classification for what I am here to do. Sun Ra is the only name that can help the planet Earth, now that words have gone bad from the Tower of Babel. I don't want anyone to worship me or my people, I just want to get this planet back on its feet.

Musical crackpot, self-deluded weirdo, hypocritical self-promoter—just a few accusations that have dogged Sun Ra and his freewheeling yet highly disciplined sounds ("I prefer to call myself a tone scientist rather than a musician") for the generation he's been making them. Along the way, he's also explored directions that, if they seemed off the map at the time, are now firmly and indelibly etched into the jazz world. Electronic keyboards, for instance, which he took up in the late '50s ("I bought one of the first electric pianos Wurlitzer made," he claims) to nearly universal ridicule, using them to create the offbeat, spacey textures his vision required. Free blowing, which took him and the Arkestra so far outside the pale when they began trying it in the early '60s that they stayed confined to a handful of venues like New York's Slug's. Using light shows and dancers and mimes and outrageous costumes as part of the celebratory swirl and vaudeville ritual that constituted, then and now, the extravaganza of a Sun Ra Arkestra performance. Reviving big-band standards and section work while good-naturedly skewering and updating the stylistic and harmonic assumptions inherited from the Swing Era and bop alike. However you trace through the past three decades, you're bound to see Sun Ra's footprints.

As he does in his impossible-to-classify music, so too in his conversations Sun Ra circles around a widening gyre of motives and topics, returning time and again to touchstones. "You don't have to turn the tape machine on or take notes right now. I'll get back to it, I always get back to it," he smiles at one point, then reiterates, "There isn't a birth certificate, 'cause I wasn't born." But the story goes that he first appeared as Herman Blount 70 or so years ago, in Birmingham, Alabama. "The first instrument I played was a kazoo," he says offhandedly, "and I came home one day and found a piano and just knew how to play it. I've always been that way: all I have to do is feel it in my heart, and I can play it. No one has ever had that talent on earth before, because the spirit couldn't find nobody who was willing to give up *every*thing, including their life, including their death—everything." Trained in high-school bands and at Alabama A&M, he continued his musical career by working as a sideman with the likes of blues belter Wynonie Harris and fiddle master Stuff Smith as well as in society bands. "Bands I was in played everything from Dixieland on up," he shrugs.

Moving to Chicago in the late '30s, he did the music for the floor shows at the Club DeLisa, that way hooking up with trailblazing big-band arranger Fletcher Henderson (his charts put the Benny Goodman Orchestra over), whose band also performed there. For about a year in the late '40s, in fact, Sun Ra was Henderson's pianist. "There aren't that many people left who know how Fletcher and Jimmie Lunceford and those leaders worked out what they did, how they led their bands. Not everybody can play their music. I can and I do, because I was there, so I can write what the old people were playing off the records."

When his tour with Henderson was up, Sun Ra began to lead his own orchestra. "I first was introduced to Sun Ra by a drummer name of Robert Barry after I had gotten out of the Air Force," recalls longtime tenor mainstay John Gilmore.

> He was playing down at Shep's Playhouse on 43rd St. in Chicago. Sun Ra and Pat [Patrick] had been working regularly, and he had used another substitute tenor player for Pat, and Barry said I might get the gig if I came out. I brought my horn, he say come back the next night, and that was it (laughs). So we built the band from three pieces on up: added Richard Evans the bass player, Dave Young on trumpet, Jim Herndon on tympani, and Bob Barry was on drums. We had about eight pieces: Johnny Thompson was on tenor for a while, Von Freeman played alto for a while, Lee O'Neill—his son is playing drums with us now.

Even then the seeds for the Arkestra were sown: the group often wore exotic costumes and played an array of African and Eastern percussion instruments. By the early '50s they were known (among myriad names) as the Solar or Myth/Science Arkestra, and on their gigs at Chicago venues like the Pershing Hotel wore beanies and white gloves and blazers. Gilmore continues,

> So we built it up to about eight pieces and started working in a place called Budland, the equivalent to Birdland in New York. Stayed there a long time, about a year. Ahmad Jamal was working upstairs, used to

come downstairs and steal Sun Ra's stuff. Every Monday for about an hour he'd be in the phone booth listening, right, Sunny? A whole lot of people came that year, everybody who'd come to town would stop in. Ray Charles came in one time, says, "I can't see these dudes but whoever they are they sure are smoking." (laughs) Sonny Rollins came through, all of the cats who lived in Chicago. It was a moving city at that time, people always in and out, a lot of things going on. We backed up all kind of people, like Dakota Staton and Sarah Vaughan, Johnny "Guitar" Watson, all kind of people.

By the late '50s the core octet had moved from being a backup band to intensive rehearsals and its own gigs.

The music they made during this period has been compared to hard-bop style of contemporaries like Art Blakey and his Jazz Messengers, but its idiosyncratic twists and turns seem more in line with what Charles Mingus was doing then: shredding big-band and bop tactics and reweaving them into something distinct by dint of his acute, probing sensibility. Like Mingus (who also accumulated long-term allegiances from key players), Sun Ra rerouted the path of the large-ensemble tradition in jazz, and thus became a precursor of younger musicians leading big groups today, like Henry Threadgill, David Murray, Craig Harris, and Olu Dara. (Harris, in fact, toured with Sun Ra for about three years, mostly in Europe, and recorded with him on *Strange Celestial Road*, Rounder CD 3035.) Among the cues Sun Ra's work offers this growing movement is how to harness the explosive language of free jazz to a larger group's more organized, rhythmically centered charts—since he is one of free jazz's inventors and has led a big band for over 30 years, there are few better places to begin that course of study.

Sun Song (originally Transition J-10, reissued as Delmark DS-411) and *Sound of Joy* (Delmark DS-414) were cut in the mid- to late-1950s, when, as the liner notes point out, Trane was an unheralded sideman and Ornette Coleman was still unrecorded. Listening to them now, after two generations of jazz experimenters have passed through the scene, is still a revealing and charged experience. Recognizable in outline as bop-influenced, the music stretches and warps that genre.

One key element Ra changed was the rhythms: layering interlocking polyrhythms via his multitudes of percussionists, shifting tempos within tunes, he reached beyond the abilities of even a sophisticated trapsman like Blakey to suggest the African underpinnings for his music. His harmonic structures more and more avoided the repeating chord cycles jazzmen borrowed from popular tunes and substituted modally based, recurrent, open-ended melodies. (That approach would later lead Miles Davis and his then sidemen John Coltrane and Bill Evans to produce classic LPs like 1959's *Kind of Blue,* which helped shift jazz's focus. Trane's self-confessed admiration for and derivations from Gilmore's tenor work are well documented.) Rather than using the piano as a polyphonic horn, the attack that dominated jazz keyboards from the days of Eubie Blake on, Sun Ra would move from boogie and stride stylings to percussive poundings ("Transition"), generating dense tone clusters and sonic bursts à la Thelonious Monk or Henry Cowell or Harry Partch.

By 1959, Sun Ra's compositions had become naked displays of hammering percussion and wildly varied instrumentation that unsheathed a new, rawer edge. At roughly the same time that Ornette Coleman and John Coltrane and Albert Ayler and Cecil Taylor were blasting free of bop's conventions, Sun Ra was leading his Arkestra into the stratosphere, helping launch free jazz. (The Arkestra of this period was captured on film, *The Cry of Jazz,* in the same year that saw the release of *Kind of Blue.*) They also abandoned Chicago for a small town outside Montreal, where a gig turned into an extended stay. A tour in Spain followed, and they landed back in New York in 1960.

Gilmore and Allen and especially Pat Patrick (who'd preceded the rest of the band to the Apple on his own, working there while they were in Canada and Spain) lined up a host of outside gigs, doing everything from jingles to pop sessions, to help support the communally housed Arkestra. According to Sun Ra, one key session found him, Gilmore, and Allen together: "We was all there to do the theme for the *Batman* TV show, but nobody ever give us no credit. And I did a record with Chief Ebenezer Obey then that the company never put out, and one with James Moody." But if they managed to hustle work, credited or released or not, the city was, as always, an extremely expensive place to live, especially for a large commune, and there were other inevitable problems. "Our neighbors started complaining about us practicing," explains Sun Ra, "and we couldn't find anyplace where they didn't complain." In 1971 they did, in the Germantown section of Philadelphia, where the Arkestra is still housed today. As Sun Ra puts it,

"Our neighbors there *like* us to rehearse, they enjoy it, they say it helps them sleep," Maybe it's better to just imagine their dreams.

Like the eternal present of a dreamscape, the music of the Arkestra has never "evolved" in the sense that their current sounds abandon their past; in what they do, all periods and styles coalesce simultaneously. "I can play everything," says Sun Ra. "I'm a Gemini; I get bored with one thing, but I have to play everything, 'cause otherwise I get bored. Whatever I'm doing, the part of me that's a Gemini be saying, Enough of that. I have to follow that. That's one reason I have the big band: I want to hear the alto, then I want to hear the tenor, then I want to hear the trumpet, then I want to hear the rhythm, then I want to hear me—keep moving, that's my nature. As long as I'm doing that, everything is harmonically balanced with me."

The early '60s found the Arkestra veering into unexplored territory. A cut like "Beginning" on 1961's aptly titled *We Are in the Future* (originally Savoy 12169, reissued as Savoy Jazz SJL 1141) points the way: dense percussion overlays support the mournful, vaguely Eastern modalities Gilmore pulls from his bass clarinet in conversation with Allen's chirping, quavering flute. At the same time, "Tapestry from an Asteroid" swoons like an Ellington ballad whose lushness has gone slightly awry, and "Jet Flight" romps like uptempo bop, reminding us that nothing disappears in Sun Ra's cavernous musical cosmos.

The big band is Sun Ra's self-described ideal vehicle; he has no use for small combos, explaining,

I always played in big bands, I know how to take a band and create for it. The bigger the band, the better. Every time my band rehearses they learn something. I'll write something they can't read, and they have to study for about six months, something very simple, maybe a fingering that they got to work out a solution. On a lot of my tunes, like "Jet Flight," they don't have to miss but one note and they'll never get back in. I always have my own style, play it differently every night. The band has to be accustomed to some strange chords. They have to play the same things that are written on somebody, but then I might think of something else to add, so I'll play it real quick and then I want somebody in the band to catch *that*. That's how it becomes deeper, more profound, and more in keeping with the exact psychic pitches of people. [One Sun Ra LP is called *Cosmic Tones for Mental*

Therapy, Saturn 408, reissued as Impulse 9291.] It works, it works all the time. I'm reaching a part of people, I don't know whether it's the soul or what you call it, it's the part of them that science don't know about. I *do* know about it. That's when the soul starts to wake.

In his entire approach Sun Ra demonstrates what he means when he says, "I know the whole history of jazz, the whole history of music. My [music] equations tell me all that." As with his music for the Arkestra, his solo keyboard work encapsulates a panorama of styles and periods. Gilmore puts it this way: "It's such a joy to hear Sun Ra play, it's like history on the bandstand: bits of Jelly Roll Morton, Fats Waller, James P. Johnson. I mean, where could you go that you could hear all that in one night—on the gig [laughs]. He's covering some territory." Then there are the echoes of Ellington himself, and Monk as well. Nor is jazz the only musical link to Sun Ra's peculiar keyboard stuff, as *John Cage Meets Sun Ra* (Meltdown Records MPA-1) indicates, connecting Sun Ra with the Ives/Cage axis that runs through American "classical" music.

And so Sun Ra and the Arkestra ("Next Stop Jupiter") continue to endure, if not exactly prosper, despite real and imagined persecutions. "I've been bypassed for a lot of things. That's why they sent the Art Ensemble to Europe before they sent me. They've invited Ornette Coleman to write symphonies and things but not me, because I talk about space and things so they think I'm a kook. That's what they think. I think so too for even bothering to explain it. We do not disagree." [1987]

chapter 48

Surfing on the Keys

For the uninitiated, a Cecil Taylor performance can be like sitting in the middle of a breaking tidal wave on a leaky rubber raft. He stalks the stage moaning surrealist incantations, his braided and beaded hair tossing. At the piano he becomes a barely seated dervish, body reeling and swaying, arms flailing, legs pumping, hands contorting and stretching impossibly as they stroke and pummel the keys. Imploded whimperings rise, sob, sink back into the instrument, explode into note clusters slamdunked by an elbow or a forearm or a fist. No clear melodies, no certain rhythms, no song structure.

At age 57, Taylor is a legend among jazzers because of his relentless pioneering, his driven dedication. Back in the '50s, still under the sway of keyboard greats like Thelonious Monk, Herbie Nichols, Horace Silver, and Lennie Tristano, the young Taylor was already developing the idiosyncratic language that makes his piano like nothing else. Learning from Monk's breakthrough use of the piano's pedals to bend notes from between the keys, adapting Tristano's drily stripped-back rhythms to his own introspective emotional emphasis, Taylor mixed jazz-derived idioms with the insights of 20th-century classical radicals like Stravinsky, Bartók, Henry Cowell, Harry Partch, and John Cage.

He's been classically trained from his Long Island boyhood. His mother, who played keyboards herself, started her five-year-old son studying piano, then timpani, with one of Toscanini's musicians. After attending at the New York College of Music, he entered the New England Conservatory in 1952 and exited after three years: he felt the curriculum was racist because it ignored African-American sounds. That refusal to compromise continued to mark his character and his music.

By the early '60s, Taylor's voice was nearly fully developed, and helped point the way for the emerging avant-garde—John Coltrane, Albert Ayler, Ornette Coleman. With Taylor's music as one of their fierce beacons, they would not only detonate the song-structure cycle-of-chords jazz had borrowed from popular music, but in the process launch into free jazz, where they reinvestigated and dramatically realigned the relationship between composition and improvisation, the dialectic motor that powers jazz.

By 1962, Taylor was widely recognized among his fellow musicians—besides his own recordings, he'd been showcased by Gil Evans on the landmark *Into the Hot* (Impulse). He'd formed his first Unit, as he usually calls his groups, with alto saxist Jimmy Lyons and drummer Sunny Murray, who were almost telepathically keyed in to Taylor's increasingly dense, emotionally structured sound as it hurtled through charged energy fields that implied, rather than stated, beats. He'd toured Europe, and the Unit had linked up there with Ayler. He'd won the prestigious *down beat* "New Star" award. And he alternated between washing dishes and welfare because he couldn't make it on his music. His father had subsidized him; when he died in 1961, Taylor's financial safety net disappeared. Stubborn and prickly and determined to make music on his own terms, he struggled through the decade on a handful of concert dates and low-paying club gigs combined with dishwashing rather than thin out his bristling conceptions.

From this period on, Taylor's manic excursions more and more resembled in intent and effect, though not in approach, the trance music of northern Africa and the Middle East. Melody, harmony, and rhythm collapsed into an eddying kaleidoscopic whirl that spewed their wreckage back out in choppy waves. The now-you-hear-them-now-you-don't fragments were what Taylor dubbed unit structures, which essentially replaced the linear development of musical ideas with a kind of multilayered call-and-response. What results can feel like a Cubist collage in motion, especially on classic albums like *3 Phasis* (New World).

For emotional motion coupled with swashbuckling technique drives Taylor's gnarled and often frustrating music. His first release on a U.S. major label in over a decade, *In Florescence* (A&M), underlines the concentrated fury of his inward gaze; it also demonstrates why Taylor's listeners, after about 20 minutes, either bend and relax into his nonstop assault or move their gritted teeth somewhere else before they break. No matter who he's playing with or what he's up to, Taylor is a supremely Romantic artist: rather than engaging musicians and audiences in dialogue, he relentlessly expands his interior monologue to try to engulf them. Now supported by foundations and academia, he's played at the Carter White House and tours prosperously. Ironically, he's followed his radical visions to success and fame—one of the few jazz prophets to be honored in his own country in his own lifetime.   [1990]

chapter 49

Music by Association

Outside, the bricks are peeling old paint and the shutters are missing, warped, or precarious, but inside Cecil Taylor's townhouse is being massively renovated. "I have the work done in stages, when I have the money," he says, by way of explaining the stacks of aluminum studs and two-by-fours, the occasional dangling loops of BX cable and the hole in the floor where a toilet will someday be. He's launched into a tour of the house, a thumbnail history of it and the neighborhood ("Five people were murdered here"), and a quick rundown of the personalities of his pets—the Akita who for three weeks shat spitefully on the parlor-level's parquet floors because Taylor was out of town, the white-pawed black cat who obsessively leaps onto the nearest available lap for stroking. What I figure is that Taylor, more cautious than his cat, is checking me out.

After half an hour or so, we gradually settle into what was meant to be the dining room. Aside from a plain wooden bench and a cracked captain's chair and an empty magnum of Freixenet champagne (where Taylor inserts his burning incense sticks) that remains placed at a strategic point on the floor, it's decorated with a handful of posters from the pianist's past, great semi-orderly piles and rows of books (*Dance of Siva*, *Broken Spears: Aztec Accounts of the Conquest of Mexico*, a biography of Oskar Kokoschka, Toni Morrison's *Beloved*, *Kaffir Boy in America*, *West Africa Under Colonial Rule*, *The History of the Persian Empire*) around the fireplace, and a semicircular table cut out like a quarter-moon, with a lone chair in its arc's center. Eventually, after fidgeting in and out of the kitchen ("Do you want some juice? an orange? I wish I had some beer"), Taylor eases into that chair and says, "So what do you want to know?" Even as he says it, his head and body begin the kind of punctuating movements familiar to anyone who's ever seen his version of sitting at the piano: he throws his head back, drastically shifts his body weight, squirms and laughs and bites off phrases and periodically, as if he's starting to feel trapped, cavorts out from behind his protective table to dance and spin.

Every interviewee with a genuine personality reveals it, each in his or her own way. Taylor doesn't actually refuse to adhere to the standard interview format—I ask you a specific question, you answer it. At one point, for instance, he glances at the yellow legal pad at my feet covered with scrawled questions and asks, wide-eyed but sly, "What is all that writing? My, my, my." But by the way he handles the few questions he allows to penetrate the swirling associative torrent virtually any query sets off, he simply makes interviewing irrelevant, a category and practice inapplicable to himself.

Which is also essentially what he's done in musical terms over the last 30-odd years. Using his "unit structure" building blocks to create varilength pieces that detonated the song-form limits that had both housed and imprisoned jazz from its beginnings, replacing the underlying drive of a basic, recognizable pulse with an extremely elastic rhythmic sense he calls "the wave," uniting in his idiosyncratic pianistic voice the breakthroughs of Monk, Bartók, Milt Jackson, Horace Silver, Harry Partch, and Henry Cowell, Taylor is an obsessive individualist, an American Romantic whose inward-gazing, relentlessly kinetic music either forces listeners to relax into its egocentric demands or drives them off. Though he no longer has to wash dishes to make ends meet—as he was doing in 1962, when he won *down beat*'s "New Star" award—he's no less compromising about his musical visions today, when he's got actual commissions, a massive 11-CD set of his work, *In Berlin* (FMP), and his first domestic release in a decade, *In Florescence* (A&M). "This is the first time," he says, between talking of spending six months touring Europe and the pieces he's been asked to write by his alma mater, the New England Conservatory, for a student orchestra he plans to perform with in the late fall, "that I know what I'm going to be doing more than a week from now."

When Taylor speaks, his voice slides fluently through emphases. He stretches syllables like a scat singer, drops his pitch an octave and his volume to a whisper, slips into a cadence that mimicks blank verse and rounds it off with gradual acceleration and rising dynamics, marks off his associative insights and false leads with a rhythmic pause or a barking laugh that seems to suggest his own surprise and delight. In that way, his rhythmic and tonal speech, and especially his thick, looping, nonlinear associative clusters, which make assertions that he seems to forget about until whole paragraphs have passed, strikingly recall his gnarled, inner-seeking musical visions. But since language, like music, has an essence that resolutely escapes notation, you'll have to imagine the slides and dips and slurs and accents. For the rest, a suspension of disbelief and patience are enough.

I was washing dishes in a restaurant at the same time that I was being written about in places like *down beat*, and it was very good for me, because I had to decide what I really wanted to do. Did I want to pursue my ideals badly enough? It was the only way to learn that I did. So I washed dishes while the guy who owned the restaurant played my records, along with Miles's records and Coltrane's records. I quit after a few weeks, though. Then I went out to a place called the Take 3, and I got the job performing. And it's been going and stopping like that ever since for me. We—me, Jimmy Lyons, Sunny Murray—worked there for thirteen weeks; it was the longest gig I ever had in America. Sometimes the magnificent Henry Grimes would come in: I remember one night he did, and we played for three hours but I thought we'd played for about ten minutes. Coltrane heard us there, and arranged for us to make our first Scandinavian tour.

But the Take 3 gig was a very important one, because I really had to understand that music, my music, was what I wanted to do. So I said to myself, you have to try to understand that pursuing music is a choice that you make, and that any anger that you feel as a result of that choice is [sings] "what makes the world go round"—that's a line from a song that Sinatra sang in the late '40s. So you then begin the process of really getting down to it: the distance between whatever excellence it is you're striving for in whatever it is you're trying to convey and the person you would like to be. That's gradually coming together. After all, ha-ha-ha, it's a life's work. But it means a minimum of confusion about life.

I've been quoted—and they're all lies, all lies—as saying that I think of my playing as being related to the kind of leaps a dancer makes in space. You know, my mother used to take me to see tap dancers when I was little. So I saw Bill Robinson, and the Step Brothers, and the Nicholas Brothers, and Baby Hodges—I saw them all. In '62, when I was working at the Take 3, I didn't have any money but the Bolshoi came to town, so I went to see them at the Met, *Swan Lake*. Now I had to work that Sunday night, but I said, "The lessons I've gotten about what music can do"—because the prima ballerina had danced the dying swan three times, and three times we'd all wept. Even in the pictures you can see that the way the Russians interpret Tchaikovsky is rhythmical, where we experience it as songs. The melodies are, after all, beautiful, but they're very rhythmical.

I spend a lot of time in discos. I love to dance. Lately, since I've been doing so much work, I haven't been listening to music very much, unfortunately. But I love James Brown, I love Aretha Franklin, I love Marvin Gaye—I thought he was extraordinary. I like music that makes me dance. Something is happening to me now—I'm not going to say what. But you ask these questions that can be taken in at least three different ways: you're not being duplicitous, you're being triplicitous, ha-ha-ha. As Billie Holiday said, "Don't explain." It's quite wonderful, actually.

Last summer, I was invited to a festival for flamenco in Spain, honoring Carmen Amaya, a flamenco dancer who was one of the most prodigious musical lights that I ever saw, like Billie Holiday. I saw her for the first time in 1965, then again later at the Village Gate. The magic that I felt was much akin to what I felt when I first saw Billie Holiday when I was 12. I could not breathe, I could not think, all I could experience was what was coming from her.

So I was invited to this festival in Begijar as a guest. They had erected this huge tent on the edge of this mountain, and in the evening there was a wind called the *tramontana* that blew from the Mediterranean, which was just over this mountain. Now, I had just come from spending two weeks on the island of Crete; the last night, my friend and I were taken way up into the mountains there for a wedding. Well . . . ha-ha-ha. That was something, but we don't want to talk about it.

So the next night, there I am in Begijar, and one of the things I see is a film of Carmen Amaya—outside, on a huge screen. I am introduced to all these different people, of different cultures. What happened was, there were some musicians from China, an extraordinary group from Pakistan, flamenco dancers, obviously. It was also like a living historical tableau. Sabicas was there, representing the older form; one flamenco group, of about six people, represented the sort of mid-century point of view; but there was a young woman of about 23 named Martine who, when she sang, Sabicas himself cried. And the intensity of her partner's dancing took me back to Amaya. One of the magical things about dancers is how they project: if they're 5'8", they can look like they're 6'4". This young woman looked like she was well over six feet.

So what I've been receiving is the wealth of different cultures. Experiences show you that not only are you an American artist, but if you are allowed to go to other countries and other cultures, you have something to bring and share and exchange. Once you do this, you begin to understand there is a commonality of human experience that transcends—of course, obviously, right—but also that if you make the commitment to the elevation of the song, then you begin to see all kinds of linkages to people everywhere.

Wherever I go, what I find is that when I perform now it always hearkens back to something that took me years to understand, something my father said to me when I was in those really very traumatic years, though all years, ha-ha-ha, are traumatic. I mean, it took me about nine years, maybe ten, to find Jimmy Lyons, or for us to find each other. For the first six years or so after that, we would average maybe three or four gigs a year. So for most of that time Cecil was being irritable, angry. My father was a sheriff when I was growing up way out in Corona, out by the World's Fair, and he supported me even then, but I would say to him, "You don't understand, you're just an Uncle Tom"—even though he put me through the Conservatory and blah-blah-blah.

But finally about four or five years ago, I was playing a concert at Carnegie Recital Hall. It was an interesting period: I was supposed to give a series of fourteen concerts in Europe, but I had to cancel them because Europe turned out to be not nice, there were chiselers behind them. I said to myself, "Here you are at your advanced age and not a pot to piss in. What are you gonna do?" So I got on the phone, and things started to move. The concert at Carnegie Recital Hall was part of a series of concerts in which you had, within the American hierarchy of different kinds of music, different cultural expressions of America. David Amram was the organizer.

So I'm grumpy. What happens is, maybe for the first time in my life I saw that it really didn't matter, because you, Cecil, were ready to do it, because you always had to overcome the shit. And then, that being done, it was wonderful to see that the hall was packed. So I finished the concert, having said to everyone through the music, "You're gonna sit there and listen, I'm gonna fix you all for ever and ever and ever and ever"—and it came that they wanted more. And I came out, and I played, and I understood what it was my father used to say to me: "I am to serve." That's what he'd told me all those years, and to finally understand it was so wonderful, because you'd pleasured so many people that there are no words.

But we've gone a long way away from Begijar. I decided, of course, that yes, I would play—they had this beautiful grand piano there. Well, Carmen Amaya was a gypsy, as you know, so I'm being asked to play first on the first night. So here I come out, and I'm gonna chant and wooooo—and the gypsies are all, "Oh no, wait a minute, what the fuck is this," and the babies started screaming ah-ah-ah-ah-ah, you know. Well, of course. But here I go. And you know, you do it for fifteen minutes, and it becomes quiet. And then I noticed that on the days when I would be practicing, different members from different groups would come and just stand there and listen. One day, a young woman from Martinique came. We all lived in this one building; you could watch the Mediterranean from the rooftop, it was on three sides of that roof.

What do I do when I go to dance? They had a party; all the dancers were there. Ha-ha-ha. A wonderful thing. So I waited, and waited, you know. Each room had different kinds of music. And then, when I got ready, I danced. And the dancers understood—which to me was the solidification of the common-ness of our purpose, and it broke through.

On that level—when I was in Boston [in early March], I wrote a piece—the first time I've been asked, ha-ha-ha, to go back to the New England Conservatory, in this capacity—that brought out that common-ness once again, only this time it was in America. We worked for two weeks for these two concerts. There was a Chinese, a Japanese-American, four women singers, one of whom was from Poland. Other people from other places.

Now, I have certain ideas about what to do, as musical theater and composition and how I set it up. So in the middle of this, I pick up the paper, and one of the people that I love, I found out, was playing at the Regatta Bar. So I take three of my musicians and we go there, and there's Milt Jackson. And he plays a piece that J. J. Johnson wrote, "First Love." It was such an extraordinary solo. It wasn't that he has changed; I mean, I first heard Milt when I was sixteen, and nothing much has changed, except that the Regatta Bar is now more money and Milt Jackson is one of the few musicians who, I am quite glad to say, has made some money. And he certainly deserves it—the joy that he's given me. To see this man so many years later still doing it. I said, "Okay now, young adults, that's one part, but here's what I want. You just wait, be patient. He's gonna play a blues for you the like of which you've probably not heard. That's why I wanted you here. You don't have to do it that way, but I want you to be aware of

242

this." So we wait, and boy, he does it. And I say, "Now, that's where I came from. I don't do it that way, but it's a part of me."

So then I decided to go to Washington, and a friend of mine and I go walking by Blues Alley, and who's going to be there the next night? I said, "Oh shit, I'm going to stay, you know." "But it's all sold out." "But you said we had passes." And some people we know say, "We can't go, take our passes." Well, I remember when I first heard Sonny Rollins: it was in 1951 when I was living in Boston, and he was playing with the demon Miles then. Well, when he came in—I hadn't seen or talked to Sonny in quite a while, though I remember when we—no, I can't tell you all the stories or you'll never come back again. Anyway, he was marvellous. Not only was he marvellous, but I learned so much from him about what I wasn't able to accept.

What I mean is, I was up in Minton's one Saturday night, I was about 21 years old, and Milt Jackson was leading a band with Sonny in it. Saturday night! In Harlem! Everybody's, "Hey, hup, ho." Then all of a sudden Milt and Sonny played this piece, and you could hear everybody breathe. I said, "Oh." That, to me, is what it's about. You play from the heart. If that's what you really love, it doesn't matter if there's one person there or ten thousand.   [1990]

chapter 50

Unplugging the Enlightenment

His music is no snap to pick up on: it has none of the glib melodic hooks of "jazz" radio stars like Kenny G, and skips an easy reliance on canonized traditions like bebop. It can be knotty and passionate, Cageian and Coltranesque, highly structured and deliberately destabilized—and usually tries to be all those things at once. Like Anthony Braxton himself, a softspoken and unassuming man who becomes eloquent about his music when speaking about it and driven to finessed traversings of sonic edges when playing it.

After 20-odd years, Braxton has refined his highly ramified musical environment without any success in the marketplace. I use the word environment deliberately. Braxton, like countless other artists, taps into pre-industrial beliefs to counter alienated Western stances like the privileged notion of technological progress, the automatic division of rational and mythic structures, the degeneration of culture into entertainment, imperialism, racism, sexism, and so on.

As a result, for Braxton, as for namers since Adam, sounds are not abstract and fleeting throwaways, but rather speak to a kind of supra-reality, function as both barometers and shapers of the time-space surrounding them. Shaman, seer, mystic—these are concepts that, devalued by our society, describe almost exactly the kind of Pythagorean belief Braxton (and almost every culture but the post-Enlightenment West) has in the power of music to affect the world.

This is not the escapist mumbo-jumbo of white middle-class New Ageism. Braxton was an early member of the Association for the Advancement of Creative Music, the catalytic cooperative that arose in Chicago in the late '60s under the leadership of pianist Muhal Richard Abrams. Basically, the AACM launched its own musical revolts from the iconoclastic sound-pioneering and cultural politics of folks like Thelonious Monk, Harry Partch, Cecil Taylor, John Cage, Sun Ra, Karlheinz Stockhausen, Charles Mingus, Ornette Coleman, and John Coltrane. Following in their soundprints, AACMers placed no more value on notes than on other sounds, from overblown whistles and shrieks to elephantine roars to low-end belching; homemade instruments like Henry Threadgill's hubkaphone, a percussion device made of hubcaps, became integrated into the expansive sonic textures. Partly as a by-product of this refocused energy, the cyclical form of chordal progressions, which had been adapted from popular music by early improvisers for their own uses and continually extended in its harmonic implications up through the bebop era, lost its privileged position as the dominant vehicle for improvisation.

The consequences—which are still being worked with and through today—were several. But maybe most crucial was the burgeoning if misnamed "free jazz" movement. Misnamed because, in fact, it dealt with new kinds of interrelations between composition and improvisation—the dialectical engine that powers what we call jazz.

That engine needed an overhaul anyway. Despite the best intentions of contemporary moldy figs like Wynton Marsalis, proscriptions about the music's future shapes have never been easily gleaned from its past. Who at the time—outside of the musicians whose project it was—would have deduced bebop, the privileged model of Marsalis et al., from swing? Or swing itself from the society and dance bands of the '20s? Or Louis Armstrong's solos from New Orleans ensemble playing? Discontinuity plays as necessary and radical a role in history as any unfolding evolutionary model.

Not so coincidentally, that's exactly the set of bifocals through which the AACMers saw their own tasks. On the one hand, they set out to expand the harmonic riches bebop had picked up from European classical as well as internal sources; on the other, they moved toward locating those harmonies in a more open-ended, explosive, dialogically reactive space than the cyclical chord progression could be bent into.

Their bifurcated approach addressed those two facets of the same problem. They paid increased attention to composition, with sheet music making its reappearance on bandstands (though at least some of that music was usually the product of band input into arrangements and solos). They also tried to create "free" improvisation. Like Ellington, Monk, and Mingus, the AACM grappled with the difficulty of reorganizing composition while using—and keeping the benefits of—the supple improvisational languages they inherited. For like any language, jazz carries within it an ideology, in its case a model of interactive, conversational democracy in which leader (the soloist) and community (the band) exchange ideas about direction.

So in a real sense, AACMers try to push that democracy farther, by erasing distinctions between frontline and backline musicians in an ensemble. At the same time, they want to reintegrate written notation and improvisation, to outline a different way for them to work together, to produce a new format that would reach outside the confines of imposed generic labels like jazz to suggest, mimic, include the fuller reality of their diversified cultural experiences as black Americans.

Braxton is so radical about his vector in this direction that he's developed a totally distinct, geometrically based notational system while trying, via his own writings and lectures, to position his music within the larger cultural vistas of history, society, and politics. So Graham Lock's book, *Forces in Motion: The Music and Thoughts of Anthony Braxton* (Da Capo), answers a real need by delving into his music and worldview. Spending two weeks on tour with multi-reedmaster Braxton and his then

245

quartet (pianist Marilyn Crispell, bassist Mark Dresser, drummer Gerry Hemingway), attending all the performances and lectures, interviewing Braxton himself each day on a wide variety of topics, Lock succeeds in both capturing a sense of the music and depicting the overarching contexts Braxton always sees himself working within.

It's not always smooth going. Braxton's own terminology, like Hegel's or Husserl's, can be gnarled and self-referential, and Lock's somewhat reductive leftist stances on everything from vegetarianism and feminism to the music industry can be more annoying than insightful. Take, for example, his rather smug note on a conversation with Crispell: "Though I smile to myself at the irony of a pro-feminist man trying to unravel this concept [he's referring to a notion that music is a male-formulated and dominated language which needs to be drastically reconstituted by women for their own use] with a nonfeminist woman, it's not a situation I feel comfortable with." For good reason.

Still, Lock translates Braxton's concerns with sympathy and excellence. Combining raw interview transcriptions, concert descriptions, historical and musical and mystical background, he places Braxton within the rich intellectual, emotional, and sociological realms that nurture him rather than defining him sheerly musicologically, formalistically. It's an invaluable look at a musician whose work is all too undervalued—even within the exceedingly undervalued jazz realm.

In part, as the book points out, that's because of the racist/imperialist assumptions that underlie (however unconsciously) most of what passes for music criticism. Braxton's music has frequently been attacked as overintellectual, not swinging enough. The charge may seem incoherent to folks who have witnessed him on the bandstand, where he almost invariably explodes his material past its limits with the force of his intensity. But thanks to what Braxton calls "the reality of the sweating brow," black musicians—especially when they can be pinned with the label jazz—aren't supposed to think, just sort of squirt out carefree improvised noises with a Sambo grin; that's their natural talent as well as their preordained upper limit of cultural achievement. Of course, that viewpoint also reduces the music to a kind of sexual gymnastics overheard as exotica by slumming tourists. So it hits home when Braxton says,

"I mean, it's taken for granted that a European or a European-American jazz musician has borrowed some aspects of African-American language: why should it be such a big thing that I've learned from Europe? I'm a human being, just like Ronnie Scott or Derek Bailey [two white English improviser/composers]. Why is it natural for Evan Parket [a white English jazzman], say, to have an appreciation of Coltrane, but for me to have an appreciation of Stockhausen is somehow out of the natural order of human experience? I see it as racist. . . .

"That's part of the dilemma of the African-American intellectual. James P. Johnson wrote several operas—I think there's been *one* performance in North America and that not long ago. Most of the performances he had in his lifetime were in South America. Why isn't this information known? I'll tell you—because there's a real interest in suppressing African intellectual dynamics. . . . It's a taboo subject, and we have all paid for it."

Including Braxton, who lived with his wife and children in the grinding poverty all too typical of jazz musicians until he got a gig teaching at Mills College. But poverty drove him to learn, to ponder, to articulate. Along with his mixed-race and mixed-media pantheon of heroes, Braxton's assertions about suppressed Western history—the attribution of cultural breakthroughs by the ancient dusky civilization of Egypt to the Mediterranean but whiter Greeks by the even whiter slave-trading nations of Europe's Imperial Age, the claims that Haydn and Beethoven were black—reiterate scholarly attacks by George G.M. James (*Stolen Legacy*, Philosophical Library), Yosef A. A. ben-Jochannan (*Black Man of the Nile and His Family*, Alkebu-lan Books), and Martin Bernal's *Black Athena: The Afroasiatic Roots of Classical Civilization*, Rutgers) on the cultural hegemony of northwestern Europe—or anywhere else.

One excellent way to start an acquaintance with Braxton's music—which is so marginally available it might as well be suppressed—is with the just released *Quartet (London) 1985* (Leo Records), which chronicles two sets recorded live with the very quartet Lock toured with. Its six sides offer many entry points into Braxton's formidable sonic universe, and Lock's liner notes are useful and informative.

But in the end, as critics are supposed to say, the music is what matters, and Braxton's matters a lot. Listening to it in this extended format lets it surround you with its varied preoccupations and goals in a useful and provocative way: the sheer length forces/allows you to react to its kinetic changes of mood, texture, form, concept in a kind of flowing dialogue, the way the musicians onstage have to. Look at it as a chipping away at the barrier between audience and performer, observer and participant, people and culture, that has haunted Western civilization since the Industrial Revolution and its intellectual arm, the Enlightenment. [1989]

chapter 51

Child Is Father to the Music

"Music is like a child," says Henry Threadgill. His nine-year-old daughter watches TV in the next room, while we sit amid a collection of instruments that ranges from a baby grand piano through his army of reeds to a harp. "The way a child comes into the world, a mother's and father's genes, which they have inherited from all the generations before them, are all put back together again to create something new. So the child has got all the genes of its ancestors, but it's also got genes none of them ever had."

So it's natural enough that in the music Threadgill composes for and performs with his trio Air, his Sextett, his WindString Ensemble, his Orchestra, and his dance band, as well as the film and radio and dance projects he's scored, you'll catch echoes of the damnedest things caroming off each other. Whether in his dense, swinging compositions or in his virtuosic excursions on reeds and flute, those meetings—between Stravinsky and King Curtis, B-movie soundtracks and Muddy Waters, Bach and Mingus and Ornette Coleman—help create a unique and powerful voice.

That voice filters through its contemporary concerns and vocabulary elements of whatever Threadgill heard when he was a child in a Chicago ghetto. "Music used to be put out in a more democratic way, before radio got commercially institutionalized," he says.

It was more or less a hodgepodge of everything. I remember hearing programs for Mexicans, Polish shows, Serbian, country & western, black gospel groups, rhythm & blues, jazz, classical music—plus regular programming like theater pieces and detective shows, outer space shows. Television was freer like that in the beginning too: *The Kate Smith Show, Ted Mack's Amateur Hour, GE Theatre* with Noel Coward plays, Nat King Cole's show—there was some of everything. In a way they didn't know what they were doing, because it was uncontrolled—which is the way it really should be. The minute the controls come in, so many people and so much talent get cut out because of the so-called taste of one group who think that they're doing the public a service. I *know* they're doing their pockets a service, because if you just push one thing people are gonna have to get into it. If you're only selling Coca-Cola, and you're taking up all the space in the store and all the ads in the Sunday *Times*, the other people who aren't putting things out on that level get swamped.

Henry Threadgill has spent his life making sounds that render categories superfluous. Trained as a child on piano in a house filled with music ("My aunt was studying to be an opera singer"), Threadgill was initially drawn to the bass, but abandoned it for the sax after hearing Charlie Parker records. Concerts at his high school exposed him to players like Stan Getz and Sonny Rollins, and he doubled on tenor and baritone in the school band. Soon he'd added alto, clarinet, and flute to his growing instrument arsenal. And when he wasn't playing in school, he was working out in local r&b bands, mastering that swooping, throaty wail that still resonates in his playing.

A stint in the Army was followed by study in a series of music programs, where he pursued his craft from unexpected perspectives like composition and voice training, classical piano and clarinet. "I knew what I didn't know," he says, "how much I couldn't take apart theoretically. I wasn't in those programs the way most students were, to get their degree; I was there just to take everything they had." His schooling outside school continued too, in gigs with VFW bands, marching bands, polka bands, light-classical orchestras, Dixieland combos, and blues bands.

The earthiness of the blues remains at the core of his writing and playing:

> The blues as I understand the blues is different from what a lot of jazz players play as the blues. Chicago is a blues town, with people like Muddy Waters and Howlin' Wolf, the blues that come up from the South—I don't mean these twelve-bar blues that Charlie Parker and them were playing a lot of different progressions on. I'm talking about country blues, which might happen in any amount of bars, even or uneven. And spiritual gospel music too: it's that emotional thing where you get inside the note and *work* it.

You can hear what he means on "Do Tell" (Air, *80° Below '82*), where he digs that trio into a Cannonball Adderley-style gospel vamp; or "Black Blues" (Sextett, *Just the Facts and Pass the Bucket*), which kicks off like a boozy Salvation Army band and lurches into gutbucket squalling; or "Bermuda Blues" (Sextett, *You Know the Number*), where he formulates a melody so seemingly familiar it's scary. "It's like enticing you into the spookhouse with a piece of candy," he grins.

Just as the country-blues players wrote of their times and places, the floods and droughts and insect plagues and broken hearts, so does Threadgill see his music—indeed, all music—as bound to reflect social reality in some way. Thus bebop, with its virtuosic displays, didn't grab him:

> That music was not the music for me to express what was happening at that time, in the late '50s and early '60s. That was over for me, it was a whole new world in the United States culturally for everybody. What Charlie Parker and them were playing about in the '40s after the war, after these black soldiers had come back from travelling all over the world and getting another realization of themselves and started making contacts again with the people of this country, and everybody's head opened up on a different basis—well, they expressed all of that for that period, and it took 'em all the way over to the '50s, when the McCarthy era started to shut America back down after it got opened up from the war. So when the '60s erupted it was a whole new day again, and the music moved too. Trane had moved his music to an emotional spiritual plane, and had come off the plane of playing progressions that everybody was comfortable with. Ornette Coleman, Cecil Taylor,

Mingus—the whole scene had changed, and emotionally I could feel it. So bebop couldn't service me: it didn't have anything to do with people standing up for their rights, it didn't have anything to do with the Vietnam war, didn't have anything to do with the Gray Panthers, the Black Panthers—that music couldn't express that. The language had opened up and expanded. Artists like Charlie Parker knew that happens, which is why before his death he started getting into Edgard Varese—he knew that things were gonna change. Any sensible artist is in tune with what's going on around him, he knows that the language has to expand.

Not surprisingly, Threadgill has no patience for nostalgia mongers:

All this revivalism that we're experiencing, I'm really against. It's funny to see a lot of musicians involved with music that's older than they are—that's rare in the history of jazz, where they're playing stuff that isn't relevant today. It's actually musical fascism, all this neo-this and neo-that. These young traditionalists that make a whole lot of talk about understanding tradition—forget that. The tradition only becomes a background of ingredients. Whatever element you want to bring into your music, you've got to understand ontologically and then synthesize it in musically. Just in itself, it's nothing; if you can't make something out of it, the world can do without it.

Nor does he have patience for empty musical posturing:

A lot of young musicians get a lot of credit for being musical athletes, contortionists, like it's hip to be a virtuoso. Ain't nothing hip about that: music is not about that, it doesn't say anything, it doesn't even make you musical to be the fastest-playing person on earth or make the biggest leaps on your instrument. That is not music. Music has to do with expression, how to play now musically. There are no rules about how to do that, no laws: anything goes, so long as it works. Music is organized sound, that's all, and it's got nothing to do with purism. You can't create music for your time by speaking an archaic language that makes reference to other sociological and spiritual and emotional values in the society—the whole thing is connected symbolically in the tones.

Those complementary ideas—that the language of music must reflect its environment, that musicianship is the means of expressing that relationship, and that any sound could be a part of that language—were developed in Threadgill during his participation in the Chicago-based

Association for the Advancement of Creative Musicians. A nonprofit group that sponsored performances and recording sessions for its members, the AACM grew out of the Experimental Band led by pianist Muhal Richard Abrams, a large free-jazz ensemble in which Threadgill played during the early '60s. Its ranks included such musical daredevils as Lester Bowie, Joseph Jarman, and Roscoe Mitchell of the Art Ensemble, Julius Hemphill, Oliver Lake, Leroy Jenkins, Anthony Braxton, and Steve McCall—a Who's Who of younger jazz players. What they shared was a sense of musical change. Notes per se became less important to play than the effects that could be conjured up via instrumental sounds, any sounds from bleeps and blatts and burps to childlike whimpering and sobbing sighs and whinnying overblown shrieks. Coming in the wake of experiments by Trane and Ornette and Dolphy and Ayler, the AACM further enriched jazz's vocabulary and bequeathed the music some enormous talents.

But like David Murray, in whose original Octet he played, Threadgill is not only an original explorer but also an heir to the approach favored by great jazz composers and arrangers like Ellington and Mingus. "I always have particular players in mind when I'm writing music. It's like a basketball team, where the guard has particular strengths, and so the defense is keyed around him. I think that's very important, and that all good ensembles use that. And I write different pieces for the different ensembles, because I have that particular orchestration and instrumentation in mind." How much of the music is written and how much improvised varies from group to group, and piece to piece. "My music is not complete until the musicians are finished with it" is the one general rule he has. "Until I hear everything that happens in rehearsal, anything is subject to change."

One musical constant, especially in the case of his Sextett and Air, is how Threadgill draws on his free-jazz background to obliterate the division between soloist and accompanist. Take most of *Airsong*, where he deliberately feeds foregrounded lines to agile bassist Fred Hopkins. Or "Apricots on Their Wings" (*Air Show No. 1*), where he uses the supple voice of Cassandra Wilson as another instrumental line at the same time he is playfully deconstructing the classic Ella Fitzgerald renditions of Cole Porter songs. "Democracy is part of this country, and it's gotten into the arts. I use that, highlight all the instruments at different points; why have all these instruments if only one of them is important?"

252

In the case of the Sextett, one result of the musical democracy that leads him to spread detailed parts around equally is that the group's sound swells beyond its numbers, as the LP called *Just the Facts and Pass the Bucket* demonstrates. Listen to how the title track and "Higher Places" revamp big-band notions of how to treat ballads with power to spare. Ponder the murky, *noi*rish atmosphere that periodically bursts into Stravinsky-ish rituals on "Cover," or the way "Cremation" explodes from its dirgelike string opening to the cello twittering like a spook over madly riffing horns. Combine the improvisational talents of stellar members like cornetist Olu Dara, who can mix Louis Armstrong and Lester Bowie with ease, or trombonist Craig Harris, who boasts a full range of smears and whinnies and yelps as well as amazing agility, with Threadgill's own unpredictable and catchy compositions, and you can get some sense of the force this supple and idiosyncratic lineup can unleash. "It's such a good pallette to write with," he grins. "The range of strings from the bass to the cello goes all the way from the top of the treble clef to the bottom of the bass clef. With the brass I've got the same thing. Percussion, too, with two drummers—that gives me 12 drums. And with all the reeds I play, it's like having a little orchestra. So I approach it like a reduction for orchestra." And audiences love it.

And so he returns to a favorite motif. "I'm not a pessimist," he concludes. "I'm a dreamer, and a dreamer is an optimist by definition. But I have to face the facts around me. Decomposition and reintegration is what's needed in music today." Characteristically idiosyncratic, he combines the facts of birth and death, recurrent themes in his work, with his desire to have a permanent ensemble gig that would allow him to write constantly for a set group of players. "America is so afraid of death," he begins.

All these devices—plastic surgery, cryogenics, storage of organs, moving further and further away from the graveyard—just show a fear of life and reality. I'd like to put a band in a funeral parlor and work there. That'd put me in position to be like Bach, to have an ensemble to write for weekly. It'd be special, something for each person who's getting married, something for each person who's died. We've got to accept the idea that death is part of life. A healthier understanding of that would give us more material to express ourselves in a larger way, and keep us out of the kind of ignorance that enslaves. [1987]

chapter 52

In and Out of the Tradition

Brilliant improviser, adept multi-instrumentalist, talented arranger, and gifted composer: these are the major talents David Murray has used to carve out a unique place for himself in modern jazz. Along with such innovators as Henry Threadgill, Butch Morris, and Olu Dara, he is among the brightest potential stars to emerge from this generation. Drawing on his understanding of the past's best, like the big-band music of Ellington and Mingus, he forges composed structures that can accommodate the improvised onslaught of the explosive sonic and harmonic languages devised by the experimenters of the last generation, the Ornettes and the Coltranes, the Dolphys and the Aylers. They also swing hooky melodies like mad, as the bobbing heads and kicking legs and tapping feet during even the farthest-out solos demonstrate. That reconciliation of what had seemed, since the end of the Swing Era, to be two opposing aspects of jazz—its need to explore relentlessly and its ability to attract a truly popular audience—is one of Murray's highest achievements.

It's a synthesis that finds its roots in his own musical beginnings. His mother plays piano in a Pentecostal church, his older brother studied clarinet, and Murray himself started on alto sax at age nine. "Then I heard Sonny Rollins play at a Berkeley jazz festival," he recalls, "and after that I started playing tenor. The alto just couldn't accommodate what I knew I could do after I'd seen Sonny." He found out what he could do playing professionally through high school in various r&b bands, and by his 20th birthday had made a name for himself with several experimental jazz outfits around his Berkeley home.

As it inevitably does for jazz musicians, the Big Apple loomed large in Murray's ambitions, and so at 21 he packed his horn and headed east, where he arrived in time for the hard-blowing loft sessions of the 1970s. Characteristically undaunted, he plunged into working with such explorers as Ornette, James Blood Ulmer, Lester Bowie, and Sunny Murray, recording edge-city discs with trios and quartets. Equally characteristic, though, is how he both played his way through the cutting contests and began harnessing the raw energy unleashed by that scene to power his own evolving vision.

That vision had its first translation to reality at the Public Theater in 1978, when Murray was offered the venue for a big-band performance. "That was the beginning of it," he feels now. "I'd done ensembles before, like six or seven pieces, but I never *thought* of them as a big band. I never thought that I could actually *lead* all these people to somewhere. So I wrote all this music, [trumpeter] Butch Morris conducted it, and it came out pretty well." Well enough to set critics raving and a cult to following him as he began moving in this new direction.

Murray himself puts his move into historical perspective:

> Duke Ellington in his era synthesized a lot of the big band sounds that were happening before him and while he was there, and to me he took them into a new era, a modern age, with a much slicker harmonic base; he used technical things that maybe somebody like a Jimmie Lunceford didn't have time to explore. Mingus, coming after Ellington, created a resurgence of the "jungle rhythms" of Ellington's band from around 1927, that African feel, and he refined it, rejuvenated it. That's kinda what I'm doing in this time and day. I'm not *comparing* myself to Duke Ellington or Charlie Mingus, but I *do* see myself as one link in a chain of great organizers who can take from the past and put it into a fresh perspective in the present.

Clearly Murray's project is not neocon nostalgia; unlike the embalmer's attitude toward the past boasted by, say, Wynton Marsalis, Murray's gaze is inevitably directed forward by jazz's key attribute, improvisation. "A lot of cats who talk that large ensemble stuff can't really play that well," he asserts.

> I think I'm in the middle: I can play well and I can write well, which sets me apart already. See, in each generation each of those organizers has been a great improviser as well as a great arranger and writer. Since I'm a player first, what I play on what I write is going to sound good. And with the kind of improvisers I've got in my bands, I'm hoping that what I write inspires them to a level of performance beyond what they've already done.

Given that the players he's talking about include high-caliber types like Threadgill, Morris, Dara, trombonist Craig Harris, sax masters Hamiett Bluiett and Steve Coleman, bassists Wilber Morris and Fred Hopkins, drummers Steve McCall and Billy Higgins, that's no small hope. It's also the lifeblood of his music, even though the days are long gone when a Duke Ellington could keep a stellar band together by gigging night after night. "I've got to keep people like that around," he says,

> because on any given night I might play better than them, or they might play better than me. It's that *challenge* that makes the music happen. You've got to read people, what's happening in their lives; that's what enables you to inspire them with your music. Take the Ellington orchestra, a cat like Paul Gonsalves. Paul never sounded that way with any other orchestra; neither did Johnny Hodges. They all came back to Duke because he made them search inside themselves and find the genius that was in there. *That's* what my music is about: you've *got* to play, you can't be half-steppin'. A bunch of notes on a page don't mean nothin' to me; what you're gonna play on it after you finish the composition, that's what *I* want to know. A composition has got to inspire you to another level, because otherwise you might just as well be playing classical music.

That intersection of the planned and the spontaneous is displayed most obviously on his recordings with the Octet and his 12-piece Big Band. Not surprisingly, the tunes, their arrangements, and their improvisational glosses resonate with historical gestures that are constantly bent into new shapes by new contexts. On *Ming*, for instance, the material ranges from a pull-out-the-stops update of the loft blowing scene ("The Hill") through not-so-oblique references to old standards like "Misty" ("Jasvan") to scrambled reworkings of bop influences ("Dewey's Circle"). *Home* includes everything from lullabyish melodies that evoke Ellington ("Home") to strutting multiple melodies that evoke Ives ("3-D Family"). The title track of *Murray's Steps* both refers to and renovates Coltrane's famed "Giant Steps"; the lushly voiced melodies and dissonant flute echo on "Sweet Lovely" at times seem to picture a meeting between Duke and Dolphy; and the exuberant calypso stomp called "Flowers for Albert" in honor of Ayler never fails to blow the roof off Sweet Basil and get the crowd to rollicking happily even as the music extends slyly beyond their harmonic pale. The two-volume *Big Band*

Live at Sweet Basil offers other crowd-pleasers, like the full-throated Dixieland bash called "Bechet's Bounce."

It would be hard to overstate the impact of this music: it dazzles the mind with its complexity, touches the soul with its unleashed singing, and shakes every booty in sight. As the man himself puts it, "I like big bands because of the power you can come in with: it's so much more magnified. It's like the difference between getting hit with a tennis ball and getting hit with a hard ball. It leaves people breathless."

As does the apparent ease with which Murray moves his concept and material from a big to a small band. With his trio or quartet, for example, he becomes the primary soloist with room to spare, and so he croons his Coleman Hawkins-ish vibrato, warm and wide, on a classic like "Body and Soul," or pulls out his bass clarinet for a creamy, occasionally belching rendition of Fats Waller's jokey "Jitterbug Waltz." Or take the eight-year-old World Saxophone Quartet, which he forms with fellow reed aces Bluiett, Oliver Lake, and Julius Hemphill. As you'd expect from its personnel, the WSQ commands a delirium-inducing array of styles, from raucous riffing that features four deftly independent lines spiraling outward to the smoothly and lushly interwoven section work of *Plays Duke Ellington*, a beautiful if unslavish reworking of Ellington and Strayhorn tunes. Or the similarly styled *Clarinet Summit* LPs, where he joins forces with greats Alvin Batiste, John Carter, and Jimmy Hamilton for tunes by them and the Duke. Or there are his free-jazz-style excursions with Blood on *Children*, for instance, where they dismember the chestnut called "All the Things You Are" with such savage good humor that they make it impossible to listen to some lounge lizard idle over its changes for the umpteenth time without laughing.

Which brings us to our second question: Why has no major U.S. label signed such a volcanic talent? The answer to that one, unfortunately, rattles lost in the minds of the MBAs who run those companies. The only certainty is that Murray's supple and wonderful music will outlast them all.   [1987]

chapter 53

The Knitting Factory

Scene is a word musicians use to describe their world, but as its theatrical metaphor implies, a scene needs a place to happen, a staging area where players can try out their ideas on each other and an audience. Each generation discovers that kind of venue, whether it's the Cotton Club for budding swing bands or Minton's for incipient beboppers.

Basically, that history is repeating itself for the eclectic music coming from the hungry and honed young players based largely in downtown Manhattan and Brooklyn. When 25-year-old Michael Dorf arrived in New York in 1985 from Wisconsin, he wanted to open a club that would mesh performance art, poetry readings, and music with his interest in Flaming Pie Records, which he ran with bassist Bob Appel. They found a funky second-story streetfront space with a bay window overlooking Houston Street, put a small stage and sound system next to the window, clustered folding chairs and homemade tables around, tucked a small bar and some basic kitchen facilities in a back corner, hung for-sale art all over, and dubbed the results the Knitting Factory.

What followed illustrates the diverse vitality of the New York music scene—and, not so coincidentally, demonstrates how younger audiences are, despite industry disbelief, willing to take at least an occasional chance on what they might hear. When Appel tired of touring and became the club's engineer, and Jerry Liebowitz formulated the college-radio series *Live at the Knitting Factory*, the support systems to create a forum for the eclectic, overlapping scenes around the Apple were in place.

Initially progressive-rock college-radio faves dominated the venue, but that shifted as Dorf began a kind of private crash course. "I'd studied jazz history up through the hard-boppers and the 5 Spot, but I didn't really know anything about the new music," Dorf admits. "But Wayne Horvitz, John Zorn, and other people began playing here and really turned me on to what was happening around town now, both in jazz and in improvisation as a genre distinct from jazz."

Dorf's enthusiastic on-the-job training led him to book some of the scene's most interesting sonic explorers. Since, as he implies, jazz is an increasingly misleading tag for up-and-comers, none of the jazz venues in town regularly booked emerging musicians unless they were sidemen to established older artists. That left them scuffling to showcase their music; if they were among the lucky, they periodically wound up at a grant-funded arts venue like the Kitchen. "That's fine for what it is," says Dorf, "but I think it's just as important to show that these kinds of music are commercially viable in a commercial setting. It gives them a quasi-legitimacy that they don't get, for whatever ephemeral reasons, at a place like Roulette—even though the show and the crowd might be the same."

His club's success underscores the point. As Dorf's knowledge of the scene broadens, so do his booking policies. Key elder statesmen of the new avant-gardes have begun to show up: Sun Ra crammed his entire Arkestra in to mix his otherworldly musical alchemy; Cecil Taylor spun through his mind-warp with a fiery vengeance; Julius Hemphill brandished his alto; organ great Big John Patton reprised his soul jazz with Zorn, Frisell, and Previte.

That last event indicates how the Knitting Factory has become a nexus where the many distinct strands of non-mainstream music around New York can twine in unusual and rewarding ways. In such an intimate space, with relatively low fees and cover charges, the pressure to package the music is off; players can take chances with their stuff while the audience listens in and learns. Maybe most telling is the way younger musicians (and critics, and record company folk) now routinely stop in just to check out whatever might be going on.   [1988]

chapter 54

Monk Goes Downtown

"Jazz"—a word the musicians saddled with have hated from its beginnings—covers a multitude of sounds and styles. One result is that as the music moves through history its heroes, movements, truisms are constantly being re-evaluated in terms of contemporary trends, needs, potentials.

Take bebop as a prime example. In the '40s the unwelcome term described musical revolutionaries who were forging a new language in reaction to the then-mainstream as well as to the dramatically shifting social conditions of the postwar world. Now bebop *is* the mainstream, a language that can still be astonishingly supple and can still tell amazing stories but that is, like Beethoven's classical idiom, hardly revolutionary any longer. A product of its time and place, it's become a generally accepted set of musical propositions, the basic grammar and syntax taught in the supermarket-style music schools that have prospered in the last decade or so.

In the larger world, academies exert their sanctioned views of the past via dictionaries and canons as they attempt to control the natural riot of development that sprawls into linguistic and cultural growth. In some ways—and with no little historical irony—that's how the music schools have used bebop. Its vocabulary and formats and tunes have been elevated to the status of holy writ, its upstarts transformed into an unassailable pantheon, its internal tensions papered over with dogma.

And yet, despite the codifiers, history moves on and takes bebop with it. Outstanding young players like Ralph Moore and Roy Hargrove, who see themselves "in the tradition," inevitably echo more recent harmonic and conceptual developments even as they revive bebop-style jams and call the period's standards; self-described revolutionaries like Steve Coleman and John Zorn inevitably echo earlier voices like Bunky Green and Ornette Coleman. Each meeting with the past creates a kind of two-way funhouse mirror in which past and present distort, blur, and merge.

It's an image Thelonious Sphere Monk would have appreciated. Drawing on his deep roots in stride piano while pursuing outrageously shifting harmonies, tautly angular melodies, and jagged rhythms, Monk obviously knew better than to try to tie up all his energizing loose ends into some consciously neat bundle. In fact, it could be argued that the enduring power of his music explodes out of the collisions between his loving debts to earlier traditions and his refusal to view them as sacrosanct. If, thanks to his membership in the pantheon, his own tunes have been incessantly trivialized in cocktail lounges the last few years, Monk's understanding of tradition and its relation to his music has made him an ongoing inspiration for explorers like Sonny Rollins, John Coltrane, Ornette Coleman, and the AACM.

It's no coincidence that Monk himself first started to win public acceptance with his *Monk Plays Ellington* (Riverside). At the time, his musical stock was pretty low: he had no cabaret card, his previous records barely sold, and most jazz fans and musicians thought his playing was at best charmingly primitive; at worst, incomprehensible and illiterate.

In his invaluable *The Jazz Tradition* (Oxford), veteran jazz historian Martin Williams observes,

> To make his playing as personally expressive as he wished, Monk had even altered his way of striking the keys, his finger positions, and had largely converted his piano into a kind of horn which was also capable of stating harmonic understructures. And he did not fake, doodle, decorate, or play notes only to fill out bars or fill time.
>
> The core of Monk's style is a rhythmic virtuosity. He is a master of displaced accents, shifting meters, shaded delays and anticipations. Therefore he is a master of effective pause of meaningfully employed space, rest, and silence. Fundamentally his practices in harmony and line are organized around his insights into rhythm. And as rhythm is fundamental to jazz, so one who develops its rhythms also develops jazz along just the lines that its own nature implies it should go.

And though critics cried sellout, *Monk Plays Ellington* not only garnered Monk a new public but also demonstrated his acute insights into the relationship between composition and improvisation—the dialectic engine that drives jazz's development—as well. Monk approaches classic Duke tunes with obvious respect and no deference. His arrangements and solos evoke Duke's own stride roots, lilting sense of swing, and hard-won harmonic idiom, but they're totally unwilling to be museum pieces.

Instead, "It Don't Mean a Thing (If It Ain't Got That Swing)"—to take just the leadoff track as an example—becomes a showcase for Monk's preoccupations as well. The original melody shadows his solo whether he's fitting his serrated ideas into its rhythmic contours and harmonic motion or deliberately going completely against where it breaks into a rest or negotiates a harmonic turn; the fact that he never simply takes the changes opportunistically both makes his highly idiosyncratic attack more accessible and puts it into sharp relief. As he was later to insist others do with his own material, he demonstrated clearly that a real composition demands a different improvisatory treatment from a collection of chords limned by a head.

Monk was trying, in a real sense, to translate jazz composition from the big-band format to the small group—a project that made him closer to Ellington than to Bud Powell. That meant restructuring an improvisational language into a compositional one without emasculating it, and at the same time redefining the relationship between musical piece and improvised solos.

In this sense, Monk was no bebopper. Though he was present at the creation and shared many of bebop's harmonic explorations and preoccupations, he wasn't motivated by the same concerns that drove Diz and Bird and Bud. His melodies, however skewed and gyring, are hummably accessible as few bebop heads are. In place of extended solos that zigzag at hurtling speed over extended changes, he offers short, pointed expositions that are more like variations on melodic themes. His slamdunk chords, squashed seconds, and curling rests—which at the time were heard as his inability to sprint like Bud Powell, whom Monk had ironically helped tutor—actually form a different, if related, vocabulary, From these perspectives, Monk's concept can be related to another mislabeled bopper's, since Miles Davis—whose airier attack and honed melodies were precisely what drew Bird to the younger man's playing, so different from his own—was redefining even the most hackneyed Tin Pan Alley standards at the same time Monk was redoing Duke.

But, aside from Miles and Monk, a generation of "little Birds," in thrall to the genius of Charlie Parker, spent their time and talent chasing the chimera of speed through bebop's cyclically repeating harmonic mazes. Not coincidentally, melodies were reduced to "heads"—little more than an excuse to link a set of changes. Think of the many Bird recordings (especially live) where he either filigrees the head into rococo abstraction or just dispenses with it altogether, and you'll get the sense of how far jazz's internal balance had tipped away from composition at the time.

Monk's emphasis on his writing accounts for much of his impact on the loose amalgam of younger players corraled as "the downtown scene," since for them writing and arranging have regained a status unthinkable during the '70s loft-session era. But that historical pendulum swing beats at the heart of jazz's evolution. On the one hand, jazz has developed the dazzling scores and orchestral voicings of key innovators from Jelly Roll Morton to Duke Ellington to Charles Mingus to Henry Threadgill; on the other hand, its players have insisted on the right to spontaneity within a community, the democratic interaction of voices that can either defy anarchy or deliberately incite it.

The balance between charts and blowing has been tipping back again partly because a younger generation of musical explorers has been re-evaluating the past and trying to forge languages that can speak to today while today's purists cry "sellout." Broadening their sonic and rhythmic vocabularies with reggae and rap and funk and punk, they pen pieces that interweave improvisation and writing in such a seamless way you can't always distinguish the two. They exchange the head/string-of-long-solos/head bebop format for more scripted, sculpted varieties of ensemble crosstalk, shape solos via oddly floating space and off-balance rhythms rather than breakneck spews of eighth and sixteenth notes, push their instruments' sounds with deliberate abrasiveness. Overall, it's a combination that Monk would have understood—indeed, it echoes his own efforts and draws inspiration from them.

So it's no accident that two of the best of the emergent generation, Geri Allen and Bill Frisell, can be found side by side on drummer Paul Motian's tribute album *Monk by Motian* (JMT). Listening to Frisell's throaty, careening guitar and Allen's now-stabbing, now-twisting piano combine on two such diverse cuts as "Ruby My Dear" and "Off Minor" may open some ears for these composer-players just as Monk's Ellington gambit did for him. For while they demonstrate how well they understand Monk's dicta about the seamless relationship between melody and solos, about the use of space and cunning silences, they filter those lessons through their own sensibilities and sounds—as Mink filtered Duke.

Allen first. Born in Detroit to a Bird-loving father, she counted funksters like James Brown and George Clinton among her musical heroes. That gradually expanded when she studied ethnomusicology at Pitt, where she turned on to worldwide ethnic sounds as well as AACMers like Lester Bowie, Joseph Jarman, and Oliver Lake, who were adapting their own interests in Africa and the Caribbean to their fierce, distinctly un-bebop brands of jazz. Perhaps not surprisingly, her thesis avoided pianists and dealt with Eric Dolphy.

Like the AACM folks she admires, Allen's music, especially on *In the Middle* (Minor Music), is bristling with varied ideas but keeps its energy harnessed and focused. Where Ellington drew on the blues and the church, on Broadway and Tin Pan Alley, Impressionism and Afro-Latin sounds as contemporary ingredients for his compositions, where Monk mixed blues, the church, stride, bebop, and romantic ballads, Allen juxtaposes salsa, funk, cubist sonic collages, Impressionistic études, and more. Like Ellington and Monk, Mingus and Threadgill, she fills her groups with players she's worked with for years, so that she knows how to write for their strengths and they know how to play her music, with its demanding angles and dense, crosstalking arrangements.

Her own piano attack combines the forceful key-slamming and incisive pedal manipulation that made Monk's piano technique so repugnant to bebop fans. In Allen's hands, as in Monk's, the piano is goosed into the kind of jarring, warped overtones and clusters that defeat its well-tempered tuning. Her sense of harmony, and the spareness with which she comps, recall the Ellington-Basie-Monk-Lewis axis, and when she solos she avoids the predictable—holding her breath when you expect a sprint, blitzkrieging a few bars where you expect a pause, squashing a whole-tone phrase into a crushed delight.

Not that Allen's piano is a Monk clone. Overall, her approach resides somewhere between Monk's, Herbie Nichols's, and Cecil Taylor's—which is not as odd a place as it might seem at first reading. Consider, for instance, that Nichols, who earned his keep mostly by playing in society bands, wrote the first published article on Monk, and on his relatively few gigs as a leader used Monk's lunging rhythmic displacements as the launching point for his solos. Consider, too, that Taylor, after Monk, has been the most dogged pioneer in altering the actual physical mechanics of eliciting sound from between the cracks, of pursuing a horn-like flexibility while working the keyboard's near–unique ability to make simultaneous harmonic statements. Consider that all three approach the keyboard as an orchestral reduction. Then you'll have a context for how, whether she's comping astringently à la Monk or even when she's flurry-ing notes à la Taylor, Allen will veer with Monk-like suddenness against the pulse, hold a space open or fracture it brutally, play with and against the shape of the themes she uses to conjure life in our fragmentary, information-barraged age.

Her versions of "Bemsha Swing" and "Round Midnight" on her solo album *Homegrown* (Minor Music), like Monk's versions of Ellington classics, serve both to link her to a tradition and to display her unique contemporary voice. Unlike Marcus Robert's devout neoclassic reading of "Blue Monk," which genuflects respectfully before a historical giant, Allen reimagines Monk's music in terms of what's happened to Ameri-can ears since Monk's day, from Nichols and Taylor to Herbie Hancock and the hammering conveyor belts of Detroit assembly lines and the metallic arpeggiated arc of African mbiras.

Like Allen, Frisell is now beginning to come into his own as both a player and composer-arranger, and as with her, that's partly due to his grappling with Monk's music and its still pivotal position in jazz's van-guards. Born in Baltimore, raised in Denver, schooled in the blues, rock, and Berklee's bop, Frisell has worked in such an astounding diver-sity of contexts that it's hard to keep them straight. From Paul Motian to Leni Stern, from Bass Desires to Power Tools, from Tim Berne to Vernon Reid, Frisell has kept expanding his technical facility; he's now at the point where his patented bleary, attackless sound can hover gracefully or spin like a demented frisbee ringed with razor blades, lurch dissipatedly into space or sledgehammer a note into oblivion. Wrapping his bluesy roots in a cloud of delay, he reimagines on the guitar the kind of arcing space Monk coaxed and yanked out of the piano via his idio-syncratic fingerings and pedal-pumping.

But even beyond his extraordinary detonation and reassembly of the electric guitar's sound, what links Frisell as a player most clearly to Monk is his off-balance sense of rhythm, where he mixes Monk's whiplash aggressiveness with Jim Hall's supportive understatement. Lis-ten, for instance, to *Monk in Motian:* working mostly between Motian's melodic drums and Joe Lovano's spiraling sax, he covers the vast ground opened up and makes it coherent by floating Monk-like spaces that he'll suddenly puncture with fiercely bent, split-toned notes, abrupt register shifts, provocative intervals and chord shapes. Add his Monk-like insistence on structuring his solos around thematic motifs, rather than riding the changes, and as with Allen it becomes easy to hear what's exciting younger players and critics about Frisell's work. He's about as far from fusion's macho noodling as you can get.

His compositions make that even clearer. Where Monk is grounded in blues and Allen in the blues' funkier updates, Frisell takes country twangs and East Village noise barrages and melts them down into a vicious but charming combo that often finds itself cruising various disguised blues, like his "Some Song and Dance" medley on his latest *Before We Were Born* (Nonesuch). Stalking over tripwire beats, his pieces revolve around melodies—idiosyncratic and gnarled, but like Monk's hummable, even unforgettable once they penetrate your ears. Tunes like the two-themed "Little Brother Bobby" and the haunting "Lonesome" from *Lookout for Hope* (ECM) tuck into their apparently simple structures the surprising turns Monk made seem so inevitable in his own because of the flowing melodic shape. Augmented by the propulsive crosstalk of his charts, Frisell's music speaks of late 20th-century dreamscapes in scarred, apocalyptic tongues.

Which brings us to the underlying quality of Monk's music that appeals across generations to vanguard after vanguard: a coruscating, searing irony that can laugh at itself, that unsettles rather than soothes. The music schools can't teach that; it's dangerous, because it undermines notions like canons and pantheons and aesthetic hierarchies of whatever kind, then pokes gleefully among the pieces. It shatters expectations about sound and how to process it—and hence expectations about the world. That's a task music can perform only when it's not so freighted with nostalgia and so overburdened with its own history that it's always checking out its own shadow.   [1989]

chapter_heading
chapter 55

The Nurturer

Her piano can dart over curving lines with the jackrabbit agility of a McCoy Tyner, crush note clusters like a French Impressionist, or float spare lines over telling spaces with the wit of a Thelonious Monk. Her versatility has made her a very-much-in-demand side person. Since 1984, she's worked with jazzers as diverse as Oliver Lake, James Newton, Lester Bowie, Arthur Blythe, Paul Motian, Wayne Shorter, and Steve Coleman.

But it's her stunningly individual writing that is propelling her emergence as a leader. Her conpositions range easily over broad musical terrain; jazz and funk and international sounds percolate through them without degenerating into pastiche. Beginning with efforts like the trio *Printmakers* (Minor Music) and solo *Homegrown* (Minor Music), she resolutely extended her approach to larger ensembles for *Open on All Sides in the Middle* (Minor Music) and *Twylight* (Minor Music).

But now, with *The Nurturer* (Blue Note), Geri Allen has a U.S. major-label release. Even though the deal came through the back door—Blue Note's Japanese partner Toshiba approached Allen about the project—it gives her a shot at a larger audience.

Though it bristles with ideas, Allen's music is very catchy and hardly forbidding. But it's also sui generis, not a retread of an older style in the mode currently popular among many younger jazzers. As the thoughtful, soft-spoken, 30-something Allen sees it,

> I think younger people see somebody like Wynton Marsalis and say, I want to do this too. That's positive in a lot of ways.
>
> Artistically these kids—I'm not that much older than some of them, but it's really a different generation—are playing on a real high plane. That's a big plus. But I also think that there's this romance with the history now. It's really difficult to go for something that is not a traditional sound *per se*. Today, chances are people aren't gonna want to hear it. Maybe they're not as patient, maybe the record com-

panies aren't interested, and if they don't put it out nobody gets to hear it.

You can make a decision to be great and sound great by getting as close to what John Coltrane sounded like as you can. Or you can make a choice and say, People are gonna identify with John Coltrane because he pulled his weight—you know what I'm saying?—and it's still fresh. So you can think, Why should I go through all this when I can really feel good about my playing and not have to go through the frustrations of doubting myself? Because if I'm gonna play like Trane, nobody's gonna put me down. How can you put something that great down?

So in a way I think that attitude is a safety valve. It's more the feeling of being a really good player and getting out there and dealing right away, because people understand that language. It's clear and it's been around long enough; it's not fumbling around trying to find a better way to say itself. It's already there.

I can see my own music taking some time to be accepted that way. I mean, I play Mary Lou Williams's music, which I love to do; I play Thelonious Monk and Herbie Nichols. That's always an education for me. It's like reading a piece of classic literature. It's always fresh, you're always getting a lot back. But at the same time, it'll never be greater than it was at its origins, as far as I'm concerned. It can be different, it can be interesting, but it was unadulterated when it came. It was in its time then. It was one living thing; it was culture fluctuating itself. So it has a different weight than me playing it today. There's a distance today that wasn't there then; me playing it today is a historical act, which it wasn't then.

For Allen, *The Nurturer* is a deliberate historical act of a contemporary kind. It reaches back to her Detroit upbringing—her parents encouraged her and her brother to be interested in the arts—and her education in the Motor City's famed Cass Tech High School, which has turned out players like harpist Dorothy Ashby, bassist Ron Carter, and Eric Clapton sideman Greg Phillingames. There in 1972 she joined saxist Kenny Garrett, bassist Robert Hurst, and percussionist Eli Fountain to study with trumpeter Marcus Belgrave. Belgrave was Cass Tech's jazz-artist-in-residence and led an ensemble he called the Jazz Development Workshop. With compositions and performances from Belgrave and his now matured students, *The Nurturer* is in fact meant to be a belated record of those Detroit days.

The Nurturer

Says Allen,

Marcus, of course, is reflecting all his years: he played with Clifford
Brown, studied with the same teacher, worked with Charles Mingus
and Ray Charles—there's a whole history there. We worked together
on this like we always worked together; it was very natural. And it's important for us to get a chance to play with Marcus and have it documented.

From Cass Tech, Allen went on to Howard University's Jazz Studies
Program in 1975, where she studied with classically oriented composer
Thomas Trilling and ex-Billie Holiday accompanist John Malachi,
who'd also worked with Charlie Parker in Billy Eckstine's big band. After
graduating in 1979, Allen headed to the Big Apple, where she used her
NEA grant to study with undersung piano great Kenny Barron. Six
months later, though, she changed direction.

Allen recalls,

Nathan Davis (of the University of Pittsburgh music department) called
me and said, "Come on to Pittsburgh, I've got this situation for you
here." The situation was a job as a teaching assistant and a place in
the master's program of ethnomusicology. . . . I felt like I needed to
go, 'cause I was slipping, you know? I didn't really feel ready to be in
New York, I didn't feel like I could sustain myself after the grant ran
out. It was a great opportunity to work with Kenny, and have the cush-
ion of knowing I had the grant to get me through. But I wasn't working, and I didn't see how I was going to be working. I didn't feel like I
was playing well enough to be working in New York.

Her four years at Pittsburgh polished her up so she felt ready. She
listened to jazz's then cutting edge and immersed herself in various
world musics as well as continuing to follow her long-standing interests
in classical music. In 1982, she headed back to New York much less
tentative than she'd left it.

Jazz is still a relatively small world, and even one solid connection
can open many doors for a musician with solid chops. For Allen, her
New York connection took the form of fellow Motowner Dwight An-
drews, with whom she'd studied at Cass Tech's extension program at the
University of Michigan. Andrews, who has penned the music for all of
August Wilson's acclaimed plays, including *The Piano Lesson*, intro-
duced the neophyte to Oliver Lade and Lester Bowie. Once she cut *Plug
It* with Lake's reggae-funk outfit Jump Up, the phone started ringing.

But for her first six months back, it didn't ring consistently enough for Allen to give up her steady gig as a side person in ex-Supremes vocalist Mary Wilson's band. Playing straight-ahead soul music wasn't the problem for Allen, who grew up on the stuff. The fact that the gig didn't give her room to pursue her own ideas and work very often with others was. On the other hand, it was a steady paycheck. Allen finally took a deep breath and jumped off the Wilson train, teetered near financial disaster for a year, and then sighed with relief when the phone began to ring steadily enough so she didn't have to worry about the rent every month.

Now, married, a mother, a working side person, and a leader, Allen has left those fears behind. But her ambitions remain the same as they were at Cass Tech:

> I've always felt comfortable about trying to do things my own way, whether it succeeded or not. All my teachers were saying, That's what the history is about, people trying to do it their way. That's really the tradition.
>
> I like to hear people who are really studied, who have really worked it out, and continue to work it out, but they're not thinking about it when they're playing. It's so well ingrained and they work it out so well that by the time you start playing they don't deal with it any more. Just the music comes out, that moment and what's happening. Life comes out, and not the technique, not the ego. It's unconscious. That's what impresses me. I don't care what the genre is; if that's there, I want to hear it. I'm looking for that human quality.   [1991]

chapter 56

The Clark Kent of the Electric Guitar

Even non-music freaks can identify Bill Frisell's guitar within a couple of seconds. His patented tone is unmistakable—a bleary, gritty, echoing surge—and his snaky, off-balance solos float unexpected spaces and spear wickedly warped notes instead of running through flashy scales. But though he's usually pigeonholed as a jazz player, Frisell's music overrides categories. Trained on clarinet and music theory from age nine, the 37-year-old grew up on classical music, marching bands, blues, rock, soul, and jazz—a mix typical of his generation. So he combines raw emotion and barbed wit, rock-flavored raunch and jazz skills, to create a musical patchwork all his own.

Which is why he's appeared on dozens of albums over the last few years. His deft diversity becomes clear from even a brief sample of his work. Whether he's playing Kurt Weill songs behind Marianne Faithful on *Strange Weather* (Island) or rampaging like a jackhammer on Power Tools' *Strange Meeting* (Island), roaming pastoral glades on his own first album, *In Line* (ECM), or cruising the siren- and construction-strewn cityscape on Tim Berne's *Fulton Street Maul* (Columbia), Frisell's touch and tone somehow adapt to the material's special needs without losing the idiosyncratic individuality of his instrument's voice.

Baltimore-born and Denver-bred, Frisell didn't pick up the guitar until two years after the clarinet; and where his reed training was by the book, he deliberately kept his early six-string fumblings casual. "At first I couldn't read music at all for the guitar," he says. "I was using a whole different part of my brain, just playing along with records." The period's favorites, like Dylan, the Beatles, and the Stones, eventually led him to the blues, which became—and remain—a major love.

He was musically restless right away. "My school was about as perfectly integrated as you can get, so I ended up playing in soul bands backing up singers doing their James Brown things. It must've been pretty strange to see me up on stage playing 'I'm Black and I'm Proud.'" A school talent show turned him on to jazz when he had to learn a tune by guitar great Wes Montgomery to accompany a group of girl dancers. He was hooked, and began devouring jazz from Bird on up and transferring his formal training to the guitar.

Not that that made his musical road any straighter. After his band won an intercollegiate jazz contest, he made an abortive stab at Berklee, a prestigious Boston music college, then holed up in Denver for a couple of years, where he taught music and played rare gigs while becoming, in his own disbelieving words, "a young old fogey. I thought anything other than the old-style jazz-guitar sound, any kind of sound that was contemporary on the guitar, was just bad. Then—I don't know what happened—it just started to seem weird to me that I'd shut off the whole world that had made me want to play in the first place." So he started cranking the volume and reincorporating non-jazz moves into his music again, and soon he was putting together his one-of-a-kind sound.

By 1975 he was ready for another crack at Berklee. Guitarist Pat Metheny, among his other teachers, was struck by his promise; and when Frisell headed to New York in 1979, Metheny got him his first real gig with drummer Paul Motian—an association that continues. And though another couple of years passed before Frisell could leave behind the weddings and bar mitzvahs that underemployed musicians depend on for cash, he began working steadily with a wide variety of lineups.

In fact, with all the groups he's been in and sessions he's done it's amazing Frisell could keep his own musical focus. That he did is clear from the growing depth and sophistication of his composing and playing—despite small budgets that allowed only a couple of days to record and mix each album. By his third, *Lookout for Hope* (ECM), his range became formidable: some hair-raising, metalloid tunes could be soundtracks for *The Road Warrior*, while others paint trail-drive cowpokes squatting around the campfire amid bean farts beneath a psychedelic sky.

Changing labels partly to win the freedom (and budget) to stretch even further, Frisell took over a month in the studio on *Before We Were Born* (Nonesuch). "I'd never made a record where people got the whole picture. So the idea was to use people from all the different areas I go into." The result is a kinetic, cinematic potpourri of styles from the blues to serialism that collide in unpredictable, thought-provoking ways. Funny and intense and full of surprises, *Before We Were Born* holds up a slightly fractured musical mirror to the 30-something crowd.   [1989]

chapter 57

Downtown Scenes

Jazz—whatever that means—is headed in some fascinating directions. Younger musicians keep shifting the balance in their music between composition and improvisation—one of jazz's innermost tensions, providing it with a lot of its propulsive power. To a large extent, that is now helping to rearrange the concept of the band. In the wake of the flat-out blowing sessions of the '70s, sheet music is appearing on stages more often, reflecting what in some ways is a return to the older swing-based jazz bands, where players worked off charts for what they played, often including their solos night after night. Not accidentally, that coincides with the rock-and-roll sensibility most younger musicians have grown up with—the notion of a band fitting the music together in a formatted way.

Also crucial is the harmolodic revolution led by Ornette Coleman. "Free" jazz is democratic in the way it approaches composing and arranging—the emphasis is on the band's movement as a whole, rather than on a star soloist and supporting players—but what results is not a chaotic outpouring of raw, unpremeditated musical power. Ornette insists on the priority of composing even during the unleashed group improvisations, and claims that the larger percentage of what you hear on his Prime Time records is written. Like much of what he says, this is subject to interpretation, but it's more important that younger players see his work as a vital source for what they do, and know his formulations about it.

Of all the Colemanesque offshoots tendrilling through the new music scenes around New York, one of the most consistently fascinating and provocative centers around alto saxophonist Tim Berne and guitarist Bill Frisell. They've worked as a duo; Frisell was all over Berne's first Columbia recording; and the bands they lead share overlapping members—cellist Hank Roberts and drummer Joey Baron. In many ways, the sounds in their respective heads couldn't be more different.

273

Frisell's music is shot through with a mutant Western strain, as if a bunch of cowpokes around a dying fire under an open sky were swapping stories of cattle drives and Mexico after downing lots of Jack Daniels and peyote. Berne, on the other hand, revels in the relentless industrial sounds of the cityscape: he's the street-smart hipster bopping past a 12-car pileup, eyes and ears wide open and probing with an avid love/hate.

What they share is reflected in their sharing bandmates, and is in turn shared by those players on their own outings. First is a love of sheer electronic noises, and a deliberate avoidance of the "normal" rock or jazz instrumental lineup—they're looking to redefine the sound of music per se. Second is their general approach to making music, which turns on improvisation but proceeds from heavily composed and arranged scores that sometimes annotate even solos. The coiled tensions of that combination give their work a power that can twist music and listeners alike into knots. As they range from the swaggering to the subtle, they, along with the Brooklyn-based crew that includes altoists Steve Coleman and Greg Osby, keyboardist Geri Allen, and trombonist Robin Eubanks, are mapping some of the main lines for this generation's musical growth, much as the AACM did 20 years ago.

In Berne's case especially, that's no accidental linkage: he learned his alto sax and compositional skills at the hands of alto master Julius Hemphill, one of the key members of Oliver Lake's Black Artists Group, the AACM's St. Louis analog. (Now Hemphill, Lake, David Murray, and Hamiet Bluiett comprise the finally acclaimed World Saxophone Quartet.) Picking up the sax in his late teens, Berne wanted to cross the rawboned r&b/soul horns he loved (he still listens primarily to soul music) with his interest in broader composition. That's why he sought out Hemphill, who was doing just that.

Cutting albums for his tiny Empire label and then for the Milan-based jazz label Black Saint/Soul Note over the last several years, Berne doggedly set about forging his own idiom. His two Columbia discs leave no doubt he's succeeded. The punningly titled *Fulton Street Maul* (the gentrifying construction of downtown Brooklyn pounded for years right outside Berne's windows) sears and jangles and scrapes and slashes and even occasionally soothes as it hurtles through the urban landscape and gleans jarring, unlooked-for bits of beauty from the wreckage and endless change. Frisell's arching guitar smears its fat tones across the picture just before tailing off into the cracks of the piano keyboard—he's learned his lessons about un-well tempering well indeed. Roberts's electrified cello skitters and jags and sings like an unsheathed sawblade, and Alex Cline's drums are always stirring up trouble.

For his second major-label release, Berne shifted his lineup, replacing Frisell with trumpeter Robertson and bassist Mark Dresser, and Cline with Baron. Not surprisingly, some of his turbulent music's emphasis shifted too. It's as if on *Sanctified Dreams* Berne no longer has to wedge the splinters of urban life under your fingernails; he can relax a bit and ride the sheer energy always about to burst from any corner of his tightly plotted, incrementally organized compositions and arrangements. While the music is no less intense than on *Maul*, it's more accessible, and offers diced-up bop ("Velcho Man") and ruminative melodies ("Sanctified Dreams") as well as raging snarls. Baron, in particular, skews any beat he plays with such off-handed authority that there's no danger of a piece settling into predictability; he prods and pokes the band into navigating the music's antic mood swings—from smokily mutant blues to finessed bebop to gritty near–heavy metal—with strutting exuberance.

Frisell has had more trouble documenting his extraordinary growth on his own records. ECM's Manfred Eicher, an eccentric wizard of sorts, insists on swaddling all his recordings in the equivalent of a hyper-reverberant medieval cathedral. Somehow Frisell has managed with his latest effort, *Lookout for Hope*, to capture the jabbing, feinting, greasy raunch he pours out with endless invention—I've rarely heard him repeat a lick—and country soulfulness onstage.

His music is kaleidoscopic, a shimmering blur of gentle seduction and ferocious attack. Over the never-on-the-one beats tripwired by drummer Baron and the loopy, off-kilter bass of Kermit Driscoll, Frisell and Roberts fly daredevil loop-de-loops through a cloud of electronic enhancements, now strafing each other and the tune, now executing precise split-second formations, all the while spinning a dizzying web of sound that hangs before your astonished eyes. That's no mere conceit—part of the music's catchy genius is the way it becomes tactile, insinuates a literal sound sculpture.

More and more, Frisell's abilities as a composer are equaling his guitar prowess. That's clear from the way his tunes can stand next to Monk's "Hackensack," the one cut on *Lookout* not from his pen. From the metallic slash-and-burn of "Remedios the Beauty" to the minimalism-meets-bebop "Hangdog," from the reggae-inflected "Alien Prints" to the achingly sweet country sights of "Lonesome," Frisell never lets his songs get stuck in a single groove. He writes melodies, not just vamps that are excuses to solo, unfolds sequences of ideas across kinetic juxtapositions, uses spaces as daringly as he does his electronic effects to create an unmistakable voice.

Nor is the versatile and much-in-demand Frisell limited to his own music. His extensive jazz training and outstanding chops make him one of the few players who can confidently crisscross from downtown N.Y.-style freneticism to mainstream jazz without a serious misstep. His recordings and live dates with famed drummer Paul Motian and young guitarist-composer Leni Stern show off his idiosyncratic guitar vocabulary in more conventionally unconventional jazz settings. His disc with fellow guitar flamethrower Vernon Reid, *Smash and Scatteration*, reworks the history of guitar duos from Lonnie Johnson and Eddie Lang on up with barbed, witty intensity, while the aptly named Power Tools, his collaboration with ex-Ornette Coleman drummer Ronald Shannon Jackson and *his* ex-Decoding Society bassist Melvin Gibbs, rips and roars with all the grace of a ramaging jackhammer. One hilarious number is called "The President's Nap," while "Howard Beach Memoirs" is the gently pastoral piece you'd expect.

As a composer, cellist Hank Roberts leans more toward the pastoral than any of his colleagues, although his musical landscape harbors whining ghosts that can leap out from behind the smallest bush without a hint of warning. His debut, *Black Pastels*, pulls together Berne, Frisell, Dresser, Baron, and Eubanks, along with trombonist Ray Anderson and bass trombonist Dave Taylor, for yet another oddly weighted lineup.

Roberts's cello is an extension of his voice, and vice versa; he wears a headset with microphone and sings along, usually in a keening wordless style that deliberately echoes Tibetan chanting. As his voice veers from drone to wail, the cello haunts it, then sidesteps it to trade places in the foreground, a shadow becoming substantial. Couple this introspective dialogue with the group exchanges ricocheting all around him, and you've got the essence of his music's motive power.

He drives the combination far. The ambitious, gnarled composition called "Granpappy's Barn/Dance Death Dance" kicks off with a trombone choir in a bleary round beneath Berne's screeching alto, and segues through one inventive, contrasting section after another, from tottering waltz to burbling, grumbling trombone strut. "Scarecrow Shakedown" takes off from a basic blues lick to land on the far side of Alice's mirror; "Lucky's Lament" forges edgy metallic textures into a modern AmerIndian dirge. Meditative and waspish and always moving, *Black Pastels* offers another set of possible clues about the shape of music to come.   [1988]

chapter 58

Fractured Fairy Tales

If you're 30-something like Tim Berne and most of the outstanding players he's assembled here, the title Fractured Fairy Tales conjures up a world. A childhood world, that is, of Saturday mornings in front of the tube—Cartoon Heaven.

Up at the pinnacle of Cartoon Heaven ranks the repository/sampler of arcane jokes and groaning puns and scrambled eclecticism, *Rocky and His Friends*, starring a somewhat intelligent flying squirrel and his dumb-moose sidekick who battled bumbling Russian spies Boris Badenov and Natasha Fatale in epics by weekly installment. Mixed in with the adventures of Canadian Mountie Dudley Do-Right and the harebrained time travels of the dog-scientist Mr. Peabody and his pet boy Sherman, Fractured Fairy Tales was a treasured segment on the show, featuring Bullwinkle's oddly twisted reworkings of Mother Goose and the Brothers Grimm that ended inevitably with a series of groaners-as-morals.

The allusions fit the mutant serio-comic sounds this crackerjack band spins out. Slashing an opening somewhere between Ornette Coleman, musique concrete, Carl Stalling, the Velvet Underground, Henry Threadgill, and Henry Cowell, Berne & Company then fracture your perceptual frame into a post-cubist collage that's strident and energizing and moving and provoking and edgy and insistent and very, very funny.

Berne's compositions reflect his continuing astonishing growth; he's evolved a language that conveys a hyper-hip, tongue-in-chic sense of a world that's surrealistically playful and painful by immediate turns.

Kinda like a world that's so skewed that George Bush is president, Dan Quayle is vice president, and Ronald Reagan collects piles of cash on trips to Japan for telling the Japanese film industry that it's making good old-fashioned American-family-type movies. Kinda like a Saturday-morning world, where Rocky and Bullwinkle, Boris and Natasha, Mr. Peabody and Sherman and the Wayback Machine unfold absurd, hilarious, and telling allegories for kids of all ages. [1990]

chapter 59

Caos Totale

Caos Totale is Italian for just what it looks like. It also describes the brink Tim Berne's latest group skates along with considerable finesse and wit on *Pace Yourself* (JMT). Inspired by the AACM's expanded sonic pallette and idiom-stretching, the altoist scrambles angular boppish heads, offbeat harmonies, dangling meters, *noir*ish atmospherics, raucous blowouts, and worldbeat patches that twitter and drone with a wink. The subtle backing riffs and textures—Berne likes goosing his soloists and matching unlikely instruments—buttress and contrast with the improvising. Even the solo sections twist mainstream expectations. They veer away from running-the-chords to juxtapose a cappella breakouts and stretches of understatement or near silence with plotted free-for-alls. The result: a compelling and highly inflected language that reflects the leader's own wryly hip sensibility and the hyperventilating perspective shifts that define life and culture in our time.

Lately the mainstream press has been trumpeting jazz's return from the grave thanks to young neoboppers. But Berne reminds us that jazz didn't die or stop evolving. Looking around with a lopsided but knowing grin, he orchestrates post-free-era jazz with a focused compositional eye and a cartoonist's catchy sense of caricature—his last album was called *Fractured Fairy Tales*. In the process, he creates a sonically and emotionally volatile soundscape of the late 20th century that is ominous and ironic, unexpectedly funny and brutally assaultive, and yet coherent. The soloists personalize its imagery: guitarist Marc Ducret's scrabbling skids and lunges, omnibrassman Herb Robertson's brilliant comic yawps and stuttering speechifying, drummer Bobby Previte's rhythmic and coloristic sense, bassist Mark Dresser's sonically inventive agility, trombonist Steve Swell's smears-to-silken moves, Berne's own slippery-to-edgy-to-raging alto. Skirting total chaos as they conjure its abyss, their voices fill *Pace Yourself* with the resonant depth that lets us recognize ourselves in its kaleidoscopic whirl. [1991]

chapter 60

On the Street Where You Live

Here's the scene. King Curtis decides to do a Charlie Parker tribute on location in Tibet, where the monks, having blasted their unwanted Chinese visitors back to Beijing with the spiritual force of their chanting, are now busy with jackhammers and cement mixers trying to rebuild the rubble before the Dalai Lama returns. Got it?

If that sounds like a might-have-been painting by Bosch, so does the music alto saxist Berne's been making these last ten years. Although what he writes and performs is about as far from ezy-listening yuppie wimpers like Spyro Gyra as you can possibly get, Berne has managed to land a contract with a major label (Columbia) and record two albums (*Fulton Street Maul* and *Sanctified Dreams*) that slash and burn musical categories with the textural élan and flash-fried wit of New York's best graffiti artists.

Berne's music is simultaneously street-smart and intelligent. That's partly because he studied with altoist Julius Hemphill, in the late '60s one of the prime movers behind the St. Louis-based Black Artists

Group. Like its Chicago model, the Association for the Advancement of Creative Musicians (AACM), BAG was a cooperative organization that both sponsored concerts and recording sessions for its members and investigated the entire landscape of sound; filling in the templates laid out by revolutionaries like John Coltrane, Ornette Coleman, and Albert Ayler, they expanded their notions of musicality beyond well-tempered and blue notes, dove headlong into the cracks between the piano's keys and blew whinnies and bleets and blatts and wordless whooshes on instruments that were traditional to jazz, homemade, and from around the world, and drew on sources as diverse as Dixieland and r&b, blues and African rituals.

So when Berne gave up the fast breaks and teamwork of basketball (his previous main squeeze) for a different kind of sprinting, group-oriented play, Hemphill was the mentor he sought out. "I loved the fact that Julius could play and write all this complex stuff and at the same time get such a great throaty r&b tone from his sax," is how Tim puts it. "I studied the horn and composition at the same time, so for me playing and writing were always closely linked."

That linkage manifests itself repeatedly on his last two albums. While there are openings for improvisation in the traditional jazz sense (Berne calls them "coups" and says, "Anybody in the band can pull one at any time, but there'd better be a good reason"), much of the music is through-composed in the dense, heavily structured, definitely urban idiom that Berne has been evolving since recording on his own small Empire label. Now that his unusually voiced lineup has gelled—Herb Robertson's off-kilter trumpet and weird assortment of mutes, Hank Roberts's electrified cello enhanced by spacey delay loops and Tibetan-style wordless vocals, Mark Dresser's bass moving from arco whalesong to two-handed skidding, Joey Baron's never-on-the-one, about-to-blow-at-any-time percussion—he's got a group that packs the disciplined taut-ness, near-telepathic communication, and spark-to-flare firepower his fractured mosaics of sound demand. What results ranges from slippery ballads to twisted bebop to industrial-strength grunge, all clearly in tune with the jagged but endless rhythms at the heart of life in the Apple. [1988]

chapter 61

East Village Jumpcuts

More than a dozen years after he first began playing his music around the East Village, composer/saxophonist John Zorn is still living on the economic and musical margins of mainstream culture, but with an ironic twist. More and more, the kind of generic/geographical border-hopping he's pursued and the kinds of hybrids he's been breeding reflect a central method of transmission across the world's cultures. This is not vapid New Ageism: no transcendentalist goals lurk in Zorn's closet, and his plugged-in feel for noise and speed and form preclude him from dwelling on the inexorable beauty of pentatonic pablum. Even "eclectic" is far too weak a word to descrbe Zorn's intensely demanding yet playful sonic assaults. If a whiff of *epater ie bourgeoisie* hovers about his work, it's not there just to titillate or shock, but to raise questions and rearrange expectations about how music can go about being whatever it is.

Zorn's own attack on that vast subject takes multiple forms that all hinge on both massive collisions between musical genres and heady encounters at the borders of improvisation and composition. He's been honing that attack since his Webster College days in the early '70s, when he first came in contact with the Chicago-based AACM and its St. Louis analog, the Black Artists Group, one of whose leading lights, saxman Oliver Lake, taught at Webster. And so Zorn was introduced to the work of jazzers like Anthony Braxton, Roscoe Mitchell, and Leo Smith, who were exploring different ways of mixing freedom and form.

The result:

> It was a real inspiration that helped me break free of the traditional classical mold, and I began incorporating improvisation into some of the structures I'd been working on, which ranged from traditionally notated stuff like Elliot Carter- and Charles Ives- and Edgard Varese-influenced pieces to improvisational works coming more from John Cage or Earle Brown or Stockhausen.

That combination of elements created some unusual strategies, such as the game structures Zorn employed in pieces like *Archery* and *Cobra* to decenter both the process of improvising and the composition itself:

> The game pieces are something very special meant for improvisers working in a live situation. They weren't really meant to be recorded because they're like a sport—it's an exciting thing to see, it's very visual when all the musicians are making signs at each other, trying to get each other's attention. It creates a *more* spontaneous situation than there would be if you just told ten or twelve musicians, "Okay, go out there and improvise completely," because if you did that all you'd get would be a big muddle. With this system, you can give a downbeat and have no idea what's going to happen—you might be playing with no one or one person or ten people, or you might give a downbeat where you'll have a pretty clear idea *who* you'll be playing with but no idea of what kind of music is going to happen, or you can give a downbeat and have a clear idea of what's going to happen musically by using different modifiers like fast or loud. My role there was to set up rules so that the people in the band have to make decisions, have to communicate. All I'm concerned with there is that people make the most possible decisions in the smallest amount of time, so that everything is jam-packed together and the music changes incredibly fast.

Zorn's anarchic approaches to the nexus of improvisation and composition have grown as varied and unpredictable as the tangle itself demands. But there are two attributes that virtually all Zorn pieces share. The first is how, like many of the best younger composer-musicians currently emerging, Zorn works in true partnership with the group of players he calls his family, who bring their own special talents and insights to shape and fill in the outlines the leader has sketched. This rebirth of the band concept—which owes much to rock's influence on this generation—not so coincidentally cuts to the heart of what composition can mean. As Zorn puts it in the liner notes for *Spillane*,

> Whether we like it or not, the era of the composer as autonomous musical mind has just about come to an end. . . . Over the past 40 years, many of the great composers have worked with collaborators. Ellington had Billy Strayhorn as well as his amazing band, John Cage had David Tudor and Takehisa Kosugi. . . . Philip Glass and Steve Reich work closely with their ensembles. The collaborative aspects of the recording process make this even clearer. When the Beatles put to-

gether *Sgt. Pepper* with George Martin, or Frank Zappa worked with the Mothers of Invention of the early Verve recordings, the collaboration helped produce a musical statement greater than the sum of the individuals involved.

Zorn explains the connection with his own work:

In the studio it's just pieces of tape that you can splice or not splice together. So the way I work in the studio now is by creating a collaborative environment with the band I've picked for this piece. The way the piece is written is unusual, in the sense that I write images and ideas down on filing cards, order them, and that's basically the composition. Then it gets scored: I decide this card will be a solo for the guitar, and the card following it will have the full band, and the card after that will be the two drummers—see what I'm saying? That scoring doesn't really get committed until I'm in the studio and I hear what's going on. As all the musicians are working and coming up with their own ideas, throwing them into the pot with mine, I realize, "Well, that next section that I thought was going to be so good has to get ripped up and thrown away because now that this happened I've got to go right to the card after that." So it's something that's sketched out in my head at home, and may even have been notated musically, but it's not until I'm in the studio that the actual constructing begins.

It's done with the people that I've chosen as the band, the same way that Duke Ellington worked with his band: he'd bring in a head chart, or just play the piano and everybody would find their note [within the section]—"I'll take the third, you take the fifth"—and so it would just kinda *happen*, because he'd hired an incredible band that worked that way, and they knew each other and the music. I'm sure he heard melodies the guys were blowing and took them, but they were on salary to him, and he was the ultimate producer, the guy who was putting it all together: Duke Ellington and his band. That's why I say it's a collaborative environment, and I call the musicians a family, because through working with me on these different pieces everybody has learned their different roles. Each of the musicians has his own musical world in his head so that, whether he likes it or not, as soon as he gets involved with something, is interested and excited, he's gonna add his world to it. That makes my piece, my world, deeper. I think that's what helps give my music a kind of filmic sweep.

One way Zorn makes sure those minds will interact with his more than once is by cutting the musicians involved in his projects equal slices of the artists' royalties.

The other attribute structuring Zorn's work is velocity, the sheer relentless speed driving the late 20th century. Zorn's art of the quick-change and the juxtaposition of the apparently incongruous from liter-ally around the world—a baroque harpsichord flourish next to a spew of guitar screeches or a circus motif or a strangled human cry or computer-generated bleeps, a rumba pattern alongside a bit of shakuhachi or a Brazilian *batucada* ensemble or diced-up fragments of Beethoven's *Für Elise*—finds its best analog in the jumpcuts and channel-hopping so natural to the first generation that grew up on TV. Think of what Firesign Theater did with that conceit on record, and you'll realize what you're definitely *not* hearing in John Zorn's music is a bored lack of attentiveness, a self-indulgent and superficial meandering. Just the op-posite, in fact: it's a provocative representation of and challenge to the hurtling, increasingly atomized bombardment of information that marks life in our hurtling, decontextualizing times.

If you keep those emphases in mind, it's clearly no accident that Zorn's recordings like *The Big Gundown* and *Spillane* spend their time at the movies and on TV. The first LP collects key players on the East Village scene—guitarists Robert Quine, Jody Harris, Bill Frisell, Ver-non Reid, Fred Frith, and Arto Lindsay, turntable mixer Christian Marclay, altoist Tim Berne, accordionist Guy Klucevsek, bassist Melvin Gibbs, keyboardists Anthony Coleman and Wayne Horvitz, and percus-sionists Bobby Previte and Anton Fier among them—for brash and witty reworkings of music by spaghetti-Western scorer Ennio Morricone. Zorn takes the Italian's brooding, twangy atmospherics, themselves witty reworkings of Duane Eddy and the Ventures, and skews them into scorching surrealism, redistributing the voicings of the original charts over utterly different instruments and players to produce wild, apocalyp-tic renditions that refract—Zorn calls them "recompositions"—the still-recognizable material. If the album's working title was *Once Upon a Time in the East Village*, it's because the jagged atonal bursts of noise alternating with moodier, more melodic feels capture what Morricone might have written had he been exiled to these margins rather than the Leone-imagined Wild West.

Spillane's mosaic of a title piece—it charges through 60 sections in its 25 minutes—traffics mainly in variants of the moody *noir*ish sounds that accompanied TV detectives in the '50s. The subject grew from several Zorn obsessions: detective fiction, New York, sleazy soundtracks, and jazz. Another species of Zorn composition is represented here by "Two Lane Highway," the "portrait" of blues guitar great Albert Collins that teams Collins with Zorn family members like Quine, Gibbs, Horvitz, and Previte as well as keyboard master Big John Patton and drummer Ronald Shannon Jackson. While the piece's dozen sections move from shuffle blues to funk to New Orleans r&b in alternation with rip-'em-up rumbles, they build a powerful impetus; it peaks with its allusion to the classic organ-trio format in a segment that unites Texans Collins and Jackson with Kansas City-born Patton, all of them coming from their region's long blues traditions in very different ways.

While Zorn may be best known as a composer-arranger, his alto sax playing is as chameleonic and supple as his writing. There are the duck calls and squeals (often generated by his literally deconstructed sax) on things like *Ganryu Island*, his alternately melodic and raucous duo with shamisen master Michihiro Sato. (Zorn lives half the year in Tokyo, and finds the richly hybrid Japanese culture fascinating, which is why he brought some of its on-the-edge performers to the Kitchen for the Hidden Fortress series he curated in 1987.) Then there are the freewheeling Ornette Coleman tributes Zorn stages with fellow altoist Tim Berne at clubs like the Knitting Factory. Or there is the bop-based but idiosyncratic fluidity displayed on *The Sonny Clark Memorial Quartet/Voodoo* (Black Saint).

Along with innovators like Henry Threadgill, whom he admires a great deal, Zorn disdains neocon pseudo-traditionalism:

> It's really that music the way it should be played today—exciting, on the edge. Bebop is not just running changes the way Sonny Stitt or Bird did; there's no point to just copying that, you can take out the record and play it if that's what you want to hear. It's tunes and changes and a certain tradition that needs to be updated to keep it alive. I think that music is great today, and I'm trying to play it today. [1987]

chapter 62

Naked City

The Weegee photo on the cover of *Naked City* (Elektra/Nonesuch) sets you up for downtown composer/alto saxist John Zorn's latest musical onslaught. Yanking deliberately harsh and grainy shots out of the mix-and-match sonic grab-bag called pop history, Zorn compresses their essences into odd-angled Info-Age soundbytes, shuffles, then hurtles them gleefully, assaultively by. Though patches of relative calm and even snatches of innocence sometimes hover, ironic subversion lurks at every turn of phrase.

Naked City was formed to give Zorn a focused vehicle for his omnivorous compositions and rearrangements. Taking its name from the gritty pulp TV show ("There are six million stories in . . ."), this collection of downtown all-stars—Zorn, Bill Frisell on guitar, Wayne Horvitz on keyboards, Fred Frith on bass, Joey Baron on percussion—did a four-night, eight-set stint at a packed Knitting Factory last summer; they never repeated a tune. Now tightened and toughened by roadwork, they jumpcut—often within a single piece—from surf-music buoyancy to reggae punch, country twang to *noir*-movie sleaze, hardcore slamdunk to second-line strut with the kind of urgent, methodical grin you'd expect from a chainsaw murderer in a rush-hour subway car.

Imagine the resulting spatter as a Jackson Pollock, and you'll begin to understand how they transform everything they touch. Take jazz great Ornette Coleman's "Lonely Woman." Coleman, a Zorn hero, wrote and played it as a brooding, off-balance elegy, but in Naked City's hands it comes out as a contemporary "Peter Gunn" played by Booker T and the MGs: the bass line is the structuring riff from Roy Orbison's "Pretty Woman," and Zorn closes it out by flourishing Ornette's "Dancing in Your Head" theme. Or take "The Sicilian Clan" (from *The Godfather*) by another Zorn fave, spaghetti-Westerner Ennio Morricone: here it curls up in a cocktail lounge with a cheesy Farfisa organ out of "Telstar." Then there are Zorn's originals: raging grungers like "Hammerhead" and mutant cartoon memories like "Snagglepuss," skewed beach-blanket-bingos like "Batman" and infectious r&b party-downs like "Latin Quarter," each produced to mimic its genre's classic sound.

Think of Zorn as a rapid-fire dial twirler—the LP has 23 cuts; the CD and cassette, 26. Part of the listening fun comes in hanging on for dear life whenever he hits the button. Catch your breath when you can. [1990]

chapter 63

A *Star Is Made*

When altoist/composer Steve Coleman hitchhiked from his native South Side Chicago to New York, on May 22, 1978, a couple of months short of his 22nd birthday, he didn't bring much with him except a saxophone and a game plan. He still had the radio-transcription recording of Charlie Parker his father, a Bird fanatic, had slipped into his suitcase when Steve left for Illinois Wesleyan four years earlier. And he carried his own addiction to blues and funk and Coltrane, some tunes he'd been playing with different bands in Chicago, a consuming curiosity about the Apple's music scene, and a fierce desire to burn to the heart of it.

And that was about it. Even his game plan was simple and lean. The $150 in his pocket was enough to cover his room at the Vanderbilt Y on East 47th Street for a while—he'd dialed New York City information from Chicago to get the address of the YMCA closest to the center of town—since rates ran $10 a day ($11 if you wanted a room with a TV, which he didn't). It turned out to be a pretty close to ideal location—until he got kicked out for practicing on the roof.

Every morning he'd grab some breakfast on his way to the corner of 50th and Broadway, where he parked himself in front of the tall black skyscraper in Paramount Plaza and rolled out pop tunes like "Alfie" and "Mr. Bojangles" and hits by Stevie Wonder and Roberta Flack that brought in the spare change. He'd pull in about $30 a day, drop some of it for dinner at the Tad's Steaks down the block, then hop on the IRT and head downtown to haunt the Village's jazz spots.

Early August 1988, and the phone rings in Coleman's Brooklyn apartment. It's Herbie Hancock's people; they want him on the tour the keyboardist was planning for fall. It's tempting. Prestige. Good exposure. Very good money: the weekly salary Hancock's tour would offer is several times what he can make leading his own group. But it's out of the question. Coleman politely but firmly refuses.

He has his own plans for the fall. His first major-label album, *sine die*, has been getting favorable reviews since its release in June. He and his band, Five Elements, have booked time in the studio in September to record the follow-up to *sine die* before hitting the road themselves, starting with a gig at the Knitting Factory on October 8 and 9. And in December Coleman will make his debut in the Brooklyn Academy of Music's Next Wave Festival, leading a 16-piece big band in two concerts billed as "M-BASE Jams at BAM." So money or no, prestige or no, it's a question of commitment—and if there's one thing Coleman possesses, it's commitment to his music. He can be so focused and single-minded about it, in fact, that he can drive even the folks working with him either to distraction or to opposition. So the outcome of the phone call with Hancock isn't very surprising.

But it does measure how far Steve Coleman has come in the jazz world's estimation over the decade since he arrived in New York. It's a long way from playing for chump change on the street and living at the Y to laudatory features in the *New York Times*'s Arts & Leisure section and touring with Sting. And while Steve Coleman isn't exactly looking to buy Trump Tower, he's certainly got a lot more options than he had even a year ago.

Unlike the pop world—where the right record and the right video can take an artist from obscurity to international stardom in less than a year (see Tracy Chapman)—jazz stars aren't made every day. When it happens, it's because of a gradual convergence of elements: talent (of course), paid-up dues, connections, a new voice, press buzz. Steve Coleman's got all those. He's an exciting and thoughtful sax player. And in his compositions, jazz, African concepts, and funk snake in a double helix that creates a new idiom. He's apprenticed with masters, and he's attracted a like-minded cadre of explorers who agreed the scene was ripe for change: keyboardist Geri Allen (to whom he was briefly married), trumpeter Graham Haynes, altoist Greg Osby, drummer Marvin "Smitty" Smith, vocalist Cassandra Wilson, guitarist Vernon Reid. Tipped off by the European-released albums and the grapevine, the press picked upon this group and dubbed them "the Brooklyn crew," a designation that makes Coleman grumble. "We just live here because we can't afford to live in Manhattan," he says. "It's not like there's some 52nd Street-type scene happening out here. There aren't even any clubs."

More important than their mailing address is what these musicians share conceptually, the musical idiom they call M-BASE. Coleman grabs listeners with a muscular sound that reflects the *Zeitgeist*. Like most emerging players his age, Coleman was raised on pop culture: an early fascination with science-fiction and comic books, a later passion for computer technology, and always rock and roll—in his case, funk stylists from Stevie Wonder to George Clinton. His earliest outings as a fledgling musician were in South Side funk bands; his hero was Maceo Parker, the alto titan who wails on the greatest hits of James Brown. But the jazz tradition also shaped Coleman. His father's gentle persistence converted him to the Bird cult, and he got tuned on to Coltrane once he began playing with jazz bands like Von Freeman's in Chicago. Seeking a territory for himself that could encompass all these influences and others he'd picked up along the way—African polyrhythms, rap's punch, kung-fu soundtracks—is what Coleman and M-BASE are all about.

The search for this sound is what brought Coleman to New York. Playing on the street and sitting in at jam sessions in downtown lofts led Coleman into club work. The Chicago connection helped. Chico Freeman, Von's son, brought Coleman down to tenor great Sam Rivers's Bond Street loft not long after his arrival; Rivers liked what he heard, and soon Coleman found himself playing lead alto in Rivers's swaggering big band. Bassist Dave Holland, a veteran of Miles Davis's *Bitches Brew* band who was in Rivers's Big Band at the same time, recalls that the young altoist distinguished himself: "Sam never said much, so it was very much up to the players to catch what the phrasing should be. Steve was really quick about that."

A gig like that, in jazz terms, can be like the outside ring of a spider web—for the skillful player with any ambition, one strand leads to another. There are traps, to be sure; some get stuck as perennial side-men, some push too hard and burn out. Building on personal loyalties and staying away from the perils of substance abuse, Coleman began working his way to the center. At Rivers's rehearsal studio in the West 30s, he met five-string cellist Muneer Abdul Fataah, a big, muscle-bound, furry-bearded Muslim whose hypnotic atonal compositions captivated him. Muneer introduced Coleman to drummer Doug Hammond, and the trio—sometimes with Coleman's fellow Chicago émigrés guitarist Jean-Paul Bourelly and bassist Lonnie Plaxico—began playing around Harlem, mostly at a hole-in-the-wall West 125th Street loft called Zola's or tiny clubs like Lickety Split at West 137th and Adam Clayton Powell Boulevard. They made demo tapes on a cheap cassette deck in the Harlem basement of a friend's house. It was this group that in 1982 began to attract the charter members of M-BASE, younger players like Haynes and Allen, to Coleman's ideas. His zeal for probing other musicians' gifts matches his own inner drive. That, and the intensity of his sound, made converts like Osby and Wilson.

The Hammond-Muneer-Coleman trio evolved into the first version of Five Elements, and Coleman got a taste of leading a band. They made a studio tape and took it around to clubs. RT Firefly, a punk-rock venue on Bleecker Street, was on their hit list. When the booker asked Coleman what kind of music his band played, the altoist shot back, "What kind of music do you want? Punk-rock? That's what it is." When the booker listened to the tape, he loved it: "Sounds great. A couple of tunes remind me of jazz, but you can just leave those out of the set." It was a strategy that set the scene for introducing M-BASE to the music world. Whatever flavor club owners asked for—free jazz, rock, bebop—Coleman assured them he could deliver. He got away with it because he redefined what they thought they wanted to hear and left them begging for more.

When Hammond and Muneer left for Europe in 1982, Coleman moved to Brooklyn and started getting involved heavily with building a sense of musical and political community. Younger black players began getting together to share strategies to overcome racism, indifference, and artistic conservatism in the music industry. The Musicians' Referral Agency, which started out as a jobs bulletin board with political overtones, evolved quickly into a revolutionary jazz workshop. While the typical jazz workshop (whether informal master classes with the likes of

Max Roach or an impromptu group reading big-band charts) focuses on problems of intepretation and improvisation, this workshop set different goals, more like the famed Mingus workshops, where the maestro forged new musical ideas from the creative heat of the interaction among musicians.

A basement on Sterling Street was headquarters for this Monday afternoon workshop. "That way we didn't bother the working people," notes Coleman, "and we had a real homey atmosphere." (Five Elements still rehearses there.) Whether 4 or 40 players showed up, the process remained fairly constant. Rather than recycle classics like "Nefertiti" or "Groovin' High" all day, the key participants (Coleman, Smith, Allen, and Haynes) decided to explore and build on their own musical ideas.

The workshop spurred Coleman's rapidly evolving ideas and honed his developing leadership skills. But other gigs paid the rent: a slot with the Cecil Taylor Big Band, the alto spot in David Murray's Octet and Big Band, a Far Eastern tour with Rivers's sax ensemble Winds of Manhattan. A turning point came in 1984. Bassist Holland was recovering from a heart ailment: at a benefit for him Coleman turned up at, Holland talked about putting a band together to tour and record, and he wanted Coleman in on it. Coleman shrugged mentally; that kind of talk is SOP among musicians, and doesn't necessarily lead to anything. A couple of days later, though, he picked up his phone to find Holland's trace-of-an-English-accent on the other end asking, "Why don't you come up to my house here in Saugerties for a couple of days. We can jam and play some tunes, feel each other out, see how we'd work in a band." The sessions went off so well that Holland asked Coleman if he knew any hip young drummers to recommend. Coleman brought Marvin "Smitty" Smith, a Zola regular whose drumming conveyed an African sense of interlocking rhythmic parts. The chemistry's been so successful that they're still working together.

Most people have no idea how difficult it is for an aspiring musician—especially a jazz musician—to get demos heard at a record company when he's got no track record. The albums Coleman began cutting with Holland for ECM, and the continental tours the group did to promote them, put him on the European musical map. When Stefan Wynter, then engineer for enja and now head of his own JMT label, first heard of Coleman, the altoist was still paying his journeyman's dues, doing a studio session in New York for flugelhornist Franco Ambrosetti. Sitting in the control booth while the tapes rolled, Wynter got smacked by the bluesy tone that had escaped vinyl until then. The way he recalls it, "I'd heard his stuff with Dave Holland on ECM and liked it, but the sound of his saxophone live was like the feeling you get on your back during a cold shower—that was what attracted me to him initially."

After listening to the Five Elements demo tape, Matthias Winckelman, Wynter's boss at enja, wanted Coleman but not the context he'd been developing. Like many self-described purists, Wincklemann then (he's changed his tune now) refused to accept electric instruments in a jazz context. Yet electronics are obviously crucial to the postwar generation's notion of sound, from Buddy Holly to Michael Jackson, and that's the very group Coleman targets. "Too many jazz musicians talk about how they want to make music that's all for the head," he says. "They don't want people to understand it, like that's hip. I want my music to reach people in every way. I want to give them something for their bodies and something for their minds."

Coleman won a compromise: he could pick his own band, but it had to play acoustic. It was from the M-BASE pool of talent that Coleman drew his collaborators for his 1985 album, *Motherland Pulse*. When Winckelmann decided he didn't want the album, Stefan Winter used it to launch his own label; Coleman and Five Elements cut two subsequent albums for him, *On the Edge of Tomorrow* and *World Expansion*.

But small European labels, however loyal to the music, can't back musicians with the distribution muscle of a major multinational like CBS or Warner Bros. Coleman, like most musicians, wanted to see his records available beyond New York and a handful of hip record boutiques around the country. Sure, his records might continue to sell on the 10,000-unit range, a handsome figure for labels accustomed to selling 2000 copies or less of most titles. But that's still a fraction of what Wynton Marsalis, powered by the world's biggest jazz label (CBS), sells. So while Coleman continued his handshake deal with JMT, he began shopping his next demo around at American jazz labels to see if he could land a deal.

That was why mid-1987 found him walking into the midtown office of Pangaea Records, the label created by Sting that is distributed via MCA's huge pipeline. Despite its marketing motto, "Creative Anarchy," Pangaea's greeting was chilly. Pangaea president Christine Reed barely looked up from her desk when she took his tape—not unlike any major label's attitude toward a young, relatively unknown jazz-based player. But unpromising as that brief encounter seemed, it planted seeds. On a brief teaching stint at Banff College in Alberta, Canada, Coleman got a message from New York that a Christine Reed had called and could he please call her back. As he puts it, "That wasn't enough for me to call long distance." Two days later, the message was more urgent: "I've played your tape for Sting; we both love it. Please call right away. Don't talk to anybody else until you talk to us." He didn't, but he did hire a lawyer and begin the serious negotiations that resulted, nearly five months later, in a record contract.

Meanwhile, Branford Marsalis, Coleman's neighbor in Fort Greene, couldn't make the Brazilian leg of Sting's tour accompanying his latest album . . . . *Nothing like the Sun.* So Marsalis recommended Coleman to the ex-Policeman. Nobody told Steve, though. When the phone rang in his Fort Greene apartment in November 1987 and the caller said, "This is Sting," he figured it was Osby, who loves practical jokes.

> STING: "I'd like to ask you to join the tour I'm going to be doing starting in January, because Branford can't make it."
> COLEMAN: "Aw, c'mon, Greg, cut it out, man."
> STING: "Greg?"
> COLEMAN: "Okay, man, you've had your fun."

And so on, until the Laurel-and-Hardy routine got straightened out.

> COLEMAN: "I don't want a gig where I'm supposed to play just like somebody else, whether it's Branford or David Sanborn or anybody."
> STING: "The reason I'm hiring these musicians for this band is that I want all of your input. I could hire anybody to read charts—I want people who can interpret creatively and rearrange where it makes sense."

It was a deal. Coleman packed his alto in its case and headed up to the heavily trafficked SIR rehearsal studios, pretour launching pad for the likes of David Bowie. The photo tacked up on his wall—Coleman in a Trouble Funk T-shirt and a bare-chested Sting clutching a soccer ball backsage at their Rio gig with famed Brazilian vocalist Milton Nascimento—tells one side of the tale, the glamorous life. But Coleman got work done, too. The sinuous "First Sunrise" on *sine die* grew out of it, written on the plane ride back from the Rio beaches, where Coleman says, "People there walk to that kind of groove—that's why I wrote it."

Written partly during Sting's tour, recorded right afterward at Systems Two studio in Brooklyn, *sine die* not only introduced Coleman to the major-label music leagues but also closed a kind of circle: its stuttering, funkified opener, "Destination," features Coleman and Branford Marsalis romping through tag-team solos.

August 1988, and Coleman's back in the city after three days' fishing on a Minnesota lake with his father. He's sunburned and wired up already: meetings, meetings, meetings. There's the promo taping for VH-1, interviews and PR pit stops to push his latest album, the page proofs from a Steve Coleman songbook that need comparing and checking. Not to mention rehearsals, studio dates, the BAM gig.

But tonight is computer-nut night. In the back rehearsal room at Martin Audio, a studio on West 55th Street, the weekly meeting of a music-computer group is gradually subsiding from friendly hubbub to attentiveness. Coleman's up on the small stage with his pal and co-programmer Joe Ravo, and they're snaking coils of wire from one computer to another to ready Coleman's demonstration of a futuristic piece of software he's spent three years designing. The program does what many musicians can't: fed a chord sequence, it improvises over it, logically and musically, in two variants of Coleman's own alto attack.

Bugs crop up in the studio's gear, the audience buzzes, the duo onstage works frantically. Finally the demonstrations, and gasps of astonishment mingle with looks of incomprehension. Terms fly around the room: Pythagoras' Golden Section, Symmetry, the Fibonacci sequence, machine language, MIDI and SMPTE. "My concept of a computer," he tells the 50 or so programmers in his best Jack Benny deadpan, "used to be *Lost in Space*—y'know, 'Danger, danger, danger.'"

When the meeting's finally broken up, an hour past its usual endpoint, the inevitable knot of questioners tails him down nearly to the D train before he lugs his heavy synthesizer-sax back home to Brooklyn. [1988]

chapter 64

Master of Tributes

"I always felt I ended up producing records because it was convenient," says Hal Willner in his characteristically offhanded way. "It could have been anything else. I'm not really in any one musical world. Music coming from a social place isn't where I come from—kids getting together. I'm someone who sees music as a book, something you do at night when no one else is around. Or an extension of film."

That perspective has made Willner well suited for his groundbreaking series of "tribute" albums that use a wide range of often unlikely musicians to reimagine disparate sounds: *Amarcord Nino Rota*, *Lost in the Stars* (Kurt Weill), *That's the Way I Feel Today* (Thelonious Monk), *Stay Awake* (Walt Disney cartoon soundtracks; all on A&M), and *Weird Nightmare* (Columbia), a Charles Mingus outing. But he's also produced albums like Marianne Faithful's comeback, *Strange Weather* (Island); in addition, he was music director of TV's lamented *Night Music*, and provides musical atmosphere for *Saturday Night Live*.

The bulk of the Mingus dates were in late spring at Astoria's Master Sound studio with Willner's "house band"—Bill Frisell, Don Byron, Art Baron, Greg Cohen, Michael Blair, Don Alias, and Francis Thumm. Guest artists like Henry Threadgill, Vernon Reid, and Robert Quine came in with agreed-on songs that they'd reconceptualized; after explaining their ideas to Willner and Cohen, who was functioning as pit boss, the guests led the sessions. Willner said almost nothing when things were going well—which was most of the time. When they weren't, he found tactful ways around impasses. Low-key and laid-back but clearly in control, he provided the overall frame of vision. When the ideas of those he'd asked aboard the project struck that frame, creative sparks flew.

But before the Mingus album came out in late 1992, he released an atypical offshoot of his tribute series, *The Carl Stalling Project* (Warner Bros.). Stalling was one of American culture's classic eccentric geniuses.

295

An organist who accompanied silent movies in Kansas City, Stalling met a young animator named Walt Disney. When Disney came up with "Steamboat Willie," one of the first sound cartoons, he turned to Stalling for the music. Using the markings animator Ub Iwerks made on the film to act as a metronome, Stalling crafted the screwball musical effects that would become his signature. "Steamboat Willie" opened on November 18, 1928; an instant smash, like *The Jazz Singer*, it guaranteed the end of silent animation. Stalling was Disney's music director until 1930, creating "The Silly Symphonies" series when he suggested using Edward Grieg's "March of the Dwarfs" for a cartoon graveyard goof.

Then Stalling moved to Iwerks's MGM-distributed cartoon studio, which boasted the now forgotten Flip the Frog and Willie Whopper. But in 1936, he was hired by Warner Bros. animation producer Leon Schlesinger; he stayed at that studio until he retired in 1958. Working from the huge trove of popular tunes Warner owned, with a full orchestra for recording whenever he needed and sometimes only a few days to compose for a new six- or seven-minute cartoon, he raised the soundtrack to an art form.

The Carl Stalling Project proves it. After you've listened for a few minutes, even if you're a Looney Tunes fanatic you forget the images flickering in your head to concentrate on the zany jumpcut sounds. Stalling brilliantly sliced and diced music history and salted it with wit: his often weird voicings and delightfully knowing parodies cut with vaudevillian timing.

Says Willner,

I think the album works historically and on a fun level. There are the montages, and a few complete cartoon tracks to break things up. It's a 78-minute album you can get through without going crazy. "Hillbilly Hare," which opens it, is the typical Warner Bros. sound without effects. Then we went right into early Stalling—the montage from his first scores. Then "The Good Egg," which is not a very good cartoon but a great score. Then a typical Bugs Bunny medley. Then we started jumping all over the place: that complete Roadrunner score, "There They Go Go Go." Unbelievable. Then we end with "Porky in Wackyland," one of the most popular scores.

The events that hatched the album began in 1985, when producer Mary Salter called Willner about *The Looney Tunes 50th Anniversary Special*. Salter and executive producer Lorne Michaels knew him from

Saturday Night Live, where he scores sketches with old music. According to Willner,

> Obviously I knew who Carl Stalling was: I'd spent a lot of time at the old Thalia Monday night animation festivals. Just watching the stuff for the show I thought, "I can't do this without the original music. We've gotta find it." People said, "It doesn't exist." I said, "It has to exist; how'd they put the cartoons into Italian?" So I pressed, pressed, pressed. Oh yeah: there are these things called M & E tapes—Music and Effects, together. So we sat around and picked out 40 cartoons for the show. Then the tapes showed up. They blew me away. Separated from the animation, they were incredible—aggressive and quick-changing, all these emotions packed into a few minutes.

Greg Ford, one of the special's writers, had programmed the festivals Willner haunted at New York's old Thalia theater. When the duo sat down with the music and effects tracks, which leave off the dialogue but keep everything Stalling wrote, Willner had not only what the show needed but another idea.

He recalls,

> The idea of a record fit something I'd had in my head a long time. So I let Lorne and Mary know. Greg made two shorts for Warners, "The Duxorcist" and "Night of the Living Duck." We did that together. Meanwhile Rich Gehr, who works for Warners Animation, came across these four boxes labelled "music tracks," which had about 20 minutes of complete music sessions from four cartoons, like "Hillbilly Hare." Alternate takes, everything. We used a lot of those for "Night of the Living Duck," which opened the New York Film Festival.
>
> Meanwhile, more vaults were opened, and more tapes were found. I think we've got just about all of it now: Stalling's last score, for instance. Other record companies were interested, but I wanted it at Warner Bros. Partly that's because I wanted to appeal to the largest possible audience: everybody should be able to get into this somehow.

It took some brutal work to ensure that accessibility. Willner continues,

> Greg went through and picked out what he thought were the best scores: there were about 250 seven-minute soundtracks to choose from. So I went to California for a week—it was like going cold turkey. Put myself in a Santa Monica hotel by the ocean and listened to 250 cartoon soundtracks, taking notes. After listening to 60, the obsession with

the music was over. After 90, I wanted to die. But then Greg came out, and we mapped out the record.

Originally it was going to be Stalling in chronological order. Instead it got more like the other albums I've done, became a little journey. I came up with the idea of the jungle scenes, Greg latched onto the anxiety montage idea. We picked out the parts we liked and built these montages over a week; our first edit came to about 110 minutes. CDs can only fit about 78. The cassette is actually longer than the album: "Stupor Duck" isn't on the CD.

Stalling blithely ignored divisions between high and low culture, so besides being fun, listening to *The Carl Stalling Project* is like hearing music history and your own past collide in front of a funhouse mirror. As John Zorn—who was initially slated to co-produce the album with Willner—writes in his liner notes, "[This] will go a long way to elevating Stalling to his rightful position as one of America's great composers. Like Charles Ives, a true original. A visionary who created the music most of us were *weaned* on. The music of our subconscious."   [1990]

chapter 65

The Big Apple Avant-garde

The last few years have brought a spate of stories in the mainstream press about jazz's alleged resurgence. Writers like Tom Piazza have spotlighted young musicians who have dug back into hard bop for their inspiration. But while they've been recycling the past, others have been scoping out possible futures for the collection of improvisatory languages we lump together as jazz.

Piazza and his ilk are right about one thing: it's a rare and exciting time in jazz. But they're right for reasons they can't appreciate. Rules and concepts are being discarded and reworked, and the results are revitalizing musicians and audiences alike. One center of creative ferment is the so-called downtown New York scene—a misleading label.

The scene's influences are as varied as its players. There's Monk's notion of space and close-interval angularity. There's Mingus's Rabelaisian sprawl and eagerness to redefine the relationship between composition and improvisation. There's Ornette's melodic emphasis, discarding of bebop's cycle-of-chords cage, and transformation of funk into harmolodics. There are the expansive sonic idioms pioneered by Miles, Ayler, Trane, and Dolphy. There are the early, heady fusion of Weather Report and off-the-wall mélanges of Captain Beefheart. There are slick Motown backbeats and fatback Stax-Volt soul, the jazz-tinged funk of James Brown and the satiric cartoon sci-fi of Parliament-Funkadelic. There's game theory, post-Viennese atonality, spaghetti-Western and kung-fu soundtracks, African-derived slants on polyrhythmic interdependence, and post-punk savagery.

Nearly all of these concepts were fed through the AACM and BAG, musicians' cooperatives formed in the '60s in Chicago and St. Louis. They combined and extended idioms in ways that sparked the loft-jazz and no-wave scenes of the '70s and early '80s, when they effectively transferred headquarters to the Apple. Composer/performers like Muhal Richard Abrams, Lester Bowie, Henry Threadgill are still active around town, both as working musicians (somewhat sporadically) and mentors.

The younger players are no less difficult to categorize, because they emphasize jazz's traditional freedom of choice, the right to synthesize a musical language from whatever shards of the past you choose. So John Zorn furiously jumpcuts soundbites with Dadaist aggressiveness and an eye toward TV attention spans. Tim Berne slamdunks postpunk noise, soul-music alto, and Ornette into an urban-hipster argot. Bill Frisell bleeds post-apocalypse raunch into a keening pedal-steel longing for a big sky. Wayne Horvitz swirls The Band and Monk and Sonny Clark together. Marty Ehrlich jumps off from Muhal and Braxton.

M-BASErs Steve Coleman and Greg Osby combine different branches of funk and jazz in drastically diverse ways. Cassandra Wilson updates Ella and Betty Carter with angular originals and dramatically recast standards. Geri Allen's piano enfolds Ellington through Monk up to Cecil Taylor and Andrew Hill, while her compositions rove around the world. As do Bobby Previte's, which shuffle Nigerian juju, Moroccan rai, and Elvin Jones. Countless others like Don Byron, Matt Shipp, Craig Harris, Michelle Rosewoman, Michael Formanek, Thomas Chapin, Mark Helias, Joey Baron, Mark Dresser, Gerry Hemingway,

Graham Haynes, Gary Thomas, Andy Laster, Ivo Perelman, Curlew, and New Winds scramble new ideas.

For all the scene's musical openness and promising vitality, there are a couple of disturbing undercurrents, like the tendency among some black and white players to put unirace bands together. Unfortunately, only part of the reason is musical. And then there's getting work in the clubs.

"Scene" is a theatrical metaphor that implies a staging area. When the Knitting Factory opened in 1986, the loft scene was long dead and sonic explorers were relegated mostly to grants-funded venues like the Kitchen and Roulette. For all their virtues as sheltered labs, such showcases have the disadvantages of those virtues: drawing the already converted, they rarely expand the cutting edge's audiences.

According to Knitting Factory co-owner Michael Dorf, they have other drawbacks too:

> Often it seems like the motivation, the whole way of presenting music when it's done from a nonprofit perspective, is different from at least trying to break even. I have to worry about getting decent attendance and a way to pay the groups I book based on the market, rather than just aesthetic or political reasons—although those things definitely enter into the formula. But nonprofit spaces just keep trying to get bigger budgets so they can spend 'em and lose 'em. That's great; it's like getting a major gift and blowing it on CDs and then giving them away. But it seems to me you could take that money and put on the same thing and at least come out with what you went in with, and still have the shows be great.

The Knitting Factory's policy of booking college-radio rockers, downtown pioneers, and outside jazzers (like Braxton and Taylor) that no mainstream club would touch created a stage the fragmentary vanguards and their overlapping audiences could call home. Its critical and PR success—it's still skating on thin financial ice—helped lead other Apple clubs to broaden their booking policies. Visiones puts downtown types in a few times a month. The Time Cafe, which recently opened a club in its basement, plans to offer the likes of Perelman and Chapin and Berne. And the venerable Village Vanguard has begun showcasing young 'uns like Frisell and Allen. Max Gordon's widow Lorraine follows talent old and new: "I listen to all kinds of music, and bring in individuals I like and that I think the room will embrace—it's got a ghostly mind of its own, and can be very obstinate. I love Bill and Geri, and so does the room."

Meanwhile, an outgrowth of the London acid-jazz scene has been struggling in the basement of the Metropolis Cafe, an upscale Union Square eatery. Every Thursday after midnight DJs jam with live musicians as the audience dances to jazz. It's early days yet: the musicians and DJs, who change week to week, vary wildly in ability. But execs like Antilles's Brian Bacchus and Blue Note's Matt Pierson are enthusiastic about this idea's prospects for expanding jazz's audience.

"It's not a jazz scene," notes Bacchus.

> But it's a gas to watch kids dancing, whether it's to Trane records or a DJ putting grooves under a live sax quartet. One problem is the level of improvisers. In the U.S. we're used to a higher quality of jazz musicianship. I think it needs support from the industry: bring down artists, bring down vinyl. The DJs are spinning really hip stuff, and with the right musicians there could be a real explosion. The most important thing is that clubgoers get opened up to music they've never heard before, and so the music gets a shot at reaching a new audience.

The major U.S. labels have barely started to touch a lot of the most creative stuff spilling off these stages. (Most so-called avant-garde releases are on small labels, often European or Japanese.) In fact, until recently the majors' jazz divisions have seemed remarkably unwilling to invest in cultivating these small but rabid-out-of-proportion-to-their-numbers audiences. It's remarkable because the majors' rock arms are doing just that with college-radio bands, for instance, by the score. Using the analogy with broadcast and cable TV, rock execs have realized that their marketplace is fragmentary and cultish; that only a few blockbusters can sell across the listening spectrum; and that luring buyers back into the stores means narrowly targeting their tastes.

BMG's Steve Backer sees the selling of jazz's vanguards as part of a larger historical cycle that is coming around once again:

> We signed Steve Coleman about two years ago. I felt that as we got into this decade, the sociology I think this type of music follows would allow us to record more adventurous and less in-the-pocket type music. The '80s were ultraconservative: yuppie-ism, investment bankers, New Age, all that. The first six months of this decade, on the other hand, were about enormous change all over the world, things that nobody

expected to happen. It's like the '60s, with the Vietnam war and black power, when people were buying Trane and Shepp. If the music follows the sociology, then more adventurous and difficult music can be embraced a bit more than in conservative times.

Blue Note's Matt Pierson agrees, and feels that younger artists can bridge several audiences because of the breadth of their influences. "People like Osby and Coleman and Allen were brought up on the Stylistics and P-Funk. What they are doing is putting out the black American music experience; it's not just jazz," he insists. "It's very sophisticated music, but it presents itself in a way that isn't lofty or arcane. This is a really good time for that, because I think boundaries are opening up all over again now."

If the reins that have been holding in jazz execs' creative license are the majors' armies of bean counters, the blinders that have been keeping the accountants happy are the massive reissue programs, which generally account for well over 50 percent of major-label releases. It's wonderful to have all these vintage recordings available again. (It's ironic, of course, that it took the CD's higher profitability to push the majors into opening up the vaults.) But it can also mean that when a major-label jazz exec looks at his current roster (no, no women run major jazz divisions), he may well want continuity with his catalog. That way, to some extent he has a pre-sold market. From this perspective, the ongoing corporate (and corresponding press) push behind the hard-bop revivalists has a certain logic.

Blue Note executive Michael Cuscuna disagrees:

> We don't look at scenes; we look at individuals. We want the range of what's out there pretty well represented. Each month we release three new things and six reissues. We separate them by two weeks. We don't want a new artist to be treated by the stores as a reissue; they have to have more attention and be sold differently. Besides, reissues don't sell as much as people might think. Aside from the obvious exceptions, they only sell within the five to ten thousand range.

Of course, the overhead involved in prepping a reissue is a fraction of a new release's. And it's hard to deny that right down to the dress code, the neo–hard boppers look like the covers of reissues their music mimics. What's behind the logic of that presentation is shortchanging jazz's future.

The majors dominate distribution and retail like never before, so it's not enough to shrug that jazz's cutting edge has always relied on indies. Given the largely conservative lockstep of the majors, retail, radio, and most club and festival booking policies, jazz's new idioms have to work harder than ever—and be luckier than ever—to find their audiences. It could only help if the majors reinvest even a small percentage of their reissue profits in what they see as marginal sounds. Some of those sounds are heralding the music's next directions. [1990]

Index

Index

Index